THE YOUNG LEIBNIZ AND HIS PHILOSOPHY (1646–76)

ARCHIVES INTERNATIONALES D'HISTOIRE DES IDÉES

INTERNATIONAL ARCHIVES OF THE HISTORY OF IDEAS

166

THE YOUNG LEIBNIZ
AND HIS PHILOSOPHY (1646–76)

edited by
STUART BROWN

THE YOUNG LEIBNIZ
AND HIS PHILOSOPHY
(1646–76)

edited by

STUART BROWN
The Open University, U.K.

KLUWER ACADEMIC PUBLISHERS
DORDRECHT / BOSTON / LONDON

A C.I.P. Catalogue record for this book is available from the Library of Congress.

ISBN 0-7923-5997-6

Published by Kluwer Academic Publishers,
P.O. Box 17, 3300 AA Dordrecht, The Netherlands.

Sold and distributed in North, Central and South America
by Kluwer Academic Publishers,
101 Philip Drive, Norwell, MA 02061, U.S.A.

In all other countries, sold and distributed
by Kluwer Academic Publishers,
P.O. Box 322, 3300 AH Dordrecht, The Netherlands.

Printed on acid-free paper

Printed in the Netherlands.

Table of Contents

Acknowledgements

This volume had its beginnings in a conference on *The Young Leibniz and his Philosophy* held in 1996 as part of the celebrations of the 350th anniversary of Leibniz's birth. I am grateful to Philip Beeley, Christia Mercer and Harry Parkinson for encouraging me to organise this conference and to the staff of in Woburn College in Bedfordshire for providing us with an ideal environment for our discussions. The Conference was sponsored by the British Society for the History of Philosophy and supported by grants from the B.S.H.P, the Mind Association and the Open University Arts Faculty Research Committee, which is gratefully acknowledged.

The task of preparing the collection for publication was greatly facilitated by the support of colleagues in the Faculty of Arts at the Open University. I am especially grateful to two Secretaries of the Department of Philosophy, Wendy Clarke and Miriam Selwyn, for their willing advice and support. I am also grateful to the Faculty IT Co-Ordinator, Angela Redgewell, for technical assistance, and to Sophie Reid, who helped me in the curiously difficult task of adding accents over Greek characters.

Grateful acknowledgement is made for permission to quote from the following works: *Gottfried Wilhelm Leibniz. Philosophical Papers and Letters*. Translated by Leroy E. Loemker. Second Edition. Copyright © 1969 by D. Reidel, Dordrecht. Reproduced here by kind permission of Kluwer Academic Publishers. Also from *G. W. Leibniz. De Summa Rerum. Metaphysical Papers, 1675-1676*. Translated by G. H. R. Parkinson. Copyright © Yale University Press. Reproduced here by kind permission of Yale University Press and G. H. R. Parkinson.

A CHRONOLOGY OF THE YOUNG LEIBNIZ (1646-76)

1646   Born in Leipzig, 1 July (NS).

1653   Enters Nicolai School in Leipzig.

1661   Enters University of Leipzig.

1663   Defends and publishes *Metaphysical disputation on the principle of individuation*. Becomes Bachelor of Philosophy.

Spends summer semester at the University of Jena.

1664   Graduates Master of Philosophy from Leipzig with a dissertation on philosophy of law.

1665   Studies law, receiving bachelor's degree in law.

1666   Works on *Habilitationsschrift*, resulting in the *Dissertation on the art of combinations*.

Refused doctor's degree by Leipzig and moves to the University of Altdorf.

Publishes dissertation on *Difficult cases in law*.

1667   Receives doctorate in law from Altdorf.

Meets Baron Johann Christian von Boineburg.

Moves to Frankfurt and publishes his *New method for learning and teaching jurisprudence*.

1668   Moves to Mainz, where he is appointed to the High Court of Appeal by the Elector of Mainz.

Catalogues Boineburg's library and writes anonymous tract supporting the Elector's candidate to be elected king of Poland

1669   Engaged in ecclesiastical diplomacy and in writing about theology and philosophy of religion, including the drafts known as *The Catholic Demonstrations*

Confession of nature against atheists published anonymously

1670   Produces for Boineburg an edition of Nizolius's *Anti-Barbarus*

Works on physics and studies Hobbes

1671   Publishes *New physical hypothesis*

Completes his *Justa dissertatio* and his *Grundriss*

1672   Goes to Paris on a diplomatic mission to keep peace in Europe

Meets Antoine Arnauld and Christiaan Huygens

Death of Boineburg

1673   Travels to London in hope of setting up peace conference

Meets Henry Oldenburg and demonstrates a model of his calculating machine

Elected Fellow of the Royal Society in London

Death of Elector of Mainz

Returns to Paris and begins intensive study of higher mathematics

Writes *Confessio philosophi*

1674   Working on mathematical problems and on completing his calculating machine

1675   Makes breakthrough with infinitesimal calculus

Meets Nicolas Malebranche and Ehrenfried Walther von Tschirnhaus

Begins writings that form the *De summa rerum*

1676   Decides to accept employment with Johann Friedrich, Duke of Hanover

Revisits London and shows his calculating machine to Oldenburg

Visits Antoni van Leeuwenhoek in Delft and Benedict Spinoza at the Hague

Arrives and takes up posts in Hanover

References to works are given in an abridged form, without publication details, where these details are given in the bibliography In addition the following abbreviations have been used:

(a) Editions of Leibniz's works-

A   German Academy of Sciences (auspices). *G. W. Leibniz: Sämtliche Schriften und Briefe.* Berlin: Akademie Verlag, 1923-. (Referred to by series and volume number.)

AG   Ariew, R., and Garber, D. (trans. & ed.). *G. W. Leibniz: Philosophical Essays.* Indianapolis, Hackett, 1989.

C   Couturat, L. (ed.). *Opuscules et fragments inédits de Leibniz.* Paris: Alcan, 1903; repr. Hildesheim: Olms, 1961.

D   Dutens, L. L. (ed.). *G. G. Leibnitii ... Opera Omnia.* (6 vols.) Geneva, 1768.

FC   Foucher de Careil, A. (ed.). *Nouvelles lettres et opuscules inédits de Leibniz ...* Paris: Durand, 1857; Hildesheim: Olms, 1971.

G   Gerhardt, C. I. (ed.). *Die Philosophischen Schriften von Gottfried Wilhelm Leibniz.* (7 vols.) Berlin: Weidmann, 1875-90; repr. Hildesheim: Olms, 1965.

GM   Gerhardt, C. I. (ed.). *Leibnizens Mathematische Schriften.* (7 vols.) Berlin: A. Asher/Halle: H. W. Schmidt, 1849-63; repr. Hildesheim: Olms, 1965.

Gr   Grua, G. (ed.). *G. W. Leibniz: Textes inédits d'après les manuscrits de la Bibliothèque provinciale d'Hanovre.* Paris: Presses Universitaires de France, 1948.

K   Klopp, O. (ed.). *Die Werke von Leibniz.* (11 vols.) Hanover: Klindworth, 1864-84.

L   Loemker, L. E. (ed. & trans.). *G. W. Leibniz: Philosophical Papers and Letters.* 2nd edition. Dordrecht: Reidel, 1969.

M   Mollat, G. (ed.). *Mittheilungen aus Leibnizens ungedruckten Schriften.* Leipzig: H. Haessel, 1893

MB   Martin, R. Niall D. and Brown, S. (eds. & trans.). *G. W. Leibniz: Discourse on Metaphysics and Related Writings.* Manchester: Manchester University Press, 1988.

PDSR Parkinson, G. H. R. (ed. & trans.). *G. W. Leibniz: De Summa Rerum: Metaphysical Papers 1675-76.* New Haven & London: Yale University Press, 1992.

PW   Parkinson, G. H. R. (ed. & trans.). *Leibniz: Philosophical Writings.* London: Dent, 1973.

RB   Remnant, P. and Bennett, J. (trans. & ed.). *G. W. Leibniz: New Essays on Human Understanding.* Cambridge: Cambridge University Press, 1996.

R   Riley, P. (ed. & trans.). *The Political Writings of Leibniz.* Cambridge: Cambridge University Press, 1972.

Ru   Russell, C. W. (ed. & trans.). *System of Theology.* London: Burns & Lambert, 1850.

VE   Leibniz-Forschungstelle der Universität Münster (eds.). *G. W. Leibniz: Vorausedition zur Reihe VI (Philosophische Schriften).* In der *Ausgabe der Akademie der Wissenschaften der Berlin,* Münster, 1982-.

W   Wiener, P. (ed.). *Leibniz Selections.* New York: Charles Scribners, 1951.

b) Other titles

BH   Bodemann, E. (ed.). *Die Leibniz-Handschriften der Königlichen Öffentlichen Bibliothek zu Hannover.* Hanover: Hahn, 1895; repr. Hildesheim: Olms, 1966.

SL   *Studia Leibnitiana.* Stuttgart: Franz Steiner.

SL Sond. *Studia Leibnitiana, Sonderheft.* Stuttgart: Franz Steiner.

SL Supp. *Studia Leibnitiana, Supplementa.* Stuttgart: Franz Steiner.

STUART BROWN

LEIBNIZ'S FORMATIVE YEARS (1646-76):

AN OVERVIEW

Education

Gottfried Wilhelm was born in Leipzig on 1 July[1], 1646, the son of
Friedrich Leibniz, a Professor of Moral Philosophy. His father, who
had given him every encouragement in the direction of piety and
learning, died while Gottfried was still a child. His library was, for a
while, locked up, but the child's relations were prevailed upon to
allow him access at the age of eight. Leibniz, in an autobiographical
fragment, gave this account of what the privilege meant to him:

> This announcement made me exult greatly, as though I had
> found a treasure. For I was eager to see the many ancients who
> had been known to me only by their names, – Cicero and
> Quintillian and Seneca, Pliny, Heroditus, Xenophon, Plato, ...
> Augustine, and the numerous Christian fathers, both Greek and
> Latin. I occupied myself with these as my inclination
> prompted; and was delighted by their wonderful variety. Thus,

---

[1] 10 days earlier, according to the calendar still in use when Leibniz was young.
Leibniz lived through a time when some countries had gone over to the new,
Gregorian, calendar but others, including the Protestant states of Germany, had not
yet done so. In this volume, however, dates will be given in accordance with the
modern calendar.

S. Brown (ed.): The Young Leibniz and his Philosophy (1646-76). 1 – 18.
© 1999 Kluwer Academic Publishers. Printed in the Netherlands.

before I was quite twelve, I readily understood Latin and had begun to stammer in Greek.[2]

Leibniz was, not surprisingly, a long way ahead of his contemporaries at school and claims to have read Suarez with as much ease as they would have read fairy tales and romances.[3] He was already interested in Scholastic philosophy and immersed in writers such as Fonseca and Zabarella. His mastery of Aristotelian logic was advanced for a schoolboy and he was well read in theology.

After completing the *trivium* at the Nicolai School, Leibniz claims to have encountered the Moderns and, at the age of fifteen, to have taken up the new philosophy.[4] But scholars are mostly of the opinion that his adoption of the mechanical philosophy did not happen for another two years.[5] He entered Leipzig University in 1661 and was particularly influenced by two of his teachers there – Jakob Thomasius and Johann Adam Scherzer – from whom he learned what Christia Mercer calls a "conciliatory eclecticism".[6] In a letter to a correspondent late in life he himself claimed that his facility for harmonising very different points of view was one he acquired while still very young:

---

[2] Quoted (my translation) from the autobiographical fragment '*Vita Leibnitii a se ipso breviter delineata*', FC 381.

[3] FC 383.

[4] "After having finished the trivial schools, I fell upon the moderns, and I recall walking in a grove on the outskirts of Leipzig called the Rosental, at the age of fifteen, and deliberating on whether to preserve substantial forms or not. Mechanism finally prevailed and led me to apply myself to mathematics." (L 655: G III 606) Leibniz later wrote to a friend in 1676 that Bacon and Gassendi were the first modern authors he read. He admitted that he still knew Descartes mainly from popular expositions and had "not yet been able to read his writings with all the care I had intended to give them". (L 152: A II i 247)

[5] See, for instance, W. Kabitz, *Die Philosophie des jungen Leibniz*, Heidelberg: Karl Winter's Universitätsbuchhandlung, 1909. See also E.J. Aiton, *Leibniz. A Biography*, Bristol & Boston: Hilger, 1985, p. 15.

[6] See below, p. 20. Mercer discussed both Scherzer (pp. 24-28) and Thomasius (pp. 28-33).

I have tried to uncover and unite the truth buried and scattered under the opinions of all the different philosophical sects, and I believe I have added something of my own which takes a few steps forward. The circumstances under which my studies proceeded from my earliest youth have given me some facility in this. I discovered Aristotle as a lad, and even the Scholastics did not repel me; even now I do not regret this. But then Plato and Plotinus also gave me some satisfaction, not to mention other ancient thinkers whom I consulted later ... [7]

His early education encouraged him to read widely, to have very broad philosophical sympathies and yet at the same time to develop his own thoughts in an independent way. Leibniz probably exaggerated the extent to which he was self-taught[8] and under-acknowledged the importance of particular teachers for his intellectual development. But it is likely too that he was already in the habit of reading very widely as a boy and already disposed to look for what he could agree to. The University provided him with an opportunity to immerse himself in some of the problems of scholastic Aristotelianism.[9] This is clear from the dissertation he wrote in 1663, under the supervision of Thomasius, entitled *Disputatio metaphysica de Principio Individui*.[10] Though this dissertation was a *juvenilium*, it is noteworthy that its preoccupations were ones that remained central to Leibniz's later

---

[7] L 655: G III 606.

[8] "I was thoroughly self-taught (αὐτοδίδακτος)..." (G VII 185).

[9] This was the time when, as he put it in his *New System*, he "penetrated deeply into the land of the scholastics". In a letter to Herman Conring he admits that he "read them [the scholastics] more immoderately and eagerly than my teachers approved". (L 190: A II i 401) As well as the principle of individuation, Leibniz claimed that he also worked on the composition of the continuum and the concurrence of God. Scholasticism was much influenced by a Christian theological agenda and Leibniz's debt to Aquinas and later Thomists such as Francisco Suarez was considerable. Thomasius, however, encouraged him to read Aristotle for himself and to recognise that his doctrines were often distorted by his scholastic followers.

[10] 'Metaphysical Disputation on the Principle of Individuation' (A VI i 3-20).

metaphysics. Indeed it already anticipates his later logic and metaphysics to a remarkable extent.[11]

Leibniz spent the summer term of 1663 in Jena and attended the lectures given by the Professor of Mathematics there, Erhard Weigel. Weigel had published a book[12] in which he sought to reform philosophy through a reconciliation of Aristotle with the Moderns, such as Bacon, Hobbes and Gassendi. Weigel was an important influence[13], and Leibniz himself[14] was to take up just such a project in the late 1660s. This concern to reconcile ancient and modern philosophy remained a central one in his later philosophy.

On returning to his home town Leibniz extended his studies into 'practical philosophy'[15] and, in 1664, graduated Master of Philosophy with a dissertation on the relationship between philosophy and law. In the following year he received a bachelor's degree in law, for which he wrote a dissertation with a strong philosophical emphasis – on hypothetical judgements.[16]

During his stay in Jena and in the next few years Leibniz read and came to be influenced by a group known as the Herborn Encyclopaedists[17] – in particular, Johann Heinrich Alsted[18] and

---

[11] For instance, the principle of the identity of indiscernibles is already implicit in Leibniz's solution to the problem, as is his view that the complete concept of every individual substance contains everything that is predicable of it. See Laurence B. McCullough's *Leibniz on Individuals and Individuation* (Dordrecht: Kluwer, 1996).

[12] *Analysis Aristotelica ex Euclide restituta*, Jena, 1658.

[13] This is argued, for instance, by Christia Mercer, pp. 33-36 of this volume. See also K. Moll, *Der junge Leibniz*, vol. 1 (Stuttgart-Bad Cannstadt: Fromann-Holzboog, 1978).

[14] See particularly his letter to Jakob Thomasius of April 1669 (L 93-105: G i 15-27: A II i 14-24), which he had published in the following year. This phase of Leibniz's career is discussed by Christia Mercer in her 'Mechanizing Aristotle: Leibniz and Reformed Philosophy', in *Oxford Studies in the History of Philosophy* 2 (1997): 117-52.

[15] He wrote extensive notes, for instance, on Thomasius' *Philosophia practica* (A VI i 42-67).

[16] *Disputatio juridica de conditionibus* ('Legal Disputation on Hypothetical Judgements'), in two parts (A VI i 97-150).

[17] See L.E. Loemker, 'Leibniz and the Herborn Encyclopedists', *Journal of the History of Ideas* 22 (1961): 323-38.

Johann Heinrich Bisterfeld[19]. The Herborn Encyclopaedists stimulated Leibniz's interest in the *ars magna* of Ramond Lull[20] and in particular the idea that there might be an 'alphabet of human thoughts' – "a catalogue of those things that are conceived through themselves and by whose combination the rest of our ideas arise".[21] In 1666, while he was working on his *Habilitationsschrift* in the Faculty of Philosophy[22], Leibniz began to develop these ideas in his own way and produced his first truly original work, his *Dissertatio de Arte Combinatoria*[23]. In this dissertation it is possible to see the beginnings of an interest he was later to develop in constructing a universal characteristic and a logical calculus.[24]

A related idea and one fundamental to the Herborn Encyclopaedists is that human knowledge constitutes a harmonious whole. It is embodied in Alsted's *Encyclopaedia* (1630), which Leibniz considered as a peak of achievement for its time.[25] He came to share Alsted's vision of the perfection of the sciences and, in this way, of the perfectibility of man – a view which in Alsted's case shaded off into his explicit millenarianism. Leibniz made a careful study of Alsted's

---

[18] See H. Hotson, 'Alsted and Leibniz: A Preliminary Survey of a Neglected Relationship', in *Proceedings of the VIth International Leibniz Congress, Leibniz und Europa* 1 (Hanover: G. W. Leibniz Gesellschaft, 1994), pp. 356-63.

[19] Leibniz's studies of Bisterfeld are detailed in Maria Rosa Antognazza's paper in this volume (pp. 41-64 below).

[20] See Catherine Wilson, *Leibniz's Metaphysics* (Princeton: Princeton University Press, 1989), pp. 19-29.

[21] C 430: PW 240. This sentence was deleted from the manuscript in which it occurred, perhaps because in that context he was about to declare that only God can be conceived through himself.

[22] The purpose of this project was to establish himself as qualified to teach the subject.

[23] This is given the English title 'Dissertation on the Art of Combinations' by Loemker for his selections from this work. (L 73-77) It might be better, however, to translate *ars combinatoria* as 'the art of combining' or 'the combinatorial art'.

[24] Leibniz referred back to *De Arte Combinatoria* with some satisfaction on a number of occasions in his later writings. See, for instance, A VI i 279: L 88, G VII 185: AG 7, G VII 293: L 229f., G III 620: L 657, C 157: W 16.

[25] "Ioh. Henr. Alstedius, cujus Encyclopaedia mihi pro captu illorum temporum certe laudanda videtur". (G VII 67)

Diatribe de mille annis apocalypticis (1627)[26] and it may be that this encouraged in him a sympathy for millenarian ideas.

The idea of the harmony of knowledge corresponds with a conception of the universal harmony or connection between all things, an idea which was to be important for Leibniz as it had been for Bisterfeld.   In her paper in this volume, Maria Rosa Antognazza considers the theological foundation of this idea in Bisterfeld's thought and the relationship of Leibniz's conception of harmony to his own theological ideas.[27]

Leibniz sought, but was refused, the degree of Doctor of Law by the University of Leipzig and so he moved to the University of Altdorf, where he matriculated in October 1666. He soon completed and published a dissertation on difficult cases in law (*De Casibus perplexis in Jure*) and received his doctorate the following February. His dissertation and his brilliant oral defence resulted, on his own account, in his receiving broad hints that, were he to remain in Altdorf, he could be assured of early promotion to a professorship.[28] But Leibniz's mind by this stage seems to have been set on a legal career. He had already met and made a very favourable impression on Baron Johann Christian von Boineburg, who was to become his patron. Boineburg was himself a minister of the Elector of Mainz and it was most likely on the Baron's advice that Leibniz dedicated his next publication to the Elector. This was his *Nova Methodus discendae docendaeque Jurisprudentiae*.[29] The first part of this work belongs to the philosophy and psychology of education and reflects Leibniz's broad view of the curriculum. The second part puts forward views about natural law and justice that are reflected in other works of this period. The book seems to have made the right impression on the

---

[26] As Howard Hotson points out (see below, p. 173, fn. 14), Leibniz's awareness of Alsted's millenarianism is indicated by the underlinings and marginalia on his copy of the *Diatribe*.

[27] The theological roots of Leibniz's notion of harmony is also a theme of Konrad Moll's paper, though he focuses on writings of a few years later, particularly 1671.

[28] Leibniz apparently had this assurance from the leading clergyman of the nearby city of Nuremberg. (FC 385)

[29] 'New method for learning and teaching jurisprudence'. (A VI i 259-364: selections from Part I in L 85-90)

Elector, since Leibniz moved to Mainz and shortly took up employment there.

Philosophical and Religious Writings
of the Mainz Period (1668-72)

Context

In 1668 Leibniz moved to Mainz, where the Elector appointed him as a judge in the High Court of Appeal. His talents were soon used also for other projects of a more political and diplomatic kind. He wrote an anonymous tract[30] supporting the Elector's candidate on the occasion of the election a King of Poland. His *Specimen Demonstrationum* was innovative in adopting the mathematical method of demonstration favoured by Hobbes and Spinoza, as well as by his former teacher, Weigel.[31]   Later on, when Louis XIV planned to attack the Netherlands, he wrote a piece[32] proposing instead an attack on Egypt and it was in the hope of averting war in northern Europe that he was sent to Paris.

Leibniz's involvement with Boineburg was particularly close and, as well as becoming a friend, he served the Baron in a number of roles, including secretary and librarian. At Boineburg's instigation he wrote, in 1670, his *Dissertatio praeliminaris* for a new edition of a work by the Italian humanist, Marius Nizolius – his *Anti-Barbarus seu de veris principiis et vera ratione philosophandi contra Pseudophilosophos* (1553).[33] Leibniz agreed with many of Nizolius' criticisms of the

---

[30] His *Specimen Demonstrationum politicarum pro Rege Polonorum eligendo ...* . Vilna, Lithuania (pseud.), 1668. ('Specimen of Political Demonstrations for the Election of a Polish King ...') A IV i 3-98. Some of the ethical aspects of this work are discussed by Francesco Piro in his contribution to this volume.

[31] Leibniz mentions all three, amongst others, in a writing of the late 1670s advocating the extension of the mathematical method to other areas. (C 175-82: W 50-8)

[32] A I i 252-4. Leibniz wrote a good deal on his 'Egyptian plan'.

[33] 'The Anti-Barbarian or On True Principles and the True Method of Philosophising against the False Philosophers.' (G IV 138-76: selections in L 121-130) The *Dissertatio praeliminaris* is commonly referred to, following Loemker, as the 'Preface' to an edition of Nizolius.

scholastics – especially regarding the obscurity of their language. However, he drew the line at imputing these same faults to Aristotle. He argued, moreover, that, of the older scholastics, the most profound were the nominalists, whose thought was "the most consistent with the spirit of our modern reformed philosophy".[34]

Boineburg had converted to Catholicism but shared with Leibniz an earnest desire to see the Lutheran and Catholic Churches re-united. This provided the context for the large number of writings on religious topics that Leibniz produced during his time in Mainz.

Writings on Religious Themes

Chief amongst Leibniz's religious writings of the Mainz period are the group known as the *Demonstrationes Catholicae* (1668-71).[35] These included a number of pieces of a theological character as well as others that belong to the philosophy of religion. Amongst the theological writings was a defence of the doctrine of the Trinity against a Socinian who had written to the Baron.[36] An important early work in the philosophy of religion was his *Confessio Naturae contra Atheistas*.[37] In the first part Leibniz argues that corporeal phenomena cannot be explained without an incorporeal principle. He takes the view of 'the Moderns' that physical phenomena are to be explained in terms of the primary qualities of bodies – magnitude, figure, and motion – but argues that these primary qualities themselves have to be derived from an incorporeal principle. In the second part he offers a demonstration of the immortality of the human mind which makes use of the argument that since the mind is not in space, it cannot be dissolved and is therefore incorruptible.

In her contribution this volume, Ursula Goldenbaum gives particular attention to a work (known as *De transsubstantiatione*) on the

---

[34] A VI ii 427: L 127.

[35] A VI i 489-559.

[36] Andrzej Wiszowaty. Leibniz's reply was his *Defensio Trinitatis* (A VI i 518-30).

[37] 'Confession of Nature against Atheists' (A VI i 489-93: L 109-13).

Catholic doctrine of the Eucharist.[38] The philosophical explication of this doctrine of 'transubstantiation' proved to be a serious difficulty for the 'Modernes'. The French Cartesians tried to show how transubstantiation was compatible with the mechanical philosophy but were widely thought to have failed. Goldenbaum suggests that it was because of his concern with the theological implications of science for the defence of the Christian revelation that Leibniz started his serious work on physics and mathematics in this time.

Leibniz's concern to defend the Christian religion led him to consider on what basis the authenticity of the Bible as the revealed word of God could be defended. In his *Commentatiuncula de judice controversiarum* (1669-71) he claimed this authenticity was founded "reason and history".[39] According to Leibniz, as Daniel Cook points out in his paper on 'The Young Leibniz and the Problem of Historical Truth', ancient history alone can demonstrate the truth of Christianity and its superiority over other religions. Thus empirical considerations played an important part, so far as Leibniz was concerned, in deciding whether or not the claims of revelation were acceptable.

There are other religious writings of the Mainz period that are of particular philosophical interest, including a memorandum on the possibility of the resurrection which Leibniz wrote for Duke Johann Friedrich of Hanover. In this memorandum and in a covering letter Leibniz sought to show how the resurrection of the dead was in conformity with processes to be discovered in nature. He suggested that no substance was altogether destroyed in nature, even by fire. Instead it was reduced to a nucleus or essence too small to be visible but from which it could be re-constituted. This idea is transformed in Leibniz's later writings into his doctrine that no animal, strictly speaking, ever dies, which is an integral part of his later monadology.[40]

---

[38] The doctrine requires that the wine in the sacrament strictly becomes the blood of Christ and the bread strictly becomes his body. Leibniz argues that this is possible if transubstantiation is taken to involve a change of substantial form.

[39] 'Brief Commentaries on the Judge of Controversies', para. 16 (A VI i 549f.).

[40] See my 'Some Occult Influences on Leibniz's Monadology', in *Leibniz, Mysticism, and Religion*, Coudert, A., Popkin, R. H. and Weiner, G. (eds.) (Dordrecht: Kluwer, 1998).

But, though there is much continuity between the writings of the early and the later Leibniz, there are also significant changes. The young Leibniz, like other scientifically-inclined contemporaries, was well-informed and at least open-minded about alchemy.[41] It seems to have been partly on this account that he made such a good impression on Boineburg when they first met. But attitudes towards alchemy changed during Leibniz's lifetime and he ceased to rely, as he had done in his writings on the resurrection[42], on alchemical ideas and put much more weight on the evidence of the microscopists.[43]

The complexity of this pattern of change and continuity in Leibniz's thinking on ideas fashionable in his youth but more suspect in his later years is evident again in the case of millenarianism, the theme of Howard Hotson's chapter in this volume. As Hotson argues, the major diplomatic work of Leibniz's Mainz period, the *Justa dissertatio* of 1671-2, rises to a climax which can only be described as millenarian. Returning from Paris with his diplomatic efforts a failure, however, Leibniz seems to retract this millenarianism completely in the little-known *Summaria apocalypseos explicatio* of 1677. But a host of still later passages attest Leibniz's continuing interest in millenarianism, and among these are statements which collectively suggest, as Hotson argues, that he retained a subtly and uniquely modified interpretation of the doctrine as long as he lived.

Scientific Writings

Leibniz's scientific work of his Mainz period was partly motivated by his concern with religious apologetics and can be seen as an extension

---

[41] See the papers by George MacDonald Ross on 'Leibniz and the Nuremberg Alchemical Society', *SL* 6 (1974): 222-48; 'Leibniz and Alchemy', *SL Sond.* 7 (1978): 166-80; and 'Alchemy and the Development of Leibniz's Metaphysics', *SL Supp.* 22 (1982): 40-5.

[42] Leibniz had not only appealed to the results of alchemical experiments but had used the alchemical phrase 'flower of substance (*flos substantiae*)' to express his central thought that there was something indestructible about the human body.

[43] See Catherine Wilson, 'Leibniz and the Animalcula', *Oxford Studies in the History of Philosophy* 2 (1997): 153-75.

of the project of his *Confessio Naturae*.[44] An important influence and stimulus for the young German was the work of Thomas Hobbes[45], especially his *De Corpore*. Leibniz wrote to Hobbes in 1670 that the "foundations" the Englishman had laid for the abstract theory of motion seemed to him "remarkably justified".[46] He agreed that one body is not moved by another unless the second body touches it and is itself in motion. He also agreed that bodies, once set in motion, continue to move unless impeded by something else. It seemed to him, however, that Hobbes' theory could not account for the observed cohesiveness of bodies, i.e. the fact that the parts of a body remain together rather than departing from it. He suggested that Hobbes' own concept of *conatus* (endeavour) could be used to explain this phenomenon. Hobbes seemed to him glaringly deficient in his account of mind. That is one reason why Leibniz formed the project of adding to Hobbes' *Elementa de Corpore* with his own *Elementa de Mente*, which would demonstrate the need for imperishable incorporeal beings to explain the laws of motion. In this way he intended that God and immortality would be established against the atheism and materialism many found implicit in Hobbes' system.[47]

Although Leibniz had not really mastered modern mathematics and physics at this stage, he produced two treatises with which he hoped to make his mark on the scientific world. These are commonly referred to as his *Hypothesis physica nova* (1671) and consist of his *Theoria Motus concreti*, which was dedicated to the British Royal Society[48],

---

[44] See the papers by Ursula Goldenbaum (pp. 79-102) and Konrad Moll (pp. 65-78) in this volume.

[45] See, for instance, Bernstein, H. M. 'Conatus, Hobbes and the Young Leibniz', *Studies in the History and Philosophy of Science* 11 (1980): 25-37; Moll, K. 'Die erste Monadenkonzeption von Leibniz und ihr Ausgangspunkt in Conatus-Begriff und Perzeptionstheorie von Thomas Hobbes', *Proceedings of the Vth International Leibniz-Kongress*, Hanover: Leibniz-Gesellschaft, 1988; Tönnies, F. 'Leibniz und Hobbes', in *Studien zur Philosophie und Gesellschaftslehre im 17. Jahrhundert*, E. G. Jacoby (ed.), Stuttgart-Bad-Cannstatt: Frommann-Holzboog, 1975, 151-68; and Watkins, J. W. N. *Hobbes' System of Ideas*, London: Hutchinson, 1975.

[46] L 106: A II i 57.

[47] See Konrad Moll's paper in this volume, particularly sect. 4, for an account of Leibniz's use of Hobbes' ideas for apologetic purposes.

[46] Leibniz became a member of the Society in 1673.

and the *Theoria Motus abstracti,* which was dedicated to the French Royal Academy.[49] In the latter work Leibniz addressed one of what he later described as the two great "labyrinths" in which the human mind is caught: the problem of the continuum.[50]

Leibniz's distinction between an abstract and a concrete theory of motion raises the question of how he conceived of the natural sciences and of the place of metaphysics and mathematics within them. Philip Beeley, in his chapter on 'Mathematics and Nature in Leibniz's Early Philosophy', argues that the reason mathematics plays such a crucial role is that nature, as conceived by Leibniz, has a metaphysically pre-determined structure.[51] By basing this structure on the continuum, Beeley argues, Leibniz is able to claim not only that every body is actually divided into smaller parts but that no part is so small that it does not itself contain an infinity of creatures. These claims were ones Leibniz continued to make in his later philosophy.

Writings on Ethics and Politics

In his paper on 'Leibniz and Ethics; the years 1669-72', Francesco Piro claims that in the political and juridical works of the Mainz period, Leibniz introduced most of the ideas around which his moral philosophy developed in later years. Nevertheless, these ideas are introduced through a discussion of philosophical traditions, such as Epicurean hedonism and Renaissance philosophy of love, which are not discussed in Leibniz's later essays. Piro argues that the young Leibniz's attempt to create a synthesis between very different traditions of moral philosophy derives from his desire to reply to the challenge of moral scepticism and to ground political philosophy on alternative anthropological principles to those of Hobbes. In Piro's opinion, this eclectic approach to ethics has important consequences

---

[49] The Akademie editors published the *Theory of Concrete Motion* under the *Hypothesis Physica Nova* (A VI ii 220-57) and the *Theory of Abstract Motion* separately (A VI ii 258-78: extract in L 139-42).

[50] In a paper of around 1679, FC 180: L 264. The other labyrinth, with which this particular paper was concerned, was the problem of freedom and contingency.

[51] Such a structure is already evident in the *Dissertatio de arte combinatoria* and indeed provides the basis for the application of combinatorics.

for Leibniz's metaphysics, since it let emerge a way of considering affections, will and deliberations which is deeply influential on Leibniz's doctrine of human freedom and on his later philosophy of monads.

Though Leibniz preferred absolutism over anarchy, he did not like to concentrate on power as the main attribute of rulers. In an important (but neglected) early work, the *Grundriss eines Bedenckens von Aufrichtung einer Societät in Deutschland* (1671)[52], he sharply distinguished between reason and power. A harmony of mind and power is not only the foundation of beauty and justice but of true statesmanship: "if power is greater than reason, he who possesses it is either a lamb who cannot use it at all, or a wolf and a tyrant who cannot use it well". On the other hand, the man in whom reason is greater than the power to use it is "overpowered". Accordingly, Leibniz urged, "those to whom God has given reason without power...have the right to be counsellors", whilst those who have power alone "must listen patiently, and not throw good counsels to the winds". What is ideal, however, is a union of power and reason within a single person: "Those to whom God has given at once reason and power in a high degree are heroes created by God to be the promoters of his will, as principal instruments." Of the three ways of honouring God – through good works, good thoughts and good actions – the last is best, and is accomplished (if ever) by moralists and statesmen; as "governors of the public welfare" they "strive not only to discover the brilliance of the beauty of God in nature", but to imitate it.

The *Grundriss*, as Patrick Riley has argued, foreshadows much of the mature Leibniz.[53] The definition of love is not yet complete (as in the 1690s); and the notion of God rests on prime causality rather than on the ontological proof which Leibniz later preferred to stress. But even in 1671 the emphasis on charity, even "wise charity" or enlightened benevolence, is fully present in his praise of moralists and statesmen who attempt an *imitatio dei* through good works. The importance of science and enlightenment are fully there too. The

---

[52] 'Foundation for a Proposal for the Establishment of a Society in Germany' (A IV i 530 ff.).

[53] See his *Leibniz's Universal Jurisprudence*, Cambridge, MA: Harvard University Press, 1996.

Grundriss is thus a foretaste of the Leibniz to come and shows that his fundamental moral, political, and scientific ideas were more or less in place by his twenty-fifth year.

Philosophical Writings of the Paris Period (1672-76)

Context

Leibniz arrived in Paris in early March, 1672, on his secret mission on behalf of the Elector of Mainz and in the hope of diverting Louis XIV from his plans for military expansion in Europe. This mission, though unsuccessful, allowed him to stay in Paris for some time and gave him the chance to get to know some of the intellectual luminaries of that great city. He met Antoine Arnauld (1612-94), who enjoyed the highest standing as a philosopher and theologian, and who was later to prove one of the most penetrating contemporary critics of his developing system.[54] He also met Christiaan Huygens and it was during this period, partly thanks to Huygens' guidance, that he properly mastered modern mathematics and physics. In early 1673 he visited London for a few weeks. The primary purpose was diplomatic but he met Henry Oldenburg, to whom he demonstrated a model of his calculating machine, and he was, largely on the strength of his *Hypothesis physica nova*, elected a Fellow of the Royal Society.

Leibniz had planned to return to Mainz but, because of the untimely death of the Elector, he decided to return to Paris, where he engaged in the intensive study of higher mathematics which was to result, in 1675, in his breakthrough with the infinitesimal calculus. During this period he met with other philosophers, including Nicolas Malebranche, whose *Recherche de la Vérité*[55] caused a stir in Paris when it was published in 1675-76. He also became a friend of one of the most persistent critics of Descartes and Malebranche, the sceptic

---

[54] See R. C. Sleigh, Jr., *Leibniz and Arnauld*, New Haven & London: Yale University Press, 1990, for an account of their relationship and a commentary on their correspondence.

[55] The *Search after Truth*, including the *éclaircissements* added later by Malebranche, is available in a modern translation by Thomas M. Lennon and Paul J. Olscamp, Columbus, Ohio: Ohio State University Press, 1980.

Simon Foucher.[56]   Foucher was to become Leibniz's main contact in Paris in the next twenty years, after he had left the French capital in October, 1676, for what was to be the last time.

Leibniz was disappointed in his failure to secure a suitable position for himself in Paris and decided to enter the service of Johann Friedrich, Duke of Hanover.   He travelled via England, taking the opportunity to show his completed calculating machine to Oldenburg. Passing through the Netherlands he visited the microscopists Jan Swammerdam in Amsterdam and Antoni van Leeuwenhoek in Delft. He also took the opportunity to visit Benedict Spinoza in the Hague.

Leibniz had initially put Spinoza down as a Cartesian and continued to think of his great contemporary as profoundly influenced by Descartes.[57]   In 1675, however, he became friendly with a young nobleman from Saxony, Ehrenfried Walther von Tschirnhaus (1651-1708), with whom he collaborated in some mathematical projects. Tschirnhaus, who had met Spinoza and some of his circle, told Leibniz about Spinoza's as yet unpublished metaphysics, which he became eager to read for himself.   In his contribution to this volume, Mark Kulstad looks at a key aspect of what he regards as a three-way dialogue between these men.   Leibniz's attraction to Spinozistic metaphysics in this period is also taken up by Catherine Wilson in her paper.   He wrote notes for his meetings with Spinoza but there is little record of what the two philosophers said to one another.[58]

By the time Spinoza's *Ethics* was finally published, after his death, Hanover had become Leibniz's base, which it continued to be for the

---

[56] For some account of Foucher and of Leibniz's association with him, see Richard A. Watson, *The Breakdown of Cartesian Metaphysics*, Atlantic Highlands, N.J.: Humanities Press, 1987, chs. 3 and 9.

[57] Leibniz originally knew Spinoza as the author of an exposition of Descartes presented in geometrical form – *Renati Descartes Principiorum Philosophiae* (1663) but by 1670 he had dropped him from his list of Cartesians. In 1697, however, he could still claim that "Spinoza has done nothing but cultivate certain seeds of the philosophy of Descartes ..." (G II 563).

[58] Leibniz offered Spinoza an improvement on the Cartesian ontological argument (A II 271-2: L 167-8) which he claimed the latter thought was "sound". There is also a note written by Leibniz after a meeting with Spinoza. (See C 529-30: L 168-9.)   He claimed to have talked to Spinoza "several times and at great length" (A II i 379).

remaining 40 years of his life. Despite his relative isolation, of which he complained, he was able to keep up through correspondence many of the contacts he had made in his formative years.

Philosophy of Religion

Leibniz's most important work in this area during his Paris period is his *Confessio Philosophi* (1672-3),[59] which is devoted to problems of what he later called "theodicy". In this dialogue he presents a defence of human freedom which is interesting in its own right and also anticipates some of his later views. The problem he discusses is whether free will is possible, given the truth of the principle that everything that exists and happens has a sufficient reason. In his contribution to this volume, G. H. R. Parkinson notes that this principle of sufficient reason (for which Leibniz advances two arguments) seems to imply that God is the ultimate cause of sin and damnation, in that our will is subject to external factors which can be traced back to Him. Leibniz argues that the solution to the problem lies in a satisfactory definition of free will. His definition is that free will is the power of acting and not acting, given all the *external* necessary conditions of action. He also states his definition in Aristotelian terms, saying that 'free' means "spontaneous with choice". Leibniz also offers another, and quite different definition of freedom, according to which freedom consists of the proper use of the faculty of reason. None of this affects the truth of the principle of sufficient reason, nor is its truth affected by the fact that a person whose action has been predicted can always act in a way which is contrary to the prediction. Finally, the discussion addresses the problem of the justification of punishment. People may argue that they sin because of the kind of person they are, and that they cannot be blamed for what is in effect their bad luck. Leibniz replies that if a person is to be justly punished, it is sufficient that there should be a known, evil and deliberate will; the external causation of the will is irrelevant.

---

[59] 'The Confession of a Philosopher' (A VI i 115-49).

Metaphysics

During much of his stay in Paris Leibniz wrote relatively little on metaphysics. But in the period from December, 1675 to April, 1676, he wrote a series of metaphysical papers generally referred to as *De summa rerum.*[60] As Parkinson observes in his introduction to the Latin-English *en face* edition, these writings represent "Leibniz's first major attempt at presenting his philosophy in a systematic form".[61] Though Leibniz's discussions in these writings are often compressed and pose difficulties of interpretation they must surely figure more prominently in discussions of his philosophy than they have hitherto.

In the first of two papers in this volume that centre on these texts, Catherine Wilson suggests an approach to the *De summa rerum* via what she calls "the Contouring Problem". Materialistic schemes (like Hobbes') and monistic schemes (like Spinoza's) contain few intrinsic resources to carve out 'contoured' individuals – bounded in space and in the scope of their experiences. Spinoza and Hobbes do some contouring through the notion of *conatus* or endeavour and Spinoza tries further with his theory that the mind is the 'idea' of the body. However, their failure to solve the problem is in part deliberate and serves their moral-political ends. Wilson argues that some fairly baffling sections of *De summa rerum*, particularly those to do with 'vortices' are addressed to this Contouring Problem. Leibniz tries to figure out how persons are bounded in the scope of their experience but persist forever. The soul-body relation turns out to be modelled on the relation of God to the world. Leibniz does not approve of the 'new' moral-political subjects of Hobbes and Spinoza.

In the final chapter of the volume I argue that the *De summa rerum* already contains many elements of his later monadology. For this purpose I take a 'monad' to be an entity which is (1) simple and

---

[60] These were edited and translated by Parkinson under the title *De Summa Rerum. Metaphysical Papers,* 1675-76 (New Haven & London: Yale University Press, 1992) and are referred to here as 'PDSR'. The papers are all translated from A VI iii, but the Akademie editors have grouped together a larger, though overlapping, set of papers under the same title. Parkinson translates *'De summa rerum'* as 'On the highest of things', i.e. 'On the supreme being'. (PDSR xiv)

[61] PDSR xii.

irreducible; (2) eternal or at least not naturally destructible; (3) spontaneous or self-determining; and (4) the source of all other beings. A monadology is a system of monads organised according to certain principles of which perfection, harmony and plenitude are amongst the most characteristic. I claim that Leibniz was already committed in the *De summa rerum* to a number of key monadological principles. He did not yet embrace the doctrine of spontaneity by which his system was later distinguished from that of the occasionalists. But much of what the author of the *De summa rerum* has to say about minds anticipates what he later said about monads.

This introductory overview has presented the first thirty years of Leibniz's life as his 'formative years'. This phrase should not be taken to imply that there were no other important influences on him subsequently or that his ideas did not change or develop later in significant ways. Leibniz sometimes distanced himself in his later writings from the views he had adopted in the period covered by this volume.[62] He apparently thought he had not arrived at his metaphysical system until 1686[63] and many scholars have noted significant changes in the last thirty years of his life.[64] Nonetheless there are, as we have seen, many important principles that Leibniz had already adopted by 1676 and many important ideas that had largely taken shape by that stage.

---

[62] For instance, in a paper from the late 1680s, he identified in his earlier views a tendency to the view that "all things are absolutely necessary" and that "security from compulsion is enough for freedom" (PW 106: BH 115). It is interesting, however, that his determinist letter to Magnus Wedderkopf, in which he says that "God is necessitated to do the best by the very ideality of things", already hints at his later solution through the consideration that not all possibles exist (A II i 117-8: L 146-7).

[63] In the *New System* of 1695, Leibniz claimed that he had arrived at it "several years ago". Foucher, replying in the *Journal des Sçavans*, claimed it was not new but that Leibniz had told him about it "more than ten years ago" (G I 424: WF 41). Leibniz had in fact outlined his theory about the mind and the body to him in 1686 (G I 380: WF 52).

[64] See, for instance, Broad, C. D., *Leibniz: An Introduction* (Cambridge: Cambridge University Press, 1975); Brown, S. *Leibniz* (Brighton: Harvester & Minneapolis: Minnesota University Press, 1984) and Garber, D. 'Leibniz and the Foundations of Physics: The Middle Years', in Okruhlik, K. and Brown, J. R. (eds.) *The Natural Philosophy of Leibniz* (Dordrecht: Reidel, 1985).

CHRISTIA MERCER

THE YOUNG LEIBNIZ AND HIS TEACHERS

In the spring of 1661 Leibniz entered the Lutheran university in his hometown of Leipzig at the age of 15. Before graduating in 1663 he spent a semester at the Lutheran university of Jena. Upon the completion of his undergraduate studies Leibniz had accepted a set of assumptions which he learned from his university professors and which he would retain for the rest of his very long life. In this paper I will summarise some of the views of three professors with whom Leibniz came into contact during his undergraduate days and then describe briefly the philosophical lessons which they bequeathed to their precocious student.

In the 1660s two of the most prominent professors at the university of Leipzig were Johann Adam Scherzer and Jakob Thomasius. At the university in Jena, Erhard Weigel dominated the intellectual scene. As a group, Scherzer, Thomasius, and Weigel are enormously interesting. They are conciliatory eclectics who believe that the philosophical truth, which they assume to be consistent with Christianity, is discoverable within the (apparently) conflicting philosophical schools.[1] They believe that the ancient pagan texts in general offer the key to that truth and that Plato and Aristotle in particular are to be used as source material for the correct metaphysics: Aristotle for his views about substance, Plato for his views about divinity. Scherzer, Thomasius, and Weigel produced an impressive amount of work on a stunning array of topics. I cannot offer even a quick overview of their work here, but I will present a summary of their methodological

---

[1] I use the somewhat vague designation 'conciliatory eclecticism' to refer to any eclecticism that attempts to combine the views of some group of apparently incompatible philosophies into a coherent system. It is not terminology used by Renaissance and early modern thinkers and so it is free of complicating connotations.

S. Brown (ed.): The Young Leibniz and his Philosophy (1646-76). 19–40
© 1999 Kluwer Academic Publishers. Printed in the Netherlands.

proposals. Before doing this however it will be helpful to place them in their rightful historical circumstance.

Early Modern Humanism

Renaissance and early modern humanism is an enormously complicated intellectual movement.[2] We may bypass its complications and focus on a set of methodological assumptions which are particularly relevant to our discussion of Scherzer, Thomasius, and Weigel. Many humanists believed that the ancient philosophies could be combined into a single unified whole. Many practised and preached conciliatory eclecticism among the ancient schools, and some extended their eclectic scope to include more recent authors. Because the proposals of even the mightiest of ancients (e.g., Plato and Aristotle) did not obviously cohere, these thinkers engaged in elaborate interpretative schemes. For all such philosophers, the assumption was that the diverse philosophical traditions were not as incompatible as they at first appeared; the goal was to forge a reconciliation among the worthy schools; the result was a mixture of ancient and modern ideas; and the hope was that the proper synthesis would effect peace among contemporary philosophers.

---

[2] For standard accounts of Renaissance humanism, see P. O. Kristeller's *The Classics and Renaissance Thought* (Cambridge, MA: Harvard University Press, 1955) and *Studies in Renaissance Thought and Letters* (Oram: Storia Letteratura, 1956); E. Gilson, 'Humanisme Médiéval et Renaissance', *Les Idées et les Lettres*, (Paris: Vrin, 1932); and E. Garin's *Ritratti di umanisti* (Florence, 1967). For some recent discussions and for references to the vast intervening literature on the topic, see A. Grafton, *Defenders of the Text: the Tradition of Scholarship in an Age of Science, 1450-1800* (Philadelphia: University of Pennsylvania Press, 1990); *The Transmission of Culture in Early Modern Europe,* ed. by A. Grafton and A. Blair (Cambridge, MA: Harvard University Press, 1991); and *The Impact of Humanism on Western Europe,* ed. by A. Goodman and A. Mackay (London: Longman, 1990). In the latter collection, P. Burke defines humanism and offers a brief survey of its dissemination throughout Europe in his article 'The Spread of Italian Humanism'. According to him, humanism "is the movement to recover, interpret, and assimilate the language, literature, learning and values of ancient Greece and Rome" (p. 2). For a lengthy discussion of the humanist background to Leibniz, see L. E. Loemker, *Struggle for Synthesis* (Cambridge, MA: Harvard University Press, 1972).

The early Renaissance philosopher, Giovanni Pico della Mirandola (1463-94), formulates one of the defining statements of Renaissance eclecticism in his *De hominis dignitate* of 1486. Pico demands that we not devote ourselves "to any one of the schools of philosophy" and notes that "it was a practice of the ancients to study every school of writers, and if possible, not to pass over any treatise". He declares: "I have resolved not to accept anyone's words, but to roam through all the masters of philosophy, to investigate every opinion and to know all the schools".[3] According to Pico, each philosophical tradition had a share of the truth so that, once the truths in each were discovered, they could be combined into one comprehensive and true philosophy. One of the main points of his project was to show that "the philosophies of Plato and Aristotle should be reconciled" and "a concord" between the two systems effected.[4] In fact, Pico's texts are more steeped in Platonism than in Aristotelianism, but it is important that unlike many of his contemporary humanists he speaks favourably of Aristotle and the scholastics. He was prepared to add Aquinas, Scotus, Avicenna, and Averroes to his eclectic mixture. Pico was also the most prominent humanist to include Jewish and Kabbalistic teachings in his syncretic vision.[5]

---

[3] G. Pico della Mirandola, *De hominis dignitate, Heptaplus, De ente et uno, e scritti Varii*, ed. Eugenio Garin (Florence, 1942), pp. 138-40. For an English version, see Pico, *On the Dignity of Man, On Being and One, Heptaplus*, trans. Charles G. Wallis and others (Indianopolis: Bobbs-Merrill, 1965), pp. 21f.

[4] *De hominis dignitate*, pp. 144, 162 or *On the Dignity of Man, On Being and One, Heptaplus*, pp. 24, 33.

[5] For a summary of Pico's interest in the Kabbalah and citations of the vast literature on the topic, see B. P. Copenhaver and C. B. Schmitt, *Renaissance Philosophy*, (Oxford: Oxford University Press, 1992), pp. 171-3. The young Leibniz was familiar with Giovanni Pico (see, e.g., A II i 176) and with another widely known Renaissance syncretist, Agostino Steuco (1497/98-1548) whose most important syncretic work, *Perennis philosophia*, Leibniz cites (see A VI ii 137 and also A II i 176). The mature Leibniz had books by each in his private library; see G. Utermöhlen, 'Die Literatur der Renaissance und des Humanismus in Leibniz' privater Büchersammlung', *SL* XXIII (1983): 221-38. For an interesting discussion of the similarities between the methodological assumptions of Leibniz and Steuco, see C. B. Schmitt. 'Perennial Philosophy: From Agostino Steuco to Leibniz', *Journal of the History of Philosophy* 27 (1966): 505-32.

For many conciliatory eclectics, the philosophy they proclaimed had a religious goal : because they assumed that one truth 'flowed through' all philosophical schools and that this truth was Christian, they firmly believed that the ancient texts contained religious truths. Two obvious questions faced the concilatory humanist: if there is a single truth to be discovered within the ancient philosophical schools, then why had it not previously been discovered?; if the truth is fundamentally Christian, then how did the philosophies of pagans like Plato and Aristotle come to contain some of those Christian truths? Although the details of their explanations differ, most early modern humanists agreed that it was the development of new philosophical, theological, and/or intellectual tools that made it possible for them, in a way that it had never been before, to excavate the buried truth. There were however (at least) two rather different answers given to our second question. Many accepted an account of history that allowed them to sanctify pagan learning. This historiography, usually called *the prisca theologia* or ancient theology, was a brilliant melding of religion and philosophy. The story runs roughly as follows: Moses did not write down all the wisdom bestowed on him by God, but transmitted it in an oral tradition that continued until it found its way into the writings of Plato, Pythagoras, and others; moreover, Plato and other ancient authors intentionally obscured these divine truths because they were not appropriate for the uninitiated.[6] In the post-Christian era, with the help of the newly discovered texts and the proper scholarly and

---

[6] The standard text on the ancient theology remains D. P. Walker's *The Ancient Theology: Studies in Christian Platonism from the Fifteenth to the Eighteenth Centuries* (New York: Cornell University Press, 1972). Copenhaver and Schmitt in *Renaissance Philosophy* also neatly summarise the tradition and cite more recent studies. See esp. pp. 146-8. As they note, the theory that Plato was heir to an esoteric theology existed before the Renaissance, but it became "a major element in Western historiography only in the later fifteenth century" when Marsilio Ficino and Pico made it famous (p. 136). There were various elaborations on the story just given. For example, some humanists maintained that Plato had acquired his esoteric wisdom during travels to Egypt where he met and conversed with Jewish wise men. One of the more amusing variations on the theme developed in France where some humanists argued that the ancient (French) Druids were the original source of this wisdom and that most of the major players in the genealogy were French. See Walker, *The Ancient Theology,* pp. 74-9.

philological tools, humanists like Pico believed that the wisdom in the ancient theology could be recovered and the single unifying philosophy forged. This philosophy would of course be firmly rooted in Christianity so that the unique truth of the Judaeo-Christian tradition would coincide with philosophical truth. According to Pico, for example, the Jewish Kabbalah was an important source of knowledge which was ultimately about Christian truths. On this reading of history, Jewish thinkers like Maimonides became a source of Christian wisdom. Pico and many other humanists insisted that, with 'the divine light' of Christian revelation, the wisdom of the ancients could be fully discerned.[7]

The ancient theology was wildly popular. But it would not do for all. Many conciliatory eclectics were wedded to the ancient texts but offered another explanation for how the one truth could 'flow through' all philosophical schools so that even pagan philosophers like Aristotle and Plato could contain Christian truths. For these philosophers, the divine truths could be read in the 'Book of Nature'. That the ancient pagan texts were a proper source of some divine truths was a tradition with a long respectable history. Many philosophers cited Paul who wrote in *Romans* about the Greek philosophers: "That which may be known of God is manifest among them; for God hath shewed it unto them. For the invisible things of him from the creation of the world are clearly seen, being understood by the things that are made, even his eternal power and Godhead".[8] The philosophical profundity of the texts of Plato and Aristotle gave dramatic support to this thesis. Many humanists assumed that superior intellects, whether pagan or not, were able to glimpse God. Pico nicely expresses this point when he writes: "In every age there have been a few predominant thinkers, supreme both in judgement and knowledge

---

[7] I have left out many important details in this brief account of the ancient theology. One of these is worth noting because it bears slightly on our discussion. An important part of the argument for the genealogy was the collection of texts entitled the *Hermetica* which foresaw Christianity and yet were believed to be very ancient. When Isaac Casaubon argued persuasively in 1614 that these texts were post-Christian, the defenders of the ancient theology lost ground that was never regained. See Walker, *The Ancient Theology,* pp. 17 ff. Scherzer, Thomasius, and Weigel were aware of Casaubon's argument; Thomasius took it to undermine the theory.

[8] *Romans* I 19-20.

... who all agreeing together, not only believed these things, but also powerfully proclaimed them".[9] For Pico and subsequent conciliatory eclectics, two doctrines that at first seem incompatible may often, after careful study and full analysis, be made to cohere.[10] To twentieth-century sensibilities, the resulting coherence may seem a perversion of the original tenets; to the sincere humanist conciliator, the coherence was a step towards philosophical truth and intellectual peace. There were conciliators who proclaimed coherence where none is recognisable. For thoughtful eclectics like Pico however the proper analysis would involve a comparison of the views of one philosopher with those of other great philosophers. If one doctrine seemed to conflict with another, then it was appropriate to re-examine the interpretation given to each. After thorough re-examination, the ingenious eclectic could often forge an agreement. Scherzer, Thomasius, and Weigel were such eclectics.

Johann Adam Scherzer (1628-83)

As professor of philosophy, Hebrew, and theology, Scherzer was a leading figure at the University of Leipzig in the early 1660s.[11] Although he was thoroughly familiar with the proponents and canonical texts of the *prisca theologia,* he did not accept that theory entirely. He refers frequently to Plato, Plotinus, Philo, Proclus, Augustine, Maimonides and Johann Reuchlin, but he warns against the

---

[9] Quoted in Walker, *The Ancient Theology,* p. 49.

[10] For a brief introduction to Giovanni Pico and other Renaissance eclectics and for the standard literature on these topics, see Copenhaver and Schmitt, *Renaissance Philosophy,* Chapter 3.

[11] I have not come across any accurate account of Scherzer and his work in the secondary literature. Wundt and Leinsle offer the most complete accounts, but like Fischer incorrectly place Scherzer among the Protestant Aristotelians. See M. Wundt, *Die deutsche Schulmetaphysik des 17 Jahrhunderts* (Tübingen: Mohn, 1939), pp. 141f.; U. G. Leinsle, *Reformversuche protestantischer Metaphysik im Zeitalter des Rationalismus* (Augsburg: Maro Verlag, 1988), pp. 20-6 and K. Fischer, *Gottfried Wilhelm Leibniz: Leben, Werke, und Lehre* (Heidelberg, 1920), pp. 38-9. In fact, Scherzer is more interested in Kabbalistic and Platonic doctrines than those of Aristotle.

dangers of "the most sinful syncretists".[12] He was deeply committed to the importance of Jewish thought in general and the Hebrew language in particular, but took them to be tools with which the careful student could expose the Biblical truths. In one of his textbooks he asks how "will the bare truth ever be revealed"? His answer in short is: in "the words of the scripture ... properly understood".[13] Besides the important contribution which 'the Hebrews' could make to the discovery of the truth, Scherzer also believed that the ancient philosophers could contribute significantly. In one of his most interesting texts, the *Vade mecum sive manuale philosophicum quadripartitum* (Leipzig, 1686) he offers a sketch of a metaphysical system that relies most heavily on Aristotelian tenets in the areas of metaphysics and physics, but uses Platonic notions as soon as the topics shift to God and the relation between the divine and mundane. According to Scherzer, his proposals will lead to philosophical agreement, Christian faith, and religious harmony.[14]

There are then four basic ingredients in Scherzer's eclectic mixture: his native Lutheranism, the thought and language of "the Hebrews", the metaphysics and physics of Aristotle, and the metaphysics of Plato. Let's treat each of these briefly. Scherzer was acutely aware of the religious crisis of his time. He bemoans the fact that there is so much disagreement among the faithful and so many "pernicious theological controversies". The only way out of this intellectual chaos is to convince people of the correct theological positions, namely, those consistent with Lutheran teachings. For our purposes, we may avoid the details of this Protestant theology and simply note that for Scherzer

---

[12] For a more thorough account of Scherzer's views on the *prisca theologia* and general methodology, see my 'Humanist Platonism in Seventeenth-Century Germany', *Humanism and Early Modern Europe,* ed. J. Kraye and M. Stone, *London Studies in the History of Philosophy*, vol. 1 (London: Routledge, forthcoming).

[13] Scherzer, *Collegii anti-Sociniani,* preface. Leibniz speaks favourably of Scherzer (e.g. A VI i 15, 310).

[14] The *Vade mecum* went through at least five editions; the one cited here is the fourth. In the introduction to this edition there appear a number of reviews which proclaim the importance of Scherzer's book. One of these is by Thomasius; another claims that Scherzer has offered the "lost youth" of today an Ariadne's thread out of the "labyrinth" of present day philosophy.

'the truth' about theological and metaphysical matters was consistent with Lutheranism. What Scherzer intended to do was to forge an agreement among thinkers by means of careful definitions and proper methodology. With sources ranging from Aristotle, Aquinas and Suarez to Plato, Porphyry and Augustine, he attempts to give a thorough analysis of the basic elements of philosophy and to arrive at "the knowledge of all things".[15]

For knowledge about Biblical things, Scherzer insisted that we turn to the insights of "the rabbis". His attitude toward Jewish thought is nicely exemplified by an edition he did of three commentaries on the Hebrew Testament. The *Trifolium orientale,* which was published in Leipzig while Leibniz was still an undergraduate, contains three commentaries, each of which is in Hebrew, each of which is on a Biblical text, each of which is by a Jewish 'theologian', and each of which is translated into Latin.[16] It was Scherzer's belief that such philosophical and philological commentaries on the Bible would help the thoughtful Christian properly interpret that text and then grasp the truths within. By such means, "the pernicious religious controversies" could be avoided and peace among the faithful attained.

For knowledge about metaphysical matters, Scherzer turned to the ancient philosophies where he maintained a strict division of labour. To Aristotle and the scholastics, he assigned the job of constructing an accurate account of substance and nature. Scherzer makes much use of Spanish scholastics like Suarez and the Coimbrans, though earlier scholastics like Aquinas, Scotus, and Albertus Magnus are also frequently mentioned. For example, he cites the Coimbrans when he first defines a real cause as "that from which an effect receives its being", he cites Suarez when he offers as a second definition "the per se flowing of being into another".[17] But whatever his source his account of substance and the principles of nature are thoroughly Aristotelian. For example, he explains that *entelechia* was invented by

---

[15] *Vade mecum*, Part I, p. 131.
[16] *Trifolium orientale, continens commentarios R. Abarbenelis in Haggaeum, R. Sal. Jarchi in Parsch. I. Geneseos, & R. Mos. Maiemonidae Theologiam, cum versione, notis philologico-philosophicis & Appendice Specimenis Theologiae Mythicae Ebraeorum, junctis Autoritatum SS Scripturae ...* (Leipzig, 1663).
[17] *Vade mecum*, Part I, p. 24.

Aristotle and signifies form or "what acts and has one end"; and he defines *forma* as "what gives being to a thing" and is such that "with matter" it constitutes a per se being.[18]

Given this thorough-going Aristotelianism, it is striking that, when the topics turn to God or the relation between the supreme being and creatures, Scherzer's sources are almost entirely Platonic. For example, he says that he is following Plato in Book II of the *Republic* when he defines God as what "remains simple" while being "most beautiful ... and most good". Embracing the Plotinian causal doctrine of emanation, Scherzer claims that the supreme being is the principle of all things and their constant source: "in acting ... [God] is neither changed nor depleted" and yet "is that through which things live". He claims to follow the Renaissance Platonist Marsilio Ficino in conceiving of God as "the light itself.., the reason of reasons, the fount and maker of all things, the uniform and omniform form ..., the unity in the multitude". According to Scherzer, the supreme being contains all things while remaining fundamentally simple, and acts constantly to conserve creatures while "nothing in him is changed, nor is it depleted".[19] Scherzer stands in a long line of Platonist theists, both Jewish and Christian, when he distinguishes between the archetypal world and the created world, where the former is the Idea of all possible things as they exist in the mind of God and the latter is the coordinated aggregate of created things. The conception of the divine and its relation to the created world is clear. The mind of God contains the Platonic Ideas or archetypes; the creatures of the world are (somehow) the manifestations of these Ideas. The former are perfect, the latter are not; yet the perfection of God is evident in the composition and harmony of created things.[20] The frontispiece of Scherzer's *Vade mecum* constitutes a delightful summary of his position. In this elaborate engraving, we find two robed figures – one marked Aristotle, the other Plato – who stand on either side of and jointly hold a sphere on which a triangle is inscribed. The triangle, a symbol of the Trinity, emits rays of light which fall on a lone stag, a

---

[18] *Vade mecum*, Part I, pp. 69-70.
[19] *Vade mecum*, Part I, pp. 52-3.
[20] *Vade mecum*, Part I, p. 137.

symbol of the faithful Christian.[21]   The point of this pictorial summary of Scherzer's proposals seems clear: the truth will shine on the faithful Christian and illuminate the right path only when the thought of Aristotle and Plato have been made appropriately consistent with one another and with the insights afforded by ancient revelations and Christian doctrines.

Jakob Thomasius (1622-84)

Jakob Thomasius was professor of rhetoric, dialectic, and moral philosophy in Leipzig.[22]   His contemporaries considered him an 'erudite' historian of philosophy and important conciliatory philosopher.[23]   Leibniz describes him as "the most celebrated German Peripatetic"[24] and often refers to him as "our most famous Thomasius".[25]   We may glean from Thomasius' books the philosophical and methodological lessons he taught his students.[26] First and foremost, Thomasius was a conciliatory eclectic who rejected both syncretism and the *prisca theologia*.   For Thomasius, the new scholarly skills were the key with which to open the ancient texts; the reformed theology was a means by which the truth could be recognised.   He believed that the true philosophy could be constructed

---

[21]   This engraving is reproduced in my 'Humanist Platonism in Seventeenth-Century Germany'.

[22]   Wundt, *Die deutsche Schulmetaphysik des 17. Jahrhunderts*, p. 142.

[23]   Johann C. Sturm, *Philosophia eclectica* (Altdorf, 1686), pp. 72f.

[24]   A VI ii 426.

[25]   A VI i 186; see also A VI i 300.   There has been little scholarly work done on Thomasius.   The work that has been done has categorized him as an Aristotelian. See Leinsle, *Reformversuche*, pp. 139-49; E. J. Aiton, *Leibniz: A Biography* (Bristol & Boston: Hilger, 1985), pp. 13-14 and Wundt, *Die deutsche Schulmetaphysik des 17. Jahrhunderts,* pp. 142-3.

[26]   My discussion is based on several texts by Thomasius, cited more fully in the bibliography.   The most relevant of these are his (1) *Origines historicae philosophiae & ecclesiasticae*, (3rd edition, 1699); (2) *Schediasma historicum... ad historiam tum philosophicum ...* (Leipzig, 1665); and (3) *Dissertationes LXIII & varii argumenti magnam partem ad historiam & ecclesiasticam pertinentes*, (Leipzig, 1693).   The latter, which were written in the 1650s, 1660s, and 1670s, reveal a good deal about his attitudes towards philosophy and the proper philosophical method.

from the raw materials of apparently diverse philosophical schools, but he insisted that those raw materials be chosen with great care.

Thomasius complained bitterly about the propensity among his predecessors and colleagues to collect ideas without thorough analysis, to assume that all philosophical schools could be made to cohere, and then to force a synthesis between doctrines where there was none. It is important to grasp the subtlety of Thomasius' approach to history. He believed that ancient philosophers offered the primary raw materials for the proper conciliatory philosophy, but he was prepared neither to force their views into Christian doctrine nor to accept the mistaken interpretations of their ideas promulgated by the less discriminating humanists. He encouraged his students to take the texts of Aristotle and other historical figures on their own terms.[27] The result of this historically informed analysis of ancient philosophy was to make the 'true' views of the ancients available for careful scrutiny. Once the ancient doctrines were properly interpreted, they could be thoroughly evaluated. The evaluative procedure involved two steps: first, the Christian orthodoxy of the doctrine had to be noted, then both its philosophical merit and potential for conciliation among philosophers had to be determined. For example, Thomasius' *Exercitatio de Stoica mundi exustione* of 1676 is an extended unveiling of the heresies of the Stoics.[28] He makes a thorough analysis of Stoic philosophy, compares its tenets to those of the Platonists, Aristotelians, and Epicureans, and then identifies its "many errors". While identifying the heretical views of the Stoics, he clarifies those Platonic and Aristotelian doctrines which conform to Christian teachings. Only through the careful analysis of the views of the ancients can we recognise the difference between "the light of true doctrine" and the "shadows of the pagans".[29]

---

[27] See e.g., Thomasius, *Dissertationes,* pp. 466, 478f.
[28] The full title of the work is *Exercitatio de Stoica mundi exustione: cui accesserunt argumenti varii, sed imprimis ad historiam Stoicae philosophiae facientes, dissertationes XXI* (Leipzig, 1676). As Guhrauer puts it, Thomasius began the "scientific study of the history of philosophy in Germany" (*Gottfried Wilhelm Freiherr von Leibniz. Eine Biographie* (2 vols., Breslau, 1846; repr. Hildesheim: Olms, 1966), Vol. I, p. 27).
[29] Thomasius, *Exercitatio,* p. 3.

Thomasius had no doubt about the superiority of Aristotelian philosophy, but he subjected that philosophy to the same scrutiny that he applied to other ancient sources. He was fond of reminding his students that, however brilliant Aristotle might have been, he was a pagan whose philosophical insights lacked the full aid of "divine light".[30] He writes in his *Schediasma,* for example: "For those people who repeat the same old song that the ancient Aristotle can be reconciled with sacred scripture, they should be met with derision".[31] For Thomasius, it was an important though arduous task to uncover Aristotle's real views. As many humanists had done before him, he argued that the bad translations of Averroes and the misinterpretations of the scholastics had made the excavation of the real Aristotelian philosophy especially difficult.[32] But Thomasius also insisted that the philosophy of Aristotle, once properly understood, had enormous merit. As he wrote to Leibniz in 1668, "I think no one in the history of philosophy has hit the mark better than Aristotle".[33] According to Thomasius for example the true importance of Aristotle's *Nicomachean Ethics* had long been hidden behind the misinterpretations of the scholastics. By offering his own translation and edition of the Greek text, he hoped that Aristotle's actual views might "bring some agreement" about ethical matters.[34] He maintains that Aristotle's ethical proposals offer nothing less than the foundations for virtue in the community and perfection within humanity.[35]

The favouritism that Thomasius showed to Aristotelian thought did not prevent him from making good use of other philosophies.[36] His eclectic mixture contained large parts of Platonism and to a lesser

---

[30] Thomasius, *Schediasma,* p. 13.

[31] Thomasius, *Schediasma,* p. 22.

[32] Thomasius, *Brevarium,* p. 75.

[33] A II i 13.

[34] Thomasius, *Brevarium,* pp. 72f.

[35] Thomasius, *Brevarium,* p. 82.

[36] That Leibniz's acclaimed teacher was a serious student of Aristotle has been noted by other scholars. What has not been properly understood however is that Thomasius' philosophical project was not merely Aristotelian; it was motivated by a commitment to a critical eclecticism and borrowed heavily from Platonism and other ancient sources.

degree other ancient ideas as well. It did not however draw heavily from contemporary philosophy: the major raw materials for Thomasius' conciliatory concoction were almost exclusively ancient. This conservatism was coupled with an impressive erudition. Thomasius' texts display a familiarity with a wide range of philosophical schools and doctrines, both Renaissance (e.g., Piccolomini, Steuco) and ancient (e.g., Parmenides, Democritus), Christian (e.g., Augustine, Origen) and Jewish (e.g., Philo, Maimonides). Although Thomasius clearly has some knowledge of the new mechanical philosophers, he does not take seriously the thought of the most important 'modern' thinkers (e.g., Descartes, Gassendi, and Hobbes); he writes to Leibniz at one point that he "despises" their thought.[37] His strongest approbation however is saved for the promoters of the *prisca theologia* who "have wrapped that [Platonic] philosophy in mystery and obscurity".[38] In his *Schediasma,* he insists that "it is a fiction that Platonism [and not Aristotelianism] is the closest of ancient philosophies to Christianity".[39] According to Thomasius, the central position assigned to Plato by so many humanists is based on a thoroughly mistaken interpretation of his thought.[40] Once we take Plato on his own terms, we discover both that he was mistaken on a number of important points and that Aristotle has more to offer in all areas of philosophy than does Plato.[41] But Thomasius also insists that the Platonist tradition is an important source of truths, especially about God's relation to the created world.[42] For example, in the *Exercitatio,* Thomasius agrees with the Platonists against the Stoics in their account of "the flowing of creatures from God".[43]

---

[37] For Thomasius's views about the moderns, see *Physica,* 69-87; *Origines,* p. 14. On Hobbes, see *Dissertationes* # 8, entitled 'de statu naturali adversus Hobbesium', which was written just prior to the beginning of Leibniz's undergraduate studies. For Thomasius' comment to Leibniz, see A II i 13.

[38] Thomasius, *Dissertationes,* p. 478.

[39] Thomasius, *Schediasma,* p. 38.

[40] Thomasius, *Schediasma,* p. 52.

[41] Thomasius, *Dissertationes,* pp. 465-80.

[42] Thomasius, *Schediasma,* pp. 13, 28.

[43] Thomasius, *Schediasma,* pp. 249-52.

For Thomasius, the goal of his eclecticism is the construction of the true philosophy firmly rooted in Christianity. In his *Schediasma,* he congratulates Luther for having understood that the ultimate sources of truth are the Bible and the doctrines of the church.[44] But Thomasius also maintains that as long as we carefully distinguish between sacred and profane doctrine and remain alert to the heretical teachings of both Christian and non-Christian authors, we will be able to construct a philosophy out of Christian and pagan texts. As misguided as some humanists might have been in their account of philosophical history and historical texts, their fundamental belief in the wisdom of the ancients was sound. Thomasius insists in his *Schediasma* that "there has been abundant pouring forth of divine wisdom" in ancient philosophy and that the profundity of the Aristotelian philosophy is due to the fact that Aristotle, more than any other philosopher, understood that "God speaks through the book of nature".[45] As he concludes the preface to his textbook on physics, which is thoroughly Aristotelian:

> there is the most elegant nexus among things and the finest order [which acts] as a ladder for us to ascend to God. This [order] ... reveals the glory of the supreme Craftsman.... Assuredly, whoever glimpses the single harmony and beauty of ends will therefore grasp the Wisdom of the most Benevolent Architect.[46]

For Thomasius, the wisdom of the ancients is due to their ability to discern "God himself" in nature and the proper conciliatory eclecticism will be built out of Christian doctrine and these insights of discernment.

---

[44] Thomasius, *Schediasma,* p. 74.

[45] Thomasius, *Schediasma,* p. 479.

[46] Thomasius, *Physica,* preface.

Erhard Weigel (1625-99)

Erhard Weigel was professor of mathematics and astronomy at the university in Jena.[47] It was to study with Weigel that Leibniz went to Jena for the summer semester of 1663.[48] Unlike Scherzer and Thomasius, Weigel took seriously the new mechanical philosophy according to which all corporeal properties are reducible to and explainable in terms of matter and motion. The degree to which he influenced the young Leibniz's ideas about logic has been much discussed.[49] What concerns us here is the eclecticism of Weigel's most important book, *Analysis Aristotelica ex Euclide restituta,* of 1658. Rejecting the sectarianism of both scholastic and contemporary philosophers, he chooses a conciliatory approach. According to Weigel, the present unfortunate state of philosophy is due to ignorance on the part of the scholastics about the proper mathematical method. As he explains in his 'Dedicatio', with the rediscovery of the thought of Euclid and the perfected mathematical method that it engendered, we now possess the key with which to enter "the most valuable Palace of that very ancient philosophy".[50] By applying the mathematical method to all the parts of philosophy, Weigel proposes to remove philosophy from its present "ruins" and to construct a single coherent and true system. His ultimate goal is "first and foremost" to present

---

[47] Lewis White Beck makes some interesting biographical remarks about Weigel, but seriously miscategorises him. See L. W. Beck's *Early German Philosophy: Kant and his Predecessors* (Cambridge, MA: Harvard University Press, 1969), pp. 194-5.

[48] For the fullest account of Weigel, see Leinsle, *Reformversuche*, pp. 63-87. For a brief account of Weigel and of Leibniz's stay in Jena, see Aiton, *Leibniz*, pp.15-6.

[49] See W. Kabitz, *Die Philosophie des jungen Leibniz*, Heidelberg: C. Winter, 1909; Guhrauer, *Gottfried Wilhelm, Freiherr von Leibniz: Eine Biographie;* Belaval, *Leibniz: Initiation à sa Philosophie* (Paris: Vrin, 1962); and especially K. Moll, *Der junge Leibniz* (Stuttgart: Frommann-Holzboog, 1978), vol. 1, for various views about the influence Weigel had on the young Leibniz. All of these scholars believe that Weigel influenced Leibniz's logic and Moll argues that a great part of the young Leibniz's logical plans arose out of Weigel's thought.

[50] Weigel, *Analysis*, 'Dedicatio'. Fischer notes Weigel's conciliatory approach and claims that Leibniz was influenced by it, though he does not describe that influence in any detail. See Fischer, *Gottfried Wilhelm Leibniz: Leben, Werke, und Lehre*, p. 40.

what is "true, real, and most accurately demonstrated".[51] Weigel is even more insistent than were Thomasius and Scherzer that clarity in both definition and argumentation is the bedrock of the true philosophy.[52] But he also claims that "the most accurate way and method" to the truth is that "of the ancient philosophers".[53] According to Weigel, "today it is possible to abandon the ignorance of the former [scholastic] philosophers" and "to complete" the work begun "by the ancients". It is to this end that his book "is chiefly directed".[54]

Weigel's conciliatory system is a complicated mixture of Platonic, Aristotelian and mechanical ideas. He explains that it was Aristotle who first "laid down the mathematical steps to human knowledge" and that some of the insights of the new philosophers (e.g., Descartes) are merely extensions of Aristotelian ideas.[55] His physical proposals are fascinating in that he endorses mechanical explanations of physical properties and yet places this 'modern physics' within an Aristotelian account of nature. According to Weigel, what the ancients called natural philosophy is the study of those things which are constituted of two principles, "one is called *Matter,* the other *Form*".[56] For Weigel, matter is extended stuff which is indeterminate and which combines with a source of motion to produce an individual corporeal object; form is what actualises the potential in matter and turns it into a determinate thing "from which its affections flow".[57] To oversimplify somewhat, the ultimate principles of nature are the Aristotelian ones of matter and form; yet the corporeal properties of natural objects are to

---

[51] See the 'Praefatio' [v].

[52] The demand for accuracy is a motif that runs throughout German Protestant texts of the period. Like many of their contemporaries Scherzer, Thomasius, and Weigel believed that the intellectual and religious chaos would only be resolved when philosophy acquired a high degree of clarity. Although I mostly ignore this important methodological matter here, I briefly discuss the views of Scherzer and Weigel on the topic in my 'Humanist Platonism in Seventeenth-Century Germany'. More work needs to be done on this unknown part of seventeenth-century philosophical methodology.

[53] *Analysis*, p. 2.

[54] *Analysis*, p. 94f.

[55] *Analysis*, p. 4.

[56] *Analysis*, p. 193.

[57] *Analysis*, p. 196.

be explained in terms of matter and motion. This is an ingenious combination of Aristotelian metaphysics and modern physics; it is also a position quite similar to the one developed by the young Leibniz.[58]

Despite Weigel's commitment to this blend of Aristotelian metaphysics and mechanical physics, he is happy to make thorough use of Platonism. We find the same division of labour in Weigel's proposals that we saw in Scherzer and Thomasius: when his topics are natural philosophy and substance as an active thing in nature, the source is primarily Aristotelianism; when he turns his attention to the relation between God and creatures, his source is Platonism. Although the details of Weigel's Platonism differ from Scherzer and Thomasius, the basic conception of the supreme being and its relation to creatures is the same. God, who is the only self-sufficient being, is fundamentally unified and immutable.[59] The divine mind contains attributes which are like Platonic Ideas and which constitute the ingredients out of which the objects of the world are formed.[60] According to Weigel, the attributes of God "flow" into creatures and constitute the essences of created things[61] so that the perfection of the divine is "most immanent in everything".[62]

The Young Leibniz

Leibniz was profoundly influenced by the pronouncements of his teachers. He disagreed with them on important details, but he never wavered from his commitment to a conciliatory eclecticism in which Christian doctrine and ancient ideas were combined. In particular, the professors of Leipzig and Jena bequeathed to the young man three methodological lessons: first, that the true philosophy was to be discovered beneath the major philosophical schools and would be consistent with Christian doctrine; second, that the philosophy of

---

[58] For more details on Weigel's natural philosophy and its relation to Leibniz, see Moll, *Der junge Leibniz,* Vol. I, and my *Leibniz's Metaphysics: Its Origins and Development* (Cambridge: Cambridge University Press, forthcoming), chapter 3.

[59] *Analysis*, p. 175.

[60] *Analysis*, p. 182.

[61] *Analysis*, p. 183.

[62] *Analysis*, p. 177.

Aristotle would constitute the primary source for the accurate account of nature; and third, that the Platonic philosophy would inspire the proper understanding of God and the relation between God and creatures.

When we survey Leibniz's early years, we see him struggling to accomplish the complicated goal implied by these lessons. During the 1660s, Leibniz contemplates the widest possible variety of (respectable) philosophical options in order to forge a metaphysics that is Aristotelian in its account of substance, Platonist in its account of God and the relation between God and the world, consistent with Christian doctrine, and true. As I argue in detail elsewhere, the philosophical proposals which he formulated in the late 1660s are carefully crafted to conform to Christian doctrine in general and to revealed truth (e.g., about the Incarnation and the Eucharist) in particular. His conception of substance and what I call his metaphysics of substance is derived from the Aristotelian tradition. His account of the relation between God and the world, what I call his metaphysics of divinity, is clearly derived from Platonism. Where the metaphysics of substance treats substance as an active self-sufficient thing, the metaphysics of divinity sees each substance as a created thing into which the supreme being constantly emanates its power and essence. Although there is insufficient space now either to present the details of Leibniz's development or to explore the exact extent of his debt to his teachers, I would like to offer one example of his early conciliatory eclecticism.[63]

During the late 1660s Leibniz wrote a group of essays on theological topics. One of the most important of these is the *De transsubstantiatione* of 1668 in which he presents an account of transubstantiation that he hoped would appeal to Protestants and Catholics alike. Although Leibniz's solution to the grave metaphysical problems posed by the 'mystery of the Eucharist' is interesting, we may bypass these complications and focus on the general features of his metaphysical proposals. He presents here for the first time in explicit detail his Aristotelian conception of substance

---

[63] In my *Leibniz's Metaphysics: Its Origins and Development*, I argue that many of his most basic metaphysical tenets are in place by the end of the decade. See esp. chapters 2, 4, 6 and 7.

according to which an individual corporeal substance is constituted of matter, which is the corporeal principle and is essentially passive, and form, which is the incorporeal principle and is essentially active. Leibniz writes: "*Substance* is being which subsists per se... *Being which subsists per se* is that which has a principle of action per se.... But the essence or definition of a body [qua matter] is being in space".[64] There are two sorts of created substances: human substances which have their own principle of activity and non-human ones which receive their activity from God by way of an Idea. According to Leibniz, "the substance of bodies which lack reason is union with the universal mind, or God. The Idea is the union of God with creature".[65] Although the details of Leibniz's views are quite unlike anything that Aristotle himself proposed, the basic conception of substance is recognisably Aristotelian in the sense that a passive principle combines with an active principle to constitute the nature of an individual corporeal substance which itself acts as a *suppositum* and a source of the activities of the substance.[66] As Leibniz himself proclaims: "These theorems of ours differ very little from the accepted philosophy of Aristotle".[67]

Leibniz also insists in this essay that his account has much in common with Platonist views. According to Leibniz, his proposal is similar to "Plato in the *Timaeus* about the world soul", to "Aristotle in the *Metaphysics* and *Physics* about the agent Intellect", to the Stoics and others. Like these other philosophers he maintains that God is "diffused through everything". Leibniz is fairly clear about how this diffusion occurs: God chooses "among the infinitely really diverse

---

[64] A VI i 508: L 115.

[65] A VI i 509: L 116. The text here is difficult and makes things look slightly more complicated than they are. For example, Leibniz does not use the Latin term *materia* for the passive principle; instead he uses *corpus* to denote both the passive principle and the individual corporeal object that is constituted of the passive and active principles. For a thorough discussion of the details of this essay, see my *Leibniz's Metaphysics: Its Origins and Development,* chapters 2 and 6; for a summary of the view, see Mercer and Sleigh, 'The Early Metaphysics to the *Discourse on Metaphysics*', in Nicholas Jolley (ed.) *The Cambridge Companion to Leibniz,* (Cambridge: Cambridge University Press, 1995), sect. 1.

[66] A VI i 508: L 115.

[67] A VI ii 510: L 117.

Ideas" in his mind to create some so that "[t]he substance of each [non-human] thing is not so much mind as it is an Idea of a concurring mind".[68] For each non-human substance, there is a corresponding Idea in God's mind. In some marginal notes, Leibniz claims:

> Ideas are the same thing as the Substantial forms of things. Ideas are in God as an action is in an agent, as Creation is in God. If someone should ask: Is an Idea a created thing or not? It should be responded: Is a creature a created thing or not?[69]

According to Leibniz, the substances of non-human things are products of God which flow from his nature and belong to that nature. The Ideas are distinct from one another, but they are all Ideas in God. In the *Confessio naturae contra atheistas* of 1668, Leibniz defines an action of substance as a variation of essence. In *De transsubstantiatione,* each Idea is a variation of the essence of God and in that sense it 'flows' from the divine nature.

In an attempt to construct a conciliatory response to the theological problem of transubstantiation, Leibniz has produced a brilliant combination of Aristotelian and Platonist ideas. That is, he has offered a conciliatory philosophical and theological position as a way of encouraging a religious reconciliation. He has assigned the Idea associated with each non-human substance two tasks: each Idea is both an emanation of the essence of God and the substantial form of an individual non-human substance. For Leibniz here, the fundamental attributes or Ideas of God, which are simple Platonic-like Forms, are combined to create the more complicated Ideas or essences of possible individuals. When such an Idea or individual essence is actualised, it functions as the set of instructions for the activities of the substance. Perfectly in keeping with the Platonist (especially Plotinian) theory of emanative causation, the essence of God 'flows' into creatures and each creature manifests the attributes of God though in a way greatly inferior to their divine source. By such means, the divine essence is 'diffused' through every created thing in the world. So far, Leibniz's position conforms to the general account of the relation between God

---

[68] A VI i 511-12. Leibniz does not italicise these titles.
[69] A VI i 510.

and creatures proposed by Scherzer, Thomasius, Weigel, and many other Platonists. But Leibniz also insists in *De transsubstantiatione* that each Idea contains the principle of activity of the substance and therefore acts as the substantial form of the substance. That is, perfectly in keeping with an Aristotelian theory of substance, each substantial form constitutes its principle of individuation.[70] According to Leibniz, these proposals are consistent with "Aristotle himself and the noblest of his followers".[71]

Even this brief summary of a mere part of the *De transsubstantiatione* displays the depth of Leibniz's commitment to conciliatory eclecticism. Like his teachers, the young man was firmly committed to the wisdom of the ancients. The richness and profundity of their thought amply justified the use of their philosophies. In this sense Leibniz was conservative: he thinks more highly of past authors than present ones and never relies entirely on any philosopher who could be considered either modern or radical. While he was enormously impressed by Hobbes, Descartes, Gassendi, and other 'moderns', he always 'corrects' them with the help of some ancient author. Also like his teachers, Leibniz divided his most important metaphysical labour between Aristotelianism and Platonism: he borrowed more heavily from the former on worldly topics while he used the latter as a constant source for inspiration concerning divine ones. Like Scherzer and Thomasius, Leibniz insisted on distinguishing between the heretical and non-heretical tenets in any philosophy. In this sense he was a thoroughly discriminating eclectic: he was prepared to accept for his eclectic mixture only those philosophical ingredients which in his opinion were strictly orthodox. But Leibniz was less conservative than Scherzer and Thomasius concerning important religious matters. Although the young man remained a Lutheran, he became committed during the 1660s to a reconciliation among religions and embraced an ecumenicalism that

---

[70] Leibniz is aware of the fact that Aristotle's views about individuation had been debated among the schoolmen. He cites Averroes and Zabarella as philosophers who "also assert that substantial form is a principle of individuation" (A VI i 510: L 117). Of course, for the rest of Leibniz's very long philosophical career, he interprets the Aristotelian conception of substantial form in this fashion.

[71] A VI i 511: L 118.

went beyond the conciliatory goals of either Scherzer or Thomasius. *De transsubstantiatione* bears witness to his intense desire to promote peace among the faithful. The young man also went well beyond these Leipzig professors in his interest in the modern physics. Like Weigel, he extended the scope of his eclecticism to the mechanical philosophy. It is well-known that Leibniz concerned himself with the new experiments and contributed significantly to seventeenth-century physics. For the basic raw materials of his conciliatory proposals, he turned to modern as well as ancient sources. In this sense, Leibniz's conciliatory eclecticism extended farther than that of Scherzer and Thomasius: the true philosophy would combine a major part of the Aristotelian philosophy, with a major part of Platonist thought, with a component of modern physics.

Despite the dissimilarities between Leibniz and his teachers on some matters, he never wavered from the fundamental philosophical goals which he learned from them. He intended to construct a true metaphysics that would solve all the mighty philosophical problems, that would explain the phenomena of nature, and that would be consistent with Christian doctrine. The metaphor of construction is appropriate here in that the metaphysics would be made out of pre-existing components. One of the overlooked aspects of Leibniz's brilliance is his success in building such an original and sublime philosophical edifice out of re-cycled materials.

MARIA ROSA ANTOGNAZZA

IMMEATIO AND EMPERICHORESIS. THE THEOLOGICAL

ROOTS OF HARMONY IN BISTERFELD AND LEIBNIZ

1. Introduction: Bisterfeld and the Young Leibniz

Of the countless documents which will eventually fill eighty volumes
in the Academy edition of his works, one of the dozen earliest is the
series of underlinings and marginalia which Leibniz penned as a
teenage student in Leipzig in three recently published posthumous
works by the obscure central European philosopher, Johann Heinrich
Bisterfeld.[1] For evidence of the young Leibniz's high estimation of
these works, one need turn no further than the title-pages of his extant
copies of them.   On the title-page of Bisterfeld's *Phosphorus
Catholicus* he wrote simply "Ingeniosissimus Libellus".[2] On the title-

---

[1] The three works in question are J. H. Bisterfeld, *Philosophiae Primae Seminarium
ita traditum, ut omnium disciplinarum fontes aperiat, earumque clavem porrigat*
(Lugduni Batavorum: Apud Danielem et Abrahamum Gaasbeeck, 1657); J. H.
Bisterfeld, *Elementorum Logicorum Libri tres: ad praxin exercendam apprimè
utiles. Atque ita instituti, ut Tyro, trimestri spatio, fundamenta Logices, cum fructu
jacere possit. Accedit, Ejusdem Authoris, Phosphorus Catholicus, Seu Artis
meditandi Epitome. Cui subjunctum est, Consilium de Studiis feliciter instituendis*
(Lugduni Batavorum: Ex Officina Henrici Verbiest., 1657).   These works were
published posthumously by Adrian Heereboord.   Leibniz's copies are in a
Sammelband: Niedersächsische Landesbibliothek, shelf-mark Leibn. Marg. I. The
marginalia and underlinings are published as 'Notae ad Joh. Henricum
Bisterfeldium' (1663-66; A VI i, No. 7).

[2] Cf. A VI i 160. A citation of *Philosophiae Primae Seminarium* is found as early
as the annotations made by Leibniz between 1663 and 1664 in his copy of D. Stahl's

S. Brown (ed.): The Young Leibniz and his Philosophy (1646-76). 41-64
© 1999 Kluwer Academic Publishers. Printed in the Netherlands.

kind I have not seen".[3] Two of Leibniz's earliest works – the *Dissertatio de Arte Combinatoria* (1666)[4] and the *Nova Methodus discendae docendaeque Jurisprudentiae* (1667)[5] – contain still further praise of the *Phosphorus Catholicus*.[6] His high opinion of these works was maintained during the years that followed: two decades later, writing from Hanover to his brother Johann Friedrich, who was organising the auction of belongings relating to their family, Leibniz inserted in the list of books which he wished to conserve for himself the works of Bisterfeld which he had read in his youth.[7]

The importance of this youthful reading in the formation of Leibniz's thought is a subject now well established within the literature. The first to draw sustained attention to it was Willy Kabitz in his classic monograph on the philosophy of the young Leibniz.[8] Kabitz identified as the fundamental idea of Bisterfeld's philosophy the notion of the most perfect universal harmony, of unity in variety, of the consonance and difference of all parts from the smallest to the largest, and he noted especially the importance of this conception as a source of Leibniz's *Ars combinatoria*. Paolo Rossi, in his study of the art of memory and combinatorial logic from Lull to Leibniz, likewise highlighted the importance of Bisterfeld among the sources of Leibniz's *combinatoria*: "It is certainly back to this last author", he wrote, "as well as more generally to the tradition of Lullism, that we must trace the idea, fundamental for the establishment of Leibniz's *combinatoria* itself, of an alphabet of human thoughts or a catalogue of primitive notions from the combination of which all complex ideas

---

[3] A VI i 151. Unless otherwise stated, translations are my own.

[4] A VI i, No. 8.

[5] A VI i, No. 10.

[6] Cf. A VI i 199 and A VI i 279.

[7] The list of philosophical and philological books includes "Bisterfelds Elementa, phosphorus, philosophia prima" (A I iv 681).

[8] W. Kabitz, *Die Philosophie des jungen Leibniz. Untersuchungen zur Entwicklungsgeschichte seines Systems* (Heidelberg: Karl Winter's Universitätsbuchhandlung, 1909), pp. 6-8.

can be derived."[9] In both his seminal article, 'Leibniz and the Herborn Encyclopedists' and his major monograph, *Struggle for Synthesis*, Leroy Loemker emphasised Leibniz's enthusiasm for Bisterfeld's posthumous works during his youth;[10] and in the latter work he extended it into the period of fuller maturity of Leibniz's philosophy: "It was many decades after reading Bisterfeld", he wrote, "that Leibniz succeeded in fully adapting these insights, along with others of Hobbes, Bacon, and Galileo, into his own mature monadology."[11] Leibniz's debt to several further aspects of Bisterfeld's conception has been pointed out by Antonio Lamarra in his article on Leibniz and the concept of περιχώρησις and in the recent important studies by Donald Rutherford and Thomas Leinkauf.[12] The most thorough examination of the relations between Bisterfeld and Leibniz, and of the concept of harmony as the key term of that relationship, remains an article by Massimo Mugnai. Regarding the importance of the concept of harmony for Bisterfeld, Mugnai notes how Leibniz himself, in his reference to the *Phosphorus Catholicus* in *De Arte Combinatoria*, identifies the idea of a universal relation and connection of all things with all things as the foundation of Bisterfeld's thought. And in summarizing the influence of this concept on Leibniz, Mugnai concludes:

---

[9] P. Rossi, *Clavis Universalis. Arti mnemoniche e logica combinatoria da Lullo a Leibniz* (Milano-Napoli: Riccardo Ricciardi, 1960), p. 238. Further remarks concerning Bisterfeld's philosophical alphabet are found at pp. 197-200.

[10] L. E. Loemker, 'Leibniz and the Herborn Encyclopedists', *Journal of the History of Ideas* 22 (1961): 323-38, especially p. 324 and pp. 334-5: "It was Bisterfeld's posthumous works which aroused Leibniz's greatest enthusiasm. ... It is Bisterfeld's conception of the harmony or convening of distinct individuals in the universe, however, which most evokes his consent"; *Struggle for Synthesis. The Seventeenth Century Background of Leibniz's Synthesis of Order and Freedom* (Cambridge, MA: Harvard University Press, 1972), especially pp. 143-5, 190-3.

[11] Loemker, *Struggle for Synthesis*, p. 193.

[12] A. Lamarra, 'Leibniz e la περιχώρησις', *Lexicon philosophicum. Quaderni di terminologia filosofica e storia delle idee* 1 (1985): 67-94; D. Rutherford, *Leibniz and the Rational Order of Nature* (Cambridge: Cambridge University Press, 1995), pp. 36-40; T. Leinkauf, '"Diversitas identitate compensata". Ein Grundtheorem in Leibniz' Denken und seine Voraussetzungen in der frühen Neuzeit', parts I and II, *SL* 28 (1996): 58-83 and 29 (1997): 81-102, especially part II, pp. 88-93.

It is very significant that the description of harmony which one finds in *De arte combinatoria* agrees almost exactly with that of Bisterfeld, and it is still more important that the concept of harmony defined by Leibniz in this youthful work remains in its essential content unchanged in the later development of Leibniz's thought.[13]

While further affirmations of this and similar points could be provided,[14] enough has been said to illustrate a consensus which lays the foundation for this paper: namely, that the idea of harmony present in Bisterfeld was very important for the development of the notion of universal harmony central to Leibniz's thought. In this paper, I propose to carry this line of investigation two stages further: first, by examining the theological foundation of the idea of harmony in Bisterfeld's system; and second, by considering the relationship of Leibniz's conception of harmony to his own theological ideas. Such a discussion will enhance, I believe, our understanding of the origins and significance of the idea of harmony in the context of Leibniz's

---

[13] M. Mugnai, 'Der Begriff der Harmonie als metaphysische Grundlage der Logik und Kombinatorik bei Johann Heinrich Bisterfeld und Leibniz', *SL* 5 (1973): 72.

[14] E.g. D. Mahnke, *Leibnizens Synthese von Universalmathematik und Individualmetaphysik*, Halle: Max Niemeyer, 1925, especially pp. 68, 218, 266n., 231-2n.; F. Barone, (ed.) *G. W. Leibniz: Scritti di logica* (Bologna: Zanichelli, 1969), p. 126; H. Aarsleff, 'Bisterfeld', *Dictionary of Scientific Biography* (New York: Charles Scribner's Sons, 1970); W. Schneiders, 'Harmonia universalis', *SL* 16 (1984): 27-44, especially pp. 28-9; F. Piro, *Varietas Identitate Compensata. Studio sulla formazione della metafisica di Leibniz* (Napoli: Bibliopolis, 1990), especially pp. 24, 65n., 94, 95n., 99, 231; G. Varani, 'I "Loci Topici" nel pensiero di G. W. Leibniz. "Nouvelles ouvertures" di un concetto consunto', *Annuario filosofico* 9 (1993): 171-94; G. Varani, *Leibniz e la "topica" aristotelica* (Milano: IPL, 1995), especially p. 152; K. Moll, *Der junge Leibniz* (3 vols., Stuttgart-Bad Cannstatt: Fromann-Holzboog, 1978, 1982 and 1996), especially vol. 3, pp. 223-4. Special attention to Bisterfeld's thought has been paid by M. L. Bianchi, *Signatura rerum. Segni, magia e conoscenza da Paracelso a Leibniz* (Roma: Edizioni dell'Ateneo, 1987), especially pp. 144-54; U. G. Leinsle, *Reformversuche protestantischer Metaphysik im Zeitalter des Rationalismus* (Augsburg: Maro Verlag, 1988), especially pp. 27-40; M. Muslow, '*Sociabilitas*. Zu einem Kontext der Campanella-Reception im 17. Jahrhundert', *Bruniana & Campanelliana. Ricerche filosofiche e materiali storico-testuali* 1 (1995): 205-232, especially pp. 218-32.

thought. But first, a biographical word or two might be welcome by way of introduction, since Bisterfeld is such an obscure figure today: indeed were it not for the young Leibniz's praise of him, he would probably still be almost completely forgotten.[15]

Born around 1605 in Siegen, the largest town in the tiny German principality of Nassau-Dillenburg, Bisterfeld completed his studies at the Calvinist academy at Herborn under the guidance of the leading philosopher of the school, Johann Heinrich Alsted, whose *Encyclopaedia* was also a source of inspiration to Leibniz.[16] Alsted had attended the famous Synod of Dordrecht with Bisterfeld's father, the Ramist theologian Johann Bisterfeld, who died unexpectedly there in early January 1619;[17] and after returning to Herborn Alsted formed exceptionally close relations with the young Bisterfeld, who subsequently regarded him virtually as an adoptive father. After extensive academic travels which took him to Geneva, Oxford and Leiden, Bisterfeld returned to Herborn for a brief stint of teaching as an extraordinary professor of philosophy. But by this time the Thirty Years' War in general and the Edict of Restitution in particular had thoroughly undermined the viability of the once thriving academy, and

---

[15] The principal account of Bisterfeld's life is J. Kvacsala, 'Johann Heinrich Bisterfeld', *Ungarische Revue* 13 (1893): 40-59 and 171-97, which reworks an earlier paper published in 1891 in the Hungarian journal *Századok*. Cf. also J. Seivert, *Nachrichten von Siebenbürgischen Gelehrten und ihren Schriften* (Pressburg: im Weber und Korabinstischen Verlage, 1785), pp. 34-7; J. F. Trausch, *Schriftsteller-Lexikon, oder biographisch-literärische Denk-Blätter der Siebenbürger Deutschen* (Kronstadt: J. Gött und Sohn), vol. 1, 1868-1870, pp. 152-4; *Allgemeine Deutsche Biographie*, vol. 2, pp. 682-3.

[16] On Herborn, see G. Menk, *Die Hohe Schule Herborn in ihrer Frühzeit (1584-1660). Ein Beitrag zum Hochschulwesen des deutschen Kalvinismus im Zeitalter der Gegenreformation* (Wiesbaden: Selbstverlag der Historischen Kommission für Nassau, 1981). A monograph on Alsted by H. Hotson is forthcoming from the Clarendon Press, Oxford. For an overview of the relationship between Alsted and Leibniz, see H. Hotson, 'Alsted and Leibniz: A Preliminary Survey of a Neglected Relationship', VI Internationaler Leibniz-Kongress, *Leibniz und Europa*, vol. 1, (Hanover: G.W. Leibniz Gesellschaft, 1994), pp. 356-363.

[17] The most extensive discussion of Bisterfeld's father is F. W. Cuno, *Geschichte der Stadt Siegen* (Dillenburg, 1875), pp. 145-51. On his death, see *Acta Synodi Nationalis ... Dordrecti habitae anno MDCXVIII et MDCXIX* (Lugduni Batavorum, 1620), pp. 115, 145.

Alsted accepted the invitation to lead the newly founded Calvinist academy in Alba Julia, Transylvania, in 1629, taking the young Bisterfeld with him,[18] who subsequently married his eldest daughter. For the rest of his career before his death in 1655, Bisterfeld would be engaged in philosophical and theological instruction at the academy, regularly interrupted by diplomatic missions on behalf of his prince.[19] Bisterfeld's isolated geographical position is a partial explanation for his obscurity. Another, related to it, is the extreme rarity of most of his most interesting philosophical and theological works.

2. The Theological Roots of Harmony in Bisterfeld

Among these works, those read by Leibniz, and especially the *Philosophiae Primae Seminarium*, are central for the elaboration and presentation of Bisterfeld's metaphysical thought. At the very outset of that work, Bisterfeld appeals to the existence of a complete harmony between things, minds and notions as the foundation of the possibility and the necessity of metaphysics or first philosophy.[20] *Panharmonia*, in other words, viewed from an ontological standpoint, characterizes and governs the entire universe and, viewed from an epistemological standpoint, provides the possibility of universal wisdom concerning being.

Now, the key to this *panharmonia* is located by Bisterfeld in the concept of 'order'. According to the definition proposed by Bisterfeld, "Ordo, est multitudinis in ente congruentia"; "Order is the congruence of multitude in a being".[21] Order, in other words, is the

---

[18] G. Menk, 'Die Restitutionsedikt und die kalvinistische Wissenschaft. Die Berufung Johann Heinrich Alsteds, Philipp Ludwig Piscators und Johann Heinrich Bisterfelds nach Siebenbürgen', *Jahrbuch der Hessischen Kirchengeschichtlichen Vereinigung* 31 (1980): 29-63.

[19] G. Murdoch, 'International Calvinism and the Reformed Church of Hungary and Transylvania, 1613-1658' (unpublished Oxford D. Phil. dissertation, 1996), ch. 3.

[20] *Philosophiae Primae Seminarium*, pp. 1-2: "PHILOSOPHIA PRIMA, est universalis, seu de Ente, sapientia. Vel, est disciplina, notiones caeteris communes, explicans: vulgò, METAPHYSICA, rectiùs, CATHOLICA, vocaretur ... [Regula] I. Posse et debere esse philosophiam primam, rerum cognoscendarum, mentium cognoscentium, humanarumque cognitionum, panharmonia, demonstrat".

[21] Cf. *ibid.*, pp. 123-4.

principle of that unity to which every multiplicity can and ought to be recalled.[22] It is due to order that unity can be found in multiplicity; and unity in multiplicity is in turn the very hallmark of harmony.

Bisterfeld proceeds to analyze this concept of order further in a distinctive fashion crucial for the development of our argument. According to Bisterfeld, in every order there are at least three terms: the *terminus primus* or *terminus a quo*; the *terminus medius* or *terminus per quem*; and the *terminus ultimus* or *terminus ad quem*.[23] Bisterfeld justifies this three-fold division of order in the following manner: without the first term, the *terminus a quo*, beings would come from non-being (*entia essent à non-ente*). Without the second term, the *terminus per quem*, beings would be through non-being (*entia essent per non-ente*). And without the third term, the *terminus ad quem*, beings would be for non-being (*entia essent propter non-ens*).[24] To this triadic order, he maintains, all other order can and should be reduced. It is the key of all nature, both spiritual and corporeal, and of all knowledge, that is, of the *universa encyclopaedia*.[25]

From this point, moreover, Bisterfeld proceeds one crucial step further: this triadic order finds in turn its ultimate foundation in the mystery of the Trinity. This is nothing less than the central thesis of Bisterfeld's metaphysics: namely, that "the panharmony of all things"

---

[22] Cf. *ibid.*, p. 132.

[23] *Ibid.*, pp. 123-4: "Terminus est entitas, intra quam est ordo; seu, extra quam non est ordo. Terminus est, extremus, vel medius. Extremus est, intra quem totus ordo est: estque, à quo, vel ad quem. Medius est, intra quem non totus ordo est. Vel, Terminus est primus, à quo, medius, per quem, ultimus, ad quem, ordo est"; *ibid.*, p. 128: "In omni ordine, saltem sunt tres termini".

[24] Cf. *ibid.*, pp. 130-1.

[25] *Ibid.*, pp. 128-9: "Hic terminorum ternarius est planè μυστηριῶδης , summique per universam encyclopaediam momenti; nec immeritó ipsum totius naturae, spiritualis, et corporeae, clavem, dixerim. Ejus veritas, necessitas, et utilitas, magis declarabitur in specialibus: interim consule Aristotelem. l. I. de coelo. t. I. et seq. Hinc quoque fluit, quód in omni effectu necessarió occurrat triplex causa, nempe efficiens, exemplaris, et finalis. Dito saltem: quia etsi haud raró plures termini medii esse videantur, attamen, omnes vel ad unum revocari possunt; vel est ordinis repetitio aut combinatio. Atque; hunc veré sacrum ordinis ternarium, Dei nomen ..., Jehovah, divinissimé exprimit, juxta illud Pauli Rom. II. 35. Ex ipso, per ipsum, et in ipsum, sunt omnia."

("omnium rerum panharmonia") is founded in the Trinity, which is the source, norm and end of all order:

> Every multiplicity can and must be recalled to unity. For this reason it is necessary that there be, in turn, a first term, a middle term and a final term of the universal order. And so, if we do not wish to do manifest violence to the truth, it must be admitted that the panharmony of all things is founded in the most holy Trinity and that this itself is the source, norm and end of all order. When this is acknowledged and affirmed, the whole of nature and Scripture is pure light; when this is not known or denied, there is nothing but darkness and horrible chaos.[26]

That the doctrine of the Trinity holds such a central place in Bisterfeld's metaphysics is in keeping, we might add parenthetically, with the general shape of his work and the context in which he was working. Transylvania was one of the east-central European regions in which anti-Trinitarianism first and most firmly took root in the post-Reformation era.[27]   As a good Calvinist, the prince of Transylvania, György Ráckóczi, was anxious to distance himself clearly from this heretical tradition.[28]   Alsted dedicated to his prince the single largest book of his Transylvania period: a massive folio of over one thousand pages, which undertook to answer the major statement of the Socinian position written by Johann Volkel.[29]   The

---

[26] *Ibid.*, p. 132.

[27] Two useful introductions are G. H. Williams, *The Radical Reformation* (3rd. rev. ed., Kirsville, MO: Sixteenth Century Journal Publishers, 1992), ch. 28; and E. M. Wilbur, *A History of Unitarianism in Transylvania, England and America* (Cambridge, MA: Harvard University Press, 1952), pp. 28-126.

[28] Cf. Wilbur, *A History of Unitarianism in Transylvania ...*, pp. 113-20; Murdoch, 'International Calvinism ...', ch. 4.1; H. Hotson, 'Johann Heinrich Alsted: Encyclopaedism, Millenarianism and the Second Reformation in Germany' (unpublished Oxford DPhil dissertation, 1991), ch. 6. iv.

[29] J. H. Alsted, *Prodromvs religionis trivmphantis. In qvo methodicè repetuntur et breviter examinantur libri sex de vera religione; qvorum primus à Johanne Crellio, quinq; reliqvi a Johanne Volkelio sunt conscripti* (Albae Juliae: Typii Celsissimi Principis Transylvaniae, 1635). The work attacked here is *Iohannis Volkelii Misnici*

largest work ever published by Bisterfeld, *De uno Deo Patre, Filio, et Spiritu Sancto*, was a kind of appendix to this work: its purpose was to refute the work *De uno Deo Patre* by Volkel's lieutenant, Johann Crell, which was prefixed to the work refuted by Alsted.[30] Trinitarian analogies and language also permeated occult traditions such as Lullism, alchemy and Paracelsianism in which both Alsted and his prize student were steeped, and from which their concepts of universal harmony and *combinatoria* also partially derived.[31] In short, Trinitarian theology was thus no mere concession to orthodoxy for Bisterfeld but a key component of his thought.

Bisterfeld's central thesis of the foundation of universal harmony in the Trinity finds its fullest expression in his choice of the unusual term, *immeatio*, to indicate the idea of harmony itself. *Immeatio*, Bisterfeld writes, is the various concourse, combination and complication of relations, the variety and association of which link together all things with all things and of which the whole of logic is a mirror. In other words, *immeatio* is that universal relationship and linkage of all things with all things which constitutes the idea of harmony itself. But this concept of *immeatio* is nothing other than the translation into the domain of logic and metaphysics of the theological concept of ἐμπεριχώρησις or *circumincessio*, which is traditionally

---

de vera religione libri quinque: Quibus praefatione est Iohannis Crellii Franci liber de Deo et eius attributis, ita ut unum cum illis opus constituat (Racoviae: Typis Sebastiani Sternacii, 1630).

[30] J. H. Bisterfeld, *De uno Deo Patre, Filio, ac Spiritu Sancto, Mysterium Pietatis, contra Johannis Crellii, Franci, De uno Deo Patre, libros duos, breviter defensum* (Lugduni Batavorum: ex Officina Elzeveriana, 1639).

[31] R. Pring-Mill, 'The Trinitarian World Picture of Ramon Lull', *Romantisches Jahrbuch* 7 (1955-6): 229-56; W. Ganzenmüller, 'Das Buch der heiligen Dreifaltigkeit. Eine deutsche Alchemie aus dem Anfang des 15. Jahrhunderts', *Archiv für Kulturgeschichte* 29 (1939): 93-146; H. Buntz, 'Das "Buch der heiligen Dreifaltigkeit". Sein Autor und seine Überlieferung', *Zeitschrift für deutsches Altertum und für deutsche Literatur* 101 (1972): 150-60; H. Rudolph, 'Kosmosspekulation und Trinitätslehre. Ein Beitrag zur Beziehung zwischen Weltbild und Theologie bei Paracelsus', *Beiträge zur Paracelsusforschung* 21 (1980): 32-47. On the influence of these traditions on Alsted, see Hotson, 'Johann Heinrich Alsted ...', esp. chs. 5-6.

employed to explain the relation of 'coinherence' of the three persons
of the Trinity in the divine essence and in each other:[32]

> Both the variety and the connection of relations are truly
> astounding. ... [T]he whole of Logic is nothing other than a
> mirror of relations. This variety takes on the wonderful
> connection of relations which the Greeks call ἐμπεριχώρησις,
> circumincession, and which we are accustomed to call
> *immeatio*, which is nothing other than the varied concourse,
> combination and complication of relations. This governs both
> throughout the entire encyclopaedia and especially in the
> deeper anatomy of things. See our Logic, chapter three. But
> what is truly wonderful, is that both the variety and the
> connection of relations from beginning to end are founded in
> the venerable mystery of the most holy Trinity.[33]

A deeper explanation of the concept of *immeatio* and in particular
of its derivation from the Trinitarian relations, is found in the book
one, chapter three of the *Elementorum Logicorum Libri Tres*, to which
Bisterfeld refers in the passage just quoted. *Immeatio* is defined there
as "concourse of relations" (*relationum concursus*). It constitutes the
key and the nucleus of the whole of logic. Because of its rarity,
Bisterfeld continues, the term *immeatio* requires an explanation both
of its origin and of its usage:[34]

> (1) *Immeatio* is the mutual union and communion of things.
> Theologians first observed this in the most holy Trinity, and
> this they called ἐμπεριχώρησις, that is to say, mutual inter-

---

[32] Cf. R. A. Muller, *Dictionary of Latin and Greek Theological Terms. Drawn
Principally from Protestant Scholastic Theology* (Carlisle: Paternoster Press, 1985),
pp. 67-8, 102.

[33] Bisterfeld, *Philosophiae Primae Seminarium*, pp. 185-6.

[34] Cf. Bisterfeld, *Elementorum Logicorum Libri Tres*, pp. 6-7: "Immeatio est,
relationum concursus, quo unum argumentum admittit aliud. Haec quoniam
universae Logicae ἐυποριας clavis, nucleus et colophon est, nonnullisque ob vocis
raritatem videtur obscurior, necessum est, ut ejus originem et usum tradamus paulò
explanatius."

existence. Provoked by their industry, certain sharp-witted philosophers discovered that *immeatio* is diffused throughout nature and also throughout the picture of nature, the *encyclopaedia*. *Immeatio* is (2) either real or mental, and in either case it is most efficacious. *Immeatio realis* is the mutual union and communion of things occurring in nature, which reveals itself in the highest degree in higher things, such as in divine or spiritual things ... (3) *Immeatio mentalis* is the mutual union and communion of human thoughts.[35]

It is worth emphasizing, that we are not here concerned merely with the transposition of a theological concept into the domain of philosophy. Rather, this discovery of *immeatio* also within nature and knowledge involves for Bisterfeld the recognition of a true and proper *analogia Trinitatis*. According to this idea, the triune nature of God is reflected in the ontological constitution of his creation. To the Trinity, therefore, can and must be traced the ultimate roots of the structure of the universe. This is expressed by Bisterfeld in the *Philosophiae Primae Seminarium* in the thesis that the variety and connection of relations – *immeatio* or *panharmonia* of all things – is founded in the Trinity.[36]

A further, final clarification of the concept of *immeatio* comes from Leibniz himself. In the passage from *De Arte Combinatoria* in which he refers to Bisterfeld, Leibniz emphasizes the centrality of this concept in Bisterfeld's thought, and indicates that the principle of *immeatio* and περιχώρησις is found in relations.

We shall at least briefly indicate that everything is to be traced back to the metaphysical doctrine of the relations of a being with a being ... I think that this has been seen much better than usual among writers of compendia by the most solid Johann Heinrich Bisterfeld in his *Phosphorus Catholicus, seu Epitome artis meditandi* (Leiden, 1657), a work totally founded in what he calls the universal *immeatio* and περιχώρησις of all things

---

[35] *Ibid.*
[36] Cf. Bisterfeld, *Philosophiae Primae Seminarium*, pp. 132 and 186.

in all things, in the similitude and dissimilitude of all things with all things, the principle of which is relations. He who reads this little book will more and more fully perceive the utility of the *ars complicatoria*.[37]

In his recognition of the universal *analogia Trinitatis*, Bisterfeld was certainly not alone. Rather, he was working within a long tradition rooted in Augustinian thought. The peculiar manner in which this analogy is developed here, however, derives in a more specific fashion from the school in which Bisterfeld was formed, the school of Johann Heinrich Alsted, which pursued a weighty work of synthesis, collecting in numerous and voluminous works the ferment of ideas circulating in the German Reformed community of the late sixteenth and early seventeenth centuries. It is no coincidence that ideas similar to those of Bisterfeld are to be found in that other and still more illustrious student of Alsted: Jan Amos Comenius.[38] In the works of Bisterfeld, Leibniz therefore encountered and treasured a complex and flourishing tradition of which the writings of Bisterfeld were but one expression.

3. Trinitarian Theology and Universal Harmony in Leibniz

So much, then, for the theological foundation of the concept of harmony in Bisterfeld's thought. What then of Leibniz? We have surveyed the consensus in the secondary literature that Leibniz retains essentially unchanged certain key features of Bisterfeld's concept of

---

[37] *De Arte Combinatoria*, A VI i 199.

[38] Comenius too wrote extensively against the Socinians, and trichotomies structure much of his system, particularly within his recently rediscovered masterwork, *De rerum humanarum emendatione consultatio catholica*. A good example of the combinatorial development of his Trinitarian pansophia is the posthumously published *Sapientiae primae usus triertium catholicum appellandus hoc est humanarum cogitationum, sermonum, operum, scientiam, artem, usum aperius clavis triuna* (1681), reprinted in *Dílo Jana Amose Komenského*, vol. 18 (Prague: Academia, 1974), pp. 239-366, which refers directly to Alsted, Bisterfeld and other members of this tradition, pp. 297, 318, 346. For Comenius' studies under Alsted, see most recently G. Menk, 'Johann Amos Comenius und die Hohe Schule Herborn', *Acta Comeniana* 8 (1989): 41-59.

harmony. Is a link of some kind between this concept and a Trinitarian theology among them?

In attempting to answer this question, we must proceed with circumspection. To the best of my knowledge Leibniz nowhere asserts such a link with a clarity and explicitness comparable to Bisterfeld. It must be conceded at the outset, therefore, that this question cannot be answered for Leibniz with the same simplicity and certainty as it can for Bisterfeld. Nevertheless, Leibniz has left us a trail of evidence with a more and less direct bearing on this issue. It is to an explication of this evidence that the final main section of this paper is dedicated.

3.1 Preliminary Observations

Three preliminary observations can be made with certainty. The first is that Leibniz was aware that for Bisterfeld the foundation of universal harmony was to be found in the harmony of the three persons of the Trinity. Clear evidence of this is contained in Leibniz's copy of the *Philosophiae Primae Seminarium*, where several of the passages in which Bisterfeld explains the Trinitarian foundation of his concept of harmony most clearly are underlined. One underlined passage, for instance, is Bisterfeld's affirmation that

> if we do not wish to do manifest violence to the truth, it must be admitted that the panharmony of all things is founded in the most holy Trinity and that this itself is the source, norm and end of all order. When this is acknowledged and affirmed, the whole of nature and Scripture is pure light; when this is not known or denied, there is nothing but darkness and horrible chaos.[39]

Another underlined passage (also mentioned already) reads as follows: "But what is truly wonderful, is that both the variety and the

---

[39] *Philosophiae Primae Seminarium*, p. 132.

connection of relations from beginning to end are founded in the venerable mystery of the most holy Trinity."[40]

A second preliminary observation is that Leibniz was capable of detecting and explicating the Trinitarian foundation of Bisterfeld's metaphysics even when this was left tacit by Bisterfeld himself. Three examples of this from the marginalia in the same volume are particularly striking.[41] In the passage in which Bisterfeld argues that the triadic order is the key of all nature and of the whole encyclopaedia, he quotes in support Romans 11: 36, where Paul writes of God that "from him and through him and to him are all things", "ex ipso, per ipsum, et in ipsum, sunt omnia". Leibniz underlines 'ex' and writes above it, "Pater principium"; underlines 'per' and writes above it "Filius medium"; and underlines 'in' and writes above it "Sp[iritus] S[anctus] finis".[42] In doing so he is interpreting in a Trinitarian sense both the scriptural passage itself and the classification of terms proposed by Bisterfeld at the beginning of the chapter: "Terminus est primus, à quo, medius, per quem, ultimus, ad quem."[43]

A second example is Leibniz's comment on Bisterfeld's statement that in the *appetitus operativus primarius* there cannot be infinite regress. Here Leibniz notes, "unde patet Ternarius in Trinitate".[44] In doing so, he is evidently supplying Bisterfeld's own doctrine that it is the three principles (prime, middle and final), corresponding to the three persons of the Trinity, which prevent order from regressing infinitely.[45]

Still more complex is the third example. In *Philosophiae Primae Seminarium* Bisterfeld proposed a definition of *habitudo* as "entitas, quâ entitas est ad entitatem". While the *analogia Trinitatis* underlying this definition may not be immediately obvious to most readers today, it evidently was to Leibniz: he underlined the passage twice and wrote

---

[40] *Ibid.*, p. 186.
[41] A fourth is discussed below, p. 57 f.
[42] Cf. Bisterfeld, *Philosophiae Primae Seminarium*, pp. 128-9 and A VI i 158.
[43] *Ibid.*, p. 124.
[44] Cf. *ibid.*, pp. 116-7 and A VI i 157.
[45] Cf. *ibid.*, cap. VIII 'De Ordine', pp. 123-32 (especially pp. 130-1).

above it, "Trinitas".[46] We shall return to explicate the Trinitarian analogy at work here shortly.

A third preliminary observation follows from this second one. It stands to reason that the young Leibniz would have been able to detect the Trinitarian theology lying several layers under the surface of such dense metaphysical passages as these only if he were already well-versed in Trinitarian theology in the mid-1660s. No independent evidence exists of the young Leibniz's preoccupation with questions regarding the Trinity in the dozen or so surviving texts which antedate these annotations to Bisterfeld; but the years which immediately followed them provide numerous testimonies of such familiarity. In the *Demonstrationum Catholicarum Conspectus* of 1668-9 the young Leibniz pledged to wage theological warfare against the Socinians, the followers of the leading antitrinitarian, Faustus Socinus.[47] This immediately resulted in two extant texts – the *Defensio Trinitatis contra Wissowatium* of spring 1669, and the *Refutatio Objectionum Dan[ielis] Zwickeri contra Trinitatem et Incarnationem Dei* of 1669-70 – both of which undertake to defend the mystery of the Trinity against the objections of leading Antitrinitarians.[48] In the youthful period Leibniz would return to the subject of the Trinity in passages long and short over a dozen times, and his abiding mature interest in it is manifested in countless passages scattered throughout his later life.[49] It can therefore also be stated with certainty that the young Leibniz possessed a highly refined knowledge of Trinitarian theology and took an active interest in expounding and defending it, and this interest can be traced back with some confidence to the years in which he first read Bisterfeld.

This seems to provide the most appropriate line of approach to the question of the relationship of Trinitarian theology to metaphysical

---

[46] Cf. *ibid.*, p. 38 and A VI i 153.

[47] Cf. A VI i 495.

[48] Cf. respectively A VI i, N.16 and A VI i, No.17. For further detail, see M. R. Antognazza, 'Die Polemik des jungen Leibniz gegen die Sozinianer', *Leibniz und Europa: VI Internationaler Leibniz-Kongress*, vol. 1, pp. 17-24.

[49] For an overview, see M. R. Antognazza, 'Die Rolle der Trinitäts- und Menschwerdungsdiskussionen für die Entstehung von Leibniz' Denken', *SL* 26 (1994): 56-75.

conceptions of harmony in the case of Leibniz. Leibniz repeatedly stated throughout his life that the Trinitarian conception of God is the true one. What then is the relationship between these statements and his fundamental metaphysical concept of universal harmony? Three general possibilities present themselves. First, there is the possibility that these two positions contradict one another. In this case most philosophers would presumably be inclined to suppose that his professions of support for the doctrine of the Trinity are disingenuous attempts to win or preserve the favour of his patrons. Second, there is the possibility that these theological and metaphysical doctrines are entirely unconnected with one another. In this case it would remain possible that Leibniz took Trinitarian theology seriously, but there would be no reason for historians of metaphysics to take any interest in it. Finally, there is the possibility that his views on Trinitarian theology and universal harmony are themselves in harmony with one another, that is, that the Trinitarian conception of God and the metaphysical conception of universal harmony are neither contradictory nor unconnected but actually coexist comfortably or even closely in Leibniz's thought, and perhaps even reinforce one another. In this case, the closer the relationship between these two aspects of his thought, the more philosophers can learn from considering his theology.

The following discussion of this key question will be confined to two main points: first, that traces can be found in Leibniz's metaphysics of one feature crucial to the theological foundation of Bisterfeld's concept of harmony, namely the *analogia Trinitatis*; and second, that there are numerous points of parallelism between Leibniz's statements regarding universal harmony on the one hand, and those regarding the relations of the three persons of the Trinity on the other.

3.2 The *Analogia Trinitatis* in Leibniz's Metaphysics

As we have seen, the idea of an *analogia Trinitatis* plays a vital role in linking Bisterfeld's Trinitarian theology with his metaphysics of universal harmony. It is because the creator is reflected in his creation that nature and knowledge manifest the three-fold order analogous to the three persons of the Trinity. Since our question here is precisely whether Leibniz's Trinitarian theology is linked to his metaphysics of universal harmony, it is interesting to note that his metaphysical thought too is occasionally presented in terms of the *analogia Trinitatis*. Let us consider two particularly relevant examples to begin with: the first from the so-called *Systema Theologicum*, the second from the *Theodicy*.

In the *Systema Theologicum*, Leibniz rereads the traditional doctrine which sees the distinction between power, wisdom and will in the Trinity in the light of his fundamental distinction between the essence of things (depending on the divine intellect) and their existence (depending on the divine will).

> Antiquity was accustomed, and in my view wisely and [in a way] accommodated to our capacity, to illustrate the mystery [of the Trinity] by analogy to the three principal faculties of the mind or the requisites of action which are *posse, scire, velle*; so that Power was ascribed to the Father, as source of the divinity; Wisdom to the Son as Word of the mind; and Will or Love to the Holy Spirit. For from the virtue or power of the divine essence proceed the Ideas of things or the truths which wisdom comprehends, and which then at last according to their perfection become the objects of the will; and from this is also made manifest the order of the divine persons.[50]

The converse approach is found in the *Theodicy*. The discussion of the Manichaean doctrine of two principles in that work provides for Leibniz, on the one hand, the occasion to propose once again his typical solution to the problem of evil in the world through the familiar thesis that, while the divine intellect contains the ideas of

---

[50] 'Examen Religionis Christianae (Systema Theologicum)', VE 2419: "Solita est autem antiquitas, atque ut mihi videtur sapienter, et ad captum nostrum accommodate, mysterium hoc illustrare analogia trium potissimarum mentis facultatum, sive agendi requisitorum quae sunt, Posse, Scire, Velle; ita ut Patri tanquam fonti divinitatis Potentia; Filio tanquam Verbo mentis, sapientia: Spiritui sancto autem voluntas, sive amor ascribatur. Nam ex divinae essentiae virtute sive potentia promanant ideae rerum sive veritates quas sapientia complectitur, atque inde postremo pro cujusque perfectione objecta voluntatis fiunt, unde ordo quoque divinarum personarum declaratur."

infinite possible worlds, the divine will, which wants only the good, gives to our world existence proper because it is the best of all possible worlds. But it is also, perhaps less familiarly, the occasion to reread this same doctrine in a Trinitarian sense:

> There are in truth two principles, but they are both in God, to wit, his understanding and his will. The understanding furnishes the principle of evil, without being sullied by it, without being evil; it represents natures as they exist in the eternal verities; it contains within it the reason wherefore evil is permitted: but the will tends only towards good. Let us add a third principle, namely power; it precedes even understanding and will, but it operates as the one displays it and as the other requires it. ... Many have even believed that there was [in these three perfections of God] a secret connexion with the Holy Trinity: that power relates to the Father, that is, to the source of Divinity, wisdom to the Eternal Word, which is called λόγος by the most sublime of the Evangelists, and will or Love to the Holy Spirit. Well-nigh all the expressions or comparisons derived from the nature of the intelligent substance tend that way.[51]

With these examples in mind, a very similar application of the *analogia Trinitatis* can also easily be identified in the *Monadology*, in the passage in which Leibniz writes,

> There is in God the *power* which is the source of everything, there is also the *knowledge* which contains the variety of the ideas, and finally, there is the *will* which makes changes or products in accordance with the principle of the best. This corresponds to what is in created monads the subject or basis, the perceptive faculty, and the appetitive faculty.[52]

---

[51] *Essais de Théodicée*, §§ 149-50 (G VI 198-9). Translation by E. M. Huggard (London, Routledge & Kegan Paul, 1951), p. 217.

[52] L 647: G VI 615. Cf. also the 'Préface' of the *Theodicy* (G VI 27): "Les perfections de Dieu sont celles de nos ames, mais il les possede sans bornes: il est un

In this case the analogy is tacit; but, as the two previous passages alone suggest, the association of Father, Son and Holy Spirit with power, knowledge and will or love is such a well-established theological commonplace that it nevertheless represents – here, at the very heart of Leibniz's metaphysics – an unmistakable allusion to the Trinity. Leibniz himself is a witness to this: when Bisterfeld derived from the theological tradition a metaphysical doctrine strikingly similar to that expressed in the previous quotation from the *Monadology*, Leibniz immediately recognized its tacit allusion to the Trinity. In *Philosophiae Primae Seminarium*, Bisterfeld wrote that patristic and scholastics writers "wisely attributed wisdom to every entity, and formulated this most useful and profound axiom: power, wisdom and love are proper to every entity": "Omni enti competit potentia, sapientia, et amor."[53] Above the word 'potentia' in his copy of the book, Leibniz wrote "Pater"; above the word 'sapientia', he wrote "Filius"; and above the word 'amor', "Sp[iritus] S[anctus]".[54]

3.3 Parallel Formulations in Leibniz's Theology and Metaphysics

What then of the final and most crucial question: the question of the relationship between Leibniz's Trinitarian theology and his metaphysics of universal harmony? We have already suggested that Leibniz nowhere clearly and explicity links the two. In several places, to be sure, he goes so far as to *equate* God with harmony: "God or the Mind of the universe", he writes, "is nothing other than the harmony of things",[55] "the greatest harmony of things",[56] the "Universal

---

Ocean, dont nous n'avons receu que des gouttes: il y a en nous quelque puissance, quelque connoissance, quelque bonté, mais elles sont toutes entieres en Dieu."

[53] Cf. Bisterfeld, *Philosophiae Primae Seminarium*, p. 86: "Atque ut haec omnia veteres quidam Patres ac Scholastici indicarent, sapienter omni enti tribuerunt sapientiam, hocque constituerunt utilissimum ac profundissimum axioma; Omni enti competit potentia, sapientia, et amor."

[54] Cf. A VI i 156.

[55] 'Demonstrationum Catholicarum Conspectus', A VI i 499.

[56] Cf. A IV i 532: "Harmonia maxima rerum".

Harmony".[57]   What appears to be lacking, however, is a more complete and explicit account of the conception of God employed in this equation and its precise relationship to universal harmony. In the absence of a more thorough exposition by Leibniz, it is left to his students to consider the two terms of this equation and their possible relationships with one another.   This is the task of this final subsection. First we shall look at Leibniz's two standard definitions of harmony and consider how they might relate to the Trinitarian conception of God.   Then, conversely, we shall examine the terminology he applies to the Trinity and consider how it might relate to his conception of harmony.

In the *Elementa Juris naturalis* (1670-1) Leibniz writes that "Major harmonia est cum diversitas major est, et reducitur tamen ad identitatem".[58] The greatest harmony, in other words, is to be found where the greatest diversity is reduced to identity. Leibniz developed this idea further in *De conatu et motu, sensu et cogitatione* (1671), where harmony is defined as *unitas plurimorum* or *diversitas identitate compensata*.[59]   A letter to Arnauld of November 1671 employs the same formulation,[60] which recurs a third time in the *Confessio Philosophi* (1672-3), where *harmonia* is defined as "Similitude in variety, or diversity compensated by identity".[61] Drawing on passages such as these, Francesco Piro has argued that in the early 1670s harmony for Leibniz means essentially 'unity in multiplicity'[62] and that the many definitions of harmony offered by Leibniz can be condensed into the one formula, *varietas identitate compensata*.[63]   More recently still, Thomas Leinkauf has proposed that Leibniz's basic concept of 'harmony' as a *diversitas identitate*

---

[57] Cf. A II i 162: "Harmonia Universalis".

[58] A VI i 479.

[59] Cf. A VI ii 283.

[60] Cf. A II i 174.

[61] Cf. A VI iii 116.

[62] Cf. F. Piro, 'Leibniz e il progetto degli *Elementa de mente et corpore*', *Il Centauro* 11-12 (1984): 114.

[63] Piro, *Varietas identitate compensata*, p. 9. Cf. also F. de Buzon, 'L'harmonie: métaphysique et phénoménalité', *Revue de Métaphysique et de Morale* 100 (1995): 95-120.

compensata is both a "hermeneutical key to nearly all of his philosophical writings and of his thinking in general" and "an expression of a thoroughgoing concept of thinking in early modern philosophy from the Renaissance onwards".[64]

Now both of these formulations – 'unity in multiplicity' and *diversitas identitate compensata* – can be related very closely to Leibniz's conception of the Trinity. In the case of harmony as 'unity in multiplicity', the language is strikingly similar. In writings such as *De Scriptura, Ecclesia, Trinitate* and *Sceleton Demonstrationis* the mystery of the Trinity is characterized precisely as "in unitate pluralitatem".[65] On the other hand, it is not difficult to argue that, when harmony is defined as 'diversity compensated by identity', the most perfect available example of it is to be found in the traditional doctrine of a Trinity of three distinct persons in one essence. In the Trinity, the unity in plurality is so perfect, the diversity of persons, while remaining distinct, is so perfectly compensated by the identity of essence, that the being in question surpasses the limits of human comprehension and therefore qualifies itself not as a doctrine of philosophy, but as a mystery of theology. To state that the Trinity is the most perfect conceivable fulfillment of this concept of harmony, in other words, is in fact not to state enough; for it is precisely an even *more* perfect compensation of diversity by identity than the human mind *can* comprehend, which is precisely why it is a mystery.

Beginning from the other side of the equation – from terms and formulations developed to express the Trinitarian conception of God – yeilds results equally closely related to Leibniz's conception of harmony. Underlying the philosophical term *immeatio* which expressed the core of Bisterfeld's metaphysics was, as we have seen, the theological term ἐμπεριχώρησις used by patristic theologians to express the relation of the three persons of the Trinity. In his later years we find Leibniz employing this term to indicate the idea of universal harmony. In *Tractatio de Deo et Homine* (c. 1702), he

---

[64] Cf. 'Summary' in Leinkauf, '"Diversitas identitate compensata". Ein Grundtheorem in Leibniz' Denken und seine Voraussetzungen in der frühen Neuzeit'.

[65] Cf. 'De Scriptura, Ecclesia, Trinitate', VE 433, and 'Sceleton Demonstrationis', A I xi 234.

explains how the harmony and περιχώρησις of all things proceed from God:

> from the combination of Wisdom and Goodness originated the choice of the best series of things, and moreover from it has proceeded the marvellous harmony and περιχώρησις of all things, by virtue of which all things are most closely connected.[66]

Writing to Des Bosses in November 1710, he elaborates this idea further:

> it is all too true that there is no part of nature which we can understand perfectly; the very περιχώρησις of things proves this. No creature, however excellent, can at once distinctly perceive or comprehend the infinite; on the contrary, indeed, whoever were to understand a single part of matter would understand the whole universe, by virtue of this same περιχώρησις of which I spoke.[67]

The "περιχώρησις rerum" of which Leibniz writes in 1710 seems to correspond to his account in 1702 of the "harmony of all things, by

---

[66] G III 34-5. Cf. also the 'Synopsis' of the 'Tractatio de Deo' (Gr II 475): "Origo rerum. Ultima ratio rerum. Inspicit omnia possibilia, et eligit optimum. Rerum perichôrèsis." In another text, composed around 1708, Leibniz appeals to the περιχώρησις rerum against the Epicurean negation of final causes (D II ii 132): "causas efficientes concedunt philosophi omnes: sed finales negant Epicurei, et horum sequaces; qui putant, inter innumeras alias combinationes materiae quasdam casu contigisse caeteris commodiores, atque ita animalia esse orta; et oculos non structus esse visûs gratiâ, sed videre animal, quia evenit, ut oculi aptè structi essent. Verùm enim verò, haec sententia, ex altioribus quibusdam principiis de rerum ortu et περιχωρήσει, demonstrativè refutatur."

[67] L 599: G II 412. Loemker translated περιχώρησις as "interdependence", providing the original Greek in square brackets. This letter and its use of the term περιχώρησις have been noted in G. Tognon, 'G. W. Leibniz: Dinamica e Teologia. Il carteggio inedito con Jacques Lenfant [1693]', *Giornale Critico della Filosofia Italiana* 61 (1982): 278-329 and Lamarra, 'Leibniz e la περιχώρησις'. The word περιχώρησις recurs also in Gr II 797 and in D II ii 154.

virtue of which all things are most closely connected".[68] It is precisely because in nature every one of an infinite number of things is linked with every other that it is impossible for the finite human intellect to come to an adequate comprehension of any part of nature. Conversely, this same 'περιχώρησις rerum' is the reason why the adequate comprehension of any one part of nature would correspond to the comprehension of the whole universe, which is possible only for an infinite intellect. It is significant that Leibniz should have chosen to use, not the normal philosophical term 'harmonia', but the far less usual term 'περιχώρησις' in discussing the reason which hinders the finite human mind from perfectly comprehending the 'mystery' of the universe. Moreover, it is worth mentioning that in paragraph 23 of the 'Discours preliminaire' to the *Theodicy* universal harmony explicitly takes the features of a 'mystery', in analogy among other things to the mystery of the Trinity.[69]

Finally, let us consider one further Trinitarian formulation, this time one stemming, initially at least, from Bisterfeld. We have seen that Leibniz recognized a description of the Trinity in Bisterfeld's formula, "entitas, quâ entitas est ad entitatem".[70] What does this formula mean? An "entitas, quâ entitas est ad entitatem" is evidently a being an essential constituent of which is to be in relation, to be *ad aliud*. Leibniz later reformulated this idea from the standpoint of relations, when he described the relations between Father, Son and Holy Spirit as being 'essential' or 'substantial' relations,[71] relations which are (so to speak) an ontological constituent of the three persons of the Trinity.[72] Now if at this point we recall Francesco Piro's statement

---

[68] Cf. G III 34-5.

[69] Cf. G VI 64.

[70] Cf. 'Notae ad Joh. Henricum Bisterfeldium', A VI i 153.

[71] Cf. 'De Scriptura, Ecclesia, Trinitate', VE 433; 'Examen Religionis Christianae (Systema Theologicum)', VE 2419; 'Sceleton Demonstrationis', A I xi 234; 'Remarques sur le livre d'un Antitrinitaire Anglois', in M. R. Antognazza, 'Inediti leibniziani sulle polemiche trinitarie', *Rivista di Filosofia neo-scolastica* 83, 4 (1991), p. 549.

[72] Cf. 'Ad Christophori Stegmanni Metaphysicam Unitariorum' in N. Jolley, 'An Unpublished Leibniz MS on Metaphysics', *SL* 7 (1975): 188. For further details see M. R. Antognazza, 'Leibniz e il concetto di persona nelle polemiche trinitarie inglesi', in V. Melchiorre (ed.), *L'idea di persona* (Milano: Vita e Pensiero, 1996),

that for the young Leibniz harmony is a structure of relations,[73] then, the Trinity – a being *constituted by* these 'essential' or 'substantial' relations – seems once again to be the most perfect fulfillment of Leibniz's idea of harmony.

Of the three possible general relationships which might obtain between Leibniz's Trinitarian theology and his metaphysical doctrine of universal harmony – contradiction, indifference, and coherence or complementarity – enough has been said, I hope, to justify opting for the latter. Nor is this complementarity coincidental. The mystery of the Trinity was a central intellectual problem which had compelled many of the finest minds of the Christian world during a millennium and a half to contemplate the problem of unity and multiplicity and to push their reflections to the very limits of human comprehension. It is hardly surprising, therefore, that Trinitarian theology should have proved a fertile source of concepts and terminology for a philosopher preoccupied with precisely this problem of unity and multiplicity. Indeed, it is scarcely too much to say that these doctrines – Trinitarian theology and universal harmony – coexisted with one another in a kind of pre-established harmony. Their seemingly perfect complementarity is neither coincidental nor anomalous, but derives from the fact that they were harmonized with one another by that seminal if obscure figure whom the young Leibniz read with such enthusiasm and profit, Johann Heinrich Bisterfeld, and by the still longer tradition upon which Bisterfeld drew.

---

pp. 207-37 (especially pp. 233-5). On Leibniz's complex theory of relations, see also the fundamental study of M. Mugnai, *Leibniz' Theory of Relations* (Stuttgart: Franz Steiner Verlag, 1992.
[73] Cf. Piro, *Varietas identitate compensata*, pp.100-1.

KONRAD MOLL

DEUS SIVE HARMONIA UNIVERSALIS
EST ULTIMA RATIO RERUM: THE CONCEPTION OF GOD IN
LEIBNIZ'S EARLY PHILOSOPHY

1. The Beginnings of this Conception in Mainz

The beginnings of Leibniz's fundamental conception of our world's universal harmony are manifested in some letters and papers especially written in 1671 – one of the most creative periods of Leibniz's life. It was the so called 'pre-Parisian' time, when the 25 years old Aulic Councillor at the court of the Archbishop Elector in Mainz was employed in systematising different traditions of law in Germany's manifold territories. We may consider this as his daily work there, but perhaps at night the busy and eager young man was working at another, rather exhausting task, when elaborating his new physics: his conception of monad and harmony, his new philosophy,[1] in short, his conception of world and of God as the 'ultimate reason of all things'.

---

1   In a very illuminating chapter 'Il regno armonico delle menti', Francesco Piro points out the relation of Leibniz's juristic labour to his basic conception of sufficient reason: "In ideale prosecuzione con un settore della 'logica' giuridica leibniziana, l'analisi del concetto di 'condizione' per l'esecuzione di un atto, viene definito il fondamento puramente logico del principio di ragione: la nozione di ratio sufficiens." (Francesco Piro, *Varietas identitate compensata*, Napoli: Bibliopolis, 1990, p. 110). Piro refers to Heinrich Schepers, 'Leibniz' *Disputationes De Conditionibus.* Ansaetze zu einer juristischen Aussagenlogik' (*SL Supp.* 15 (1975): 1-17).

S. Brown (ed.): The Young Leibniz and his Philosophy (1646-76). 65– 78
© 1999 Kluwer Academic Publishers. Printed in the Netherlands.

We can find traces of his unfaltering work already in the so-called *Confessio Naturae* written in 1668,[2] and especially in his *Theoria Motus abstracti* and his *Hypothesis Physica nova*, both published in 1671. And in a more direct and often euphoric manner we find it expressed in his already international correspondence of those early years.

2. The world is Harmonious since the Source of its Existence is Harmony

I am now going to deal with some statements from letters of the young courtier and jurisprudent. In the fall of the year 1671 Leibniz wrote a very extended and detailed letter of self-recommendation to Johann Friedrich, Duke of Brunswick/Hanover, spreading out all his achievements in the sciences, in technique, in philosophy and – not to forget – in jurisprudence and natural theology. In this letter we also find an allusion to his early British connections, referring to his *Hypothesis physica nova*:

> I have published a hypothesis, which gives an account of the reasons for nearly all the main phenomena of nature ... in such a clear and easy way. ... From England I got very favourable opinions and there my hypothesis was reprinted very quickly.[3]

That is true: thanks to the Secretary of the Royal Society, Henry Oldenburg, a reprint of the young foreigner's paper appeared in London very quickly. And really there are highly interesting details in it. For example, Leibniz refers to the so-called "Micrographi" – the investigators who used the new microscopes, such as Robert Hooke (d. 1703) and Athanasius Kircher (d. 1680). He concludes from their

---

[2] Leibniz took himself very seriously as a defender of Christianity by means of science. So he wrote in 1669 to his Leipzig teacher Thomasius: "I venture to say that we never will be able to provide a solid counter-attack against the Atheists, Socinians, Naturalists and Sceptics, if this kind of philosophy is not really established, which I hold granted by God as a present in this late age of the world" (A II i 24: L 102).

[3] A II i 160.

discoveries that the notion of 'atoms' as the ultimate smallest particles of the physical world as never submitted to any atomic fission cannot be a rational notion. And let us emphasise that this took place, not as late as 1904[4], but already in 1671, when Leibniz says:

> It is to be noted, that – as Hooke and Kircher observed – if one goes on to the infinite, then every atom will be of infinite [sc. new] appearances like a world in itself and there will be worlds within worlds unto infinity. Everybody who thinks about this more deeply cannot but be affected by some ecstasy, offering his admiration to the creator of things.[5]

In this 1671 writing there occurs the notion of God as the admirable '*rerum Author*'. And a year before in the *Dissertatio praeliminaris* we find the notion of an '*autor naturae*'[6] in the context of Leibniz's profession of the modern nominalistic method of 'Ockham's razor'. In the preceding years Leibniz favoured other terms. I am quoting examples, beginning with the *Confessio Naturae*. Leibniz there asks for the ultimate cause of motion and cohesion and his answer is, in an unfailing mechanistic way:

> ... since I have demonstrated that bodies themselves cannot have any determinate figure, quantity or motion if there is no incorporeal being, it becomes quite clear that this incorporeal being must be one and the same for all [sc. bodies] because of the harmony of them all between each other,[7] especially since

---

[4] When Ernest Rutherford published his *Radioactivity*.

[5] A VI ii 241f. This interpretation of the discoveries of Hooke was treated in an illuminating study by Philip Beeley, 'Leibniz und die vorsokratische Tradition. Zur Bedeutung der Materietheorie von Anaxagoras für die Philosophie des jungen Leibniz', in *SL Supp.* 27 (1990): 30-41.

[6] 'Creator of nature'. (A VI ii 428)

[7] When Leibniz was a student of about 18 years he was excited by the little pansophic booklet of Johann Heinrich Bisterfeld, Professor of philosophy at the Protestant High School of Herborn (d. 1655). For instance, the young reader

bodies are *not* moved individually by an internal incorporeal being but by one another. No reason can be given why that incorporeal being chooses this magnitude, figure or motion rather than another unless he is intelligent, and wise about the beauty of things and also powerful in exacting their obedience. Such a incorporeal being will therefore be a mind that governs the whole world, namely, God.[8]

That is one of Leibniz's most fundamental arguments. And we find it in similar manner in a gigantic draft (presumably of the same or the following year), named *Demonstrationum catholicarum conspectus*[9]. In the third part Leibniz sketches his chapter 51 in this way:

The beatific vision or intuition of God face to face is the contemplation of the universal harmony of things since contemplation of the universal Mind is nothing else than

---

underlined in this *Philosophiae primae Seminarium* the passage "Omnis multitudo et potest et debet revocari ad unitatem. ... Itaque nisi veritati manifestam vim facere velimus, fatendum est, omnium rerum panharmoniam fundari in Sacro-sancta Trinitate ipsamque esse omnis ordinis fontem ... Ipsa cognita et agnita, universa natura et Scriptura mera lux est: ipsa ignorata vel negata, nil nisi tenebrae et horrendum chaos" (A VI i 158). Further details in Moll, *Der junge Leibniz* III (Stuttgart Bad-Cannstatt: Fromann-Holzboog, 1996), pp. 213-50. See also the contribution of M. R. Antognazza to this volume.

[8] A VI i 492: L 112. This corresponds exactly to the approach of Leibniz's influential teacher at Jena, Erhard Weigel, to Natural Science. In his *Philosophia Mathematica* Weigel emphasised (as he presumably had long taught): "But only God will be nature acting as nature ... moving all without being moved himself" (p. 81, § 6). Nevertheless there remains in the background the question of pantheism – discussed in an instructive manner by G. H. R. Parkinson in 'Leibniz's Paris writings in Relation to Spinoza' (*SL Supp.* (1978): 73-91) and in a critical response by Mark Kulstad in 'Did Leibniz incline toward Monistic Pantheism in 1676?' (*Leibniz und Europa. VI. Internationaler Leibniz-Kongess* (Hanover: Leibniz-Gesellschaft, 1994), pp. 424-8). I suppose Leibniz could not have produced his *Confessio Philosophi* (1673) and later essays intended to promote an ecumenical reunion, if he had been a pantheist. That does not mean to deny that there are in Leibniz's work outstanding so-called pantheistic traits. But what shall be the limit of 'right' or 'wrong' pantheism?

[9] 'Survey of Ecumenical Demonstrations' (A VI i 494-500).

contemplation of the harmony of things, or the principle of beauty in them.[10]

Experts knowing the Bible will notice Leibniz's use of St Paul's famous phrase in his hymn of love written to the Corinthians. Nevertheless the nucleus of this confession is 'natural theology' of high intellectual power and conviction. And a lot of Christians, I think, could learn from Leibniz to become more aware of this 'Cosmos' and not to divide God and world as many of them are accustomed to do as also Descartes was. To Leibniz the world – at least the realm of nature (*"regnum naturae"*) – is in its cosmic structure an expression of God's harmony in himself: and that means, of his rationality as basic essence of reason and existence. Dealing with Plato and Aristotle in his thoroughly elaborated treatise *De Transsubstantiatione* he proclaims: "The divine Mind exists as the ideas of all things."[11]

3. The Basic Law Producing the Best of All Possible Worlds

In the last but one quotation we noted, how Leibniz identified God as the Universal Mind (*"Mens Universi"*) with the harmony of things (*"rerum harmonia"*). To Leibniz that is no mere assertion, no 'mere faith', it is a fundamental proposition of philosophy of science and furthermore the right basis for an overdue reformation of corrupt jurisprudence. So he wrote to the famous German scholar of jurisprudence Hermann Conring in February 1671:

> I mean to have shown, that there is a certain ultimate reason of things – namely God[12] – a universal harmony, a Mind of

---

[10] A VI i 499.

[11] A VI i 511.

[12] Leibniz used this notion of God right up to his final years. See *Monadology* (1714) § 38: "... the ultimate reason as the source of things is what we call God" and *Theodicy* (1710) I, § 7: "God is the first reason of things ... It is necessary to look for

highest wisdom and power. His desire is absolutely nothing but the best and most harmonious and so just, that is to say, pleasing to God, whatever is most conformable to the harmony of things, to the common weal of the universe and – so to speak – the universal republic. And so the doctrine of Natural Right and of the best Republic of the Universe are the same... in what way and how far in our corrupted state of things we are able to approach (sc. to the best sort of republic) as near as ever possible, ... and in consequence: how all those wickednesses of judges and tricks of *rabulae* can be scattered at one stroke ... and how the sciences and arts can be promoted to increase the power and felicity of mankind ... about these matters I set down many reflections, as well as some demonstrated ones ...[13]

This passage shows that Leibniz wanted to prepare a revolution of science in his 17th century based on his conception of universal harmony.[14]

There is another instructive letter to a jurist colleague, M. Wedderkopf, presumably written some months later in May 1671. There he uses also the Greek superlative degree of harmonious *harmonikotaton* as standard for all realisations of existence in the universe. Leibniz starts his cosmological argument with a basic sentence on his rationalistic method. He tells how he made his great strides:

It is necessary to give a reason [sc. ratio existendi] for everything that exists. And one cannot stop giving reasons before arriving at the first reason, otherwise there must be admitted something that exists without sufficient reason.[15]

---

the reason for the existence of the world ... in the substance that carries the reason for its existence with it ...".

[13] A II i 79f.

[14] This conception provided Leibniz also with the warranty for the unity of sciences. See Moll *Der junge Leibniz* III, p. 236, n.233.

[15] A II i 117: L 146. Leibniz adopted this methodical principle from Erhard Weigel. Joining the pure Platonic sentence "Summum hominis bonum Scientia" Weigel started his famous *Analysis Aristotelica ex Euclide restituta* (1658) with a definition

In Leibniz's philosophy there is no place at all for any thing existing without a sufficient reason for its existence. We cannot understand the philosophy of Leibniz if we do not realise that this complete rationalistic proceeding is essential to him. So he continues, going on to the question of the ultimate reason of God's creating will, that means the reason of the existing totality of beings. This ultimate reason, he says, is God's intelligence. This intelligence governs God's will to elect those creatures which God reckons as the best ones (*optima*), or – what is the same thing – the most harmonious (*harmonikotata*). This is in creation the crucial step from infinite possibilities of being to the finite existences, by choice of the best of them. We see again that the reason for God's rationalistic choice always is *harmonia rerum*, the mutual compatibility:

> What then is the ultimate reason of God's will? His intelligence, since God intends what he perceives as best and most harmonious. He selects all that out of the infinite number

---

of real science: every object of scientific knowledge has to be deduced methodically, that means: "out of its first causes and all the intermediate causes in an uninterrupted series of consequent deductions". (Abbreviated from p. 1 f., § 2.) This compendium of Weigel was held by Leibniz in high esteem, and he followed this basic principle as the very method of real scientific progress. See Moll, 'Von Erhard Weigel zu Christiaan Huygens', *SL* 14 (1982): 63 f. This systematic frame also gives the background to Leibniz's reshaping Aristotle's notion of *physics* into his conception of monad as *"Ens vere unum"*. Leibniz says "... in Metaphysico scilicet sensu omnis enim substantia corporea omnes suas operationes exercet a principio interno, quod omnia involvit, sed primus autor seu motor est is qui substantiam rei produxit, hic autem revera non alius est nisi Deus, ostendi enim omnem substantiam veram non aliter quam creatione oriri posse" (VE i 68). C. Wilson, quoting this important fragment, stressed the fact, that Leibniz therefore gave rise to rehabilitation of Aristotle's formae substantiales, his notion of nature on the premise, that it now must be understood along his special way of interpretation of substance. See C. Wilson, '*De Ipsa Natura*, Sources of Leibniz's Doctrine of Force, Activity and Natural Law', *SL* 19 (1987): 172.

of all what is possible. What then is the reason of divine intelligence? The harmony of things.[16]

This is the basic and structural law of this existing world, the warranty for a maximum of existence or rather coexistence of all beings in the universe. Leibniz's reasonable notion of God as harmony and perfection itself compels him to the consequence, that this God cannot act but in perfect and harmonious manner. But, it should be noticed, this necessity will never be in opposition to God's freedom, for perfect freedom is identical with reason in order to give reality to the best, the best constellation of substances that is thinkable. This constitution of the best of all possible worlds is also expressed in his well known sentence: "While God calculates and exercises consideration the world comes into being."[17]

In this system God will not only be the creator of the world, but also in its further history its 'optimiser' – and Leibniz was convinced that philosophers and scientists have a special vocation to join this divine intellect in promoting this eternal process from harmony to harmony. The more perfect the philosophers and scientists become, the more they take part in the special proximity of God to freedom:

> Since God is a most perfect mind it is impossible for him not to be affected by the most perfect harmony and not to be necessitated by the ideality of things itself, to the best. That does not impair his freedom. For the highest liberty is to be compelled to the best by the right reason.[18] Who demands another freedom is foolish.[19]

If we compare this conception of freedom and progress, as related to the precious balances of harmonious existences in the world, with what is announced as 'freedom' and 'progress' in our modern upsets and

---

[16] *Ibid.* We also find the argumentation of these passages in an analogous way up to Leibniz's last years. See, e.g., *Principles of Nature and Grace* (1714) § 7-11.

[17] G vii 191.

[18] Also with this notion of 'right reason' Leibniz joins Hobbes.

[19] A II i 117: L 146f.

confusions, perhaps a hearty desire could arise to learn something more of harmony from Leibniz.

4. Leibniz's New Theory of Mental Activity

But, on the other side, we may ask whether these Leibnizian statements are more than idealistic speculations. Leibniz's answer is: indeed, because he has discovered a revolutionary provability of this harmonious order of the world, in the very laws of motion, demonstrated with a truly Euclidean rigour.

That depends on his doctrine of *conatus* (endeavour), taken over from his new master in scientific method, Thomas Hobbes.[20] I return to Leibniz's letter to the Duke of Brunswick/Hanover of 1671, where he wrote:

> In natural theology I can give a proof from the nature of motion, which I discovered in physics, that in the bodies as themselves there is no motion possible without an intervening mind,[21] and that there must be an ultimate reason of things or universal harmony, namely God.[22]

When he says "I can give a proof from the nature of motion, which I discovered", Leibniz takes us to the core of his investigation of motion. But those who know the books of Hobbes will recall that Hobbes

---

[20]   C. Wilson describes endeavour excellently as "the ruling idea" in Leibniz's *Theoria Motus abstracti* (*Leibniz's Metaphysics*, Princeton: Princeton University Press, 1989, pp. 53-5) Her striking reference to the young Leibniz's mechanism as "theomechanism" (*ibid.*, e.g., pp. 3, 53) is also worth mentioning. An explication of the length Leibniz went to adopt the notion of endeavour (*conatus*) and to rewrite this mechanistic heritage is to be found in *Der junge Leibniz* III 103-22, and 217.   In addition see 'Frühe Versuche naturphilosophischer Standortbestimmung' in the impressive book of Hartmut Hecht *G. W. Leibniz Mathematik und Naturwissenschaften im Paradigma der Metaphysik* (Leipzig: Teubner, 1992), pp. 23-9.

[21]   There are similar sentences in his *Confessio Naturae* (A VI i 492: L 112).

[22]   A II i 162.

himself had already written: "no motion arises from inside the body"[23]. The axiom was the same, but Leibniz and Hobbes differed in the reason they gave for it,[24] because Leibniz's reception of the method of Hobbes and of some notions (especially *conatus*) was a very critical one and in this critical transfer Leibniz appropriated the notion of *conatus* from Hobbes. Let us emphasise that Leibniz here argues from his studies in the laws of motion, focused on the so-called *compositio conatuum* ('composition of endeavours') and that is a very complicated doctrine.[25]

We know Leibniz followed Hobbes in using the term *conatus* and in establishing certain laws of resulting motions when different endeavours as insensible micro-impulses of motion hit each other by impact. Let us here call this endeavour 'atoms of motion', building up the universe from these smallest elements up to the whole world. This construction of the world is ruled by geometry[26] in a vectorial sense, or as Leibniz wrote, following Hobbes: "If we follow this composition of endeavours all originates from addition and subtraction [sc. of those endeavours]".[27]

In this way Hobbes and Leibniz treated the problem of composition physically by adding and subtracting certain quantities or directions of motion,[28] of endeavours in a geometrical way. But to Leibniz this is

---

[23] *Elementa philosophiae de Corpore, Opera* I 283.

[24] Leibniz put this sentence forward as basic in opposition to scholastic Aristotelianism, and also as an authentic Aristotelian one. The quoted Hobbesian words made it much easier to follow the approach of Hobbes to physical research in spite of all divergences in metaphysical frame.

[25] Details in *Der junge Leibniz* III, pp. 218, 221, 232.

[26] We can find early historical traces of Leibniz's geometrical method of examining every object in our existing world in his teacher Weigel's philosophical textbook *Philosophia Mathematica* (1693): "Every finite being is a geometrical footstep of God's thinking" (Gen. Sectio I, Def. I, Corollarium I, p. 26). Insofar Mathematics lead to the Knowledge of God: "The foremost scope of mathematics is God" (*ibid.*, Observatio II, Corollarium III).

[27] A VI ii 282.

[28] See Hobbes, *De Corpore* i 2: "Computare vero est plurium rerum simul additarum summam colligere, vel una re ab alia detracta, cognoscere residuum. Ratiocinari igitur idem est quod addere et subtrahere ... Recidit itaque ratiocinatio omnis ad duas operationes animi, additionem et subtractionem" (*Opera* I 3). In his 'Notes on Harmony', R. C. Sleigh discussed Leibniz's concept of action in the period of the

only one side of the problem of motion, for to him mental activity also is a sort of motion of endeavours. What will result, when endeavours are in concurrence with each other in my mind or in God's mind? Do they combine following the simple laws of geometry?

5. A New Mechanistic Theory of the Reasoning Mind

Here Leibniz establishes a new mechanistic theory of the reasoning mind – and it is Leibniz's very own philosophy. His approach combines modern and mechanistic as well as metaphysical traditions in a new interpretation of mental activity:

> In mind all endeavours remain, and none of them is elected by addition or subtraction, but the one [sc. resulting] that is the most harmonious.[29]

Thinking then is a participation in the universal interaction of small and big motions in the world, taking part in perception and appetite.

> 'Cogitation' is nothing but sense of (1) harmony (2) of comparison, or in short, sense of several at once or one in the many. ... 'in mind' means: one in the many. Therefore 'in harmony' that is unity of many or diversity compensated by identity. But God is one and all [sc. together].[30]

In this early paper of (presumably) 1671 we find already the famous definitions of harmony in his mature treatises, as well as the source of his identifying God and harmony. The further pursuit of Leibniz's

---

1680s as a problem of harmonious concomitance (*Leibniz-Werk und Wirkung.* Hanover, 1983, 716-23). I presume that foregoing interpretation of the metaphysical differences of the level of endeavour and the level of sensible motion in Leibniz's work can support the interpretative strategy.

[29] A VI ii 282.

[30] A VI ii 282. In this text I follow a hand-written supplement of Leibniz as noted on line 32.

system was hence a continuous development of his early studies of the compositions of motion.

In the same paper[31] we again find the young scholar full of an elevated spirit. Seeing himself in front of the philosophical and scientific peer group he says:

> I venture to say there was never a knowledge of human mind more clear and sure. Until now there was no proof of human mind. I venture to say that I as the first gave a demonstration of the nature of mind and of its indestructibility ... Henceforth the duration of all endeavours [sc. 'in mind'], yet of all comparisons among them, that means of all their constellations. That is what constitutes mind.[32]

I do not know a more euphoric statement of Leibniz concerning the importance of one of his discoveries and its bearing on the scientific revolution of his time.

There is yet to be explained a special phrase, when Leibniz writes "*In mente omnes conatus durant ...*"[33]. The explication will give another quote from Leibniz, when he says:

> N.B. Also harmony is a composition of endeavours, but at the same time one of all previous endeavours. Motion (physically) is only a composition of the last endeavours. This is an admirable and unknown [sc. fact]. But it is certain from demonstration.[34]

The background to this sentence on the arising harmony in mind is this: the perception of harmony presupposes memory and comparability of the endeavours congregated there in the whole – assembling the consciousness of all until now entered endeavours in this individual mind. Leibniz experienced this mental discovery as a

---

[31] *De Conatu et Motu, Sensu et Cogitatione* ('About Endeavour and Motion, Sense and Thought') (A VI ii 280-7).

[32] A VI ii 285.

[33] A VI ii 282.

[34] A VI ii 285, column 1, lines 14-7.

lucid and epoch-making vision of the world's basic structure. In terms of motion he was now able to provide the commensurable and comprehensive definitions of mind *and* matter showing the physical things as created by mind. The analogue composition of endeavours in the physical realm differs by its transitoriness, caused by the constantly changing transformation in physical motions. Therefore motion is defined as "only a composition of the last endeavours".

What is most important and elevating to the young investigator of motion was his conviction that he "demonstrated" this in a geometrical and mechanistic pattern – providing full satisfaction to the claims of modern scientific standards as reconstructed by Thomas Hobbes. Now Leibniz himself is making claims to a new scientific standard, based on rational analysis of motion, and so he pronounces – not for the first and not for the last time – a stiff sentence on the failing approach of Descartes to the basic problems of mind and matter.

In Descartes he criticises a philosophical one-sidedness, in spite of his well known dualism:

> Descartes did not penetrate to the innermost core, because he considered mind only in one single manner in itself, and he did not ascend to it by reflections proceeding from the corpora...[35]

That means also, that Descartes could not discover the harmonious structure of the universe, because he neglected the reciprocation and interaction of endeavours, corpuscles and minds. I am sure that, in Leibniz's view, Descartes would have done better to build up his philosophy, beginning with corporeal phenomena – of course as Hobbes and Leibniz did – and then, reflecting, step by step, ascend from physics to metaphysics. Then he possibly also could have encountered the harmonious pattern of the world. But unfortunately,

---

[35] A VI ii 285, column 1, lines 17-21.

as Leibniz's favoured *"ceterum censeo"* sounded, Descartes preferred to remain in the antechamber of the true philosophy.[36]

To discuss this harsh judgement would take us into a wide field of scientific history, beyond our present topic. Suffice it to say that, throughout his life, Leibniz gave serious attention to the fundamental connection between philosophy, ethics and science. As to the relevance of his anthropological and theological view of *Harmonia universalis* to our present cultural situation, the judgement of Leroy L. Loemker still stands:

> If the restoration of science to its proper place in an humanistic and moral culture is our chief problem, Leibniz ... is our man. ... Leibniz portrays a social universe of which the harmonising principle is the love of the wise man, that is, justice ...[37]

[36] See, for instance, the long letter to Honorato Fabri, S. J., in 1676: "Cartesii scripta vestibulum appellare soleo Philosophiae verae ... Fateor tamen multas et magnas res in Cartesio emendandas esse ..." (A II i 298).
[37] L. E. Loemker, 'Leibniz and Our Time', in *The Philosophy of Leibniz and the Modern World*, ed. I. Leclerc (Nashville: Vanderbilt University Press, 1973), p. 9.

URSULA GOLDENBAUM

TRANSUBSTANTIATION, PHYSICS AND PHILOSOPHY

AT THE TIME OF THE *CATHOLIC DEMONSTRATIONS*

Before I come to my .subject I want to draw attention to two general judgements of Leibniz research: first there is widespread agreement among Leibniz scholars about a remarkable continuity in the development of Leibniz's philosophy from the earliest manuscripts to his mature philosophy. We can find this judgement first in the writings of Guhrauer[1] and of Trendelenburg against Erdmann in the 1840s,[2] in the writings of Gerhardt against Ludwig Stein in the 1890s,[3]

---

[1] See G. E. Guhrauer: *Quaestiones criticae ad Leibnitii opera philosophica pertinentes* (Bratislava, 1842) p. 3 and 15; compare also: G. E. Guhrauer: *Gottfried Wilhelm Freiherr von Leibniz. Eine Biographie* (Breslau, 1846), vol. 1, pp. 185-7. Guhrauer argues against J. E. Erdmann: *Introduction to: De vita beata*, in *Leibnizii Opera philosophica quae exstant Latina, Gallica, Germanica omnia* (Berlin: Eichler, 1840).

[2] See A. Trendelenburg, 'Ist Leibniz in seiner Entwicklung einmal Spinozist oder Cartesianer gewesen und was bedeutet dafür die Schrift *de vita beata*?' (*Monatsberichte der Berliner Akademie der Wissenschaften*, 1847: 372-86). Trendelenburg shows that Leibniz's writing is a composition of quotations from Descartes. Furthermore he claims that there was no time in the life of Leibniz where he could be influenced by Spinoza, because he had already finished the general concept of his philosophy in the years in Mainz.

[3] See C. I. Gerhardt, 'Leibniz und Spinoza' (*Sitzungsberichte der Berliner Akademie der Wissenschaften* 49 (1889): 1075-80). This is the answer to L. Stein, 'Leibniz in seinem Verhältnis zu Spinoza auf Grundlage unedirten Materials entwickelungsgeschichtlich dargestellt', *Sitzungsberichte der Kgl.-Preuss. Ak. d. Wiss. zu Berlin* 25 (1888): 615-27; L. Stein, 'Neue Aufschlüsse über den litterarischen Nachlass und die Herausgabe der Opera posthuma Spinoza's', *Archiv*

---

in the book by Cassirer[4] and even in the first special investigation into
the young Leibniz by Kabitz from the beginning of our century.[5]
Cassirer shows us in the section about the development of the
philosophy of the young Leibniz at the end of his book that Leibniz's
work on the concept of the individual was a continuous one from his
first drafts,[6] and Kabitz, in his pioneering investigation of the young
Leibniz counts five general ideas which stayed as central ideas in
Leibniz's philosophy for his whole life: 1) a panlogism, consisting in
the idea of rationality of the universe or of its logical regularity, 2) the
idea of the independent significance of the individual, 3) the idea of a
perfect harmony of all things, 4) the idea of the quantitative and
qualitative infinity of the universe and 5) the mechanical hypothesis.[7]
But it seems to me quite unsatisfactory when Kabitz emphasises, on
the one hand, the exceptional early formation of these leading ideas in
the thinking of the young Leibniz, which then have been only
developed more and more systematically during his life, while, on the
other hand, he has to concede that what we can find even in these
central ideas of the early philosophy is "not original or peculiar to
Leibniz".[8]   Because of this Kabitz sees the originality of the
philosophy of the young Leibniz in the way of the connection of these
ideas.

Despite such contradictions, the view that there are some central
continuous ideas in the philosophical development of Leibniz appears
since the beginning of our century as the generally supported one, and
we find it still in more recent specialist works about the young
Leibniz, for example by Wiedeburg[9] (1962) and Konrad Moll in the

---

[4] E. Cassirer, *Leibniz' System in seinen wissenschaftlichen Grundlagen* (Marburg:
Elwert, 1902).
[5] W. Kabitz, *Die Philosophie des jungen Leibniz* (Heidelberg: Carl Winter's
Universitätsbuchhandlung, 1909).
[6] Cassirer, *Leibniz' System*, p. 520.
[7] Kabitz, *Die Philosophie des jungen Leibniz*, p. 127.
[8] *Ibid*, p. 127.
[9] P. Wiedeburg, *Der junge Leibniz. Das Reich und Europa*, 2 vols. (Wiesbaden:
Steiner, 1962).

1990s[10], and also in many of the presentations of the philosophy of Leibniz since the three great classics of the beginning of our century.[11]

The continuity has been seen above all in the enduring work of Leibniz on some central notions like harmony, substance (or substantial forms), and individuality; in his opinion about the activity and the dominance of the soul over the body, and, last but not least, in his insistence on mechanical principles of modern philosophy on the one hand and his embracing of Aristotelian notions on the other.

It is this opinion which I want to dispute in this paper. For the present I want only to point out that in spite of all the apparent continuities in Leibniz's philosophy, and some sentences of the early time do indeed sound absolutely similar to those of later times, it is clear that we can also find obvious differences and even strong changes in Leibniz's philosophical opinions from one period to another. The most obvious change is in my opinion Leibniz's denial of the sensations of animals or plants and others in his early philosophy until the early 70s and his later understanding of the substantial forms of animals and even plants as soul-like. It sounds really astonishing to me when I read the ironic letter of Leibniz to Tschirnhaus from 1684 where he tells about the jokes of the Dutch people about the Cartesians who believed that the whimpering of a beaten dog is nothing but the sound of a beaten bagpipe.[12] That was, after all, Leibniz's own opinion for a long time, until the early 70s.[13] There are other differences in the great significance attributed to body and matter in the earlier years and the gradual disappearance of – let me say – materialistic views at the end of the Paris time. And we can see also clear differences in the development of the central notions such as substance, substantial form, individual substance, monad as well as in the concept of harmony as it develops into the doctrine of pre-established harmony.

----

[10] K. Moll, *Der junge Leibniz*, 3 vols. (Stuttgart-Bad Cannstatt: Fromann-Holzboog, 1978, 1982 & 1996).

[11] Compare B. Russell, *A Critical Exposition of the Philosophy of Leibniz* (Cambridge, 1900); L. Couturat, *La logique de Leibniz d'après des documents inédits* (Paris: Alcan, 1900); and Cassirer's *Leibniz' System*.

[12] Letter to Tschirnhaus of November (?) 1684, A II i 541.

[13] Compare, for example, the following writings of the time in Mainz: *Elementa juris naturalis* (1670-71(?)), in A VI i, No. 12$_4$.

Nevertheless the apparent philosophical continuity of Leibniz's development has guided scholars to investigate above all the inner metaphysical motion of his thinking, seeking for the sources of Leibniz's thought especially in his early philosophy – looking from the end to see how and by what steps he could have arrived at his mature system of philosophy. The singularity of his thinking compared with the mainstream of mechanical and anti-Aristotelian philosophy in the 17th century has led to the study of his Aristotelian education at the University of Leipzig and from there to the discovery, investigation and comparison of the most important modern works that he read – like Erhard Weigel, Gassendi, Hobbes, Descartes and others. We have got by these efforts very detailed works about the young Leibniz and his dependence upon Erhard Weigel and Gassendi and recently about Hobbes from Konrad Moll. We have in the essays of Christia Mercer and of Robert J. Sleigh in the Leibniz *Companion*[14] a very exact description and clear presentation of all the steps of Leibniz's metaphysical thought and his inner development in the early years – how new problems arose and how he provided solutions at each step. And naturally we have a lot of interesting articles about special influences from other philosophers upon Leibniz.

My second remark concerns the interesting discussion among Leibniz scholars about the relation of Leibniz's metaphysical development and the influence especially of logic, but also of scientific theories of physics or dynamics and biology, by Couturat, Russell and Cassirer, as well as by Gueroult, Fichant, Garber, Parkinson and others.[15] Concerning the relation of sciences and

---

[14] C. Mercer and R. C. Sleigh, Jr., 'The early period to the *Discourse on Metaphysics*', in *The Cambridge Companion to Leibniz*, ed. Nicholas Jolley (Cambridge: Cambridge University Press, 1995), pp. 67-123.

[15] Apart from Couturat, Russell and Cassirer these questions are discussed by: A. Hannéquin, 'La première philosophie de Leibniz', in *Études d'Histoire des Sciences* (Paris: Alcan, 1908); M. Guéroult, *Dynamique et Physiques Leibniziennes* (Paris, 1934); M. Fichant, 'Neue Einblicke in Leibniz' Reform seiner Dynamik (1678)', *SL* 22 (1990): 48-68; *G. W. Leibniz: La réforme de la dynamique,* ed. by M. Fichant (Paris: Vrin, 1994); D. Garber 'Physics and philosophy', in *The Cambridge Companion to Leibniz,* ed. Nicholas Jolley (Cambridge: Cambridge University Press, 1995), pp. 270-78; G. W. Leibniz, *Specimen Dynamicum,* ed. and trans. by H. G. Dosch et. al. (Hamburg, 1982), p. IX-XX; H. Stammel, *Der Kraftbegriff in Leibniz' Physik* (Mannheim: Meiner, 1982); H. Stammel, 'Der Status der

metaphysics in Leibniz the question has been discussed, whether the logical, physical, or biological problems and theories produce the metaphysical conclusions or whether it is on the contrary metaphysics which leads to solutions in the sciences. This discussion continues even now.

While the relation between logic, mathematics, physics and biology, on the one hand, and metaphysics, on the other, has been at the centre of most scholars' considerations, there exists hardly any larger and detailed investigation about the significance of theological or juridical problems for his metaphysical work. There was always agreement about the correspondence of Leibniz's metaphysical and theological or juridical ideas, but in spite of his obvious intensive preoccupation with problems of Christian theology, and even with revealed religion, its significance for his metaphysical work was almost never discussed. His many drafts on revealed religion could no longer attract the interest of philosophers in the late 18th century, when 'enlightened theology' was focusing above all on natural religion. Reflecting on the theological interests of Leibniz, Cassirer and Kabitz even deny any importance to his metaphysical development. Cassirer says about the intensive efforts of the young Leibniz to defend the mysteries of the Christian religion by metaphysical and dynamical arguments, that these would be only an additional application on, not a deduction from theology. He explains these efforts of the young Leibniz as a pure external accommodation to prevailing dogmas. The real religious motive of Leibniz would be expressed in his central idea of harmony.[16] Kabitz also reduces the significance of religious problems to the intention of Leibniz to found the Christian religion in a more rational way. As a consequence he has to neglect the drafts on revealed religion as only external reflections, belonging to the political project of the Reunification of the Christian churches. And so Kabitz even criticises Leibniz because he held on to dogma and was not able to arrive at the consequences of the rationalists and Socinians of his

---

Bewegungsgesetze in Leibniz' Philosophie und die apriorische Methode der Kraftmessung', *SL Sond.* 13 (1984): 180-8; H. Breger, 'Elastizität als Strakturprinzip der Materie bei Leibniz', *SL Sond.* 13 (1984): 120; H. Poser 'Apriorismus der Prinzipien und Kontingenz der Naturgesetze. Das Leibniz-Paradigma der Naturwissenschaft', *SL Sond.* 13 (1984): 177-8.

[16] Cassirer, *Leibniz' System*, p. 507.

time.[17] Even this judgement seems to me a clear misunderstanding of Leibniz, who was never willing at all to follow the Socinian arguments. Also Kabitz cannot see any significance of Leibniz's works on revealed religion or on the Christian mysteries for his metaphysical development, with the exception of the problem of predestination, because of its relation to the philosophical problem of freedom.

This tradition of a lack of interest in the theological papers of the young Leibniz concerning revealed religion persists, while new philosophical works are continually being published about Leibniz's opinions on natural religion, so about his concept of God, of immortality and individuality of the soul as well as about freedom and predestination. The theologians themselves were never really interested in Leibniz's theological opinions about revealed religion: during his life time the theological ideas of Leibniz were regarded by the different confessions as more or less heretical,[18] and even the *Théodicée* was not accepted by the reformed or by the Lutheran church.[19] Later on, the Protestant theologians were less interested in the problems of revealed religion, when the tendency to reduce the Christian religion to natural religion became dominant at the time of the 'Aufklärung'. And so it is not surprising that we have only a few systematic works on the theology of Leibniz[20], which stem from

---

[17] Kabitz, *Die Philosophie des jungen Leibniz*, p. 111.

[18] Compare the evaluation of W. Sparn, 'Das Bekenntnis des Philosophen. Gottfried Wilhelm Leibniz als Philosoph und Theologe', *Neue Ztschr. f. Systemat. Philosophie u. Religionsphilosophie* 28 (1986): 139-78. See also H. Schepers' article on Leibniz in *Neue Deutsche Biographie* (Berlin, 1985), vol. 14, pp. 121-31.

[19] Compare St. Lorenz, 'Leibniz und Gottlieb Johann Hansch. Zur Frühgeschichte der Wirkung der *Essais de Theodicée* in Deutschland', in *Leibniz und Europa: Vorträge zum VI Internationer Leibniz-Kongress* (Hanover: G.W. Leibniz Gesellschaft, 1995), vol 2, pp. 206-211.

[20] A. Pichler, *Die Theologie des Leibniz* (Munich, 1869), 2 vols. Compare also J. Baruzi, *Leibniz et l'organisation religieuse de la terre d'après des documents inédits* (Paris: Alcan, 1907). See also the presentation of Leibniz in the great works of E. Hirsch, *Geschichte der neueren evangelischen Theologie im Zusammenhang mit den allgemeinen Bewegungen des europäischen Denkens* (Gütersloh: Bertelsmann, 1951), vol. 2, pp. 7-48; and of E. Troeltsch, 'Protestantisches Christentum und Kirche in der Neuzeit', in *Die Kultur der Gegenwart, ihre Entwicklung und ihre Ziele*, ed. P. Hinneberg (Berlin & Leipzig, 1909), part 1, section 4, 1, pp. 431-755.

Catholic theologians. But we have even fewer investigations of the significance of theological problems to the metaphysical ideas of Leibniz.

But these investigations stem in almost every case from the last twenty years. First (1975) Marcelo Dascal focused on the importance of Leibniz's preoccupation with the Christian mysteries for his epistemological theory, and especially for his concept of the confused idea.[21] Following on from this in 1993, Maria Rosa Antognazza investigated systematically the opinion of Leibniz about the Trinity in its significance for Leibniz's metaphysics.[22] In 1992, Daniel S. Fouke discussed the Leibnizian concept of the Eucharist in respect of its metaphysical consequences.[23] And in 1996 Philip Beeley dedicated two chapters of his book about Leibniz's concept of the continuum to his work on the explanation of a possibility of the Christian mysteries.[24] In my paper I want to take up these new reflections on the significance of Leibniz's theological work for his metaphysics and I will argue that it was his preoccupation with the problems of revealed religion, faced by the challenge of the mechanical philosophy, which initiated his systematic work on metaphysics, physics and mathematics in Mainz.

***

Since the time of my first Leibniz studies, and while reading all the interesting explanations about his early metaphysics mentioned above, which I highly appreciate and from which I have learned and understood a lot about Leibniz, I have not able to convince myself that

---

[21] See M. Dascal, 'Reason and the Mysteries of Faith: Leibniz on the Meaning of Religious Discourse', in *Leibniz: Language, Signs and Thought* (Amsterdam: Benjamins, 1987), pp. 93-124.

[22] See M. R. Antognazza, 'Die Rolle der Trinitäts – und Menschwerdungsdiskussionen für die Entstehung von Leibniz' Denken', in *SL* 26 (1994): 56-75.

[23] D. C. Fouke, 'Metaphysics and the Eucharist in the Early Leibniz' in *SL* 24 (1992): 145-159.

[24] See P. Beeley, *Kontinuität und Mechanismus. Zur Philosophie des jungen Leibniz in ihrem ideengeschichtlichen Kontext* (*SL Supp.* 30), Stuttgart: Steiner, 1996, pp. 75-81.

86 *Ursula Goldenbaum*

there was such a strong inner intellectual development from Aristotle by way of atomism, Weigel, Gassendi, Hobbes, other English philosophers (like Thomas White) and Descartes to the *Theoria motus abstracti* and the *Hypothesis physica nova* – and by way of these to the notion of the body as a *mens momentanea*, and the mind as a permanent *conatus* – and that there was a simultaneous development of the notion of substance as the unity of body and soul in other manuscripts of this time. Perhaps especially because of the difficulties I have had, finding my way through the early manuscripts of Leibniz in the four years between 1668 and 1671, I have asked myself 'What is the thread in all these so similar and still slightly different concepts; what are the reasons and also the motives of Leibniz's philosophical seeking and changing in this time?'

The intellectual development of a great philosopher or of a scientist, when viewed from the end of his life, always looks like a chain of consequences, although in fact there were often changes or even breaks in the individual's life. Such an intellectual development as a chain of interior logical consequences is at the same time at every step a decision against other possible consequences too. And so the question arises again for me – 'Why did he decide on these consequences?' And all his reading of other philosophers cannot explain why Leibniz did not become a follower of them, why he could not be content with them.[25]

Why did he choose atomism at first in Leipzig, holding from this time the mechanical principles of this modern philosophy, reading Weigel, Gassendi and Hobbes, and why did he then return in Mainz apparently to the substantial forms of Aristotle, all the while still reading above all the new philosophers? I can imagine the intellectual curiosity and the enthusiasm of the young Leibniz regarding the clarity of the principles of the atomistic philosophy against the background of the very traditional and a slightly boring atmosphere of the University

---

[25] Thus I am in agreement with Beeley's criticism of Moll's book, that it is very interesting in its details, but unsatisfactory as a presentation of the development of the young Leibniz: "Tatsächlich aber besteht der Schwerpunkt seiner Untersuchungen darin, jene Schlüsselgestalten ausfindig zu machen, die entscheidenden Einfluß auf Leibniz' frühes Denken ausgeüt haben sollen. Da der Autor auf eine zusammenhängende Darstellung verzichtet, geht die innere Dynamik der Entwicklung bis 1672 verloren." (*op. cit.*, p. 8)

of Leipzig where it was even forbidden to read the modern philosophers of Jena or Altdorf in the seminar.[26] But I cannot see Leibniz as a white page on which every reading left its traces. I would say on the contrary that he searched this literature for some philosophical hints to help him on his own way.

In my opinion his inner intellectual development as well as his choice of literature can be seen to follow only if we understand it as his more and more developed answers to his own questions. And so I had to look for such a fundamental question of Leibniz in these early years. I asked myself, what could be the central problem of a young Lutheran, who had grown up in the stronghold of Lutheranism and post-Lutheran Aristotelian scholasticism in Leipzig, but also in the warm security of a deeply religious family, gifted with excellent intelligence and a developed capacity for logical thinking and with the benefit of a good education in history of philosophy, already curious about modern philosophy and with some knowledge about it? What could be the problem of such a young person when he comes to Mainz, a strong Catholic town, getting a post from the Archbishop and invited to the Catholic circle of erudite men around Baron von

---

[26] "Konstituierend ist die Überzeugung, auf der Grundlage eines Weltbildes zu stehen, in dem sich Philosophie und wahrer Glaube in Harmonie verbinden und die Grundlage aller Wissenschaften bilden. 'Novitäten', die in der Konsequenz gewollt oder ungewollt auf eine Infragestellung dieser Basis hinauslaufen, mußten daher mit Ablehnung und Widerstand rechnen. Das zeigt sich an der Haltung zum Cartesianismus als der alle Gemüter innerhalb der Respublica litteraria in der Mitte des 17. Jahrhunderts bewegenden neuen, revolutionierenden Richtung. Der Widerspruch, auf den Descartes' Philosophie an fast allen deutschen Universitäten stößt, ist auch in Leipzig unübersehbar. Es erscheint als ganz und gar undenkbar, daß ein beliebiger Zeitgenosse es wagen sollte, seine eigene. Auffassungen der Doctrina publica aller vergangenen Jahrhunderte, d.h. der Philosophie des Aristoteles, einfach entgegenzustellen. Als daher Anton Gunther Heshusius 1662 ein Privatkolleg über Johannes Sperlings 'Institutiones physicae' anmeldet, stößt er auf den entschiedenen Widerspruch der Fakultät. Auch wenn Heshusius, wie er behauptete, Sperling widerlegen wollte, so würden doch die Studenten nur eine Bestärkung in der bei ihnen grassierenden Philosophia antiperipatetica suchen. Der Dekan (kein geringerer als Jakob Thomasius) verweigert die Zustimmung zu einer solchen Lehrveranstaltung, ja es wird sogar die Erklärung abverlangt, der Jugend allein die an der Leipziger Universtät 'diu recepta doctrine' zu vermitteln." (D. Döring, *Der junge Leibniz und Leipzig. Ausstellung zum 350. Geburtstag von Gottfried Wilhelm Leibniz* (Berlin: Akademie Verlag, 1985), pp. 67-8)

Boineburg. We can hardly imagine today the contrast between the worlds of Leipzig and Mainz. For example, it was impossible in this time to become a citizen of Mainz as a Protestant, and in the churches in the University of Leipzig you could constantly hear strong refutations of the Catholics, the Reformed and even of the so-called Syncretists.[27] It must have been something of a culture shock for the young Leibniz, in spite of his intelligent openness, conciliatory nature and curiosity. Especially the contact with von Boineburg, a personality with a high political rank, a wide erudition and a special interest in religious and theological questions, but also with obvious Catholic missionary intentions toward Leibniz[28] must have made a great impression for the young man. The close relation with Boineburg must have been a high acknowledgement of his intellectual abilities and a great career opportunity; but it was also at the same time a great challenge.[29]

It was above all through Boineburg that Leibniz gained entry into a new world, not only with regard to religion and the court of the Archbishop of Mainz, but also in the intellectual and cultural world of Catholicism. The court of Mainz was known for its religious

---

[27] "Was die von späteren Historikern häufig als Gezänk kritisierten Gelehrtenstreitigkeiten angeht, so gehören sie in jenem militanten Jahrhundert tatsächlich zum fast täglichen Brot nicht nur der Philosophieprofessoren, sondern der Angehörigen aller Fakultäten... So sind es gerade in Leipzig eine Reihe von Theologen, die einen besonderen Eifer im Ausfechten der mannigfachsten literarischen Kämpfe entwickeln. Dabei verbindet sich die Überzeugung, für den Schutz der reinen Lehre zu streiten, mit einem ganz ungebrochenen Selbstbewuß tsein, als Professor der Theologie an der lutherischen Hochburg Leipzig zur geistigen Elite, zu den tragenden Schichten der Ständegesellschaft zu zählen." (Döring, *op. cit.*, pp. 65-6)

[28] Writing a recommendation of Leibniz to Melchior Friedrich von Schönborn on the 20th May 1668 the Baron von Boineburg supposed that Leibniz was already on the way to the true religion. He even expected: "Vielleicht wird er geistlich." (Compare: *Leben und Werk von Gottfried Wilhelm Leibniz. Eine Chronik*, composed by K. Müller and G. Krönert (Frankfurt on Main: Klostermann, 1969), p. 13.)

[29] The first detailed investigation about the intellectual significance of the Boineburg circle for the development of the young Leibniz was published by Paul Wiedeburg, *Der junge Leibniz. Das Reich und Europa*, 1. Part: Mainz, 2 vol., (Wiesbaden: Steiner 1962). See particularly pp. 59-100.

tolerance.[30] Leibniz participated in the discussions of the Boineburg circle; he made the acquaintance of famous and important men like the van Walenburch brothers, Catholic Churchmen of Cologne and of Mainz[31]; he participated in the correspondence of von Boineburg with other Catholic converts of a high rank like Johann Friedrich and Ernst von Hessen-Rheinfels, and even with the head of the French Jansenists, Antoine Arnauld. Through von Boineburg he also gained contact with the famous erudite Protestant physician and lawyer Hermann Conring. And – last but not least – he got the keys to the extraordinary library of von Boineburg in order to compile a catalogue of it. There he had access not only to literature on jurisprudence necessary for his juridical work, but also to theological works of all Christian confessions: the great editions of the Royal printing office in Paris, the new publications of the Dutch printers, the recently published works from then-current religious controversies between the Jansenists and Huguenots in France, between Arnauld and Jean Claude, also the latest Socinian challenges, and last but not least the whole of the modern philosophical literature, from Descartes to Pascal and Arnauld, from all of Thomas Hobbes to Ludwig Meyer and even to Spinoza's *Tractatus theologico-politicus*, from the English Platonists to the *Philosophical Transactions*. The treasures of this library are still to be sifted for the intellectual possibilities the presented to Leibniz in these years. If you read the old Leibniz catalogue, which still exists in Hanover, you have much more

---

[30] "Sein [von Schönborn's] Hof wurde in Reichstagskreisen die 'aura laboriosa' genannt... Musikfreudig, mathematisch und physikalisch interessiert, aber kein Mäzen und bei aller geistigen Aufgeschlossenheit mehr praktisch eingestellt, bot er das Bild eines treusorgenden Landesvaters... Seine Toleranz und Konzilianz, seine Mittlerbegabung und sein bedeutender Anteil an der Wahrung einer 25jährigen Friedenszeit nach dem Drei-βigjährigen Krieg haben ihm den ehrenden Beinamen eines 'deutschen Salomo' eingetragen. Diese seine auch konfessionell und kirchlich friedsame und weitherzige Haltung mag ihn in manchen Gewissenskonflikt zwischen seinen Aufgaben als Kirchenfürst, Landesherr und Mensch gebracht haben.... Der Verfechtung römisch-katholischer Ziele und Forderungen in solchen protestantischen oder konfessionell gemischten Gebieten konnte und wollte er sich nicht entziehen, aber es war.... offensichtlich, daβ dies seiner irenischen Gesinnung wenig entsprach" (Wiedeburg, *op. cit.*, pp. 69-71).

[31] Concerning the significance of the brothers Walenburch for Leibniz, see Wiedeburg, *op. cit.*, pp. 79-92.

confidence regarding the incredible list of books Leibniz had read according to his letter to Arnauld. You can find the traces of probably common discussions about theological and metaphysical topics in the books, from the hand of both von Boineburg and Leibniz.[32]

For the Lutheran Leibniz, a new moment of such religious discussions in Catholic Mainz was the close connection of the Boineburg circle to the Western world and to religious discussions in Western Europe, France, Britain, Italy and the Netherlands. One of the great discussions was at that time the discussion about the Catholic doctrine of transubstantiation. This has been shown to be the case especially in the last ten years with reference to Galileo and his followers in Italy[33] as well as the Cartesians in France[34]. Whereas the Cartesians or other mechanical philosophers in the Netherlands, in Britain or even in some Reformed universities in Western Germany had comparatively minor problems with their churches and their theology, the philosophers in France and even more in Italy had to defend themselves against the charge that they denied the doctrine of transubstantiation and thus fell under the anathema of the Council of Trent. The attraction of the Moderns in spite of the Jesuit criticism and attacks was at the same time in France grist for the mill of the Huguenots like Jean Claude who attacked the Catholic doctrine of transubstantiation above all from his theological viewpoint, but who also used the new argument for the impossibility of transubstantiation,

---

[32] I gave a presentation of a new small 'Leibnizstück' which I found among other marginalia from the hands of Leibniz and Boineburg in a copy of Spinoza's *Tractatus theologico-politicus* from the library of the Baron von Boineburg, at a Leibniz conference in Potsdam in the summer of 1996. The papers of this conference will be published shortly in a Sonderheft of the *Studia Leibnitiana*.

[33] P. Redondi, *Galilei der Ketzer* (Frankfurt on Main & Vienna, 1989), p. 211; compare also P. Costabel, 'L'atomisme, face cachée de la condamnation de Galilée?', in *La Vie des Sciences* IV.4, pp. 349-365.

[34] Compare J.-R. Armogathe, *Theologia Cartesiana* (The Hague: Nijhoff, 1965); R. Watson, 'Transubstantiation among the Cartesians', in *Problems of Cartesianism*, ed. T. Lennon and others (Montreal: McGill/Queen's University Press, 1982); R. Specht: *Innovation und Folgelast, Beispiele aus der neueren Philosophie- und Wissenschaftsgeschichte* (Stuttgart-Bad Cannstatt: Fromann-Holzboog, 1972), pp. 84-91.

at any rate as implied by modern mechanical philosophy.[35] In this situation every discussion about physics was at the same time a discussion about theology and vice versa. An experiment like that of Huygens in 1672, to show the mechanical principles of cohesion using two polished blocks of marble,[36] or the experiments of Pascal about atmospheric pressure as an affirmation of mechanical principles could get enormous public attention as arguments in a theological-political struggle between the Jansenists and the Jesuits as well as between the Moderns and the Aristotelians.[37]

Against this background it is not very surprising that Leibniz, having entered this world already in Mainz (and not only in Paris), could be or even had to be interested in the problems of the Eucharist and especially of transubstantiation. We can imagine that Leibniz had to explain in such discussions with von Boineburg his own view about the Eucharist as a Lutheran (he tells something like that in his letter to Arnauld)[38].

Christia Mercer has drawn our attention to the fact that we can find the most metaphysical concepts of Leibniz from his time in Mainz especially in some theological drafts, about transubstantiation, incarnation and resurrection. There we will find the most interesting steps of Leibniz's work on the concept of substance and the relation of body and soul: "Although each of the essays in this collection treats a traditional Christian theological question ..., Leibniz's answers lay the foundation of his metaphysics." Mercer explains this interest in theological questions with his engagement in the plans for the Reunification of the Christian churches – Leibniz had to solve some theological questions in a sense "that would satisfy the members of

---

[35] Compare A. Arnauld: *La perpétuité de la foy de l'Eglise Catholique*, Paris, 1669; J. Claude *Reponse au livre de Mr. Arnauld intitulé La Perpétuité de la Foy de l 'Eglise Catholique touchant l'Eucharistie défendue*, Rouen 1670. Leibniz knows this discussion. We can see this from his letter to Arnauld of November 1671, compare A II i 170.

[36] Compare the announcement about the experiment by Chr. Huygens in *Journal des Sçavans* 3 (1672) (Amsterdam 1678): 112-113 (Chr. Huygens, *Oeuvres complètes*, Haag 1897, vol. 7, pp. 201-206). For the significance of the experiences of Huygens and Pascal for Leibniz see H. Breger, 'Elastizität als Strukturprinzip der Materie bei Leibniz' in *SL Sond.* 13: 115.

[37] Redondi, *Galilei der Ketzer*, pp. 273-320.

[38] Compare Leibniz to Arnauld (November 1671) in A II i 170.

both faiths and would remain consistent with the pronouncements of the Council of Trent".[39]

But in my view it is not so self-explanatory that Leibniz began by working on a defence of the Catholic transubstantiation. A defence of the Catholic interpretation of the Eucharist by a Lutheran in this time was not a small matter, and Leibniz was deeply aware of that, as we know from his plea for silence at the end of his letter to Arnauld[40].

Neglecting the sublime differences between the confessions we should expect from a Protestant in such struggles a more sympathetic feeling and support for the Protestants in France and in the Netherlands. But in reality Leibniz resolved upon a defence of the Catholic position. We know from a letter by Boineburg from 20th May 1668 that he already saw Leibniz on the way to the true religion because of that.[41] But the explanation given by Leibniz in his letter to Arnauld from 1671 is right in a certain way. Leibniz justified his support for the Catholic interpretation with its great proximity to the Lutheran notion of the Real Presence of the body of Christ in the Eucharist. And really it is so, whereas the Reformed church did not accept the real presence of Christ in the Eucharist, but interpreted the words *This is my body* more symbolically as a spiritual presence. This proximity of the Confession of Augsburg to the Catholic interpretation is not so surprising because it was already a compromise of Melanchthon to avoid the separation of the Christian church in Augsburg. But Leibniz may have been nearly the only Lutheran in this time who could see the things in this light. No other deeply faithful Lutheran, especially amongst thinking men, would see as he did the consequences for Christian theology of the quick and (in spite of all obstacles) successful development of the mechanical philosophy. In Germany – even in the Lutheran parts – the knowledge of the new science had not yet arrived and the intra-theological refutations and controversies still dominated for a long time. But Lutheran theology was clearly concerned in a really similar way with its interpretation of the Eucharist. How could the body of Christ be

---

[39] Mercer and Sleigh, *op. cit.*, p. 68.
[40] Letter to Arnauld, A II i 184.
[41] See note 31.

present in the Eucharist if only material particles and their motion in the bread and wine existed?

Leibniz became aware at this time that the mechanical philosophy would lead to the rejection of this (especially for Lutherans) most important sacrament – to an abolition of this mystery of Christianity, which was central for the Christian doctrine of revelation. In this situation he had to find a way to reconcile the new successful and useful mechanical principles with a philosophy or metaphysics which was compatible with Christian theology, and especially with the unintelligible mysteries of revealed religion. In my opinion, even his holding to the mechanical philosophy expresses the modernity of Leibniz's intention to reconcile it with revealed religion. He had to find a way to prove the possibility of the mysteries which could be accepted by modern philosophy. On the other hand he had to respect the nature of the mysteries as not accessible to human reason. His explanation of his methodical solution for this task in the letter to Arnauld expresses his deep consciousness of this difficulty:

> As the geometrician has to examine, that a possibility has thus been proven or that it explains a certain possible way and means and that the possibility was proven, if he applied them either to other exercises, which have already been resolved or to exercises which do not have to be solved, which means that he has reduced them to postulations which relate to the exercises, as axioms do to theorems.[42]

Leibniz wants to show only a possibility, how the mysteries could happen, but not the real way, in which God let them happen. In his opinion, such a demonstration of a possibility had to be convincing to the mathematical philosophers of his time. So in my opinion it was not so much the political project of reunification of the Christian churches that provided Leibniz's motive for working out his theological-metaphysical drafts, but his own interest in finding a way to reconcile, in a metaphysical concept, the accepted mechanical principles of modern science with the essentials of Christianity. I believe we have to trust in the confession of Leibniz to Arnauld that

---

[42] Letter to Arnauld, A II i 175.

he was working hard on the problem of transubstantiation all the years in Mainz until 1671.[43] He writes in the same regard also about his motive of avoiding the danger which would beset the Christian faith if a new philosophy were not found and accepted by the Church which was compatible with mechanical principles as well as with Christian doctrine. He writes in his letter to Arnauld:

> Nothing would more effectively strengthen atheism or the growing spirit of naturalism – and nothing would more effectively undermine entirely the already precarious faith in Christianity of many important but unsaved people – than the following: on the one hand to prove that the mysteries of faith have always been believed by all Christians; and, on the other hand to demonstrate that these mysteries can be shown by certain proofs in accordance with right reason, to be nonsense.[44]

In my opinion the long letter to Arnauld is in some way the key to understanding the intellectual motives of Leibniz. It is also a report about his efforts to find the solutions to the theological-metaphysical problems, and about the conclusions in all the other fields of his work at that time – from mechanics and mathematics to practical philosophy and jurisprudence. This letter gives us at the same time the explanation of the coherence of all the different fields of his work. One important reason for taking this letter as a serious confession by Leibniz about the theological-metaphysical intention of his different works, lies in its semi-public nature: it was written by arrangement with von Boineburg, and it served as confidential, but serious information about the solution of a problem, which was highly explosive for the Cartesian Jansenists in France at that time. Because of the contradiction of the Cartesian philosophy with the dogma of Trent about the transubstantiation the works of Descartes were put on

---

[43] "It remains for me to speak of the Eucharist. I have studied this problem for four years, as is known to the illustrious Boineburg, in order to prove the possibility of the mysteries of the Eucharist, or, what amounts to the same, to explain them by continuous and unchallengeable analysis, so that we shall finally arrive at the first and admissible postulations of divine power." (Letter to Arnauld, A II i 175)

[44] Letter to Arnauld, A II i 171.

the *Index Romanum* in 1663. We have to see this theological background to understand the euphoria of Leibniz, when he could write to Arnauld:

> And I think, that I have finally brought this to a happy conclusion. After I had initially understood, that the very essence of a body does not consist in its extension, as Descartes had believed, that otherwise indisputably great man, but in its motion, and that because of this the substance of a body or its nature, which accords with Aristotle's definition, is the principle of motion (as there can be no absolute rest within bodies) but as the principle of motion or the substance of a body lacks extension, there it is finally revealed in all clarity, what differentiates substance from external appearances, and thus the reason was found because of which we are enabled to realise clearly and distinctly, that God brings it about *that the substance of one and the same body can be in many different distant places, or, what is the same, amongst numerous external appearances.*[45]

And so we can explain the possibility of the presence of Jesus Christ in all different places in the Eucharist.

Compared with this great letter I cannot see the letters of Leibniz to his old teacher Thomasius as his 'Systementwurf'[46] from this time, because Leibniz therein is only defending his holding to the mechanical philosophy against the Aristotelian criticism of his teacher. That is obviously a continuation of former discussions, although in a more developed manner, because Leibniz has already accepted the mechanical philosophy in Leipzig. And it is clear that Leibniz never could discuss his at that time urgent questions about transubstantiation with his Lutheran teacher at Leipzig. Nevertheless

---

[45] See the letter to Arnauld, A II i 175 (Emphasised by me – U. G.). Compare also the letter of Fresne to von Boineburg of the 27th November 1671, who read Leibniz's letter to Arnauld and became really enthusiastic about the solution found by the "merveilleux Saxon". Compare *Commercii epistolici Leibnitiani*. recensuit Io. Daniel Gruber Tomi prodromi pars altera, Hanover and Göttingen 1745, n. 466, p. 1380.
[46] Moll, *Der junge Leibniz*, vol. 1, p. 17.

the letters give us an interesting view of the way Leibniz would interpret the Aristotelian terminology in a modern mechanical way.

Thus given Leibniz's confession that he began to work on the demonstration of the possibility of transubstantiation in 1668, we have to see all his writings in the light of this concern. We find the first answer to the problem in his *Confessio naturae*[47] where he demonstrates that the mechanical philosophy cannot explain its own central concepts: it cannot explain a certain shape [figura] of a body and its cohesion by mechanical principles of extension and size. Leibniz concluded from this demonstration that the moving principle must be another thing than the body, namely the mind, as God and as human mind. Leibniz is right in his criticism, but other solutions of the problem would be possible – for example, to place the moving principle within the bodies themselves (in some respect Leibniz will do so in his mature philosophy).

But at this time Leibniz does not accept this solution and criticises the substantial forms as self-moving principles in bodies as a scholastic distortion of Aristotle. We find in the letter to Thomasius of the same year a reduction of the substantial forms of Aristotle to the geometrical figures, without any inherent ability to move the body.[48] It sounds at first like a mere mechanical reduction of the Aristotelian substantial forms to geometrical figures in the sense of the mechanical philosophy – and in fact Leibniz had to defend his insistence on the mechanical principles of the modern philosophy against his old Aristotelian teacher; but it represents on the other hand also the establishment of his strong separation of the moved body and the moving mind. Thus Leibniz's way of thinking does not lead from the Aristotelian substantial forms to their reduction to geometrical figures and then to the notion of the moving substance. On the contrary, it is the moving mind which will be the ground for Leibniz's notion of substance as self-standing and self-acting which he develops first in the draft about transubstantiation.[49] That was the point where he remembered indeed 'the true' doctrines of Aristotle.

---

[47] See *Confessio naturae*.
[48] Compare the letter to Thomasius of 30th April, 1669 in A II i 20.
[49] Compare *De transsubstantiatione* in A V1 i 15.

In the writings of 1668 he still defines the body as space or extension, and figure as the limits of the body.[50] The body is able to be moved, but it does not have the ability to move itself. (It is in some respect the opposite of his mature philosophy!) And so it cannot be a substance, but space is a substance and figure or substantial form is something like a substantial thing. The motion through space is the action of the body, but the moving principle is the mind. The action of the mind is thinking. The letter to Thomasius of April 1669 contains again a justification of the identity of geometrical figures with substantial forms, but with some interesting differences – the substantial form [i.e. the figure] is no longer divisible and in the unpublished original version we find the concept of the instantaneous creation of these substantial forms[51] (The deletion of this formulation in the published version need not signify a giving up, but may be attributed to caution about appearing heretical.)

But one or two years later, in the *Theoria motus abstracti*[52], in the letters to Johann Friedrich[53] and to Antoine Arnauld[54], Leibniz defines the essence of the body no longer as extension, but already as motion, and the mind as conatus. This changing of the definitions of body and above all of mind, and especially the new concept of conatus is on the one hand initiated by the challenge from the results of Huygens and Wren[55] which contained the rules of mechanical motion by pure mechanical explanations. But at the same time another challenge was given to Leibniz by the opinions of Thomas Hobbes, for whom Leibniz had considerable respect. It was just the problem of mind which led him to his criticism of Thomas Hobbes.[56] Hobbes regarded

---

[50] See *Confessio naturae*; letters to Thomasius of 6th October, 1668, in A II i 10-11 and of 30th April, 1669, in A VI i 14-24.

[51] Compare the letter to Thomasius of 30th April, 1669, in A II i 18.

[52] See § 17 of Leibniz's *Theoria motus abstracti*.

[53] See the letter to Johann Friedrich of 21st May, 1671, in A II i 108.

[54] See the letter to Arnauld, A II i 171, 172, and 175.

[55] Compare Chr. Huygens 'A Summary Account of the Laws of Motion', *Philosophical Transactions* 46 (1669): 925-8; Chr. Wren's Theory Concerning the General Laws of Motion, *Philosophical Transactions* 43 (1668-9): 864-6.

[56] It is a particular achievement of Philip Beeley to dedicate one chapter of his book especially to the philosophical opinions of Thomas White and Kenelm Digby, which had obviously a great significance for the young Leibniz. Compare Beeley, *Kontinuität und Mechanismus*, pp. 82-118.

the minds as material conatus and denied the existence of mental things. Given the fundamental importance, in Leibniz's reflections, of the mind as the principle of the motion of bodies as well as for the possibility of transubstantiation, resurrection and incarnation he had to find a refutation of the Hobbesian explanation of the sensations as material conatus. He had to find another theory of mind. And in fact he speaks constantly in the papers of this time of the necessity of such a philosophy of mind.[57]

It is curious to see how Leibniz also found, even in his critical preoccupation with Hobbes, the means for his own solution to a whole set of questions in theology as well as in mechanics and mathematics, in practical philosophy, philosophy of law and in metaphysics. He simply took Hobbes's definition of conatus as an instantaneous moving of the body or of a part of a body, but he made it into the essence of the mind. The place of the mind becomes the point. And here we find the reason of the new interest of Leibniz in the mathematical discussion about the indivisibles. Leibniz, although still a greenhorn in mathematics, changed the traditional definition of 'point'. Euclid and with him Hobbes had defined 'point' as a thing, "cujus pars nulla est". Hobbes interpreted this classical definition to the effect that the point be undivided, leaving the traditional understanding of the point as indivisible.[58] As a materialist, he has so understood the point as an extended thing with parts, but with parts, which have to be left out of consideration in any mathematical reflection. Leibniz does agree with Hobbes's changing interpretation of the Euclidean definition of the point to the effect that it had parts, but he denies naturally, that a point is extended.[59] The reason for Leibniz's quite particular definition of the point as an unextended thing, which has parts, is in my opinion a mere metaphysical-

---

[57] See the letter to Arnauld, A II i 173; see also Leibniz's paper for the Duke Johann Friedrich of 21st May, 1671, *De Usu et Necessitate Demonstrationum Immortalitatis Animae,* in A II i 110-114.

[58] Compare Beeley, *Kontinuität und Mechanismus*, pp. 245-54.

[59] Beeley thinks it is possible (*op. cit.*, p. 271) that Leibniz studied the mathematics of indivisibles (Cavalieri and Wallis) through the works of Thomas Hobbes, and not in Cavalieri or Wallis themselves. I found a some support for this supposition in the library of the Baron von Boineburg. There exist many remarks and marginalia from the hand of Leibniz in the mathematical chapters of Hobbes's *De corpore.*

theological one: This new definition is useful for his task to explain the immortality of the mind, the possibility of the mystery of resurrection as well as of the possibility of transubstantiation. An unextended thing is not a body, it is indestructible and immortal. But such a definition of the point will be helpful too for Leibniz's draft of a theory of a mere abstract geometrical description of the rules of mechanical motion, which could be compatible with the Christian mysteries.

If Leibniz wanted to understand the mind as the moving principle of the body and if he wanted to do so on the level of the new mechanical theory, he had to find an explanation for the relation of mind and body within a mechanical theory. He had to introduce the mind in some way into the mechanical theory of motion itself. Leibniz also demands this in his criticism of Thomas White and other modern critics of the mere mechanical philosophy. He emphasises that it will not be enough to say that the mind is no body but it is necessary against the mechanical thinkers like Hobbes and others to explain what the mind is and how it can cause the motion of the body.[60]

Leibniz is convinced from 1670 onwards that he has found the solution for his problems in the definition of the mind as the conatus and of the body as a momentary mind. And he offers now these new definitions not only in his private theological papers and in his semi-public letters to Arnauld and Johann Friedrich, but also in the published physical writing *Theoria motus abstracti*. The definition of the body as a momentary mind allows him to explain the relation of body and mind within the mechanical theory. But on the other hand he has to argue for a clear difference between mind and body. Minds have to be indestructible, and they can be indestructible, if they are without any extension. And so Leibniz places minds in points without any extension.

The *Theoria motus abstracti* sought so to present the compatibility of mechanical philosophy (or science) and the metaphysical-theological explanations of the mysteries, whereas the *Hypothesis physica nova* sought to provide, as the complementary part, the transformations of the abstract rules of God to the motion of the

---

[60] See the paper from Leibniz for the Duke Johann Friedrich *De Usu et Necessitate Demonstrationum Immortalitatis Animae,* especially § 10, in A II i 113.

phenomenal world, which is guaranteed by God through the incoming of the Ether as the instrument of the 'divine economy' (a central theological concept of Leibniz).[61]

This – in Leibniz's view – successful grounding of all his different preoccupations as connected in the one meaningful concept of mind as conatus, in accordance with each other and especially with Christian theology, has led me to the conviction that the search for such a modern defence of Christian theology was the driving motive of the metaphysical, and in the consequence of the physical and mathematical, not to speak of the juridical work of these years. And that means not only and not primarily the rational or natural theology, as is the opinion of many Leibniz scholars, but much more the more difficult demonstrations of the possibility of the mysteries, which were attacked both by the Reformed theologians and by the modern philosophers like Hobbes. And so I see Leibniz's letter to Arnauld as the best and most convincing explanation of his work between 1668 and 1671 – of his motives, of the results and especially of the connection of all the different subjects in the central notion of conatus in the new Leibnizian sense as the mind. The intensity of the metaphysical work which leads him to his work on mechanics and mathematics (of the indivisibles) is attributed to his deep religiosity and responsibility for the defence of religion against the dangers of the new mechanical philosophy. And I see an affirmation of this interpretation as well in the euphoria of Leibniz in this letter because of the discovered solution as in the continuous significance of the notions of these theological-metaphysical results of this period for years to come. Yes, there exists indeed a continuity in his intellectual development, but it is a theological continuity whereas the metaphysical opinions may change more or less. He is always holding to the mechanical theory, but criticising its self-explanatory claim; he is always defending the Christian essentials, but criticising its cutting off from the new science and its intolerance, for example in the case of

---

[61]   Compare the full title of Leibniz's *Hypothesis Physica nova, qua Phaenomenorum Naturae plerorumque causae ab unico quodam universali motu, in globo nostro supposito, neque Tychonicis neque Copernicanis aspernando, repetuntur* (Winter 1670/71 (?)).

Galileo.[62] He develops a metaphysical theory which can be the basis for both, for the grounding of the first concepts of the mechanical theory on the one hand, and for the explanation of the possibility, that means of the consistency of the Christian mysteries, especially of transubstantiation, with the same concepts.

If I see the thread of Leibniz's work of the early time in Mainz in his theological questions, in his decisive defence of the Christian mysteries against the attacks of the Socinians, the Reformed theologians and especially of the modern philosophy by the demonstration of their possibility, so I do not at all claim that Leibniz's philosophical concepts are the result of mere theological efforts. On the contrary, I would emphasise the metaphysical achievement of Leibniz, which lies in his criticism of atomism and the mechanical philosophy, in the draft of his metaphysical concept which possesses the capacity to explain much more than the mere mysteries. We have to be aware that such an interest in transubstantiation and the other mysteries and any preoccupation with this theological subject required at this time and in the Catholic world not only a good understanding of modern philosophy, but also of the new results in mechanics and mathematics. If Leibniz wished to be accepted by the modern philosophers he had to argue on the level of the most recent results of mechanics and mathematics. So he needed, for his refutation of Hobbes' denial of minds, some knowledge of the mathematics of indivisibles and he had to understand the most recent mechanical works like those of Huygens and Wren for his criticism of the central notions of the mere mechanical philosophy and for his demonstration of the possibility of transubstantiation.

I feel a high respect especially for the strong methodical principles of Leibniz who argues against his opponents only by scientific reasons, physical or mathematical ones, on the high level of the recent scientific results, disregarding the aims of his theological enterprise within his arguments. He himself writes about his strong methodical principle to Arnauld – that he had disregarded the theological aims and even his religious feelings, only looking for rational arguments:

---

[62] Compare, for example, the letter to Arnauld, A II i 172.

I refrained from considering myself, and I am tempted to say, even religion. I even believed that everything one neglected in terms of rigour with such an important undertaking was simply negligence of duty. With great intensity I have looked for and read vigorously all those, who are regarded as particularly sharp in their opposition to our belief as indeed those who are particularly well versed in it, because I did not want at any point to have to accuse myself of the slightest negligence.[63]

I believe that Leibniz obtained in many fields of natural science and mathematics the scientific level of contemporary philosophy and science of the Western world even by his metaphysical theological work on transubstantiation and on the other Christian mysteries. His theological enterprise of Mainz was thus a preparation for his Paris time and for both the scientific and the theological discussions in France. But its metaphysical results were to be the first foundation of his own metaphysical system of the mature philosophy. The metaphysical concepts of Leibniz will still change, in Paris, and in Hanover, but the function of all these different theoretical versions of his metaphysics will remain continuously the same to explain the central notions in a way, where they can ground the mechanical science on the one hand, and to serve to explain the possibility of the Christian mysteries against the different attacks of the Reformed church and of the 'Moderns' on the other hand. I believe it is in no way chance that we find the metaphysical drafts of Leibniz even in some theological metaphysical writings – in the *Discours de métaphysique*, which was the background for his discussion with Arnauld, and in the *Théodicée*, wherein he discussed the arguments of Bayle. Even in a letter to Des Bosses in 1712 Leibniz is convinced that, on the basis of his metaphysical system, he could explain the possibility of transubstantiation.[64]

---

[63] Letter to Arnauld, II i 176.

[64] See the letter to Des Bosses of 20th September 1712, in G. W. Leibniz *Philosophische Schriften*, vol. 5, *Briefe von besonderem philosophischen Interesse*, Latin/German, ed. W. Wiater, (Darmstadt: Wissenschaftliche Buchgesellschaft, 1989), p. 271.

DANIEL COOK

THE YOUNG LEIBNIZ AND THE PROBLEM OF HISTORICAL
TRUTH

From the beginning of his intellectual career, Leibniz was concerned with proving that belief in the truth of Scriptures was a rational one. As the last major philosopher who defended the central doctrines of orthodox Christianity, the authenticity of the texts upon which they were grounded was paramount. Leibniz did not take a fundamentalist or fideist position on the truth of Scripture, but his belief in the authenticity of Biblical prophecy coupled with his opposition to the historical scepticism of thinkers such as Spinoza necessitated his investigation into, and subsequent defence of, the possibility of gaining valid historical knowledge of the Biblical period. For Leibniz, the Bible is not a self-authenticating document; it required justification from elsewhere, even if it claimed to be 'God's word' Leibniz's general approach to Scriptures as well his internal biblical exegesis was guided by the principle that an understanding of Scriptures has to be arrived at in some rational fashion, since reason itself governs the biblical narrative – as it does all other expressions of the Divine.

Contemporary treatments of Leibniz concentrate on the metaphysical and logical elements in his defence of traditional arguments of natural theology (proofs for the existence of God, the problem of evil, human freedom, etc.), or doctrines associated with them (i.e., pre-established harmony). As befits a rationalist, they usually understand 'reason' in its narrow, logical sense (as Leibniz himself usually did!). Yet Leibniz, from his earliest years, believed that belief in "truth" pointed to a need for "history" as well as "reason". Very little has been written on his efforts to defend the truths of the Christian religion on historical

S. Brown (ed.): The Young Leibniz and his Philosophy (1646-76). 103–122

rounds, or even to understand exactly what Leibniz meant by "history" and "historical knowledge".[1]

Leibniz staked much on the study of ancient history: it could demonstrate not only the truth of Christianity, but its superiority over other religions. In one of his many proposals for a *Scientia Generalis*, he makes this quite clear:

> The history of Antiquity is an absolute necessity for the proof of the truth of religion and, apart from the excellence of its doctrine, it is from its wholly divine origin that our religion is distinguished from all others which did not approach it in any fashion. Therein lies perhaps the best use of the most subtle and searching scholarship: to yield genuine evidence of the grand truths strictly verified by ancient authors, and if the Muslims, pagans and even freethinkers do not surrender to reason, we may say that it is chiefly due to their not knowing ancient history.[2]

Leibniz's interest in theological problems was awakened early in his life – in his father's home as well as his city of birth. Willy Kabitz calls 17th-century Leipzig "the metropolis of Lutheran theology".[3] Leibniz's early exposure to theological issues and his legal training conditioned much of what he wrote. It is in his early legal and theological writings that we find discussions on the authentication of

---

[1] Indicative of this neglect is the omission of the word 'history' in the recently published *Leibniz-Lexicon* and in the (admittedly provisional) index of the *Vorausedition* of Leibniz's philosophical writings. Writings of Leibniz indexed or included in these works do discuss history – sometimes at length (e.g., VE, n. 27) – but the various editors of these projects deemed it too minor or irrelevant a topic to include indexed references to it in his philosophical writings.

[2] C 226: VE 1180: W 577-8. Minor changes made in translation. Leibniz was much more upset with someone who doubted the possibility of any authentic historical evidence for corroborating Christian doctrine (e.g., the Jesuit Jean Hardouin) than someone who doubted the possibility of rational proofs for the existence of God (e.g., Pierre Bayle).

[3] *Die Philosophie des jungen Leibniz* (Heidelberg: Karl Winter's Universitätsbuchhandlung, 1909), p. 110.

Scripture and his strategies for fighting historical Pyrrhonism.[4] This paper seeks to point out the importance of history in the young Leibniz's search for truth, especially the truth of Scripture. I also will highlight some of the arguments and strategies the young Leibniz employed in his *plaidoyer* for developing an historical consciousness in the study of philosophy and religion.

1. History as an Empirical Science for the Young Leibniz

Well before he became Court Historian in Hanover, Leibniz concerned himself with the craft and methods of the historian. In the opening of his *Elements of Natural Law* (1670-71), he calls history "the glasses of time" as the recent discoveries of the microscope and the telescope are the "glasses of space". The "light of history", in Leibniz's words, "has been brought to us, so that we seem to have lived always." The discovery of printing makes paper "more enduring even than bronze"[5] putting history on a whole new footing. History is the basis for the establishment of independent truths. For the young Leibniz (1667), a *historia* is a simple, true empirical fact. Such *historiae*, expressed in singular propositions, form the basis for later observed, universal but contingent truths, or universal and necessary ones.

> Every proposition is either singular (hence *history* for example, a magnet holds the iron casket of Mohammed in Mecca – assuming for the sake of example that this is true); or it is a contingent universal, depending upon induction from singular propositions (*hence observation*; for example, a magnet lifts iron); or it is a necessary universal, demonstrable from the terms themselves (hence *science*; for example, whatever moves is moved by some other thing, or, if a magnet lifts iron, there

---

[4] The problem of historical Pyrrhonism has not received the attention in the philosophical literature that it warrants. For example, in their Introduction to the Wolfenbüttel Symposium on *Scepticism from the Renaissance to the Enlightenment* (Wiesbaden: Harrassowitz, 1987), the editors, R. H. Popkin and C. B. Schmidt admit that " ... the implications of scepticism for valid historical knowledge ... have hardly been touched in the present volume" (p. 11).

[5] L 131: A VI i 459.

must be corporeal effluvia passing from the magnet into the iron). Hence history is the mother of observation.... The same materials involve history, observation and theorems, science being the combination of these.[6]

The basis of historical truth for Leibniz was direct sense-experience.[7] If we ourselves could directly experience an event, the proposition describing that event would be true. Were we able to (re)produce the conditions for an event in the Bible, there would be no historical problem, though there might be semantic ones (e.g., do we understand the words describing the event properly?) or (meta)physical ones (e.g., whether the event violated the natural laws of physics and therefore was a miracle). Leibniz's empiricism is straightforward here, as is his adoption of a simple correspondence theory of truth. As he explains in his *Preface to an Edition of Nizolius* (1670):

> An utterance is true whose meaning is perceived through a right disposition of both the percipient and the medium: for clarity is measured by the understanding, truth by sense. This is the unique and truest definition of truth ... The sentence, 'Rome is situated on the Tiber', is true for the reason that nothing more is needed to understand what it says than that the sentient being and the medium be in a right relation. The sentient should certainly not be blind or deaf, and the medium or interval should not be too large. If this be granted, and I be in Rome or near it, it will follow that I shall at one glance *see* the city and the river and realise that this city is situated on this

---

[6] *A New Method for Learning and Teaching Jurisprudence*, L 88-89: minor changes have been made in translation and emphases. See *Nova Methodus ...*, A VI i 284. See also his earlier *De arte combinatoria* (1666), §83, where he first talks of *historia*, A VI i 199.

[7] Schneiders notes the sources of Leibniz's empiricism in late Scholastic distinctions, citing Leibniz's schematic discussion of *historia* in his brief effort at emending and completing Alsted's *Encyclopaedia* (A VI xi 394-7). See W. Schneiders, 'Aufklärung durch Geschichte: Zwischen Geschichtstheologie und Geschichtsphilosophie: Leibniz, Thomasius, Wolff,' *SL Sond.* 10 (1982): 83.

river, and I shall *hear* the city called Rome and the river the Tiber.[8]

Leibniz's attendant nominalism, as defended by him in the same Preface, allows him to see our true knowledge of the world as based on the direct experience of various atomic 'events'.[9] These individual events could be described in simple propositions and ordered chronologically.[10] Leibniz saw no intrinsic difference between the facts of nature and the facts of man: *historiae* are "singular truths of sense, like an account of a certain lunar eclipse".[11] Recent scholarship sees Leibniz's *later* efforts to include history among the empirical sciences as "a direct contribution to the contemporary philosophical discussion of the question 'How can history be possible as a science?'"[12] However, no one has pinpointed Leibniz's earlier interest in history and its role in his epistemology and theory of reason. Leibniz may indeed have examined historical questions unwillingly, as

---

[8] L 121: A VI i 409. Later in the Preface he says (assuming there are no semantic problems): "Hardly anything more will then be required for sound judgement than that the senses be protected against error by means of the right constitution of the sense organs and the medium, and the intellect by observing the rules for ratiocination" (L 127: A VI ii 420).

[9] "From this principle the nominalists have deduced the rule that everything in the world can be explained without reference to universals and real forms. Nothing is truer than this opinion, and nothing is more worthy of a philosopher in our own time" (L 128: A VI ii 428-9).

[10] See below (Section IV) where Leibniz outlines the nature of this *Book of History*.

[11] L 290, n. 3.

[12] U. Goldenbaum, 'From Adam to Alexander and Caesar: Leibniz's shift from Logic and Metaphysics to a Theory of History,' in *Leibniz and Adam*, ed. M. Dascal and E. Yakira (Tel Aviv: University Publishing Projects, 1993), p. 370. See Goldenbaum's documentation and footnotes for further sources (including, significantly, Cassirer's book on Leibniz). Also, see the discussion of Goldenbaum's article in a review (by B. Look) of *Leibniz and Adam*: "Goldenbaum argues that Leibniz will understand history to be an empirical science similar to physics or medicine, where the phenomena will be grounded in the natures of individual substances." (*Leibniz Society Review* 5 (1995): 32.)

a condition of employment or advancement,[13] but nevertheless its importance early in his life is apparent.[14]

2. Leibniz's 'Reformed' Historical Method

In some of his earlier writings, Leibniz set forth guidelines that must be followed in any effort to prove the claim of Scriptures that it is indeed 'the word of God'. In his *Commentatiuncula de Judice Controversiarum (Brief Commentaries on the Judge of Controversies)* (1669-71),[15] he said:

> But – you say – the Sacred Scripture cannot in the least be the judge of its own authenticity. That is correct, but there can be a way to decide whether the text is authentic, e.g., when there are three who provide testimony.[16] The divinity of the Sacred

---

[13] Leibniz complained (usually obliquely) of his dependence on the whims of his employers. For example, in 1671, he wrote to Arnauld: "My mode of life has itself compelled me to try to investigate moral problems and to establish the foundations of justice and equity with somewhat more clarity and certainty than is usual. I am working on a Nucleus of Roman Law,..." (L 149: A II i 173). Leibniz made the same point earlier (1667) concerning his (al)chemical studies in Nuremburg. See MK 10-11.

[14] On the importance of historical research for the young Leibniz in many areas (jurisprudence, politics), see W. Conze, 'Leibniz als Historiker,' in *Leibniz zu seinem 300 Gebürtstag* (Berlin: De Gruyter, 1951), Fascicle 6, pp. 38. Conze relies heavily on Davillé's book. Davillé notes that in 1673, while job-hunting during his stay in Paris, Leibniz capitalised on his background in history by applying for the position of court historian to Leopold I in Vienna. L. Davillé, *Leibniz Historien* (Paris, 1909), p. 26. Goldenbaum discusses "Leibniz's special interest in historical issues, which had become obvious since the middle of the 80's" (because of his work about the origins of the Guelphs), but not earlier efforts. ('From Adam to Alexander and Caesar...,' *op. cit.*, pp. 372; 375 n. 20.)

[15] The full title is *Commentatiuncula de Judice Controversiarum seu Trutina; Rationis et norma Textus*: A VI i 548-559. With corrections, I am using Marcelo Dascal's unpublished translation: *Brief Commentaries on the Judge of Controversies or the Balance of Reason and the Norm of the Text*. Hereafter I will cite this is as *Commentatiuncula* along with the relevant numbered paragraph.

[16] John, 5: 7-8 is cited by the editors of the *Akademie* edition (A VI ii 582) to explain this number, but the relevance of this Biblical passage to the text at hand is not clear.

Scripture should be proven by *reason and history,* for it cannot prove this by itself, since in such cases one's own testimony is not acceptable. Even though it declares itself to be the word of God, this should be proven another way.[17]

Earlier, in the *Nova Methodus* (1667; revised in part in 1698), Leibniz, in discussing his own principles of interpretation of legal evidence and sources (including sacred ones), defined this combination of "reason and history" simply as "truth", saying that "concerning a sacred writer ... one rejects any interpretation which would be inconsistent with *reason and history – that is to say, with truth*".[18] These parallel tracks of *reason* and *history* were a constant whenever Leibniz discussed most human endeavours.[19] For example, in his developing interest in language and the origin of words, he explicitly acknowledges the historicity of language(s) and the thoughts which are expressed. An investigation into virtually any philosophical or religious issue required for Leibniz that both *reason* and *history* be pursued. In a letter to his teacher Jacob Thomasius (1669), Leibniz closely paralleled his efforts to demonstrate the genuine connections between reformed philosophy and the "authentic" truth of Aristotle[20] with the efforts undertaken by reformed (Protestant) theology to demonstrate its correct understanding of the truth of Christian Scriptures:

---

[17] *Commentatiuncula* §16, emphasis mine.

[18] *Nova Methodus*, Part II, 66 (A VI i 338), emphasis mine.

[19] "However, we have to hold fast to the order which was provided by the incidents and accidents to which our species is subject; this order represents the history of our discoveries as it were, rather than the origin of our notions" (RB 276). C. Wilson, 'The Combinatorial Universe: Scientific Language and Metaphysics in Leibniz,' in *Leibnizian Inquiries* ..., ed. N. Rescher (Lanham, MD: University Press of America, 1989) p. 167. A recent study of Leibniz on language goes even further, concluding that Leibniz "was the one to find in the historico-natural study of language the key to the *historicity* of human experience" (S. Gensini, 'Leibniz: Linguist and Philosopher of Language: Between "Primitive" and "Natural" ', in *Leibniz and Adam*, p. 132, author's emphasis.).

[20] Cf. Duchesneau's remark: ".. [Leibniz] entend montrer que le mécanisme des modernes est compatible avec une interprétation plus 'authentique' d'Aristote" ('Une étude sur l'aristotélianisme reformé,' *Dialogue* 33 (1994): 464).

> Now that I have reconciled the reformed philosophy with
> Aristotle, it remains to show its truth per se in the same way
> that the Christian religion can be proved by *reason and*
> *experience* as well as from sacred scripture.[21]

Leibniz's method for effecting this reconciliation is worth
examining in detail.   He undertook to show how reformed
('Aristotelian') philosophy is truer to the (rediscovered) ancient
philosophy than medieval ('Aristotelian') scholasticism.   Leibniz
explicitly grounded this argument for the *"truth" of reformed*
philosophy on the same principles as that of the *'truth' of the reformed*
Protestant theology. "Indeed, what has been done by the theologians
is the same [to be done] by the philosophers."[22]

Leibniz adopted this reformed approach often in his theological
polemics; for example, he argued later with Bossuet that the Catholic
Church did not *know* its own ancient history and its documents as well
as the Protestants did.   When he argued against the insistence of the
Church that the Protestants must accept the canonicity of books that
the ancient Church did not, Leibniz made an *historical argument*
based on the documented attitudes of the ancient Church, which the
Council of Trent had in effect anathematised.[23] Leibniz also employed
this reformed historical method of argument with non-Christians,
arguing that if non-Christians did not accept Christian doctrines – in
themselves more rational than their own – "we may say that it is
chiefly due to them not knowing ancient history". So, for example, the

---

[21] L 100, emphasis mine: A II i 21: G I 24.

[22] "Scilicet quod Theologis, idem et philosophis agendum est" (G I 23: A II i 21).
This citation does not appear in the revised version of this latter to Jakob Thomasius,
published as an addendum to his *Preface to Nizolius* (1670) and is omitted by
Loemker in his translation of the original letter (April, 1669) because they "were
received by Thomasius himself in a corrupted form" (L 104 n. 18). Gerhardt notes
the obvious lacunae in the text, whereas the 1926 *Akademie* edition does not. The
latest translation of the letter into French interpolates several words or lines into this
passage without noting the textual problem for the reader. See *Leibniz-Thomasius:*
Correspondance, pp. 110-111. Leibniz was inspired by Thomasius' own writings
(*ibid*. p. 149, n. 182) in adopting his reformist approach.

[23] For a discussion on this controversy, see J. Baruzi, *Leibniz et l'organisation*
religieuse de la terre d'après des documents inédits (Paris: Alcan, 1907), p. 373.

Chinese of his day did not truly understand the meaning of their own ancient writings because they did not know their own ancient history.[24]

The invocation of an historically authentic Biblical text, whether directed to the Christian or non-Christian, was central for Leibniz, since his own religious tradition rejected the belief in "a man who has received from God the gift of infallibility – according to the partisans of the Pope". The infallible judge, he continued in the *Commentatiuncula*, for "partisans of the Evangelists" is "a text whose terms are to be retained without any addition or deletion".[25] For Leibniz then, there had to be an external, historical, textual warrant as well as an internal, rational one for validating the foundational truths of the Christian faith. Leibniz *did* allow for accepting the sacred text as the basis for faith and as a vehicle for salvation on a straightforward basis: as long as the doctrine or dogma concerned was *"expressly contained in the Sacred Scripture"*[26] even if it was not fully understood.[27] But differences about the *meaning* of 'God's word' were acceptable to Leibniz only if there were no questions about its *authenticity*: "My opinion is that one should rather side with the

---

[24] This assumption was critical to Leibniz's strategy of converting the Chinese by demonstrating to them that their ancient doctrines were compatible with Christian ones, thus preparing them for an accommodation with Christianity. The Chinese must be made aware of the true meaning of the narrative texts of *their own ancient history and doctrines* – which unfortunately has been corrupted and distorted by later writers – so that now, properly reformed and purged of later accretions and misguided interpretations, many of their distinctive ancient beliefs and rites can be accommodated, thus opening the way for their conversion to Christianity. See *Leibniz: Writings on China*, ed. & trans. D. Cook and H. Rosemont, Jr. (Chicago: Open Court, 1994), pp. 8-9.

Leibniz makes the same point regarding ancient Hebrew texts: "Who does not know in our day that Christian scholars are much better interpreters of the ancient books of the Hebrews than are the Jews themselves?" ('On the Civil Cult of Confucius', *Leibniz: Writings on China*, p. 64).

[25] *Commentatiuncula* § 36.

[26] *Commentatiuncula* §7: emphasis in original.

[27] "It can be taught that the faith of the majority of Christians consisted, and has always consisted, in the approval of propositions which are not understood" (*Commentatiuncula* § 30). Also, "... the grasping of a formula of the Sacred Scripture, accompanied by a confused understanding of its meaning and some disjunctive assent or opinion, is sufficient for salvation" (*Commentatiuncula* § 32).

[literal] meaning of the text, even if it is improbable according to reason, provided that is possible and *on the condition it is God's saying.*[28] For philosophical or historical purposes, however, such an understanding of the texts is insufficient[29] – their authenticity must first be established.

3. The Importance of History and the Historical Record

From Leibniz's earliest writings, we can clearly see the importance of ancient sources - "the historical record" - as a means for establishing truth (philosophical or religious): a characteristic which clearly distinguished him from his Cartesian contemporaries. In his explicit parallelism between the endeavours of reformed philosophy and reformed religion, Leibniz ranked Descartes' "brazen" approach of devaluing ancient philosophy (specifically Aristotle) with the schismatics who rejected the Church Fathers' interpretations of Scripture.

> One [of the three paths of reform] is quite rash – bothering little with the Ancients and scorning them openly – thus rendering suspect what is quite good in their own thoughts. Such is Descartes'.[30]

The neglect and distortion of the ancients and the heavy-handed attack on scholasticism and historical erudition in general by many of his contemporaries, especially the Cartesians, was a recurring theme for Leibniz.[31] He viewed the cavalier, if not antagonistic treatment of

---

[28] *Commentatiuncula* § 34: emphasis mine.

[29] "I agree that the text itself is not sufficient for deciding precisely questions about its meaning, unless additional support is relied on. But I think the text itself is sufficient for all religious questions concerning faith" (*Commentatiuncula* § 6). Leibniz is here defending what he calls the "textualist" position "that the judge of controversies is the text of the Sacred Scripture itself" (*Commentatiuncula* § 6).

[30] G I 23-24: A II i 21: Bodéüs, *Leibniz-Thomasius Correpondance*, p. 110.

[31] For example: "... inter caeteras gliscentes Atheismi causas etiam contentum eruditionis numero, qui hodie invalilescit" (G VII 71). Leibniz repeats and expands upon this theme in one of his earlier letters (1679) to Père Huet. (G III 16: A II i

historical sources and scholarly traditions as contributing to the efforts of the free-thinkers and atheists to undermine the Christian religion as well as the social and political order it grounded.

Leibniz thus thought it necessary to invoke historical as well as philosophical grounds for defending the truth of the Christian religion ("reason and history"). Leibniz indeed may have preferred studying general, logical truths to determining specific historical facts, but two compelling factors prevented him from doing so and forced his attention upon the need to establish the principles and guidelines necessary to demonstrate the truth of particular historical facts. First, Leibniz's research, undertaken on behalf of his (Guelph) patrons, succeeded because of his discovery of certain facts (based on his research of historical documents) about their dynastic origins in Italy. (One writer has in fact claimed that Leibniz initiated "modern historical research based on original sources".[32])

Secondly, and more importantly for our purposes, the centrality of specific historical facts (i.e., the occurrence of certain miracles) for the revealed theology of Judaism and Christianity demanded that the sacred texts that related them be authenticated. Matters of historical fact depended for their verification upon credible authorities and witnesses. Only scholars and historians of antiquity could properly authenticate such sources and therefore "it is in the interest of religion that solid erudition be preserved".[33]

Leibniz was thus prompted to study ancient, particularly Biblical, history, because of the perceived threat to religion from modern science and philosophy. In the opening paragraph of *Confession of Nature against the Atheists* (1669), he says that some

> truly capable men ... proclaimed .... .that they could find neither God nor the immortality of the soul by natural reason, but that in these matters faith must rest either on civil laws or on historical records. This was the judgement of the most

---

466-67) Belaval elaborates on this difference between Descartes and Leibniz in his *Leibniz: Critique de Descartes* (Paris: Gallimard, 1960), pp. 100-29.

[32] R. W. Meyer, *Leibniz and the Seventeenth Century Revolution*, trans. J. P. Stern (Cambridge: Bowes & Bowes, 1952), p. 204, n. 281.

[33] G III 16.

acute Mr Hobbes, ... Unfortunately there are others who have gone even further and who doubt the authority of sacred scriptures and *the truth of history and the historical record,* thus bringing an unconcealed atheism into the world.[34]

Leibniz here is defending not merely the authority of Scripture, but "the truth of history and the historical record." Leibniz echoes this plea thirty-five years later, reminding his readers that without a concerted effort to determine "the truth of history" (if only probabilistically), much of our cherished belief-structure will be severely undermined since "... nearly all historical knowledge will collapse, and a good deal more."[35]

For Leibniz (as noted in the beginning of the paper), it was the historical origins of Christianity that distinguished it, not its unrivalled theological doctrines.[36] Consequently, it is to historical studies of earlier human history (e. g., philological, etymological, numismatic, geological, archaeological, etc.) that he later turned in order to defend Christianity against its false friends as well as its declared enemies.

4. Resolving Questions of the Historical Truth of Scripture

Leibniz did not grant any privileged status to Scripture as an historical document.[37] If miracles narrated in these sacred sources, "though performed long ago, be attested to by those arguments by which, in other cases, the truth of historical fact is legitimately proved, [then] we

---

[34] L 110: G IV 195, emphasis mine. In this brief essay, however, Leibniz explicitly eschews following an historical tack: "Setting aside all prejudices, therefore, and suspending the credit of scripture and history ..." (*Ibid.*).

[35] RB 372.

[36] For example, in one of the many introductions to a Universal Science which Leibniz composed, he says: "Et cum Religio Christiana, ... non tantum excellentia dogmatum suorum intelligentibus admirabili, sed et origine sine exemplo singulari nitatur,... sequitur demonstrationem tantarum Veritatum non nisi ab Historia peti posse" (G VII 139). This selection, probably written in the late 1670s, is, like the previous point about the disdain for erudition, developed by Leibniz in the letter to Huet cited earlier (A II i 464-7). See also the first sentence in the opening citation in this paper.

[37] "... en effet la religion revelée est un Histoire" (A IV iii 551).

are bound to believe in them, just as well as if they were performed today."[38] In turning therefore to any historical texts, including sacred ones, Leibniz in effect asked three questions, whose answers would give us the truth. Firstly and most importantly, is the document an *authentic* report? Is it, in other words, an accurate and actual eyewitness account of the events at hand, or one based on them? To answer this question, Leibniz usually relied on *legal* requirements: e.g., the number and credibility of the witnesses, etc.

In his utopian Republic of "Right Reason", outlined towards the end of his *Commentatiuncula*, Leibniz thought that we can measure the degree of authenticity of secular historical documents including what he calls any "extraordinary [*peculiari*] book". In the National Library of this Republic, there will be several authoritative reference books, including

> a *Book of History,* where everything memorable would be gathered together in one book, in chronological order. The reliability of each author is to be precisely weighed, particularly in an extraordinary book, where [what] is criticised should be exactly reproduced word for word ...; even if they happened to be ambiguous, this allows for those interested to closely examine them.[39]

Earlier, when he discussed his proposed *Balance of Reason,* for resolving secular disputes through the weighing of the evidence from both sides, he concluded that, "Though in practice there are equally true reasons for each side, and of course advantageous and disadvantageous ones, their quantity can be precisely calculated, whereby the conclusion is reached."[40] While excluding religious controversies over the authenticity of Scriptures from his Republic, I nevertheless believe that he had much the same procedure in mind for assessing the authenticity or reliability of biblical authors as for 'extraordinary' secular ones. Let us recall what I cited earlier from the

---

[38] *System of Theology*, Ru 13.

[39] *Commentatiuncula* §68.

[40] *Commentatiuncula* §60.

Commentatiuncula[41] where Leibniz talked of the criteria for determining the authenticity of Scripture (e.g., "when there are three who provide testimony").

Once we can gauge the authenticity of the document in question, we ask, secondly, whether we truly understand the sense or meaning of the report? This question has, of course, *literary, linguistic* (semantic as well as etymological) and even psychological dimensions for Leibniz. In the *Commentatiuncula*, Leibniz also set up a procedure for determining the meaning of words. Its results are to be presented in what he calls "a book of definitions in the natural order".[42] Once again, I believe that Leibniz hoped to develop such a dictionary – perhaps using an improved version of his Universal Characteristic – as an instrument for resolving religious controversies over biblical terms and phrases.

Finally – assuming it is an authentic and properly understood report of an event or events – could these events have occurred as they are being reported? Is the text of the account to be taken literally? Did the events as witnessed and understood occur as the events describe, particularly the miracles and mysteries central to Christian belief? We are not talking here of Rashomon-type discrepancies, but of physical and metaphysical questions about the ultimate nature of reality. How should we understand accounts of events where the laws of science have been contravened, such as the Resurrection of Christ or the sun standing still for Joshua at Gibeon?

At various times Leibniz concentrated on different aspects of these questions about the 'truth' of Scripture: legal, literary, linguistic, scientific or philosophical, though he raised many of them in his *Commentatiuncula*. The legal approach to his defence of the truth of Scripture was, to my mind, most explicit in his formative years. Leibniz addressed specific etymological questions concerning Hebrew, Aramaic or Greek later as his interest in languages grew, but semantic questions as to the meaning of the texts are already featured prominently in his earlier *Commentatiuncula*.[43] Finally, questions as

---

[41] *Commentatiuncula* §16.

[42] *Commentatiuncula* §66.

[43] For example, after defending the "textualist" position on the central doctrines and mysteries of Christianity (see citation of *Commentatiuncula* § 12 below) he

to the objectivity of the events recounted loom larger in his thoughts once he had to defend his mature physical and metaphysical theories. Detailed discussions as to the nature and possibility of miracles (apart from Biblical ones) occur quite often in his later philosophical and theological writings, such as his correspondence with Samuel Clarke[44]. I will conclude my paper by briefly mentioning some of the strategies that Leibniz employed in arguing for the importance of the study of ancient history in defence of truth – especially 'biblical truth' – in the first part of his life.

5. Leibniz's Major Strategies in Defence of the Truth of Scriptures

It is striking to note that Leibniz's own lifetime virtually coincided with the ongoing controversy in Protestant Germany over sceptical attacks on historical sources[45] and "the discussion of the bona fides of the[se] sources remained the main method of assessing the truth of the Bible."[46] Who were better suited to determine such bona fides than those trained in law to establish the criteria for reliable evidence? Thus the same procedures used by the courts to determine the character and veracity of witnesses could be used to examine the quality of historical testimony (in particular those reporting miracles and prophecies). As A. Momigliano says:

---

immediately raises the issue of meaning, devoting the bulk of his discussion of this position to it (*Commentatiuncula* §§13-32). He leads into this discussion by asking: "But what if a question is raised about the meaning of the original text, which is dubious, as when there may be equivocations in Hebrew?" (*Commentatiuncula* §13).

[44] A good example is also found in a letter to Lacoste (1707) in AG 195-96. The problem of miracles is confronted most explicitly in Leibniz's running commentary (undated) on the story of Bileam in the *Book of Numbers*. His treatment of the strange events of this story (the talking she-ass, etc.) are influenced by his correspondence (1690-1716) with the Orientalist Hermann von der Hardt. See D. J. Cook, 'Leibniz: Biblical Historian and Exegete,' *SL Supp.* 27 (1990): 274-5.

[45] Let us not forget the Latin epigram on the original title page of his *Annalen*: "Figura veritatis triumphantis, sublato pyrronhismo historico." See W. Schneiders, 'Aufklärung durch Geschichte: Zwischen Geschichtstheologie und Geschichtsphilosophie: Leibniz, Thomasius, Wolff,' *SL Sond.* 10 (1982): 85.

[46] See A. Momigliano, *Studies in Historiography* (London: Wiedenfeld & Nicolson, 1966), p.13.

> The controversy passed from the hands of historians and philosophers to those of lawyers, who, being traditionally concerned with the reliability of witnesses, could bring a great deal of experience to bear on this subject. All these people tried to determine the characteristics of what they could call reliable evidence.[47]

The notion of a jurisprudential approach to historical problems concerning the authenticity of Scripture was thus a congenial one to the young lawyer. From his earliest writings, such as this passage from the *Ars Combinatoria* (1666), Leibniz explicitly likened theology to jurisprudence.

> The basis of terms is the same in theology, which is, as it were, a kind of special jurisprudence, but fundamental for the same reason as the others. For theology is a sort of public law which applies in the Kingdom of God among men ... the teaching of Scripture and the Word of God is like that of the laws and their interpretation; that of the canon like the question of which of the laws are authentic...[48]

Some commentators on Leibniz have discussed the various forms of *reason* that Leibniz brought to bear in defence of the rationality of the Christian mysteries, especially in his earlier writings. They have spoken of 'another Leibniz: a soft rationalist' and his 'theory and practice of soft reasoning,' as I have also spoken of the 'other Leibniz' – the one who appeals to various non-logical arguments and strategies to resolve philosophical and theological disagreements.[49] It may well

---

[47] *Ibid.* p. 11.

[48] L 82: A VI i 190-1: G IV 60.

[49] For example, see M. R. Antognazza, 'The Defence of the Mysteries of the Trinity and the Incarnation: an Example of Leibniz's Other Reason', in *Leibniz the Polemicist,* ed. M. Dascal and Q. Racionero (eds.) (Dordrecht: Kluwer, forthcoming). This paper was given in the year-long seminar (1994-95) at the Institute for Advanced Studies in Jerusalem, in which I also participated. Concerning Leibniz's 'other reason', Antognazza cites references to the work of Dascal, one of the organisers of the seminar, whose topic was 'Leibniz as

be that ultimately we will have to include Leibniz's arguments for the authenticity of Scripture as an example of some sort of 'soft' or non-logical reasoning based upon legal criteria. Among such forms of reasoning, one must include those that Leibniz adapted from his study of law. First and foremost is his use of the doctrine of presumed truth (*onus probandi*), in particular the presumed truth of received opinions or precedents. Thus one could accept the truth of various biblical accounts unless one proved them conclusively false or absurd.[50] Leibniz's *Book of Experiments,* as he called it in the *Commentatiuncula*, described the procedure for challenging the truth of experiments or experiences listed in the *Book.*[51]

Relatedly, Leibniz appealed to what were called the *"motifs de credibilité"* or "rational grounds for belief"[52] : they are the explicable reasons (based on sensation and reflection) for my belief.[53] On this basis, one might have moral certainty (i.e., a high degree of probability) that the biblical accounts were authentic: i.e., that the events described indeed occurred. Such events would thus be endowed for Leibniz with what one writer calls "juridical objectivity".[54] But authenticity alone (for example, of the words Jesus spoke) is insufficient to establish truth *for us*. We need to be able to

---

Polemicist.' Also, see D. J. Cook, 'Den Anderen Leibniz zu verstehen.', *SL* 24 (1992): 59-72.

[50] See Antognazza, *op. cit.*, pp. 12 ff.; Cook (1992), pp. 70-1.

[51] Leibniz's reliance on the doctrine of presumed truth also included the truth of hitherto received reports that at the time remained unverified. "One should compile a book of *experiments*, where all experiments of nature and the arts should be collected according to the order of things. Based on our historical and experimental book (for the latter is also historical), a challenge [*provocatio*] can be made so: a [sentence] holds (when referring to a historian, especially to those who have not copied from each other, the matter is taken on faith) until the contrary is proven. and its execution is not meanwhile suspended...." (*Commentatiuncula* §69).

[52] As Remnant and Bennett call them in their English translation of the *New Essays* (RB lxix).

[53] See also Antognazza, pp. 6 ff.; Cook (1990), p. 270 and Cook (1992), pp. 71-2.

[54] The phrase is "objectivité juridique". See M. Parmentier, 'Conceptes juridiques et probabilistes chez Leibniz', *Revue d' histoire des Sciences* 46 (1993): 439-40.

accurately determine what the words mean or signify even if they are reporting ordinary events in simple, straightforward language.[55]

Should the events described or portended appear extraordinary or miraculous - evoking scepticism and incredulity – then a deeper literary or linguistic analysis of meaning was necessary. For example, Leibniz's belief, expressed at length in his commentary (written in early 1677), that the *Book of Revelation of John* – more popularly known as the *Apocalypse* – should not be taken literally.[56]

It is my belief (to be argued for elsewhere) that Leibniz grudgingly allowed for a *literal* interpretation of New Testament passages critical to Christian doctrine (whether out of prudence or conviction) – what have been called 'faith-related propositions'[57] – but nevertheless attempted to rationalistically explain virtually all miracles by interpreting them in an allegorical fashion.[58] The only type of miracle

---

[55] "But there remains a non-negligible difficulty. Since one has faith not in words, but in their meanings, it is not enough for us to believe that the person who uttered the sentence 'this is my body' said the truth unless we also know what he said. However, we do not know what he said if we only have the words and ignore their meaning . . . nobody is able to [consider something true] unless he knows what the words signify or at least unless he think about their meaning" (*Commentatiuncula* §20).

[56] For a detailed discussion of Leibniz's treatment of the *Apocalypse*, including his distinctive strategy of criticism – see my 'Leibniz and Millenarianism,' in *Leibniz und Europa* 1 (1994): 135-42.

[57] "Concerning questions remote from practice, like God's unity and trinity, Christ's nature and person, the Presence in the supper of Christ and the bread, predestination, and the other world, no faith-related proposition is to be accepted [nulla propositio admittanda est tanquam sit de fide] unless it is expressly contained in Sacred Scripture, as translated literally [ad verbum] from the source." (*Commentatiuncula* §12).

[58] But to my mind, even this allowance was qualified by the young Leibniz. In discussing the doctrine of the Real Presence in his *Commentatiuncula,* he allowed that we should follow a literal formulaic meaning of the words in Scripture as prescribed by orthodox theology, but nevertheless understand that reason demanded we only do so to a limited extent. "But [of the presence in the bread], what about a non-literal sense *[sensu improprio]*? In that case, I think that the Christians ought to listen to the words of the text, to grasp as much truth as there is in their proper sense, yet with only as much pious candour as not to become self-defeating. And if they assume that the proposition is true in a figurative sense *[sensu tropico]*, then they will be acting in a surer way" (*Commentatiuncula* §24).

he ultimately had to accept – and the only one he seems to take seriously and literally throughout his life – is prophecy. If Scripture is genuinely prophetic – and Leibniz thought it was – then it must be God's word, because genuine prophecy is not in man's power and its efficacy cannot be explained in purely rational or natural terms.

6. Conclusion

Leibniz's treatment of miracles in Scriptures is beyond the scope of this paper, but let me conclude by simply mentioning some other strategies he employed to strengthen the hand of those who generally wished to defend the historical truth of Scriptures. First, he consistently stressed the need to study *universal* ancient history – not simply the Judaeo-Christian one – in order to show that universal history (through texts, monuments and even medals and coins) corroborated the events described in the Bible (e.g., the Creation and Mosaic chronology of the world; the Flood, etc.). It should be remembered that for Leibniz the particular history of Christianity and the truths it proclaimed did not conflict with the genuine truths of any pagan sources which Leibniz accepted (e.g., Greek or even Chinese) any more than "the light of reason" could conflict with "that of revelation".

In this context, he employed the doctrine of *Prisca Theologia* (Ancient Theology).[59] Such a doctrine served as the basis for integrating ancient pagan philosophies (e.g., Platonism or Confucianism) into Christianity or at least for showing their underlying historical and philosophical kinship. In this way – as he did, for example, with Chinese history – he was able to reconcile conflicting readings of ancient history with Biblical narratives by arguing for the Judaeo-Christian origins of pagan belief-systems and their positive religions. (By the same token, Leibniz would often use commonalities among them to reinforce his belief in the existence of a purely natural or rational religion!) More polemically, Leibniz

---

[59] This term is defined as "the assumption of a pagan tradition of religious truth derived from Moses" (D. P. Walker, *The Decline of Hell. Seventeenth Century Discussions of Eternal Torment* (London: Routledge & Kegan Paul, 1964), p. 15.)

suggested (to Père Huet, for example), that deepening our study of non-Christian ancient sources (especially Greek ones) would expose the anti-historical shallowness of many of his contemporaries, especially those seen as espousing doctrines conducive to atheism and libertinism, and consequently lessen public respect for them![60]

Another polemical or rhetorical argument that Leibniz employed in the *Commentatiuncula* to cap his arguments in defence of the truth of Scripture is a *tu quoque* one. After his contortions on the problem of literal vs. non-literal meanings of the text concerning the Real Presence, he likened the problems the committed Christian has concerning the meaning of Christ's words 'This is my body' to those the committed Aristotelians have concerning the meaning of the word 'cause.'

> .... it would be sufficient for us to understand Christ's words 'this is my body' just as the Scholastics understand their axiom that there are four types of causes. If for so long they have talked correctly about causes and have believed in Aristotle, without availing themselves of a more distinct meaning of the word, it is equally legitimate for believers in God's word without any other, more distinct, available meaning.[61]

It is striking to note that after a lengthy discussion on the problem of meaning in the *Commentatiuncula* – whether as textualists or as rationalists – Leibniz cautioned his readers again that disagreements over meaning only turn on those passages or words whose authenticity is already proven – that is "on the condition that it is God's word."[62] The truth of Scripture once again hinges first and foremost on the historical authenticity of its report as God's word. Ultimately the young Leibniz's defence of the *truth* of Scripture – and historical truth in general – rested on questions of authenticity, not analyses of meanings or arguments. To be sure he would have rejected any Christian doctrine he considered to be logically absurd – however authentic it might appear – but conveniently for him, no such ones existed!

---

[60] G III 16-7 : A II i 466-7.
[61] *Commentatiuncula* §29.
[62] *Commentatiuncula* §34.

PHILIP BEELEY

MATHEMATICS AND NATURE IN LEIBNIZ'S EARLY

PHILOSOPHY*

Leibniz's early physical hypotheses commend themselves by accounting for an infinite variety of phenomena mechanistically with simple architectonics based on a minimum of stated principles[1]. In the *Hypothesis physica nova*, his most complete model of nature, published in 1671, he believes in this way that he is able to show how all more complex phenomena can be deduced from three more manifest ones, namely gravity, elasticity and magnetism[2], and that these in turn can be explained in terms of disturbance (*perturbatio*) to the rapid flow of ether and light around the earth.[3] All phenomena are thus reduced ultimately to a singular, divine movement – taking into account that ether is described as the πρῶτον δεκτικὸν[4] – a movement so strong as to be able

---

* All dates are given 'new style', i.e. according to the Gregorian calendar.

[1] See, for example, Leibniz's remarks in his letter to Conring dated 29 March 1678 (A II i 399). In the *Hypothesis physica nova* he says that he has always believed in the admirable wisdom of the Creator, "ita res instituisse, ut paucis multa gerantur" (A VI ii 244, § 51).

[2] See Leibniz's letter to Fabri written towards the end of 1676: "Nimirum tentandum putabam an non phaenomena naturae difficiliora ex aliis quibusdam phaenomenis manifestis atque exploratis deduci possent" (A II i 290).

[3] *Hypothesis physica nova* § 58 (A VI ii 249). Sometimes in this context only gravity and elasticity are referred to – see for example Leibniz's letter to Conring of 8 February 1671: "In summa statuo, duas esse causas omnium phaenomenorum naturalium globi nostri, gravitatem et vim elasticam seu restitutivam sui post compressionem vel dilatationem, in statum priorem" (A II i 80).

[4] *Hypothesis physica nova* § 57 (A VI ii 248); Leibniz's letter to Pierre de Carcavy of 22 (?) June 1671 (A II i 126). See also his letter to Martin Fogel dated 3 May 1671 (A II i 99).

S. Brown (ed.): The Young Leibniz and his Philosophy (1646-76). 123–45
© 1999 Kluwer Academic Publishers. Printed in the Netherlands.

to naturally resist disturbance and thus incorporating in its very essence the concept of equilibrium.[5]

The material basis which Leibniz develops in 1671, but which he later considerably modifies – a development leading up to and beyond the vortex theory – is only at first glance traditional: the postulation of the four elements ether, air, water and earth.[6] These elements are in fact structurally reduced to bubbles (*bullae*) containing ether of varying amounts and density, so that what is ostensibly an element again plays the pivotal role. The imperceptible bubbles are far removed from the atomic structures they might at first suggest. Admittedly, Leibniz sometimes uses the term *atomus*[7] in this context, but he does so primarily in order to show the inconsistencies it involves. Rather, they are conceived in such a manner that there could be a second, finer ether contained in bubbles in the primary one, and that the second could contain a third, even finer ether, and so on, thus providing a theoretical foundation not only for the microscopic world discovered by contemporary scientists like Malpighi, Hooke, and Borel[8], but also supporting over and above this the idea, which indeed some microscopists themselves had put forward, that there might be worlds within worlds into infinity.[9]

The structure around which this theory is based has its origins in geometry, or to be more specific, in the geometrical continuum[10], which

---

[5] See Leibniz's letter to Fabri written towards the end of 1676: "Ubicunque motus est turbatus, conatus est ad aequabilitatem" (A II i 292). The same model is also used for example in the *Propositiones quaedam physicae* written in Paris (A VI iii 20-22) and early writings on acoustics – see Gottfried Wilhelm Leibniz, *Nachgelassene Schriften, mechanischen und technischen Inhalts*, ed. Ernst Gerland (Leipzig: Teubner, 1906), p. 29.

[6] *Hypothesis physica nova* § 52 (A VI ii 245); letter to de Carcavy of 22 (?) June 1671 (A II I 127).

[7] See for example *Hypothesis physica nova* § 43 (A VI ii 241), § 60 (A VI ii 255); *Discours touchant la methode de la certitude* (VE VI 1150, N. 259).

[8] On these discoveries see Catherine Wilson, *The Invisible World. Early Modern Philosophy and the Invention of the Microscope*, (Princeton: Princeton University Press, 1995).

[9] Letter to Malebranche of 2 July 1679 (A II i 472); *Hypothesis physica nova* § 43 (A VI ii 241-2); *De arcanis sublimium* (A VI iii 475); *Pacidius philalethi* (A VI iii 565). See also *Elementa juris naturalis* (VI i 459).

[10] *Hypothesis physica nova* § 43: "Sciendum est enim, ut praeclari illi Micrographi, Kircherus et Hookius observavere, pleraque quae nos sentimus in maioribus lynceum aliquem deprehensurum proportione in minoribus, quae si in infinitum progrediantur,

the young philosopher not only regards as being potentially divisible into infinity, but also as being actually so divided.[11] Leibniz of course – like other rationalist thinkers – holds the firm belief that God is a perfect geometrician and we find this conviction, which might equally be interpreted as representing a Platonic strand in his thought, reflected on a structural level. Put simply, nature has for the young Leibniz a mathematical core.[12] His new physical hypothesis of 1671, ostensibly put forward in the spirit of the scientific developments of his day, has in fact its roots most definitely in metaphysics. The stratified structure of Leibniz's model is not the result of observations either on his part or through the efforts of others, but instead amounts to a metaphysical decision, albeit one suggested and effectively corroborated by empirical science.

This can be seen in the young Leibniz's distinctive use of the analogical method. Hooke and his contemporaries frequently drew analogies between the microscopic world they had purportedly discovered and the world which can be immediately experienced – indeed, this was in many ways the basis for their speculations regarding the existence of a microscopic world in the first place.[13] Superficially, Leibniz also adopts this approach, since when he sets forth his explanatory model he repeatedly draws analogies to experience. For example, the mechanism at the heart of the imperceptible bubbles structure is developed in analogy to the known phenomena of expansion

---

quod certe possibile est, cum continuum sit divisibile in infinitum, quaelibet atomus erit infinitarum specierum quidam velut mundus, et dabuntur mundi in mundis in infinitum" (A VI ii 241).

[11] *Theoria motus abstracti*, fund. praed. § 1: "Dantur actu partes in continuo [...]"; § 2: "eaeque infinitae actu [...]" (A VI ii 264).

[12] The best early expression of this is to be found in the *Propositiones quaedam physicae*: "Patet ergo ex his [...] materiam non consistere in extensione, sed in motu [...]. Res est fateor paradoxa sed non minus necessaria, quam divisio continui actualis, in partes infinitas [...] aliaque naturae interioris admiranda" (A VI iii 56-7). The same idea is expressed later on for example in a text entitled *Vindicatio justitiae divinae*: "Duo sunt famosi erroribus Labyrinthi quorum unus Theologos potissimum alter Philosophos exercuit; ille de libertate, hic de continui compositione; quoniam illa mentis haec corporis interiorem naturam attingit" (VE I 46, N. 11). See also *De natura rerum corporearum*: "nam quae sic de interioribus rerum dicerentur, habenda essent non pro Hypothesibus, sed pro demonstrationibus" (A VI ii 302).

[13] See the author's *Kontinuität und Mechanismus. Zur Philosophie des jungen Leibniz in ihrem ideengeschichtlichen Kontext* (*SL Supp.* 30, 1996), pp. 197-200.

and dilation: the "two instruments of nature",[14] as he calls them. However, closer observation reveals that his metaphysical assumptions quite simply lend themselves to this application. As put across by Leibniz imperceptible areas of nature can be opened up by transferring a singular mechanistic model to each progressively finer structural level.[15] The use of the analogical method appears thereby decidedly heuristic. In fact since the structure is from the outset conceived as being infinitely replicated the analogies are not so much discovered as metaphysically in-built into the very structure itself.

Mathematics plays a crucial role in Leibniz's early philosophy first and foremost because of the metaphysically pre-determined fundamental structure of nature. By basing this structure on his concept of the continuum, Leibniz is able to create a model of nature which adequately accommodates the idea that every body is actually divided into smaller parts and that no body or part is so small that it might not itself contain an infinity of creatures. But even if nature has a mathematical core its external form cannot be expressed purely in terms of mathematics: Leibniz states quite categorically that there is nothing in nature which directly corresponds to a mathematical concept.[16] However this is not to say that mathematics cannot be applied. One of the central tasks which Leibniz sets himself in the *Hypothesis physica nova* is to accommodate

---

[14]   *Hypothesis physica nova* § 51: "[...] dicerem duorum istorum naturae instrumentorum, distenti exhaustique [...]" (A VI ii 244). There is an unavoidable circularity here. The mechanistic model is based on human artefacts, which like all natural things depend on gravity and elasticity. On the other hand it is precisely these phenomena that the model sets out to explain in the first place. See in this respect Leibniz's letter to Oldenburg dated 11 March 1671 (A II i 88-9).

[15]   See *Hypothesis physica nova* § 44 (A VI ii 242) as well as his letter to Otto Tachen of 4 May 1671, where referring to his explanation of magnetism, gravity, and elasticity he writes: "ex occultis qualitatibus factas manifestas" (A II i 100). Likewise in his letter to Oldenburg of 23 July 1670 he points out that he is able to explain chemical reactions "non atomis quibusdam, non ramentis, non abstractis, sed familiari quadam, et pene mechanica ratione" (A II i 60).

[16]   *Hypothesis physica nova* § 59: "Etsi enim per naturam rerum impossibile sit, corpus aliquod totum lucere, perspicuum, fluidum, grave, molle, tendibile, flexibile, durum, calidum etc., item motum continuum, uniformem, uniformiter acceleratum vel diminutum, rectilineum, circularem, reflexum, refractum, permutatum, exacte esse; effectum magnetis, luminis et soni, ad quodlibet punctum assignabile pervenire, etc. Evenit tamen ut summa ad sensum ἀκριβείᾳ haec omnia, etsi non sint ita, tamen sensu esse videantur, ut quantum ad usum nostrum, perinde sit ac si essent" (A VI ii 255).

and at the same time explain the remarkable successes in his day of those sciences which have high mathematical content like acoustics, optics, and physics in general.[17] It is here that reason and experience meet. But as we shall see, application constitutes not only the meeting point of reason and experience or mathematics and nature; it also has great significance for the practice of mathematics itself. The relation between mathematics and nature in the young Leibniz is therefore by no means one-sided.

A major part of the *Hypothesis physica nova* consists in providing possible explanations for phenomena by invoking physical structures and events on a deeper and therefore more arcane level of reality. But the infinite replication of a more or less singular structure raises the question of causality[18] and in particular whether there can be any causal connection between adjoining strata. Leibniz is aware that the ability to provide an adequate causal explanation ultimately determines whether hypothetical reasons for a given state or event can be transformed into more certain knowledge. Such an explanation must involve reference to efficient causes; the animalcula of the microscopists, used variously to explain things like the rotting of matter and feverous conditions, could conceivably be resolved into smaller creatures, but this would only be to provide analogies, not true causes.[19] However, even if Leibniz rejects the postulation of structural analogies as a substitute for the discovery of true or efficient causes, he recognises that physical structures and events must be assumed to obtain beyond sensible limits if his hypothesis is to succeed. Indeed, it is only by referring to an essentially similar but imperceptible level of reality that Leibniz is able to reconcile phenomena with rational knowledge. Infinite replication is effectively a necessary condition for the meeting of reason and experience.

---

[17] The passage quoted in the previous note continues thus: "atque ita incredibili Dei beneficio, Optica, Musica, Statica, Elastica, πληγικὴ (seu de impetu et percussione), Myologia seu de motu musculorum, imo et Pyrotechnica et Mechanica universa, et quidquid est mixtarum ex Physica Mathematicarumque scientiarum, ad purarum invidiam usque, non fallentibus ad sensum (nisi per accidens) theorematibus excoli possint."

[18] See *De modo perveniendi ad veram corporum analysin*: "Quanquam corpora subdividantur in infinita alia subtiliora; neque credibile sit ulla extare prima Elementa, id tamen nos non debet deterrere a causis quaerendis" (VE I 210, N. 63).

[19] See *Hypothesis physica nova* § 44 (A VI ii 242) and the author's 'Leibniz und die vorsokratische Tradition. Zur Bedeutung der Materietheorie von Anaxagoras für die Philosophie des jungen Leibniz' (*SL Supp.* 27, 1990), pp. 30-41.

From a causal point of view Leibniz makes clear cuts within the structure. Activity only takes place to the extent that quantities proportional to the senses are moved by quantities proportional to the senses.[20] Changes only occur amongst quantitatively similar things, whereby the *tertium comparationis* is defined as that which can be sensibly determined. On the question of the eventual contribution of events and structures on a lower level to those of a higher level the young philosopher states explicitly that they "do not enter into our calculation, because the phenomena are not changed by them".[21] This is clearly the limit to which he refers at the end of the *Hypothesis physica nova* at which both the philosopher and the empiricist must stop[22]: the limit of those things which can reach us on account of their strength (*virtus*) or sensible form − something which apparently also applies to ether; after all, it is part of the integral if imperceptible level immediately beneath that of direct experience assumed and at the same time put forward in order to explain phenomena.

It is important to note that Leibniz here assumes more than what he justifiably can. Phenomena express the level of human experience. As such they provide us with a clearly definable limit. On the other hand the causes of the phenomena we experience are often inaccessible, not least on grounds of magnitude. The setting of a limit in respect of what can influence the phenomena we perceive must therefore be regarded as being purely arbitrary.

Since, as Leibniz recognises, for the same phenomena numerous equally plausible possible causes can be put forward[23], he attaches great importance to scientific corroboration for his hypotheses. Indeed, on

---

[20] *Hypothesis physica nova* § 14. Contrasting the behaviour of bodies in his hypothetical system with the behaviour of bodies in a free state or vacuum, he writes: "Cum in statu libero seu naturali, quantacunque a quantuliscunque facile moveantur, in statu praesenti systematico, atque, ut sic dicam, civili, non nisi proportionata ad sensum a proportionatis" (A VI ii 227).

[21] *Hypothesis physica nova* § 49: "Sed haec in computum nostrum, quia nihil inde Phaenomena variantur, venire non possunt" (A VI ii 243).

[22] *Hypothesis physica nova* § 60: "Etsi enim possint in subtilitate et virtute dari graduum progressus in infinitum, dantur tamen summi gradus sensibiles, ita ut quod ultra est, ne virtute quidem, nedum forma sensibili ad nos pertingat; in hoc ergo limite Philosopho pariter atque Emprico subsistendum" (A VI ii 256).

[23] See Leibniz's letter to Conring dated beginning of May (?) 1671 (A II i 94). See also his letter to Fabri written towards the end of 1676 (A II i 290) and to Conring dated 18 September 1677 (A II i 377).

account of the evinced agreement not only with the results of microscopists, but also with those of chemists like Tachen, Glauber, and Boyle or with the magnetic theory of William Gilbert he claims that the explanation proposed in the *Hypothesis physica nova* is something more than simply a hypothesis.[24] In the same vein he also asserts that there are no publicly known experiments which cannot be reconciled with it.[25] But most important is the implicit agreement with reason. As Leibniz demonstrates in respect of motion, only at first sight do the phenomena differ greatly from the "principles of reality".[26] In fact, by showing that the hypothesis not only saves phenomena, but also agrees with reason, he believes that it can justifiably be said to approach and even reach the status of demonstrable truth[27] – understood in the sense of rigorous deductions from clear and distinct definitions. In this sense he later writes in Paris for example that the hypothesis of the infinite and the infinitely small splendidly agree with and succeed in geometry, and that this increases the probability that it is true.[28] Successful application and agreement with reason are the bywords of a hypothesis which aspires to truth.

Leibniz stresses time and again already in his early philosophy that there is no precise figure, that there is no circle, no ellipse, no straight line, in general nothing perfectly corresponding to mathematical figures in nature.[29] Such concepts are only definable in the intellect. In this

---

[24] *Hypothesis physica nova* § 46 (A VI ii 243); Leibniz's letter to Mariotte of early (?) 1673 (A II i 234).
[25] Leibniz's letter to Oldenburg of 18 June 1671: "Certe nihil est Experimentorum publice notorum, quae non ei, notabili harmoniae simplicissimae claritate, conciliare sperem" (A II i 122).
[26] *Hypothesis physica nova* § 46: "cum tamen plerumque experimenta, ut in motu ostendi, ab intimis rerum principiis prima specie valde dissentiant"(A IV ii 242-3).
[27] See *Specimen hypotheseos demonstrativae* (A VI iii 3).
[28] *De arcanis sublimium*: "Cum videamus Hypothesin infinitorum et infinite parvorum praeclare consentire ac succedere in Geometria, hoc etiam auget probabilitatem esse revera" (A VI iii 475).
[29] See for example *Hypothesis physica nova* § 59 (A VI ii 255); *Theoria motus abstracti,* theorem. § 15 (A VI ii 269). Similarly in numerous later texts: *Mira de natura substantiae corporeae*: "revera nullae certae figurae extant in natura rerum ac proinde nec certi motus" (VE II 294, N. 82); *Dans les corps il n'y a point de figure parfaite* (VE VII 1478-9, N. 321); *De qualitatibus quae referuntur ad extensionem* (VE VII 664, N. 367); *Principia logico-metaphysica*: "Non datur ulla in rebus actualis figura determinata, nulla enim infinitis impressionibus satisfacere potest.

sense, he says that there is no perfect similitude in nature – this would of course presuppose the natural existence of the mathematically perfect and would destroy his concept of individuality[30], – but rather that this concept belongs instead to the incomplete notions of mathematics[31]. Furthermore, this is not just true of static figures; there is also on his view no perfectly uniform and continuous curved or straight movement to be found. There might appear to be such much movements, but this is only *ad sensum*[32]. Likewise, the paths of falling bodies might appear parallel[33], but they are in fact curved: clearly as a result of the combined circular movement of the earth in the one direction and of ether in the other. It is through the fact that the path of light is always slightly curved[34] that Leibniz also partly[35] explains what in his view is the confusion concerning the laws of reflection. Since the curvature is imperceptible, it appears that the angle of incidence and the angle of reflection are equal.[36] But this is only an appearance. He is convinced

---

Itaque nec circulus, nec ellipsis, nec alia datur linea a nobis definibilis nisi intellectu" (VE VIII 2002, N. 425).

[30] In this sense there cannot be things in nature which only differ numerically. See *Elementa nova matheseos universalis* (VE V 988, N. 229); *Principia logico-metaphysica*: "non dari posse in natura duas res singulares solo numero differentes" (VE VIII 1999, N. 425).

[31] *Principia logico-metaphysica*: "Perfecta igitur similitudo locum habet tantum in notionibus incompletis atque abstractis, ubi res non omnimodo sed secundum certum considerandi modum in rationes veniunt, ut cum figuras solummodo consideramus, materiam vero figuratam negligimus, itaque duo triangula similia merito considerantur a Geometra, etsi duo triangula materialia perfecte similia nusquam reperiantur" (VE VIII 1999, N. 425). See also *Elementa nova matheseos universalis* (VE V 988, N. 229).

[32] See *Hypothesis physica nova* § 22: "Quod nullis experimentis refutari potest, quia plerique motus, qui recti apparent, reapse curvi sunt, sed ita insensibiliter ut omnia phaenomena perinde eveniant, ac si revera recti essent" (A VI ii 229). See also *Hypothesis physica nova* § 59 (A VI ii 255) and *Summa hypotheseos physica novae* § 5 (A VI ii 344).

[33] See *De firmitate, vi elastica, explosione, attractione*: "[...] uti ad sensum gravium directiones apud nos sunt parallelae" (VE VIII 1875, N. 403).

[34] See *Hypothesis physica nova* § 30 (A VI ii 235-6).

[35] A more frequently occurring reason in his view, and one which he also describes as being more compatible with the *oeconomia rerum*, is elasticity. See *Hypothesis physica nova* § 22 (A VI ii 229).

[36] *Theoria motus abstracti*, preliminary study: "Hinc sequitur falsam esse regulam, quod angulus incidentiae et reflexionis sint aequales semper. Nam ex hac regula id tantum efficitur, ut ad sensum videantur saepissime aequales" (A VI ii 174).

that on the basis of rational principles equality can only obtain in the case where the angle of incidence is 30°, and not least on this ground rejects the existence of a law of equality such as was claimed by amongst others Hobbes, Descartes and Kenelm Digby.[37]

Because of this one might wonder that more explicitly rational theories with high mathematical content should find application in nature at all. Leibniz provides us with an admirably clear answer to this and moreover an answer which, so far as we have been able to ascertain, although developed already in the early 1670s he continued to maintain with little or no alteration throughout the mature period. Probably the best formulation is to be found in a text written between 1679 and 1682 to which he gave the title *De organo sive arte magna cogitandi*. Referring to the continua represented by the straight line, the circle and movement, he writes:

> Whatever is felt about these three continua appears to depend on consideration of divine perfection. But geometry does not need to ascend to this. Then even if no straight lines or circles exist in nature, it is nevertheless sufficient that figures exist which differ from straight lines and circles to such a small extent, that the error is smaller than any given error – which is sufficient in order to demonstrate certainty as well as usage.[38]

Clearly without the approach of mathematics to experience the application of science would be impossible.[39] We must not forget that Leibniz in the *Hypothesis physica nova* calls the translation of discoveries to the usage of life for the benefit of mankind the sole aim of

---

[37] *Hypothesis physica nova* § 22 (A VI ii 228-9); *Theoria morus abstracti*, theorem. § 9 (A VI ii 269); letter to Oldenburg of 28 September 1670 (A II i 63).

[38] "Quid autem de tribus his continuis sentiendum sit videtur pendere ex consideratione perfectionis divinae. Sed Geometria ad haec assurgere necesse non habet. Nam etiamsi non darentur in natura nec dari possent rectae ac circuli, sufficiet tamen dari posse figuras, quae a rectis et circularibus tam parum absint, ut error sit minor quolibet dato. Quod satis est ad certitudinem demonstrationis pariter et usus" (VE V 1055-6, N. 237). See also *Theoria motus abstracti*, fund. praed. § 18 (A VI ii 267).

[39] *Hypothesis physica nova* § 54 (A VI ii 246).

philosophy.[40] In a similar fashion to the passage just quoted he tells us there that most movements which appear straight are in reality curved – as we have already noted in connection with gravity and reflection –, but so insensibly that all phenomena occur as if they were truly straight[41]. Mixed sciences drawn from physics and mathematics can be applied, since on account of the "incredible benevolence of the divinity" the phenomena in question "not only appear to the senses to be of the highest exactitude, but also as far as our usage is concerned everything occurs as if it were so."[42]

The key concept here, even if it is not explicitly referred to, is that of negligible error. On two accounts: firstly, we find that the appearance, although it deviates from reality, does so to such a small extent, that the sensible error can be ignored; and secondly, we are to understand that reality for its part deviates from the mathematically exact, but again that the deviation is so small as to be of no account; in particular it suffices for our purposes.

Evidently this only applies to certain phenomena, otherwise Leibniz's physical hypotheses could in principle be reduced to an abstract or mathematical model – something the young philosopher certainly does not hold. Rather, to use the trenchant metaphor Leibniz himself employs[43], abstract theory or mathematics is the source – a rather dry and meagre one, as he describes it – which leads into the most plentiful streams of the sciences, which in turn flow into an ocean of multifarious uses and methods. The image is one of progressive embellishment – Leibniz himself uses the adjective *ornatus*: it cannot be reversed. Even if

---

[40] *Hypothesis physica nova*, concl.: "[...] ac denique de translatione inventorum ad usum vitae augendamque potentiam et felicitatem generis humani, qui unus Philosophandi finis est, cogitandum esse videatur" (A VI ii 257).

[41] *Hypothesis physica nova* § 22: "[...] quia plerique motus, qui recti apparent, reapse curvi sunt, sed ita insensibiliter ut omnia phaenomena perinde eveniunt, ac si revera recti essent" (A VI ii 229).

[42] See *Hypothesis physica nova* § 59: "Evenit tamen ut summa ad sensum ἀκριβείᾳ haec omnia, etsi non sint ita, tamen sensu esse videantur, ut quantum ad usum nostrum, perinde sit ac si essent; atque ita incredibili Dei beneficio [...]" (A VI ii 255).

[43] *De rationibus motus* § 7: "Ordiamur igitur proferre Fundamenta motuum, qualia sunt in puro naturae statu, neque tamen munita demonstrationibus, neque ornata consectariis, infinitis tamen illis et illustribus; nam fontes artium, ut ariditate quadam et simplicitate delicatis displicere solent, ita decursu perpetuo in uberrima scientiarum flumina, denique quoddam, velut mare usus ac praxeos excrescunt" (A VI ii 160).

the sciences employ abstract or mathematical concepts they cannot be reduced to such concepts.

In Leibniz's view one must make a clear distinction between those propositions whose truth depends on the senses, as in the case of experiments and observations, and those which depend on a clear and distinct imagination or ideas.[44] Now, in one of his preparatory studies for the *Theoria motus abstracti*, which was eventually published like the *Hypothesis* and indeed complementing it in 1671, he cites[45] a number of cases where the senses cannot be trusted – something, we should note, which he would not say later on.[46] For example, he writes that we cannot simply through sense perception be sure if a certain body is in fact one body or numerous ones, a discontiguum or a contiguum. Nor can we be sure if a body which appears to rest is in fact motionless and not perhaps imperceptibly moving.[47] Because of this he regards the senses as being unable to ascertain the necessary circumstances of the facts; they cannot,

---

[44] See Leibniz's letter for Jean Gallois of the end of 1672: "Distinguendum ergo mihi videtur inter propositiones, aliarum enim veritatem pendere a sensu uti sunt experimenta et observationes Naturae, aliarum autem a clara distinctaque imaginatione seu ideis, vel si mavis definitionibus, nihil enim definitio aliud quam ideae significatio est, uti theoremata Arithmeticae et Geometriae" (A II I 228). See also his letter to Hobbes probably written around 1674 (A II i 244) and *Conspectus libelli elementorum physicae* (VE III 653, N 144).

[45] *Theoria motus abstracti*, preliminary study: "Tria sunt, ob quae sensualibus experimentis fidi non potest: 1.) quia nullum corpus quod sentitur quiescit, 2.) quia incertum est an corpus quod sentitur, proprie sit corpus an corpora, 3.) quia incertum est an corpus quod sentitur sit discontiguum an contiguum, 4.) quia incertum est an corpora se contingentia, contingant superficiebus, an vero tantum lineis et punctis. Quibus suppositis vel ignoratis, impossibile est prima motus principia sensu constabilire" (A VI ii 166). Cf. *Hypothesis physica nova* § 23 (A VI ii 232); the 'usus' section of *Theoria motus abstracti* (A VI ii 273).

[46] According to his later view the senses are not mendacious, but simply hide the true nature of reality. See Leibniz's letter to Oldenburg of 28 September 1670: "sensus nostros nunquam mendaces, plerumque tamen dissimulatores esse" (A II i 63) and the author's 'Les sens dissimulants. Phénomènes et réalité dans l'*Hypothesis physica nova*', in *La notion de nature chez Leibniz*, ed. Martine de Gaudemar (*SL Sond.* 24, 1995), pp. 17-30.

[47] It should be noted that even after his stay in Paris Leibniz would write that for the senses rest is the limiting state of motion. See for example *Logica transcendentium*: "Sensu etiam transcendente parabola est species ultima Ellipseos, et quies ultimum motus" (VE VIII 2048, N. 448).

so to speak, judge what is law or reason.[48] Consequently the senses are unable to establish the first principles of motion.

It comes as no surprise therefore that he rejects[49] the laws of motion put forward by amongst others Huygens and Wren. The results of the collision of bodies covered by such laws are seen by Leibniz to be dependent on the surrounding active medium. What passes as law for some turns out on his view to be simply a contingent fact. The only condition guaranteeing the necessity associated with deductions from rational principles is the presence of a resting medium or the absence of any medium at all. In this ideal state nature conforms in effect to pure mathematics.

As is well known, the young Leibniz distinguishes[50] between two types of motion: on the one hand pure or private motion, such as would occur in a vacuum or in a resting medium, and on the other the public or various forms of concrete motion such as one finds in the system set out in the *Hypothesis physica nova*, where bodies are moved, carried or blocked by what for our purposes is the universal carrier of movement, namely rapidly moving ether. The primary examples for the latter are of course elasticity, gravity and magnetism. Leibniz freely admits in his letter of 9 May 1671 to Oldenburg that when bodies collide in a free state of nature, and that is to say considered absolutely, the results of this collision can often appear paradoxical, since they diverge from phenomena.[51] Explaining, he points out that the size, shape and movement of an apparent body are one thing, of a true body another. It is evident, for example, that in a free or natural state a body with as large a

---

[48] *Theoria motus abstracti*, preliminary study (A VI ii 166). Cf. Leibniz's remarks on the senses in his drafts for the *Elementa juris naturalis* (A VI i 459-60).

[49] See for example *Hypothesis physica nova* § 20 (A VI ii 228); letter to Oldenburg of 23 July 1670 (A II i 59) and of 28 September 1670 (A II i 62-3).

[50] See *Hypothesis physica nova* § 4 (A VI ii 224); *Leges relexionis et refractionis*: "Quod antequam faciamus sciendum est duo esse genera motuum in mundo, alios puros seu privatos, alios publicos seu a systemate affectos" (A VI ii 314); *Summa hypotheseos physicae novae* § 26 (A VI ii 353); letter to Oldenburg of 28 September 1670 (A II i 62); Michel Fichant, 'La notion de système dans la physique de Leibniz' (*SL Sond.* 24, 1995), pp. 43-57; Gottfried Wilhelm Leibniz, *La réforme de la dynamique. De corporum concursu (1678) et autres textes inédits*, ed. Michel Fichant (Paris: Vrin, 1994), introd., pp. 38-41.

[51] "[...] corporum absolute consideratorum inter se concurrentium eventa saepe paradoxa, quia a Phaenomenis dissentanea; nam alia plane est magnitudo, figura, motus corporis apparens, alia vera"(A II i 102). See also *De rationibus motus* § 5 (A VI ii 161).

magnitude as one likes can be moved by a body with as small a magnitude as one likes, whereas in the system, so to speak in the civil state, bodies are only moved insofar as they are proportional to the senses[52], and that is to say that their relation can be expressed or given. As we have seen, the stratification of matter according to the model presented in the *Hypothesis physica nova* brings with it the concept of sensible limits or constraints which do not exist in the state of nature: in a vacuum the largest thing could be moved by the smallest.

On the question of relation between reason and physical hypothesis Leibniz writes that if a certain proximity to what is contrary is discovered it is preferable to look for reconciliation rather than think about overturning the whole hypothesis itself.[53] Reconciliation has here clearly pragmatic character. This is indeed what he does in 1671. In order to reconcile private and public motion, rational theory and physical hypothesis the young philosopher finds it necessary to fall back on the imperceptible ether on which the latter in any case largely depends.[54] It is of course particularly suited to fulfil this function, being conceived as something which is apparent purely through its effects.

Since reason in the form of abstract theory and mathematics represents the source in Leibniz's river metaphor, it can justifiably claim a certain pre-eminence. Indeed, as Leibniz emphasises in *De rationibus motus*, written in 1669 and representing one of numerous preliminary studies for the *Theoria motus abstracti*, the senses cannot prejudge reason, whereas the opposite certainly is true: reason may prejudge the senses, that is to say "whenever it appears that the senses contradict reason, one must conclude that something is present which cannot be sensed, except through its effects: ἐναντιοφανείᾳ ."[55]

But this relation between reason and the senses should not deceive us into falsely evaluating the importance of the senses for Leibniz. As his river metaphor suggests, in the pure state of nature everything is rather

---

[52] *Hypothesis physica nova* § 14: "Cum in statu libero seu naturali, quantacunque a quantuliscunque facile moveantur, in statu praesenti systematico, atque, ut sic dicam, civili, non nisi proportionata ad sensum a proportionatis" (A VI ii 227).

[53] *Hypothesis physica nova* § 45: "[...] ut proinde instantia quadam in contrarium reperta conciliatio potius quaerenda, quam totius Hypotheseos eversio cogitanda sit" (A VI ii 242).

[54] See for example *Elementa juris naturalis* (A VI i 480).

[55] A VI ii 159, §1.

barren, all of brute nature is determined simply by the composition of conatus. The systematic state represents a marked contrast to this: here

> all appears to occur intelligently and to enforce laws with wonderful reason towards a harmony of wisdom and justice, with the consequence that everything conspires to the use of all, everything fits together, everything flows periodically.[56]

Although Leibniz does indeed point to many cases where the senses mislead us, how paths appear to be straight, but are in fact imperceptibly curved, or how bodies appear to be at rest, but are in fact insensibly in motion – a resting body would in truth not cohere, it would not be a unity[57] –, he nevertheless does not talk by the time of the *Hypothesis physica nova* and the *Theoria motus abstracti* of the senses deceiving us, but only at most that they may conceal the truth. This is important; it is evidence of the increasing weight he puts on the evidence of the senses, and this in turn has a lot to do with the question of the application of science.

Leibniz is convinced that the meeting of experience and combined mathematical-physical theories like optics, statics and acoustics can be explained by his hypothesis. This requires that the phenomena themselves are acquitted of the charges made by certain modern sceptics – one of the reasons for Leibniz's serious interest in sceptical arguments.[58] But it requires also that the contradictions between the senses and reason are shown to be purely apparent. Here Leibniz is able to adopt an approach which has its origins in ancient law. Already an anonymous seventh-century Byzantine author, appropriately called Enantiophanes, and possibly also Photius in the ninth century, sought to show that contradictions in the Bible as well as in ecclesiastical and

---

[56] *Leges reflexionis et refractionis*: "In statu naturae puro (ut in intermundiis Epicuri) omnia sunt bruta conatuum compositione determinantur, in statu systematico omnia videntur intelligentia quadam fieri, miraque ratione ad harmoniam sapientiae et iustitiae leges exigi, unde omnia in omnium usum conspirantia, omnia sibi accomodata, omnia per periodos quasdam decurrentia" (A VI ii 315).

[57] See Leibniz's letter to Hobbes of 23 July 1670 (A II i 56) and to Oldenburg of 28 September 1670 (A II i 63).

[58] See Ezequiel de Olaso, 'Leibniz and Scepticism', in *Scepticism from the Renaissance to the Enlightenment*, ed. R. H. Popkin and C. B. Schmitt (Wiesbaden: Harrassowitz, 1987), pp. 133-167; R. H. Popkin, 'Leibniz and the French Sceptics', *Revue Internationale de Philosophie* 20 (1966): 228-48.

secular law are in fact purely ἐναντιοφανείαι. Leibniz quotes[59] the
Nomokanon of Fourteen Titles, which he attributes to Photius, but whose
most probable source was in fact the said Enantiophanes. Not
surprisingly in view of his legal training, Leibniz was also well
acquainted[60] with the writings of humanist lawyers of the late sixteenth
and early seventeenth centuries like François Hotman, Hugo Grotius,
Pacius a Beriga and Nicolaus de Passeribus, who sought to remove
contradictions in the handed-down *ius Romanum*, the so-called *ratio
scripta*, by showing that these too are only apparent. Following this
approach the young Leibniz saw it as being incumbent upon him to save
the phenomena in a much more profound sense than probably anyone
before him. It was not just a question of accounting for phenomena, of
building a mechanistic model capable of explaining observed natural
states and events, it was also a question of reconciling the phenomena
with rational knowledge as represented by mathematics and the mixed
sciences.[61] A better answer to the sceptics is scarcely conceivable.

Before concluding, we should like to return to the way the young
Leibniz sees the relationship between mathematics and nature. We
started out by indicating that the stratification of matter put forward in
the *Hypothesis physica nova* reflects his early views on the continuum –
something which remains true of the position to be found in the
monadology in spite of the fact that Leibniz later clearly distinguishes
between the infinitely divisible, but undivided continuum in the ideal
sphere of mathematics and the actual division to infinity of all bodies in
nature corresponding to the phenomenal sphere of the monads. As we
have already noted, mathematics is effectively to be found in the interior
of nature. Indeed, the young Leibniz repeatedly makes remarks to this
effect and only by looking at the models of nature which he created does
it become possible to understand the significance of these remarks. In
fact, already in the *Dissertatio de arte combinatoria* of 1666 the basic
concept of the mechanistic philosophy, that all larger things are

---

[59] *Nova methodus discendae docendaeque iurisprudentiae* § 28, nota (A VI i 314).

[60] See for example the references in *Nova methodus* § 48 and § 51 (A VI i 327-9).

[61] See his letter to Arnauld written at the beginning of November 1671: "Ego vero
videor reperisse quasdam ac pene dixerim necessarias notiones, quae Mechanicam
physicae, rationem experientiae connectant, quae ab abstractis motus legibus
transitum ad concreta corporum phaenomena faciant, quae, si experimentorum copia
et ordinatio accedat, sufficiant explicandis omnibus varietatibus naturae rerum" (A II
i 179).

composed of smaller ones, be they atoms or molecules, is seen as providing the metaphysical basis for the universal application of combinatorics, since the fundamental relation of the latter, that of whole to part, is seen as having a correspondent in reality[62]. We would suggest that from here on Leibniz more or less consistently employs a model at the core of nature so to speak which has its origins in an essentially mathematical concept.

But mathematics and nature are also connected in Leibniz's early work in another way – if less intimately. This goes back to the question of the relation between curved and straight lines or movements. As we have seen, Leibniz generally denies that there can be true linear motion in nature. In contrast, on the abstract level, and that is to say in mathematics, the straight line and linear motion are regarded as being fundamental – indeed, so fundamental, that the question of the origin of curves presents itself as a serious problem.[63] A straight line can be constructed by the flux of a point, but what about curves?[64] The

---

[62] "Istis complicationibus, non solum infinitis novis Theorematis locupletari Geometria potest, nova enim complicatio novam figuram compositam efficit, cuius iam contemplando proprietates, nova theoremata, novas demonstrationes fabricamus; sed et (si quidem verum est grandia ex parvis, sive haec atomos, sive moleculas voces, componi) unica ist via est in arcana naturae penetrandi" (A VI i 187, § 34). Cf. Leibniz's remarks on the *Dissertatio de arte combinatoria* in a draft of his letter to Gallois written at the end of 1672: "Ibi monui omnes propositiones scientiarum purarum, seu a sensu independentium (etsi earum veritas sensu quoque velut examinari confirmarique possit) quales sunt scientiae quoque de actione in universum, de ratiocinatione, de motu, utili, de iusto, nihil aliud quam pronuntiare aut definitionem partemve eius [...] de definito aut de definitione alia eiusdem definiti" (A II i 229).

[63] See *Theoria motus abstracti*, probl. spec. § 6 (A VI ii 271) and the 'usus' section (A VI ii 274-5); *De rationibus motus* § 23 (A VI ii 163); *Theoria motus abstracti*, first version § 22 (A VI ii 184-5). Cf. *De organo sive arte magna cogitandi*, dated betwwen 1679 and 1682: "Ita omnes lineae motuum in tota Geometria, revocantur ad duos tantum motus, unum in linea recta, alterum in linea circulari. His duobus enim suppositis demonstrari potest alias omnes lineas exempli causa, Parabolam, Hyperbolam, Conchoidem, Spiralem, possibiles esse. Rectam autem duci et circulum describi Euclides non docuit, sed postulare satis habuit. Quanquam posito spatio, corpore linea recta, et motu continuo, possit etiam demonstrari possibilitas circuli" (VE V 1055, N. 237).

[64] It is important to note that we are talking here about what Leibniz calls "the exact, but imaginary constructions of mathematics" (*Theoria motus abstracti*, probl. gen., A VI ii 270). In many ways a more pressing problem for him is the discovery of the "real and exact causes of figures, through which they are necessarily produced in

importance of this issue in fact goes back to debates on the *Quaestio de certitudine mathematicarum*[65] arising out of the Renaissance: whether mathematical definitions incorporate a mode of construction such as would appear to be necessary according to the *Analytica Posteriora* if mathematics is to be regarded as a true science.[66] Leibniz solves the problem simply by reducing true mathematical curves and curvilinear motion to polygons with an infinite number of sides. In his letter to Claude Perrault written probably in the first half of 1676 he states that he is certain that whatever moves along a curved path strives along the tangent to this curve, the true cause for this being that curves are polygons with an infinity of sides and that these sides are portions of the tangents.[67]

There are numerous remarks from Leibniz written around 1671 outlining similar views. In a letter to Oldenburg for example he claims that in the *Theoria motus abstracti* he has explained the origin of all types of figure and motion from mere straight lines.[68] Whatever can be

---

nature" (*Theoria motus abstracti*, first version, § 22, A VI ii 184). In the published version of the *Theoria motus abstracti* he calls such constructions physical and contrasts them with not only with mathematical but also mechanical constructions. The latter correspond to what is drawn on paper, while the term "constructio physica" refers to the mathematical core of nature. See *Theoria motus abstracti*, first version, § 22 (A VI ii 184), the section 'usus' of the published version (A VI ii 273-4).

[65] On this problem see Paolo Mancosu, 'Aristotelian Logic and Euclidean Mathematics: Seventeenth-Century Developments of the Quaestio de certitudine mathematicarum' (*Studies in History and Philosophy of Science* 23 (1992): 241-265) and his *Philosophy of Mathematics and Mathematical Practice in the Seventeenth Century* (New York and Oxford: Oxford University Press, 1996), pp. 10-33.

[66] See Leibniz's letter to Thomasius of 30 April 1669 (A II i 19-20). How seriously this problem was taken by contemporary mathematicians is reflected for example by the fact that John Wallis dedicates the second chapter of his *Mathesis universalis* (1657) to the proof that mathematics is a true science. See John Wallis, *Opera mathematica*, vol. 2, Oxford, 1695 (reprint Hildesheim and New York: Olms, 1972), pp. 21-24.

[67] "Et premierement je tiens pour assuré, que tout ce qui se meut en ligne courbe, fait effort dans la touchante de cette courbe: dont la veritable cause est, que les courbes sont des polygones d'une infinité de costez; et que ces costez sont portions des touchants" (A II i 264).

[68] Letter to Oldenburg of 9 May 1671: "Caeterum hoc loco (sc. *Theoria motus abstracti*) explicui omnis generis figurarum et motuum originem ex meris rectis" (A II i 102).

said about the circle can be understood in truth about a particular infinite polygon.[69] At times he allows a metaphysical distinction between the curve and its inscribed or described polygon[70], but the really crucial point is that it can be treated of in such a way that the resulting error is smaller than can be expressed by us or imperceptible. This he says in a letter probably written to Jean Chapelain in the first half of 1670 "is sufficient for practical use"[71]. We find the same point repeated in the *Theoria motus abstracti*[72] and in numerous other contemporary writings[73]. The significance is clear. When working with the infinite, procedures can be pursued indefinitely; we can in principle increase the level of accuracy as much as we want.[74]

---

[69] See for example *Numeri infiniti*: "Itaque cum aliquid de Circulo dicitur, intelligimus id verum esse de quolibet polygono" (A VI iii 498). See also Gottfried Wilhelm Leibniz, *De quadratura arithmetica circuli ellipseos et hyperbolae cujus corollarium est trigonometria sine tabulis*, ed. Eberhard Knobloch (*Abhandlungen der Akademie der Wissenschaften in Göttingen, Mathematisch-Physikalische Klasse*), Series 3, No. 43 (1993): 69.

[70] *Pacidius philalethi*, critical apparatus (reconstructed): "Quemadmodum polygonum regulare infinitorum laterum pro circulo metaphysice haberi non potest, tametsi in Geometria pro circulo habeatur, ob errorem minorem quam ut numero ullo a nobis exprimi possit" (A VI iii 569).

[71] "[...] quemadmodum enim post extantia Euclidis Elementa, nulla est excogitabilis figura, quae non praescripta methodo (si quem non tadeat diuturnis subiectionibus operam impendere, uti in dimensione Circuli fecit Archimedes, et qui multo longius progressus est, Ludolphus a Colonia) solui ita possit, ut error sit insensibilis, quod in praxi sufficit" (A II i 53).

[72] "At ita, inquies, Polygonum infinitangulum non erit circulo aequale: respondeo, non esse aequalis magnitudinis, etsi sit aequalis extensionis: differentia enim minor est quam ut ullo numero exprimi possit" (A VI ii 267, fund. praed. § 18). In the 'usus' section he writes in the same sense: "uti Geometrae describunt quadraticem per puncta, et Archimedes quadrat Circulum per Polygona, spreto errore nihil phaenomena turbaturo" (A VI ii 273).

[73] See for example Leibniz's letter to Arnauld written at the beginning of November 1671: "Sunt enim ad usum vitae soluta tam accurate, ut in potestate nostra sit, quantum errare velimus" (A II I 180); *De organo sive arte magna cogitandi* (VE V 1056, N. 237). See also his letter to Duke Johann Friedrich probably written in the second half of October 1671 (A II i 163-4).

[74] See *Vindicatio justitiae divinae et libertatis humanae*: "Quemadmodum tamen Geometrae et Physici esse possumus [...] modo pro indivisibilibus assumamus quantitates tam parvas, ut error qui inde nasci potest sit minor dato, seu tam exiguus quam volumus" (VE I 46, N. 11); letter to Arnauld of beginning of November 1671 (A II i 180).

He says this too in his first major work on the new infinitesimal mathematics, *De quadratura arithmetica circuli*, written in 1676 towards the end of his stay in Paris. Here he puts forward a new method of quadratures as a considerable improvement on the laborious[75] method of Archimedes using indirect proofs. Instead of using both inscriptions and descriptions, the new method using indivisibles, now more correctly termed infinitely small quantities, suffices with just one of these and moreover approaches the quality of a direct proof.[76] And here he tells us that nothing is more alien to his mind "than scrupulous details in which there is more ostentation than usefulness and which consume time like ceremonies do"[77]. To those who might question the economy of his method, the quality of his proof, he replies that the error is smaller than any giveable error and therefore null.[78] We do not need the solution so accurately, is the point he is putting across, but simply what it sufficient *ad usum vitae*. The central concept here is again that of applicability. He could in principle increase the accuracy, he could embellish the reasoning with extensive proofs. But accuracy itself is not the overriding concern, rather it is applicability, usefulness.[79]

The origin of certainty in geometry is to be found, as the young Leibniz recognises, in abstract ideas. But as the source-river metaphor shows us, the fundamentally important aspect for him is the application which mathematics finds first and foremost through the mixed sciences. There is a remarkable similarity between remarks he makes in the *Hypothesis physica nova* and those in *De quadratura arithmetica circuli*. In both works the question is of approach rather than of exact

---

[75] See Leibniz's remarks in his letter probably written to Jean Chapelain of the first half of 1670 (A II i 53). Cf. his letter for Jean Gallois written towards the end of 1672 (A II i 223).

[76] *De quadratura arithmetica circuli*, prop. VII, scholium, p. 35.

[77] *De quadratura arithmetica circuli*, prop. VI, scholium: "[...] cum nihil sit magis alienum ab ingenio meo quam scrupulosae quorundam minutiae in quibus plus ostentationis est quam fructus, nam et tempus quibusdam velut caeremoniis consumunt" (p. 33).

[78] De *quadratura arithmetica circuli*, prop. VII, def.: "Et proinde si quis assertiones nostras neget facile convinci possit ostendendo errorem quovis assignabili esse minorem, adeoque nullum" (p. 39).

[79] See Leibniz's letter to Conring of 13 January 1678: "Geometriae enim usus in applicatione consistit, abstracta autem tantum ingenio exercendo" (A II i 387). See also his letter to Arnauld of the beginning of November 1671 (A II i 180) and the 'usus' section of *Theoria motus abstracti* (A VI ii 273-4).

correspondence. In the former we see how mathematical figures are approached in nature, but that nothing exactly corresponds to them. Nevertheless this suffices; the approximation involving negligible error guarantees application *ad usum vitae*. Similarly, in the latter Leibniz emphasises that we ourselves can effectively decide how far we want to proceed, the error can be as small as we want. But the error will in any case be smaller than can be given. And this means the procedure fulfils its purpose, namely *ad usum vitae*.

The source is fairly dry and meagre, but it is also elevated: the rational principles are founded in divine reason, or to be more precise in the continuum which constitutes its base and at the same time the base of geometry.[80] However, the crucial stage according to the metaphor is what flows from this source; combined mathematical-physical sciences whose fecundity is demonstrated by their very application. The expression Leibniz repeatedly employs is *ad usum vitae*. They serve to improve the human condition. Often the use of science is couched in terms of harmony or divine benevolence: the benevolence of a geometricising God who has arranged things in such a way that the many are governed by the few. The counterpart of harmony is economy just as the counterpart of diversity is unity.

The greater the degree of agreement between his hypothesis and the important scientific disciplines of his day, that is to say, the greater degree of harmony, the higher the probability that his hypothesis is true. Metaphysical harmony is reflected in this interdisciplinary coherence. But it is also reflected in natural equilibrium. Just as crime and injustice create an imbalance requiring punishment in order that harmony be restored, so too the imbalances within the mechanistic system are taken out. The difference is simply that the harmony of the system is self-restoring. This explains the divine character attributed to the ether in the *Hypothesis physica nova*. This explains also why Leibniz in the early 1670s talks of public motion when referring to activity relevant to the balance of the system. All movement of parts of matter has consequences for the whole, in some cases more, in most cases less. This is, of course, the basis of the famous mirror metaphor: that in each mind

---

[80] The most elegant expression of this concept is to be found in a letter Leibniz wrote to Sophie, Electress of Hanover, on 30 November 1701: "La continuité uniformement reglée, quoyqu'elle ne soit que de supposition et d'abstraction, fait la base des verités eternelles et des sciences necessaires: elle est l'objet de l'entendement divin, comme le sont toutes les verités, et ses rayons se repandent aussi sur le nostre" (G VII 564).

the activity of the whole universe is reflected, most of it confusedly, but at least some to a high degree of distinctness.

It is here that an inconsistency emerges. According to the *Hypothesis physica nova* only a small number of the infinite succession of planes in the proposed model is empirically relevant. Leibniz elsewhere uses the example of the construction[81] of a defensive wall to make this clear. The presence of small stones in the earth is irrelevant to the strength of the wall; they can therefore be ignored by the constructor. However one might reply that it is conceivable that a large number of small stones could have an effect. A cut would then appear to be purely random and therefore not justifiable philosophically.

On the other hand, the actual division of matter represents the metaphysical source of future possibilities.[82] It also explains why, through research and human industry, we can approach to an ever increasing degree the hidden secrets of things, the interior of nature. We could, pursuing this path, become acquainted with the mathematical structures underlying reality and so to speak come to see the divinity face to face[83]. This is the reason why Leibniz brings together the concept of the continuum and that of the *visio beatifica*. Potentially, there are no limits to knowledge. And as he later writes in *De rerum originatione radicali*[84] the infinite dividedness of matter ensures that there are always other, smaller and increasingly undeveloped beings to be found in the depths of matter, thereby providing the metaphysical basis for continuing growth in knowledge and culture.

---

[81] See *De modo perveniendi ad veram corporum analysin*: "et qui terra utitur ad vallum ducendum, non rationcinatur de lapillis exiguis qui in ea passim reperiuntur, eumque nihil morantur: ita credibile est illorum subtilissimorum corporum in corpora nobis tractabilia ingredientium effectus non magis pertinere ad Phaenomena nostra, quam lapilli in aggere existentes vel etiam corpuscula insensibilia terram componentia ad firmitatem munimenti" (VE I 63, N. 211). Cf. Leibniz's letter to Perrault of the first half of 1676 (?) (A II i 267).

[82] See *Specimen demonstrationum de natura rerum corporearum ex phaenomenis* (A VI ii 304).

[83] *Demonstrationum catholicarum conspectus*, c. 52: "Visio beatifica et voluptas corporis, scientiaque beatorum, et contra ignorantia dolorque corporis damnatorum crescit in infinitum, crescit autem visio beatifica, tum quod prius partes earumque harmoniam cognovit, quam partium partes cognoscit, quia continuum divisibile in infinitum" (A VI i 499).

[84] G VII 308. See also the draft entitled *De mundi perfectione augente* (VE VIII 2019, N. 437).

But what exactly are the mathematical structures at the heart of nature? Clearly, the infinite division of matter is one, since this presupposes a structural analogy between the geometrical continuum and material substance. Another would appear to be the relational figures referred to already in *De arte combinatoria*. In general, the ultimate justification for *mathesis universalis* is the presence of such structures. But all this is not to say that nature has mathematical character. As we have seen, Leibniz denies that nature can be reduced to basic concepts of mathematics. But it does ensure that mathematics can be applied. The corresponding structures are inherent in nature; this is what Leibniz means when in the final section of the *Theoria motus abstracti* he refers to the inner regions of nature where accurate figures are constructed according to the pure laws of motion: "constructions which are not only possible, but also necessary"[85]. From the point of view of mathematics itself, Leibniz makes clear that we must not lose perspective. It is not just a question of developing intricate theories or extensive proofs. These certainly do have their value, albeit as a form of mental exercise.[86] Mathematics instead achieves its true significance only when its practice is subsumed to human needs. We see this reflected in the final section of the *Theoria motus abstracti* where Leibniz raises the question as to what practical purpose his purely theoretical deliberations might serve:

> Is that which we write simply a sort of mechanics for angels which possibly have relations to the finer bodies? I do not want to reply that even those who concern themselves with mechanics sometimes have the need for greater exactness than usual, for example in respect of conic sections in the making of lenses, then even if they require a very great degree of accuracy they do not need the greatest degree. Nor is it permissible here to appeal to the geometricians, since to these some would object that it is vain to seek the quadrature of the circle and so many other problems,

---

[85] "Nimirium longe aliter Natura (quaternius sensibilis est, nam alioquin interioribus eius figuras accuratas ex abstractis motus legibus secundum problemata praemissa construi, qualem constructionem Physicam voco, non possibile tantum, sed et necessarium est) et Ars haec problemata solvit, quam Geometra" (A VI ii 273, 'usus' section).

[86] See *Dissertatio exoterica de usu geometriae*: "Duplex est Geometriae utilitas, nam una ad augendas vitae commoditates pertinet, altera in ipsa Mentis perfectione consistit" (A VI iii 446) and Leibniz's letter to Conring of 13 January 1678 (A II i 387).

which even if they were solved would not bring any improvement to the human condition [...].[87]

Just as the development of theories *ad usum vitae* is for the young Leibniz in the final analysis the sole purpose of philosophy and empirical science, so too is applicability, and not excessive calculation to unnecessary degrees of certainty, the overriding principle as far as mathematics is concerned.

---

[87] A VI ii 273-4.0

FRANCESCO PIRO

LEIBNIZ AND ETHICS: THE YEARS 1669-72

1. Leibniz and Carneades' Argument against Justice

The period of Leibniz's stay in Mainz was very creative from the point of view of the development of his ideas on law, justice, and rational politics. At this stage the young philosopher wrote intensively about political problems (starting with the *Specimen Demonstrationum Politicarum,* concerning the election of the king of Poland, 1669), composed some fragments under the title *Elements of natural law* (1670-1), outlined many proposals concerning scientific academies, societies for the conciliation of the Christian Churches. He also wrote many letters on all these subjects.

The question to now ask is whether it is possible to extract from these materials a consistent set of ideas concerning good, practical reason, actions and passions and other fundamental topics of moral philosophy. At first sight, it would seem very probable. In these years, Leibniz outlines a definition of the virtue of justice ("universal justice") which was not included in his former essays: from 1670 onwards, the virtue of justice is, for him a constant love towards every mind or individual.[1] Since this change surely has a structural importance in the development of Leibniz's ideas on law and politics, as pointed out by different scholars – the most recent being A.

---

[1] The first writing in which this definition (*habitus amandi omnes*) is introduced is the first of the three fragments collected under the title *Elementa Juris Naturalis* in the Akademie-Ausgabe (A VI i 459-65). We shall call this and the following fragments *Elements of natural law* and the previous ones 'preparatory works to the *Elements of natural law*'.

S. Brown (ed.): The Young Leibniz and his Philosophy (1646-76). 147-67
© 1999 Kluwer Academic Publishers. Printed in the Netherlands.

Robinet – it would seem obvious to consider it as the point of emergence of an underlying system of moral philosophy.[2]

On the other hand, Leibniz's ideas change in ways which are not easy to clarify. According to Hostler, Leibniz's new doctrine of justice as love arises when only the 'rudiments' of the other parts of his mature moral philosophy are seen.[3]   Even if this statement perhaps goes too far, it is true that it is easier to trace the various sources of Leibniz's new doctrine of justice – the Augustinian doctrine of *caritas ordinata* and its German followers, the works of some innovative moral theologians such as the Jesuit Friedrich Spee and the Reformed Johann H. Alsted, the Platonist philosophy of love – than to clarify how he succeeded in connecting these inputs or which were the ethical problems he was preoccupied with at the time.[4]

First of all, I would like to suggest that there is one main ethical question which Leibniz was facing at the preparatory stage of his *Elements of Natural Law*. This I shall call Carneades' Argument

---

[2] See A. Robinet, *Leibniz: Le meilleur des mondes par a balance de l'Europe* (Paris: P. U. F., 1994), pp. 41-77 ("L'inversion du rapport structurel: sagesse > puissance"). The importance of the evolution of Leibniz's ideas on justice at the beginning of the 1670s was already recognised by G. Aceti, 'Indagini sulla concezione leibniziana della felicità', *Rivista di Filosofia neo-scolastica* 49 (1957):   99-145; and R. Mulvaney, 'The early development of Leibniz's concept of justice', *Journal of the History of Ideas* 29 (1968): 54-71.

[3] "Although the theory of good is thus logically prior to that of love, the historical order of their development is the reverse. For Leibniz can be seen to develop his analysis of love in a series of papers entitled *Elements of natural law* (in A VI i) during the years 1670-1, at which stage only the rudiments of his theories of goodness and volition can be found in his works." (J. Hostler, *Leibniz's Moral Philosophy,* New York: Harper & Row, 1968, p. 49)

[4] Concerning the tradition of the *caritas ordinata* and Leibniz,
see H.-P, Schneider, *Justitia Universalis. Quellenstudien zur Geschichte des 'christlichen Naturrechts" bei G. W. Leibniz* (Frankfurt on Main: Klostermann, 1967) and W. Schneiders, *Naturrecht und Liebesethik.   Zur Geschichte der praktischen Philosophie im Hinblick auf Christian Thomasius* (Hildesheim-New York: Olms, 1971), pp. 9-47. The influence of Spee and Alsted was noted by R. Mulvaney (*op. cit.*) and the possible influence of the Renaissance Platonists was suggested by Hostler, *op. cit.*, p. 49). This last case will be analysed in the next paragraph.

against Justice. I will then discuss his solutions and I will suggest that Leibniz uses, in a creative way, the ideas of different traditions of moral philosophy while working on his solution. Finally, I will consider briefly the relation between this part of his philosophy and his developing metaphysics of mind.

My story begins with Carneades. Carneades, one of the main exponents of ancient Academic scepticism, had been the ideal adversary against whom Grotius had fought in the *Prolegomena* of his *De jure belli ac pacis*. Grotius quotes many passages attributed to Carneades and, among them, this sentence: "...either there is no justice, or it is a form of supreme foolishness, since it prescribes damage to ourselves at the advantage of others".[5] In the winter of 1669-70, Leibniz found this passage in Grotius and his opinion was that Grotius had not defeated Carneades.[6] As he wrote to his correspondent Hermann Conring:

> I suppose, with Carneades (and Hobbes agrees), that to be just would be the greatest foolishness, if we were to gain no present or future utility from it; the proud pretensions of Stoics and Sadduceans concerning virtue – which would have to be performed for its own sake – are quite erroneous. Therefore, everything that is just must be privately useful. But, since the form of justice is public utility, it is impossible to give an exact demonstration of this proposition: 'every prudent man must always do what is just', without having already demonstrated that

---

[5] The formula quoted by Grotius is: "aut nullam esse justititia, aut si sit aliqua, summam esse stultitiam, quoniam sibi noceat alienis commodis consulens." (*De Iure Belli ac Pacis libri tres*, Amsterdam, 1646, *Prolegomena*) As Richard Tuck remarks: "The use of Carneades as the principal spokesman for the position which Grotius was about to attack was, I think, unprecedented in any work on the laws of nature. The medieval and sixteenth-century scholastics had never put their theories in this kind of context: their intention had always ostensibly been to interpret the ethical theories either of Aristotle or Aquinas, neither of whom saw the refutation of scepticism as their first task." ('The "modern" theory of natural law', in *The Languages of Political Theory in Early-Modern Europe*, ed. H. Pagden, Cambridge: Cambridge University Press, 1987, p. 109)

[6] A VI i 431-2.

there is a supreme revenger of public utility, namely God. Otherwise, the eyes of other men and the fear that other men inspire would not restrain the prudent man, when these other men cannot help and cannot harm him ...[7]

At first glance, this passage is only the paradoxical exposition of a very common criticism directed towards Grotius. As is well known, Grotius had affirmed that our obligation towards society derives only from our 'right reason' and therefore it would have been prescriptive even if, hypothetically, God did not exist. This opinion had been bitterly criticised by different exponents of German Lutheran moral philosophy, a current of which the correspondent of Leibniz, Hermann Conring, was one of the leaders.[8] Furthermore, Leibniz's attack does not concern Grotius exclusively, but 'Stoic pride' as such and this is a very classic *topos* in Augustinian moral philosophies.

It is easy to show, however, that Leibniz is not only using Carneades' argument in a rhetorical way. In fact, his previous *Nova Methodus discendae docendaeque jurisprudentiae* (1667) includes a doctrine of natural law which is a clear attempt at avoiding Carneades' objection. In *Nova Methodus*, natural law is considered in a purely deontologic way, namely as a series of rules or 'precepts' ('harm no man', 'give to everybody his own', 'live honestly') which are expressions of God's will. But, at the same time, God (being wise) performs the role of allowing the convergence, through the rewards and the punishments of the afterlife, of what is 'honest' and what is

---

[7] Letter to Hermann Conring, January 1670 (A II i 28: G I 160).

[8] The debates on Grotius in Germany are resumed in Schneider (*op. cit.*, pp. 122-58). Leibniz's correspondent, Hermann Conring, criticised Pufendorf's doctrine of natural law through arguments which are similar to those of Leibniz against Grotius: "... justi civilis unicum principium est utilitas civitatis; ita moralis justi est utilitatem humanae cujusque naturae. Hanc vero non posse recte constitui, nisi probe cognita humana natura, eaque humanae mentis immortalitate et praemiis, poenis a Deo ipsi decretis..." (quoted in C. Thomasius, *Paulo plenior historia juris naturalis*, Halle, 1719, p. 176). Since this passage was originally included in a letter of 1663 to Leibniz's patron, Boineburg, Leibniz could have read it. On Boineburg and his relations with Conring, see P. Wiedeburg, *Der junge Leibniz. Das Reich und Europa, Part I Mainz* (Wiesbaden: Steiner, 1962).

'useful' for the single individuals.[9] Thus, we can suppose, that if God did not exist (or were not wise), the precepts of natural law would cease to be proper obligations, just as Leibniz affirms in his letter to Conring.

At this point, let us try to see Carneades' argument through the eyes of Leibniz. From Leibniz's point of view, Carneades' argument concerns the relation between (the virtue of) 'justice' and (the virtue of) 'prudence'. Leibniz usually evaluates the moral righteousness of actions using a teleological criterion: a 'just act' (*justum*) is that which has a 'public utility' (*publice utile*). But, since the achievement of the goal of public utility may prove costly for individuals in many cases, our constant disposition to perform righteous acts (i.e., 'justice') cannot be explained starting from our own private utility. On the other hand, there is 'prudence'. Since Leibniz defines prudence as the opposite of foolishness and foolishness as 'a negligence towards one's own usefulness', we must see Leibnizian 'prudence' as the constant disposition to a careful calculation of one's own utility.[10] This is obviously a way to see prudence which is deeply different from that of the Aristotelian tradition and that seems to be influenced by authors such as Pierre Gassendi and Thomas Hobbes.[11] In the light of these definitions, only if there is a complete convergence in the long run between private utility and public utility (namely if there is a wise God), there will be no cases in which the same act is prudent and unjust or just and foolish. But, if there were such a case, 'prudence' and 'justice' could not be both constant dispositions or 'virtues' (as they must be) and our moral experience would become inconsistent or self-contradictory.[12]

---

[9] A VI i 344.

[10] A VI vi 431. See too A VI i 60: "*Prudentia* nihil aliud quam habitus ubique videndi quod utile est".

[11] See this direct quotation from Hobbes' *De Corpore* in A VI i 60: "Experientia est praeteritorum memoria, prudentia est futurorum Expectatio, similium nimirum iis quae experti sumus. Hobb. init. de Corp. P. I c.1. n.2." Gassendi's *Philosophiae Epicuri Syntagma* includes a long analysis on "prudence" which expresses a clearly utilitarian point of view (Gassendi, *Opera Omnia*, Paris, 1658, III 71-91).

[12] See the *Elements of Natural Law*: "...nemo est qui justitiam a prudentia distinguere audeat, cum enim justitia sit omnium consensu virtus quaedam, virtus

All this seems to be much more a moral proof of the existence of God than the outline of a moral theory. And this is in fact the state of affairs at the eve of the *Elements of Natural Law*. Leibniz faces a really difficult question of moral philosophy – May constant obedience to moral obligations be rational from the point of view of individuals? – but he uses it chiefly as a resource for the critics of the a-religious theories of natural law. Grotius, as we have already seen, is quite unable to solve the problem. Hobbes' solution is inconsistent or quite immoral. While basing fidelity to the sovereign on the egoistic goal of one's own safety, Hobbes has no real way of explaining why such acts as coalitions against the sovereign are always unjust from our point of view. Therefore an anarchistic tendency may easily be inferred from his principles.[13] In other words, since God is the only holder of a "right to all", the theory of "state of nature" does not apply and the political philosophy of Hobbes is wrong – but if there were no wise God, Hobbes' political philosophy would be wrong again, because the state of nature could not be surpassed.[14]

Nevertheless, a moral proof of God's existence is not a moral theory and the preparatory works to the *Elements of Natural Law*, which were written a few months after the letter to Conring, show a progressive

---

autem omnis ea affectuum frenatio, ut nihil obsistere rationis rectae imperiis possint. Ratio autem rectae agendorum cum prudentia idem sit, consequens est, nec justitiam sine prudentia esse posse" (A VI i 461).

[13] See the letters to Chapelain, April 1670: "...Thomas Hobbes...mira calliditate simul omnia dat et adimit Reipublicae..." (A I i 89); to Graevius, June 1671: "..Hobbes....fatetur alicubi cum saluti periculum aut periculi opinio ingruat, vinculum quantum ad periclitantem resolvi...Hoc si singulis concedimus, quid populo negabimus?" (A I i 154); to Lambert van Velthuysen, June 1671: "Fatetur ipse Hobbius civitatem securitatis causa ingredi homines: jus ergo suum ad omnia quae ipsis interesse securitatis videbuntur ne in statu quidem civili deponent, cur enim finem dimittant mediorum causa?" (quoted in I. Hein, 'Ein neu gefundener Brief von Leibniz an Lambert van Velthuysen', *SL* 22 (1990): 160).

[14] Leibniz sometimes considers Hobbes' "state of nature" as an useful fiction (for example in his letter to Hobbes of 1670, A II i 57-8). But, since a real state of nature is not compatible with the existence of a wise God, this statement means that Hobbes' "state of nature" is the description of a merely possible world such as the world in which elementary particles are unable to build stable bodies described in Leibniz's *Theoria Motus Abstracti*.

change of perspective in the analysis of the problem. Until the first months of 1670, Leibniz had put himself on the same ground as Carneades and Hobbes – usefulness from the single individual – while trying to determine the necessary conditions in order to make justice *rational* from this point of view. He then begins to analyse the *motives* which induce man to endeavour to perform just acts. And, remarkably, these inner motives were conceived as feelings or "affections" (*affectus*), contrary to what Aristotle himself had affirmed.[15]

Since the idea of universal love is strictly linked with that of a spontaneous activity for the sake of others, one could think that Leibniz arrived at this solution through his wish to justify the ideal of a personal involvement in the improvement of the human condition through scientific academies, philanthropical societies, legal reforms, and so on. But Leibniz could already show the existence of an obligation to universal beneficence through our personal interest to please a wise God.[16] It is more probable that the changes that intervene in his thought at the beginning of 1670 are a consequence of an attempt to give new ground to some basic ideas of classical, political and moral thinking in opposition to Hobbes' approach. In spite of his criticism of Hobbes, Leibniz admits that men engage themselves in political society with the primary goal of preserving their safety (*securitas*).[17] Nevertheless, in his opinion, when they are no longer in

---

[15] See A VI i 455: "Aristoteles collocavit virtutes omnes in affectu quodam moderando, solius justitiae medium in rebus tantum quaesivit. At si acutius introspexerit, comperies justitiam esse moderatrice amoris atque odii hominis erga hominis". In the following pages, the reference to the feeling of "hate" vanishes away.

[16] For example in the fragment *Societas Philadelphica* (1669?): "Vera *Politica* est nosse quid sit sibi utilissimum....*Utilissimum* cuique est, quod Deo gratissimum....Deo autem *gratissimum* est, quicquid facit ad perfectionem universi" (A IV i 552-3).

[17] A VI i 446: "Cum enim Civitas sit Societas securitatis, id est multitudo hominum in securitatis sibi procuratae opinione viventium". The priority of safety as "proper end" of State is often underlined in Leibniz's later writings. See: Gr. 596, 721, 763. On Hobbesian aspects of Leibniz's political thought, see the observations of Riley in R 199-217.

a situation of mutual fear, men learn to co-ordinate and connect their actions in order to obtain other "goods". This engagement for a common happiness can be ideally taken to the point where the desire to each contribute to the other's happiness becomes the basis of common life itself.[18] Of course, this "best of all Commonwealths" is a pure regulatory idea, but Leibniz often identifies this idea with the content of the *whole* science of natural law.[19]

In Aristotelian ethics, such an agreement between citizens (ὁμόνοια) was considered as the political form of friendship (φιλία).[20] The preparatory works to the *Elements of Natural Law* show us that the concept of love was introduced for the first time in connection with friendship (*amicitia*). In these first approaches, friendship is the source of those acts which are supererogatory from a legal point of view but indispensable at improving social co-operation ('equitable' acts).[21] The *Elements of Natural Law* transformed the performing of such acts into a constitutive part of the virtue of justice as such and defined moral necessity starting from equity rather than the strict 'just' acts. Equity included the obligations of legal justice but implied an effort to the maximising of common happiness too. The acts which

---

[18] A VI i 446: "Respublica est civitas quae ultra securitatis forma, habet forma *autarkeias* seu praebendae felicitatis"; *Ibidem*: "...si scilicet homines non tantum in securitatis, sed et aliorum bonorum opinione vivant, quorum maximus gradus est in optima Reipublicae forma, in qua vivunt in opinione praestantium sibi felicitatem".

[19] See A II i 79 (letter to Conring, 1671): "...eandem esse doctrinam Juris naturalis et optimae Reipublicae Universalis"; A I i 66 (to Portner, 1671): "Scientia Juris Naturalis docere est tradere leges optimae Reipublicae". See too: Gr. 614.

[20] Aristoteles, *Ethica Nicomachea*, VIII, 1, 1155a, 22-28 and IX, 6, 1167a 22 - 1167b 16.

[21] A VI i 455: "Duae sunt autem Regulae Affectus huius moderandi. 1) neminem laedere. 2) suum cuique tribuere. In illo *Iustitia* fundatur, in hoc *Amicitia* seu *Aequitas*". A VI i 456: "*Amicabilitas* est prudentia in dispensandis bonis, seu quousque prodesse debeamus". A VI i 457: "*Amicitia* est status mutui amoris". On friendship and equity in Leibniz, see W. Schneiders, "Naturrecht und Gerechtigkeit bei Leibniz", *Zeitschrift für philosophische Forschung* 20 (1966): 343.

were compatible with this effort were now called 'just' in the sense of merely lawful.[22]

Briefly, the concept of 'love' allowed Leibniz to explain both the highest forms of universal beneficence (which were implied in his definition of the 'good man') and more usual moral concepts ('friendship', 'common happiness') which ought to be refused starting from an Hobbesian (or Carneadean) point of view. Being a natural disposition of men, 'love' was able to be such a motive. Moreover, the choice of 'feeling' (*affectus*) – i.e. the interpretation of this motive as a psychologically causal motive – was in conformity with Leibniz's dynamic interpretation of the virtue of justice as a constant "endeavour" (*conatus*).[23]

At this point, one can ask whether Leibniz thought to have now resolved the problem of Carneades, which – as we have seen – both Grotius and Hobbes had let unresolved. It is easy to hypothesise that Carneades would have objected, that from the point of view of a rational egoist, 'love' cannot be a property of human nature or is only another name for what a rational egoist would call 'foolishness'. As we shall see, Leibniz was aware of these possible objections and his philosophical analysis of the concept of love has to be considered as an attempt at avoiding them.

2. Epicurean Materials in a Platonist Metaphysics

At this point, we must move to another domain of Leibnizian interest and consider Leibniz's most general ideas on human actions and their motives at this time. These ideas have no systematic form, but we can at least pick out some basic tendencies.

The first clear fact is Leibniz's sympathy for the hedonist ('Epicurean') moral philosophies: "If we divert ourselves from the

---

[22] A VI i 465-6 and 480-1. For an outline of Leibniz's deontic logic, see G. Kalinowski and J. L. Gardiés, 'Un logicien déontique avant la lettre: G. W. Leibniz.' *Archives für Rechts- und Sozialphilosophie* 60 (1974): 79-112.

[23] A VI i 454: "Justitia est constans conatus ad felicitatem communem salva sua"; A VI i 479: "Omnis vir bonus (....) est in perpetuo conatu mutandi aliquid seu novandi in melius scilicet, seu emendandi".

useless words of Scholastics and look at the facts of life, it is evident that we are driven by pleasure and discouraged by pain."[24] The authors that Leibniz quotes as modern followers of the Epicurean tradition are Lorenzo Valla, Pîerre Gassendi and, sometimes, Thomas Hobbes. The first two philosophers are really Epicurean, but an interesting question to ask is why Leibniz associates Hobbes with them. We can find the answer in the *Dissertatio de Arte Combinatoria*, in which Leibniz remarks that Hobbes admits to the existence of spiritual pleasures (*voluptates animi*), even though he reduces them to his *gloria* ('glory' or 'vain glory').[25]   We shall see later the importance of this isolated remark.   Moreover, Leibniz had read Robert Sharrock's *De Officiis secundum Jus Naturae*, quoted in 1667 but scarcely remembered in later writings.[26]   A more important source was probably the book *Del bene* (1644) by Cardinal Sforza Pallavicino: Leibniz usually quotes Pallavicino as an Aristotelian, but in fact the book by Pallavicino tries to reconcile humanist hedonism and Scholastic Aristotelianism.[27]

From this fact several questions arise; for instance: why did Leibniz think himself a hedonist? And was he effectively one, or was he more

---

[24] *Specimen Demonstrationum Politicarum pro eligendo rege Polonorum*, 1669 (A IV i 34).

[25] The passages in which Leibniz considers Hobbes as an Epicurean are A VI i 60-2 and A VI i 206. In this last case, his proof is this passage of *De Cive*, chapter I, § 2: "Quicquid autem videtur bonum, jucundum est, pertinetque ad organa vel ad animum. Animi autem voluptas omnis vel gloria est, sive bene opinari de se ipso, vel ad gloriam ultimo refertur...." (Hobbes, *Opera Philosophica* (London: Bohn, 1839), II 160. The English translation is in Hobbes, *The English Works* (London: Bohn, 1841), 2, 5).

[26] Sharrock is quoted favourably in 1667 (A VI i 342, 344) but rather critically in the letter to Lambert van Velthuysen of June 1671 (Hein, 1990, p. 160). Another author whose importance for Leibniz's theory of pleasure is hard to clarify is Gassendi, always mentioned with other moral philosophers.   His analysis of friendship from an Epicurean point of view may have been an important source (see: Gassendi, 1658, III, 91-3).

[27] Favourable references to Pallavicino's book appear in Leibniz' writings of 1667 (A VI i 342, 344), of 1669 (A IV i 35) and of 1671: "...Cardinalis Pallavicini dialogi *de Bono* mihi mirifice placuere..." (Hein, *op. cit.*, p. 161). Leibniz's exposition of the principle of sufficient reason in *Confessio Philosophi* presents some influences of the theory of the principles of knowledge exposed in *Del bene*, II, chap. 31-6.

an eclectic moral philosopher? As regards the first question, one could hypothesise that Leibniz saw hedonism as a kind of moral philosophy which is particularly close to common experience and that could be accepted even by non-Scholastic authors. But his interpretation of this doctrine is quite eclectic as many of his authors are. Already Valla's *De voluptate et vero bono* (1431) included a final conciliation between the Epicurean moral philosophy and Christian faith (or, rather, Augustinian moral theology). Valla saw the pleasures of the soul as actual anticipations of the pleasure of the afterlife, an assumption which can easily be reconciled with some forms of Platonism.[28] Moreover, Leibniz was not quite anti-Aristotelian, since he followed his master Jacob Thomasius in regarding some books of *Nicomachean Ethics* as more favourable to hedonism than others.[29] Lastly, he had some knowledge of the "innumerable contemplations of the Platonists on Beauty and Love, summarised by philosophers – mainly Italians – of the penultimate century and of the previous one...".[30] It is a pity that he does not quote some of them. He had probably read at least Marsilio Ficino, but he never quotes any masterpiece of this school, such as the *Dialogi d'amore* (1534) by Leone Ebreo (Judah Abarbanel), a possible source of Spinoza.[31] In any case, the theory of

---

[28] See *De Voluptate et vero bono*, III, 3 (Valla, Opera, Basle, 1540, 977): "Ex quo debet intelligi non honestatem sed voluptatem propter se ipsam expetenda est tam ab iis qui in hac vita quam ab iis qui in futura oblectari volunt. (....) Neque vero deest in hac vita probabilis quaedam iucunditas, ac voluptas, et ea maxima quae venit ex spe futurae felicitatis, cum mens sibi conscia recti et animus contemplandis divis assiduus, quasi candidatum se quendam putat et promissis honores sibi depingit et quodammodo praesentes facit....". Some digressions on honesty and pleasure in young Leibniz's writings are clearly reminiscent of Valla's book (for example: A VI i 464).

[29] Very critical remarks are in A VI i 61-2 and concern the doctrines exposed in *Ethica Nicomachea*, X, 3-4. But a more favourable approach to Aristotle is in A VI i 206, with reference to *Nicomachean Ethics*, VII, 12-3. On young Leibniz's critics to Aristotelian doctrine of pleasure see Aceti (op. cit., p. 101-2). On Leibniz and Aristotelian ethics, see also F. Piro, 'Leibniz et l'Ethique à Nicomaque', in *Leibniz und die Frage nach der Subjektivität,* ed. R. Cristin (Stuttgart: Steiner, 1994), pp. 179-196.

[30] A IV i 34. "Platonists" are mentioned again in A VI i 481.

pleasure explained in *Elements of Natural Law* and in *Confessio Philosophi* is quite an original fusion of these different inputs. Its main assumptions can be outlined as follows:

(i) 'Pleasure' is the effect of the perception of something as harmonious (*sensus harmoniae*). This explanation implies that even sensual pleasures are cognitive states, i.e. perceptions of some form of order or harmony. Leibniz accepts such a conclusion, even differentiating between "obscure" and "clear and distinct" perceptions of harmony.[32] This can be seen as an effort of reconciling two different postulates: (1) every pleasure is good if considered in itself (Epicureans); (2) there is a structural difference between the pleasures of the soul – including those caused by visual and auditory perceptions – and the more sensual ones and, in fact, only the object of the first ones can be judged as really 'beautiful' and not as easily agreeable (Platonists).[33]

(ii) Pleasure increases when different or various sense-data are reduced into order.[34] This assumption provides a reason for the priority of

---

[31]   Ficino is quoted mainly negatively in Leibniz's later writings. Leone Ebreo is never quoted. Of course, Leibniz could have an indirect knowledge of this tradition through the works of some later philosophers, since the philosophy of love of Leone Ebreo was considered as a part of the *Ars Cabbalistica*. See Leo Hebreaus, *De Amore Dialogi tres*, included in his *Ars Cabbalistica* (Basle, 1587).

[32]   A IV i 247.

[33]   A VI i 484. The question concerning the possibility of calling "beautiful" the objects of the senses had been widely discussed during the Renaissance. One of the most influential solutions was that of Ficino: "Voluptates auditus atque visus excellentiores sunt caeteris sensuum voluptates (..) Id autem absque proportione fieri nequit, nec absque ordine est ulla proportio. Ordo autem maxime rationis est proprius, quo sit ut in plerisque sonis figurisque, quibus ille compositionis ordo insit." (Ficino, *Opera*, Basle, 1541, I 1024).

[34]   A VI i 479: "Major harmonia est cum diversitas major, et reducitur tamen ad identitatem. Nam non in identitate, sed varietate gradus esse possunt". A VI i 484-5: "Conformitas delectat, sed nova, mira, inexpectata (...) in longe dissitis maxime grata, ubi connexionem nemo suspicaretur". A VI iii 122: "....est enim harmonia unitas in multis, maxima in plurimis; et in speciem turbatis et mirabili quadam ratione ex insperato ad summam concinnitatem reductis."

intellectual pleasures with respect to the sensual ones, since quite different phenomena can be reduced into an order only through some work of abstraction performed by the mind: for example, the remarking of analogies between different successions of phenomena rather than likenesses between the single ones. Leibniz's assumption derives from classical ideas concerning the function of dissonance in musical compositions and of the alternation of light and shadow in pictures. But his interpretation of this classical *topos* is rather original: we can prove no pleasure without a continuous harmonising of new elements with the previous ones. Therefore, pleasure becomes the momentaneous expression of a continuously changing life of the mind. But, since perceptual dissonances are the cause of pain, this idea seems to imply that the increasing (or even the preserving) of pleasure implies some element of pain. In Leibniz's later writings, this case is confronted and resolved through a distinction between the easy feeling of 'pleasure' (which cannot coexist with pain) and the more articulated feeling of "joy" (*laetitia*). Joy usually derives from a composition between little perceptions of pleasure and pain, when the former prevail.[35]

(iii) Our perceptions concerning "harmony" or "dissonance" are the consequences of a mental spontaneous activity of co-ordinating past and present sense-data.[36] This is the most important among Leibniz's

---

[35] See Gr 603: "Laetitia est excessus voluptatum praesentium supra dolores...Patet enim Laetitiam esse voluptatem totius hominis publicam sive universalem ex totius constitutione resultantem"; G VII 73: "*Laetitia* est status voluptatum, in quo sensus voluptatis tantum est, ut sensus doloris prae eo non sit notabilis".

[36] A VI ii 266: "....duobus enim actione et reactione, seu comparatione et proinde harmonia ad *sensum*, et sine quibus sensus nullus est, *voluptatem* vel *dolorem* opus est.". A VI i 483: "Quicquid agit in seipsum eius aliqua memoria est (meminimus enim cum nos sensisse sentimus); ac proinde perceptio harmoniae aut anarmoniae seu voluptatis et doloris, comparato sensu vetere et novo...". Of course, these ideas are inspired to the psychology of *conatus* expounded by Hobbes in *De Corpore*, chapter 25, but following Leibniz's general principle that "In mentes omnes conatus durant, nec eligitur aliquis addendo aut subtrahendo, sed is qui est ἁρμονικώτατος" (A VI ii 282). See on Leibniz's use of Hobbes' *conatus* in psychology: J. W. N. Watkins, *Hobbes' System of Ideas* (London: Hutchinson, 2nd edition, 1973), pp. 92-

ideas, since it clarifies why pleasure is not only to be seen as a consequence of the inner order of our perceptual contents but as a measure of the perfection of our mental performances: if we are able to anticipate future phenomena starting from past ones, we shall feel pleasure. This way of seeing pleasure demonstrates how deeply Leibniz's views on pleasure and pain depends on his analysis of cognitive processes.

Now, how could Leibniz build a theory of the motives of moral actions on these grounds? His first step was the use of the distinction between pleasure and utility, with the aim of explaining the classical concept of friendly love (*amor amicitiae*). Leibniz's ideas on this question have a quite definitive form in his *Specimen Demonstrationum Politicarum* of 1669. Love is caused by our perception of somebody as beautiful or harmonious in himself. Since a lover enjoys his loved one to become more beautiful or harmonious, he will be "delighted for his good" and this is Leibniz's definition of love. Now, since 'good' means the object of our wishes or desires (*quod appetitur*), Leibniz deduces that the loved person's good is equally important to the lover as his own good. All this would seem to mean that pleasure is not to be regarded as the *goal* of our activity, but rather as the psychological background that explains the set of goals we have. Therefore, a lover is really altruistic, since his deliberations consider the goals of the loved person as equally important as his own. An interesting remark of Leibniz is that such deliberations cannot be guided by 'prudence', which is the science of our good, but need a "science of *optimum*", i.e. of the optimal combinations between different goods, called by Leibniz by the name of "wisdom".[37] In later writings, this notion of wisdom, defined as "science of happiness", will completely replace the pre-1670 concept of prudence.

Since these ideas undergo no substantial change in later writings, we may think that the whole moral philosophy of the young Leibniz is included in those few pages. But this is not true. The main aim of this first analysis of love is to prove that no real friendship can be expected

---

4) and, more recently, K. Moll, *Der junge Leibniz*, Vol. III (Stuttgart-Bad Cannstatt: Fromann-Holzboog, 1996), pp. 220-2.

[37] *Specimen Demonstrationum Politicarum*, § 37-8 (A IV i 34-6).

where there is no possibility of close and constant relations. Therefore there can and may be no real friendship between states or even between their sovereigns. In political affairs, the only guide is the "reason of state", even if Leibniz already makes an exception in a single case, that of the friendship which would subsist between the whole of Christianity and the Polish nation. Nevertheless, no kind of "love towards every other mind" can be deduced, starting from these pages of 1669.[38]

How then could Leibniz include this same analysis of love into his philosophy of law and politics only a few months thereafter? We must now analyse the properly *metaphysical* suppositions which allowed this inclusion. The first case in which Leibniz's metaphysics was applied to the solution of a moral problem can be found in the preparatory works to the *Elements of Natural Law*. Leibniz introduces here a mental experiment. If a very powerful and unassailable giant oppressed human beings for the sake of his utility, could he be said to be unjust? It is clear that the problem concerns the possibility of distinguishing 'right' and 'power' or force. Now, if the giant oppressed men, he would giving up a pleasure of the soul, namely that of the praise of others. But this is against the most natural tendencies of minds: "Every one of us seeks the praise of others, only if we are beyond the state of mutual fear". Here is why:

> Every wise being seeks the praise of others, because every wise being seeks harmony. Praise is a big Echo of harmony, a reflection and duplication of it. If God had not placed rational creatures in the world, there would be the same harmony, but without its Echo; there would be the same beauty, but no reflection and refraction (i.e. multiplication) of it. Therefore,

---

[38] A IV i 36-41. Even if using Aristotelian materials in his description of the "true friendship", Leibniz's point of view on friendship is much more restricted than Aristotle's one. The young philosopher ignores the Aristotelian analysis of the different kinds of friendship included in the books VIII and IX of the *Nicomachean Ethics*.

God's wisdom demanded rational creatures in which things are multiplied. The mind is indeed almost a world in a mirror...[39]

This is a new set of ideas, with deep implications on every aspect of Leibniz's thought. Let us look at the different sides to the question:

(i) there is now a clear difference between 'morally possible' and 'physically possible'. An action is morally possible only if it is wise. It is wise only if it achieves the maximum of possible harmony with regard to the situation. It is remarkable that this theory is applied to God too. Until now, Leibniz had often repeated that God wants world harmony but he had never tried to prove that this fact is logically implied in its attribute of being wise. Now, the concept of wisdom is directly deduced from the assumption that minds are natural maximisers of harmony and God is treated as the most eminent application of this rule.

(ii) the Universe is seen as a network of interdependencies between the perceptual states of all minds and every mind is a "mirror of the universe". The idea that our world is a 'panharmonious' one is typical of the whole philosophy of Leibniz, since his early reading of Bisterfeld's books. But the idea that world harmony is grounded on the mirroring between minds seems to become important only from this moment on. And of course it seems to be a very similar doctrine to that of the universe as "circle of love" of the Renaissance Platonists.[40]

(iii) The importance of the desire for praise in Leibniz's moral argumentation of 1670 is probably due to the influence of Sforza Pallavicino, who saw it as an instrument through which God allowed men to become virtuous.[41]   But Leibniz uses this idea in a more

---

[39] A VI i 438.
[40] Universal circulation of love and minds as mirrors are both discussed by Leone Ebreo: "Mens enim humana est velut speculum et exemplum, vel imago et simulachrum quoddam potius ipsarum rerum..." (Leo Hebraeus, *op. cit.*, p. 339).
[41] See Pallavicino, *Del bene libri quattro* (Rome, 1644), I 24.

complicated way. On the one hand, our desire for praise can be seen as a reason for beneficence towards people who are not yet our friends (as it happens in the case of the giant and human gender). On the other hand, their praise can expand our self-esteem only if we hold them in esteem, i.e. if we consider them as possible true 'mirrors' of our harmony. A metaphor sometimes used by Leibniz in reference to this mutual relation is that of the reflection and refraction of the rays of light. But still more interesting is the word that Leibniz uses for self-esteem: it is 'glory'. "Glory", Leibniz writes to Louis XIV in 1672, "is the more intense pleasure of the soul", but a "pure glory" can be acquired only if "one converts his power into benefits for the other man".[42] Leibniz had not forgotten Hobbes' negative description of glory (or 'vain glory') as one of the proofs that we search society "not so much for the love of our fellows, as for the love of ourselves".[43] Leibniz's theory of the "pure glory" was an attempt to show that the two possibilities are not opposite and to include the desire for glory into his set of good motivations for a contribution to public good.

3. Moral Psychology as a Part of Philosophy of Mind

One may ask how many among these first experiments with moral problems will become a meaningful part of Leibniz's later collection of ideas. The view of minds as mirrors of the universe will be included in Leibniz's metaphysics but the metaphors concerning reflection and refraction of the harmony from one mind to another one will soon disappear. In this case, it can be suspected that such metaphors were an effect of the young Leibniz's wish to find an analogy between the physical phenomena described in his *Hypothesis*

---

[42] A IV i 248. See also A VI i 464: "...cum omnis mens habeat speculi instar, alterum erit in mente nostra, alterum in aliena, et si plura sint specula, id est plures mentes bonorum nostrorum agnitrices, major lux erit, miscentibus speculis non tantum in oculo lucem, sed et inter se, splendor collectus gloriam facit."
[43] Hobbes, *English Works*, II 5. The corresponding passage in the Latin edition is Hobbes, *Opera philosophica* (1839) II 160.

Physica Nova and the kingdom of minds.[44]   Even the connected idea concerning   the possibility of an "indissoluble political body" disappears quickly and has to be seen as a momentaneous effect of the reading of utopians such as Campanella.[45] Leibniz's idea of love, such as his political ideal of the "best of all Commonwealths", are so clearly dependent on a model of purely spontaneous personal relations that they may hardly have a direct application to political or social phenomena.   In these last contexts, Leibniz's usual approach is more empirical.

Even Leibniz's moral psychology was to be modified.   The continuity with the classical disputes on the pleasure of the soul and on the experience of beauty will become less intensive. Pleasure will soon be analysed as a "confused perception", even if always caused by some increase in our perfection.   Nevertheless, the basic elements of Leibniz's later analysis on affections and reason and on deliberation and choice can already be found in the ideas of the years 1669-72.

To Leibniz, the inputs of our deliberations are not merely sensual appetites, but the effects of some logical – though confused and complex – form of mental activity, such as the comparison between sense-data.   On the other hand, if appetites always presuppose perceptual states (a *sensus harmoniae*), deliberation can be seen as a kind of quasi-mechanical composition between all the appetitive endeavours or *conatus* , even if Leibniz ensures that the laws of this composition are different from the truly mechanical ones.[46] Therefore, deliberation is not only a mental operation (an inquiry or a calculus) but even a step in the process of production of the final *conatus agendi* or will.

---

[44]   See A VI i 480: "... efficit tamen DEUS addito aethere seu spiritu universali, ut omnia in corporibus, ut in mentibus evenirent".

[45]   Letter to Lambert van Velthuysen, June 1671: "Utinam delineasset Hobbius eam Reipublicae formam, quam alicubi ait ita mente designari posse, ut nequeat illa a causa interna dissolvi. Hoc qui ostenderit, ei plurimum debebit humanum genus. Egregia in hoc genere dixere Cardanus et Campanella et Octavius Pisani." (Hein, *op. cit.*, pp. 160-1). On these nearly utopian sides of Leibniz's thought, see W. Schneiders, 'Sozietätpläne und Sozialutopie bei Leibniz', *SL* 7 (1975): 58-80.

[46]   See A VI i 479-80.

Thus: (i) our intentional deliberations are only the emerging side of an enormously complicated set of mental processes. But (ii) these processes are homologous to the intentional uses of reason and can be enlightened and corrected through the latter. The discovery of new harmony or dissonance through the rational analysis of a problem can modify our feelings or desires. Therefore, the "use of reason" is the source of freedom, since it allows us to take control of our goals. But this does not mean that we are able to change deliberately our desires and wishes, since will is not under the control of the will itself.[47] That is to say, it is not through single deliberations, but through an increasing power of reason over the deliberative processes, that we become wiser.

It is easy to see that these assumptions are an important premise of Leibniz's later analysis of affections and of perceptions and appetites, such as of his doctrine of freedom, which is already expounded in the *Confessio Philosophi*. But let us come back to their functions in the economy of Leibniz's answer to Carneades.

In his more mature writings, Leibniz will once again face Carneades' objection. His solution will be that Carneades does not see that justice is the "charity of the wise". Here, 'wisdom' means "science of happiness", i.e. the science which allows us to find the best combination of goods for an individual or for more persons. Therefore, if a man can be both charitable and wise, justice is possible and Carneades is wrong since a wise man cannot be a fool.[48]

---

[47] See A VI iii 133: "Sufficit ad tuendum liberi arbitrii privilegium...quae autem bona habenda sint, amplissimo dato rationis usu, indagare possimus." A VI iii 135: "Libertas ergo a rationis usus est...". And, on the other side, A VI iii 137: "...neminem se volentem facere malum, alioquin esset malus antequam fieret; Neminem esse causam voluntariam voluntatis suam...".

[48] See *De Justitia et Amore Voluntateque Dei* (1681-89), VE 1382: "Hinc statim occurritur Carneadi, qui Justitiam dicebat summam esse stultitiam, quod per eam homines alienis commodis cum damno proprio velificarentur. Quae objectio ex ignorata justitiae definitione nata est. *Caritas* enim sapientis stulta esse non potest. Hoc ergo supererat, ut ostenderet Carneades impossibilem esse Definitionem nostram, id est caritatem cum ratione consistere non posse. Sed posse ex ipsis Caritatis et Sapientiae notionibus manifestum est. *Sapientia* enim est Scientia felicitatis, jam saepe in futurum utile, et in summa suadendum est, *felicitatem* hoc est

But in which form are these compatible qualities – wisdom and love – connected? On this point, Leibniz's affirmations are not quite clear. Sometimes, he seems to see wisdom as a kind of control of reason over love. Therefore, there could be an irrational love too. Sometimes, Leibniz denies that morally righteous men must be properly wise and define them as "*similar* to wise men".[49] Therefore, there could apparently be virtuous love which is not directly produced by wisdom.

In fact, the difficulties are produced by the fact that Leibniz sometimes uses 'love' in the sense of affection or appetite, and sometimes uses love in the sense of benevolence towards others. In any case, however, it is clear that Leibniz does not need that every morally righteous act to be actually *caused* through wise intentional calculations. Such a condition applies only to God. In the case of men, the explicitly rational inferences and decisions are always only a part of the set of requisites for our actions. Nevertheless, Leibniz is not grounding altruism on some kind of sympathetic (or rather narcissistic, if we look at his early theories on praise and glory) disposition included in human nature as such. His fundamental idea is that an altruistic attitude can be rationally justified starting from the facts that: (i) minds are cognitive systems whose primary goal is to avoid persistent discrepancies in the frame of their experience of the world; (ii) minds perceive in some form the perceptions of the other minds and are able to formulate expectations on their expectations. Starting from these suppositions, altruism is clearly a well-grounded strategy, even if it depends on single situations how far it is practicable. It has to be remarked that Leibniz's assumptions are more refined (but even more complex) than the usual commonplaces

---

laetitia durabilem quaerenti (cuius magna pars recte factorum conscientia est) alienis commodis etiam cum sua praesenti jactura favere, neque aliud a Viro justo nos desideramus, quam quod ipsimet maxime utile ostendemus. Itaque desiderium Socratis implebimus, qui honestatem et utilitatem male dissociata reconjungi optabat, illique male precabantur, qui primus disjunxisset."

[49] See Gr 608; Gr 614; and *De Cogitationum Analysi*, 1678-82; VE 964-70. Here, *justus* is defined as *similis sapienti* or as *sapientiformis*.

concerning the social attitude of men, to which Leibniz is clearly trying to give a reason through his moral psychology.

Of course, a complete rational justification of our moral dispositions requires another condition too, namely that the *whole* universe be no more than a commonwealth of monads, each of which is a mirror of the others. Without such an assumption, it would be hard to explain why *universal* beneficence is the highest form of moral activity. But, starting from this assumption, universal beneficence has to be seen as an attempt to calculate and achieve the most perfect state of the world among those imminently possible. And, of course, such a state is exactly that one which will happen. Therefore, it seems that our motivations are never completely rational, since we usually desire to do something different than contribute to what is happening. But, on the other side, from the point of view of God, it is rational that we are not completely rational and that a moral aim and a calculation of the most probable future state of the world are not identical. To sum up, Leibniz's later answer to Carneades was not in fact (nor did he wish it be) a complete change, compared with the time in which he affirmed that only God can let ethics be rational.

LEIBNIZ AND MILLENARIANISM*

1. The Millenarian Coda of the *Justa dissertatio*, 1671-2

Whether Leibniz would have been pleased by intensive scholarly scrutiny of his *juvenilia* is open to question. The pride inspired in youthful authors by their first publications is often purchased at a considerable price in later embarrassment. Even a prodigy such as Leibniz was not altogether immune to this effect: if the reprinting of perhaps his finest early publication caused him discomfort,[1] one can only imagine his reaction to the posthumous publication of his entire archive of private papers.

A case in point is the *Justa dissertatio* of 1671-2. Its secret political purpose is now well known. In a bid to shield the extensive Rhineland possessions of the Archbishop of Mainz against attack from France, Leibniz and his current patron, the elector's minister, Johann Christian von Boineberg, planned to persuade Louis XIV to divert his destructive energies outside Christendom in a crusade against its traditional arch-enemy, the Ottoman Empire. The military strategy outlined in the great bulk of the work is impressive, and comparisons of it with Napoleon's invasion of Egypt a century later are perhaps appealing for those who know little of Leibniz or of history. But its political wisdom is doubtful: a less flattering comparison is with the long, bloody, and fruitless history of crusading in the middle ages; Napoleon's Egyptian adventure did not prevent him from returning to lead far more extensive campaigns within Europe than Louis XIV ever dreamt of; and the mature Leibniz was neither a cold-blooded military

---

* It is a pleasure to acknowledge the support of the Herzog August Bibliothek, Wolfenbüttel, during a research fellowship at which most of the research for this paper was undertaken.
[1] E. J. Aiton, *Leibniz: A Biography* (Bristol and Boston: Hilger, 1985), p. 17, on the *Dissertatio de arte combinatoria*.

S. Brown (ed.): The Young Leibniz and his Philosophy (1646-76). 169–98
© 1999 Kluwer Academic Publishers. Printed in the Netherlands.

strategist nor a hot-blooded religious crusader but a mild-mannered political and ecclesiastical irenicist.[2]

The *Justa dissertatio* only begins to make political and philosophical as well as military sense if read in the light of its remarkable conclusion; but this conclusion raises problems of its own which are, if anything, even more acute. In the final pages of the work, its scope suddenly broadens to glimpse a still grander prospect, and its style correspondingly rises to alarming rhetorical heights. The military plan outlined in detail is only the initial French component of an all-embracing campaign which will reconcile France with its enemies, lead them on to still greater conquests outside Europe, and inaugurate a period of such felicity that the violence with which it was established will be forgotten. The Kaisar, the King of Poland, the Czar of Russia will also take part. All the peoples of Europe (Dutch and Jews excepted) will put aside their internecine conflicts and join together in this final great crusade. Egypt will be only the first step in a far grander campaign: at its conclusion the eastern Mediterranean will no longer form the limits of Christ's kingdom, as it had under the Roman empire; for this crusade will continue until the ancient land of China, the outermost nation of Japan, the unknown shores of Australia, and the very limits of the human race have been brought into the Christian fold. No words will suffice to describe the praise, glory, wisdom, virtue, piety and justice which will shine forth from this great adventure.

> Happy age, and worthy of the envy of all ages; happy us if we should happen to live in these times: .... The golden age of Christianity will return and we will move into the primitive Church. And we will begin the most true millennium, without all the folly of the Fifth-Monarchists. And now we will at last consider how to increase human power with machines, how to subjugate the nature of things, and how to improve at last a more effective medicine .... The rising sun of justice dissipates the clouds of uncertainty and reveals all the tricks of the pettifogging profession. Perfection in moral affairs and a

---

[2] Cf. the conclusions of the chief study of this work to date: P. Ritter, *Leibniz' ägyptischer Plan* (Darmstadt: Reichl, 1930).

certain image of heavenly life and of the desire of philosophers is transferred into human life. We express the precepts of Christ not only in name, and faith restored to its native beauty shows itself living in charity spread throughout all things.[3]

In this passage questions of political prudence are compounded by those of theological orthodoxy. That the philosophy of the young Leibniz cannot be fully understood without reference to his theology is clear from a number of other contributions to this volume. But in this text Leibniz is not dealing with a problem (such as that of evil) shared by all monotheistic religions, a mystery (such as that of the Trinity) common to all orthodox Christian churches, or a dogma (such as that of transubstantiation) crucial to resolving the differences between the two main confessions of Leibniz's Germany; he is intimating a doctrine formally condemned by all three main branches of Protestantism in the sixteenth century and marginalized within the Catholic tradition since Augustine.[4] This remarkable passage expresses many of the most passionate aspirations of seventeenth-century millenarians: the conversion of all the peoples of the earth to Christianity, the spread of Christ's kingdom throughout the whole world, the restoration of a golden age of apostolic piety, the instauration of man's dominion over nature, the radical improvement of the art of medicine and of human health as a result, the perfection of law, justice, politics, civil life, morals, and above all of faith and charity. More remarkably still, the fulfilment of these aspirations is explicitly identified as the advent of millennium: "verissimum inchoabimus ... chiliasmum." The one qualification introduced – "sine omnia Qvinta-Monarchistarum stultitia" – is limited. The Fifth Monarchists were one of the most radical and notorious millenarian groups of the English Interregnum, who looked forward to a literal Second Coming of Christ and a literal resurrection of the saints before

---

[3] *Justa dissertatio* (1671-2, A IV i 347-82, here 379-80).
[4] *Die Bekenntnisschriften der evangelisch-lutherischen Kirche*, ed. H. Lietzmann *et al.* (4th ed., Göttingen: Vandenhoeck & Ruprecht, 1959): Die Augsburgische Konfession, article xvii, p. 72. *Die Bekenntnisschriften der reformierten Kirche*, ed. E. F. K. Müller (Leipzig: Deichert, 1903): Forty-Two Articles, article lxi, p. 521.30-35; *Confessio helvetica posterior*, article xi, p. 185.3-7.

the millennium, and a literal kingdom of Christ or the saints on earth during the millennium.[5] Their 'folly' thus seems to refer firstly to the only form of 'simple' or passivist chiliasm which Leibniz explicitly identified elsewhere as erroneous: the expectation of a literal thousand-year kingdom of Jesus Christ on earth;[6] and secondly to the literal resurrection of the saints, which likewise plays no part in the scenario described in the *Justa dissertatio*. Such qualifications do not prevent this text from being designated millenarian. Rather, the first qualification would be shared by the most common millenarian position in Leibniz's day: the position commonly called 'post-millennial',[7] which awaits the Second Coming of Christ after the millennium rather than before it; and the second would be shared by a large number of late seventeenth-century post-millennialists who interpreted the first resurrection in spiritual terms and saw the onset of the millennium as a gradual process in which secondary causation rather than God's immediate intervention played the dominant role.

That the last main work before Leibniz's travels to Paris closes with a vision that can only be described as millenarian is therefore beyond dispute. Leibniz is not, of course, the first major intellectual of the early modern period to dabble in millenarianism. There is now no doubt that the doctrine played an important part in the thought of important English contemporaries such as Henry More,[8] Thomas Burnett,[9] Isaac Newton,[10] and William Whiston,[11] continental contacts

---

[5] B. S. Capp, *The Fifth Monarchy Men* (London: Faber & Faber, 1972); *idem*, 'Radical Chiliasm in the English Revolution', *Pietismus und Neuzeit* 14 (1988): 125-33, esp. p. 131; and Tai Liu, *Discord in Zion: The Puritan Divines and the Puritan Revolution, 1640-1660* (The Hague: Nijhoff, 1973), esp. chs 3-4.

[6] Leibniz, *Mars christianissimus* (1683; A IV ii 480; cf. 457 and R 128); Leibniz to Sophie, Duchess of Hanover, 23 Oct. 1691 (A I vii 36-7).

[7] See for instance B. W. Ball, *A Great Expectation: Eschatological Thought in English Protestantism to 1660* (Leiden: Brill, 1975), pp. 169-70; J. W. Davidson, *The Logic of Millennial Thought: Eighteenth-Century New England* (New Haven and London: Yale University Press, 1977), pp. 260-80.

[8] P. C. Almond, 'Henry More and the Apocalypse', *Journal of the History of Ideas* 54 (1993): 189-200; S. Hutton, 'Henry More and the Apocalypse', in Michael Wilks (ed.), *Prophecy and Eschatology* [Studies in Church History, Subsidia 10] (Oxford: Blackwell, 1994), pp. 131-40.

[9] E. L. Tuveson, *Millennium and Utopia: A Study in the Background of the Idea of Progress* (1949; New York: Harper & Row, 1964), ch. 3; M.C. Jacob and W.A.

such as Philipp Jakob Spener[12] and Franciscus Mercurius van Helmont,[13] and pansophical precursors such a Johann Heinrich Alsted[14] and Jan Amos Comenius.[15] It is also clear that Leibniz was

---

Lockwood, 'Political Millenarianism and Burnet's *Sacred Theory*,' *Science Studies*, 2 (1972): 265-79.

[10] F. E. Manuel, *The Religion of Isaac Newton* (Oxford: Oxford University Press, 1974), ch. 4; *idem, A Portrait of Isaac Newton* (Cambridge, MA: Harvard University Press 1980), pp. 361-80; J.E. Force and R.H. Popkin (eds.), *Essays in the Context, Nature and Influence of Isaac Newton's Theology* (Dordrecht: Kluwer, 1990); *eidem* (eds.), *The Books of Nature and Scripture* (Dordrecht: Kluwer, 1994). Cf. M. C. Jacob, *The Newtonians and the English Revolution 1689-1720* (Ithaca, NY: Cornell University Press 1976), pp. 100-42.

[11] On Whiston's millenarianism, see E. Duffy, '"Whiston Affair": The Trials of a Primitive Christian', *Journal of Ecclesiastical History* 27 (1976): 129-50; J. E. Force, *William Whiston: Honest Newtonian* (Cambridge: Cambridge University Press, 1985), and G. S. Rousseau, '"Wicked Whiston" and the Scriblerians: Another Ancients-Modern Controversy', *Studies in Eighteenth-Century Culture* 17 (1987): 17-44. Leibniz was informed of Whiston's main millenarian treatise the year it was published: cf. J. F. Feller (ed.), *Otium Hanoveranum ...* (Leipzig, 1718), p. 31; and G III 313.

[12] On Spener's millenarianism, see for instance Johannes Wallmann, *Philipp Jakob Spener und die Anfänge des Pietismus* (1970; 2nd rev. ed. Tübingen: J. C. B. Mohr / Paul Siebeck, 1986), esp. pp. 324-54; and D. Blaufuss, 'Zu Ph.J. Speners Chiliasmus und seinen Kritikern', *Pietismus & Neuzeit* 14 (1988): 85-108. Leibniz's references to it include A I vii 75, 103, 319, 323, 695-6; A I viii 616.

[13] Van Helmont's most obviously millenarian work is *Seder Olam, sive ordo seculorum. Historica enarratio doctrinae* (n. pl. 1693). Leibniz's two critiques of it are published in A. Foucher de Careil, *Leibniz: La Philosophie Juive et la Cabale* (Paris: Durand, 1861), 'Remarques inédits de Leibniz sur le Seder Olam', pp. 47-54. Other references to the author's millenarianism include G. H. Pertz (ed.), *Leibnizens gesammelte Werke aus den Handscriften der Königlichen Bibliothek zu Hannover* (Hannover: Im Verlage der Hanschen Hof-Buchhandlung, 1843-7), IV, 191, 193, 198; Leibniz to Lorenz Hertel, 8/18 Jan. 1695 (A I xi 22-3); Allison Coudert, *Leibniz and the Kabbalah* (Dordrecht, Boston and London: Kluwer Academic, 1995), pp. 58-63.

[14] On Alsted's millenarianism, see R. G. Clouse, 'Johann Heinrich Alsted and English Millenarianism', *Harvard Theological Review* 62 (1969): 189-207; *idem,* 'The Rebirth of Millenarianism', in *Puritans, the Millennium and the Future of Israel,* ed. P. Toon, (Cambridge and London: Clarke, 1970), pp. 42-56; W. Schmidt-Biggemann, 'Apokalyptische Universalwissenschaft: Johann Heinrich Alsteds *Diatribe de mille annis apocalypticis*', in *Pietismus & Neuzeit* 14 (1988): 51-71; Howard Hotson, 'Johann Heinrich Alsted: Encyclopaedism, Millenarianism and the

both aware of his millenarian predecessors and contemporaries and thoroughly acquainted with the doctrine itself: in fact he devoted such a huge number of passages scattered throughout his works to millenarianism and related issues that only a small fraction of them can be discussed here.[16]   What *is* open to question is whether this passage represents Leibniz's own vision of the future or merely a piece of political propaganda.   Such a question is not very amenable to direct assault.   As befits the study of a strategic document, we therefore take a more circuitous line of attack, beginning with a work written just after Leibniz's return from Paris in 1677 and returning via a consideration of other passages from the more elderly Leibniz for a second look at this early work.   An obvious beachhead for launching this campaign is offered by what is perhaps the longest sustained piece of scriptural exegesis in Leibniz's sprawling *Nachlaß* and evidently

---

Second Reformation in Germany' (unpublished D. Phil. dissertation, Oxford, 1991), ch. 7.   Leibniz's awareness of Alsted's millenarianism is demonstrated by the underlining and marginalia in his copy of Alsted's *Diatribe de mille annis apocalypticis* (Herborn, 1627): Niedersächsische Landesbibliothek shelf-mark T-A 150.

[15] On Comenius's millenarianism, see most recently Radim Palous, 'Comenius the Chiliast', *Czechoslovak and Central European Journal* 10 (1991): 1-12; J. M. Lochman, 'Comenius as Theologian', *Acta Comeniana* 10 (1993): 35-47; and M. E. H. N. Mout, 'Chiliastic Prophecy and Revolt in the Habsburg Monarchy during the Seventeenth Century', in *Prophecy and Eschatology*, ed. Wilks, pp. 93-109.   For Leibniz's knowledge of Comenius' millenarianism from 1671 onwards, cf. A I i 174; A II i 201; A IV i 373.

[16] A more complete discussion will be found in *Alsted and Leibniz on God, the Magistrate and the Millennium*, edited with introductions and commentary by Maria Rosa Antognazza and Howard Hotson [Wolfenbütteler Arbeiten zur Barockforschung] (Wiesbaden: Harrassowitz, 1999), pp. 127-215.   The present paper is a much abridged version of one of the main lines of argument of that section.

his only attempt to explicate an entire book of the Bible:[17] the little known *Summaria Apocalypseos explicatio* of 1677.[18]

2. The Irenical Praeterism of the
Summaria Apocalypseos Explicatio, 1677

In 1676 Leibniz returned from Paris, his political mission a complete failure. He had probably been unable to present his plan to Louis XIV and had certainly failed to convince him to channel his bellicose energies elsewhere. The French king had attacked Holland within days of Leibniz's arrival in Paris, had then seized Franche-Comté, devastated the Palatinate, and initiated a pattern of French invasion, subjugation and annexation of a broad swath of territory from the English Channel to Switzerland which would continue, with great loss of life and destruction of property, on and off for the rest of the century. The *Explicatio* dates from the following year. Its opening words suggest that it records Leibniz recent reconsideration of the Apocalypse.[19] And for our purposes it is all the more interesting because it seems to be advancing a position diametrically opposed to the conclusion of the *Justa dissertatio.*

The evident purpose of *Summaria Apocalypseos explicatio* is to undermine two aspects of the Protestant apocalyptic tradition which obstructed two of Leibniz's chief aspirations. The identification of the apocalyptic figure of the Antichrist with the Roman papacy aggravated the difficulties of ecclesiastical reunification; and the application of apocalyptic prophecy to contemporary political events heightened the turmoil and anguish of contemporary Europe. Recent historical research has revealed that the identification of the papacy as the Antichrist was one of the most devastating weapons of popular

---

[17] As suggested in D. J. Cook, 'Leibniz and Millenarianism', in *Leibniz und Europa* I (1994): 135-42; here p. 139. Cf. *idem,* 'Leibniz: Biblical Historian and Exegete', in I. Marchlewitz and A. Heinekamp (eds.), *Leibniz' Auseinandersetzung mit Vorgängern und Zeitgenossen* (Stuttgart: Franz Steiner, 1990), pp. 267-76; here p. 275.

[18] First published in *Oeuvres de Leibniz* par A. Foucher de Careil (7 vols., Paris: Firmin-Didot frères, fils et cie, 1859-75), II, 497-506; reprinted in VE 2065-73.

[19] *Summaria Apocalypseos explicatio* (VE 2065): "Nuper in Apocalypsin meditatus, ...".

propaganda and religious polemic and one of the firmest supports of confessional identity in the post-Reformation period.[20] The seriousness with which it was taken by Protestant theologians is illustrated by its presence in a wide range of Protestant confessional documents, including Melanchthon's apology for the Augsburg Confession, Luther's Schmalkald Articles, and the confessions of the Bohemian, French, English, Scottish and Irish (Protestant) churches.[21] The offence which this accusation offered to contemporary Catholics is indicated by the regularity with which it recurs in Leibniz's correspondence with Catholic ecumenicists.[22] When, after eight years of regular ecumenical correspondence with Leibniz, the Catholic convert, Landgraf Ernst von Hessen-Rheinfels, summarised the obstacles to ecclesiastical reunification, he selected as the greatest of

---

[20] A good introduction is G. Seebass, 'Antichrist IV: Reformations- und Neuzeit', *Theologische Realenzyklopädie*, III (Berlin: Gruyter, 1978): 28-43. For Germany, see also H. Preuss, *Die Vorstellungen vom Antichrist im späteren Mittelalter, bei Luther und in der konfessionellen Polemik* (Leipzig: J. L. Hinrichs, 1906); R. W. Scribner, *For the Sake of Simple Folk: Popular Propaganda for the German Reformation* (Cambridge: Cambridge University Press, 1981), pp. 148-89; H.-J. Schönstädt, 'Das Reformationsjubiläum 1717. Beiträge zur Geschichte seiner Entstehung um Spiegel landesherrlicher Verordnungen', *Zeitschrift für Kirchengeschichte* 93 (1982): 58-118. For the English case, see C. Hill, *Antichrist in Seventeenth-Century England* (London: Oxford University Press, 1971), which however underestimates the perseverance of the tradition into the latter seventeenth century, and D. Brady, *The Contribution of British Writers between 1560 and 1830 to the Interpretation of Revelation 13.16-18 (The Number of the Beast)* (Tübingen: J. C. B. Mohr/Paul Siebeck, 1983). An important phase in the Dutch tradition is examined in E. G. E. van der Wall, '"Antichrist stormed": the Glorious Revolution and the Dutch Prophetic Tradition', in *The World of William and Mary*, ed. D. Hoak and M. Feingold (Stanford: Stanford University Press, 1996), pp. 152-64.

[21] *Die Bekenntnisschriften der evangelisch-lutherischen Kirche*, pp. 234, 239-40, 246, 300, 364, 424, 430; cf. pp. 484-9, 488-9. *Die Bekenntnisschriften der reformierten Kirche*, ed. Müller, pp. 263.38-264.38, 536.31, 599.11; cf. pp. 32.16, 290.15, 666.7. [Jean] Aymon, *Tous les synodes nationaux des eglises reformées de France* (2 vols., The Hague, 1710), I, pp. 258-9.

[22] It features, for instance, in Leibniz's correspondence with Ernst von Hessen-Rheinfels (A I iv 358, 405-6, 425; A I vii 184-5, 203, 222, 232; and the following note), Paul Pellisson-Fontanier (A I vi 118, 147), Christoph de Rojas y Spinola (A I x 157), and Marie de Brinon (Gr 209; A I xi 381-2, 439).

"une infinité des choses et articles" the Protestant assertions that the Mass is an idolatry and that the pope is the Antichrist.[23]

Moreover, the concept of a papal Antichrist had been embedded at the heart of the standard Protestant reading of the Apocalypse. The details of this exegesis varied considerably, but the core of it was accepted virtually without question.[24] The city of Babylon against which the prophet inveighed was Rome – not pagan but papal Rome. The Whore of Babylon, seated upon the beast with seven heads, was the papal church, seated upon the seven hills of Rome. The fall of Babylon was the destruction of that church which had begun with Wycliff and Hus, was carried forward by Luther, Calvin and a host of others, and would climax with the complete destruction of the Antichrist at the Second Coming. As Leibniz explained to Ernst von Hessen-Rheinfels, 'One of the principal reasons why I believe that Mons. Spener as well as certain other well-meaning persons of his kind have such loathing for the primacy of the Pope is that they are prejudiced by the explications of the Apocalypse received by their party, which appear very plausible.'[25]

The Protestant identification of the papacy as the Antichrist, however, was merely a special case of a more general problem. This general problem is most clearly identified in a brief fragment, the *Sonderbare Erklärung der Offenbahrung*, which seems to be a first German note for what would become the *Summaria Apocalypseos explicatio*. In this note, Leibniz seems to be looking back over the previous century and a half: the era of religious bloodshed and revolt in France and the Low Countries, decades of murderous conflict in

---

[23] 8/18 Jan. 1692 (A I vii 252); repeated in more detail A I viii 169, 190-91. Cf. Leibniz's response A I vii 257.

[24] The leading surveys of the English wing of this tradition are Ball, *A Great Expectation*; R. Bauckham, *Tudor Apocalypse: Sixteenth Century Apocalypticism, Millenarianism and the English Reformation* (Oxford: Sutton Courtenay, 1978); P. Christianson, *Reformers and Babylon: English Apocalyptic Visions from the Reformation to the Eve of the Civil War* (Toronto: University of Toronto Press, 1978); and K. R. Firth, *The Apocalyptic Tradition in Reformation Britain* (Oxford: Oxford University Press, 1979). A start in surveying central European expectations has been made in R. B. Barnes, *Prophecy and Gnosis: Apocalypticism in the Wake of the Lutheran Reformation* (Stanford: Stanford University Press, 1988).

[25] [First half of March, 1684] (A I iv 324-5).

central Europe, and civil wars and regicide in Britain. Many god-fearing, well-meaning people, he wrote, have been led into all manner of violence, disruption and rebellion by highly dubious interpretations of the Apocalypse. Others, acting under the pretence of divine commands, have dared to dictate policy to kings and princes and, when their demands were refused, to excite the common people against established authority.[26] Later, Leibniz would make similar remarks with more specific reference to millenarians, who believed themselves to be ordained by God for the realisation of his kingdom on earth, and who spread mayhem in attempting to fulfil that calling.[27] The common basis of all this turbulence was the belief, fundamental to the entire Protestant apocalyptic tradition, that the prophecies of the Apocalypse were neither fulfilled in the past, nor promised for the distant future, but were being fulfilled in the era in which they lived.

In short, one root of the ecclesiastical division and political disruption so prominent in the post-Reformation era was to be found in the application of the prophecies of the Apocalypse to the recent past, the present, and the near future. Both of these problems, it followed, could be rendered more tractable if such contemporary applications could be prevented. In order to do so, Leibniz adapted the interpretation of the Apocalypse known as 'praeterism'. The praeterist interpretation maintains that most or all of the prophecies contained in the Apocalypse describe events which take place, not in the future, nor in the present, but in the past: in the era immediately

---

[26] Leibniz, *Sonderbare Erklärung der Offenbarung* (VE 2064): "Weil ich sehe daß viel gottesfürchtige und wohmeinende Leute sich durch falsche oder doch sehr ungewiße erclärungen der *offenbahrung* Johannis verführen laßen, so gar daß auch empöhrungen, meutereyen und allerhand weit aussehende anschläge, daher entstanden; auch einige unterm schein göttlichen befehls sich erkühnet Königen und Fürsten vorzuschreiben was sie thun solten, und auf den weigerungsfall oder sonst die gemeine gegen sie zu erregen. So will ich eine sonderbare erclärung der *offenbahrung* alhier mit wenigen beybringen, welche diesen gefahrlichen gedancken auf einmahl alle gelegenheit abschneidet. Nicht daß ich diese erclärung vor die gewißeste und beste halte; sondern damit man sehe wie so gar leicht sey, wenn man belesen, und hurtige einfalle hat, etwas artliches aus dem text und historien zusammen zu reimen." The final, extraordinary statement is discussed in section III below.

[27] Cf. for instance Leibniz's letters to Hermann von der Hardt, 10 (?) July) 1691 (A I vi 548) and to Daniel Larroque, 12 July 1691 (A I vi 588).

after the book was written, that is, in the first few centuries of the Christian era. The advantage of this strategy for Catholics was particularly obvious: if none of the prophecies in the Apocalypse could be applied to the present era, then none of them could be applied to the pope. From the later sixteenth century onwards, therefore, a series of eminent Catholic exegetes had developed this alternative interpretation, culminating in the massive work of the Spanish Jesuit, Luis de Alcázar.[28] In the generation before Leibniz, praeterism had also been applied to ecumenical purposes by the great Dutch jurist, Hugo Grotius.[29] In 1640, Grotius published a short work which applied all the New Testament passages concerning the Antichrist to such early opponents of the church as the magicians Simon Magus and Appolonius of Tyana, the false Messiah Bar Cochba, and the emperor Domitian.[30] Ten years later, he completed a series of annotations on all the books of the New Testament with a praeterist interpretation of the Apocalypse heavily indebted to de Alcázar.[31] Grotius's work, in turn, provided the basis of Leibniz's *Summaria Apocalypseos explicatio*. In eight pages of text, Leibniz mentions the great jurist thirteen times, and his interpretation follows Grotius in applying

---

[28] Luis de Alcázar, *Vestigatio arcani sensus in Apocalypsi* (Seville, 1604; Antwerp, 1614, 1619). F. Contreras, 'Vestigatio arcani sensus in Apocalypsi (1614). Presentación, estudio y comentarios', *Archivo Teológico Granadino* 52 (1989): 51-168. In general see I. T. Beckwith, *The Apocalypse of John: Studies in Introduction* (New York, 1919; Grand Rapids: Baker, 1967), pp. 330-33; R. H. Charles, *Studies in the Apocalypse* (Edinburgh: T & T Clark, 1913), pp. 36-42.

[29] On Grotius' irenicism, see Dieter Wolf, *Die Irenik des Hugo Grotius nach ihren Prinzipien und biographisch-geistesgeschichtlichen Perspektiven* (Marburg, 1969; Hildesheim, 1972); G. H. M. Posthumus Meyjes, 'Hugo Grotius as Irenicist', in *The World of Hugo Grotius (1583-1645). Proceedings of the International Colloquium Organized by the Grotius Committee of the Royal Netherlands Academy of Arts and Sciences, Rotterdam 6-9 April 1983* (Rotterdam: Holland University Press, 1984), pp. 43-64.

[30] Grotius, *Commentario ad loca quaedam N. Testamenti de Antichristo* (Amsterdam 1640); reprinted in his *Annotationes in libros Evangelicorum* (Amsterdam, 1641), I, pp. 1032-42.

[31] Grotius, *Annotationum in Novum Testamentum pars tertia ac ultima* (Paris, 1650), on the Apocalypse, pp. 125-286. On Grotius's debt to de Alcázar, see Wilhelm Bousset, *Die Offenbarung Johannis* (1859, 6th rev. ed. 1906, facsimile ed. Göttingen, 1966), p. 98.

successive visions to a chronological survey of Christian history from apostolic times to the conversion of the empire under Constantine in the fourth century. The seals and trumpets of the middle chapters of the Apocalypse are interpreted as various persecutions by and punishments of ancient enemies of the early Christians. The seven-headed beast of chapter 13 is pagan Rome. The number of the beast, 666, deciphered by Grotius as OULPIOS, is referred to the emperor Ulpianus Trajan. The vials of chapter 16 pertain to the growing menace of barbarians on the frontiers, which result in the destruction of Rome described in chapters 17-18. The wife preparing for the marriage of the lamb in chapter 19 is the Christian church on the eve of the conversion of the empire under Constantine.

Yet Leibniz also departs from Grotius's precedent at key points. Grotius's idiosyncratic interpretation of the Antichrist had aroused an enormous flood of hostile comment from Protestant circles without gaining favour in Catholic ones (or, for that matter, among modern biblical critics);[32] and Leibniz too rejected it.[33] More important for our purposes was his rejection of Grotius's interpretation of the millennium of Revelation chapter 20.[34] For Grotius, the millennium stretched from Constantine around 300 A. D. to the foundation of the Ottoman empire in 1300. This identified the War of Gog and Magog of Revelation 20:7-9 – the climactic struggle between good and evil after the end of the millennium and before the Second Coming – the ongoing struggle between Christendom and the Turk. Such an interpretation might have served Leibniz's purposes ideally in 1671; but his aim after returning from Paris was to undercut precisely the kind of apocalyptic politics which he had previously advanced. He therefore closed the *Explicatio* with three brief arguments designed to

---

[32] Cf. Grotius, *Commentario ... de Antichristo* in his *Annotationes in libros Evan-geli-corum*, pp. 1032-60, with his *Annotationum in Novum Testamentum pars tertia ac ultima*, pp. 74-5, 200-8, 210-12, 215-22, 244-5. For the reception of these works, see the contributions by J. K. Cameron, J. van den Berg, and Ernestine van der Wall to H. J. M. Nellen and E. Rabbie (eds.), *Hugo Grotius, Theologian: Essays in Honour of G. H. M. Posthumus Meyjes* (Leiden: Brill, 1994), pp. 159-68, 169-84, 195-215. Leibniz alludes to these attacks at A I vi 549.17-18.

[33] *Summaria Apocalypseos explicatio*, VE 2068, 2069, 2070.28-71.12, 2071.27-72.14.

[34] Grotius, *Annotationum in Novum Testamentum pars tertia ac ultima*, pp. 264-8.

show that the thousand years between Constantine and the rise of the Ottoman empire could not possibly have been the millennium. Moslems had been at war with Christians for centuries before 1300; no martyrs had been resurrected to reign with Christ in 300 A. D.; and the 'brief' interval between the end of this supposed millennium and the Second Coming was already almost four hundred years long. Rather than provide some alternative interpretation of the passage which could arouse further expectations of its own, Leibniz preferred the vague conclusion that the passage was an inscrutably obscure allegory, which alluded to ancient traditions now irredeemably lost.[35]

3. The Limits of Leibniz's Irenical Praeterism: the 'Mystical' Meaning of the Apocalypse, 1685-93

Leibniz's interest in emending Grotius' praeterist interpretation did not end here. For at least twenty years, he kept an eye out for refinements of the praeterist interpretation of the Apocalypse. He continued to make favourable mention of Grotius and his praeterist principles,[36] to rehearse certain aspects of his interpretation,[37] to pursue rumours of further scriptural annotations by Grotius,[38] and to note material for refining his arguments in commentators such as Bishop Jacques Benigne de Bossuet [39] and Thomas Smith.[40] But the

---

[35] *Summaria Apocalypseos explicatio* (VE 2073).

[36] E.g., A I iv 358, 405-6; A I vi 548; A I ix 228.

[37] The interpretation of 666 as the emperor Trajan became perhaps his favorite aspect of Grotius' exegesis (cf. VE 2069-70; A I iv 358; A I vi 549, 553-4; A I ix 228); but cf. the more purely mathematical solutions proposed in A I vi 549; *Commercii epistolici Leibnitiani typis nondum vulgati selecta specimina*, ed. J. G. H. Feder (Hanover: Sumptibus Fratrum Hahn, 1805), p. 245; and Leibniz's notes on Valentin Weigel, *Super Apocalypsin* (Frankfurt, 1619), pp. 6-7 (VE 2088).

[38] G III 303; A I ii 429, 437, 448, 481 concern a copy of Grotius' *Annotationes* supposedly corrected, altered and expanded in a great number of places by the author's own hand.

[39] Cf. Bossuet, *L'Apocalypse, avec une explication* (Paris, 1689), preface, pp. 61ff, 'Advertissement', cap. I, pp. 305-6; and A I vi 588; A I vii 184-5, 203, 222; A I ix 227-9.

[40] Smith's *Septem Asiae ecclesiarum et Constantinopoles notitia* (London, 1676; 2nd ed. Utrecht, 1694) provides a wealth of historical and topographical information

significance of this interest for the present lies not in the fine detail but in the general strategy. The application of apocalyptic prophecy to contemporary events had greatly exacerbated the turmoil, division, violence and spiritual anguish of the era preceding Leibniz and continued to do so at the end of the seventeenth century. A praeterist interpretation of the Apocalypse, based on Grotius but pursued more thoroughly, could help put an end to this turmoil.

A clear recognition of the pragmatic, political nature of Leibniz's critique of apocalyptic expectation marks a crucial turning point in our analysis, for it raises a number of important consequences, particularly with regard to assessing his views on millenarianism. As contemporary politicians too frequently remind us, political expediency and truth do not always coincide. The position best adapted to a particular set of political circumstances is not always the best position when viewed from a more detached intellectual perspective. The question thus arises: did pragmatism and theology neatly coincide for Leibniz? When interpreting the Apocalypse, did Leibniz's political needs, philological principles and theological preferences effortlessly reinforce one another? Was the interpretation of the Apocalypse best suited to calming the agitated political and ecclesiastical situation of his day also the most satisfactory in other respects?

A remarkably forthright answer to this question can be found in Leibniz's first extended statement on the Apocalypse, the *Sonderbare Erklärung der Offenbarung*. This brief text begins with Leibniz's most forceful presentation of the political rationale for defending praeterism, paraphrased above; but this is immediately followed by a remarkable qualification: "Not that I regard this interpretation as the most certain or the best; rather [my intention is that] by it one can see how very easy it is, if one is knowledgeable and ingenious, to stitch together something clever from the text and histories."[41] His attack on apocalyptic politics, as initially formulated, is therefore evidently an indirect one. He aims to demonstrate, not the best interpretation of

---

useful for a straightforward historical treatment of the first three chapters of the Apocalypse. Cf. A I xiv 709-10 (1697); VE 2066.8-9; *DNB*, XVIII. 539-41.

[41] Leibniz, *Sonderbare Erklärung der Offenbarung* (VE 2064.15-18; quoted above, note 26).

scripture, but merely how easy it is to be led into a less satisfactory interpretation by the clever and erudite weaving together of history and prophecy. His immediate purpose is not to reveal the true meaning of the Apocalypse but, on the contrary, to show how difficult that discovery is, and thereby to dampen the fires of eschatological expectation with a generous dose of scepticism.

Two things above all must be noted in this surprising qualification. One is Leibniz's remarkable candour in acknowledging that he does not necessarily regard the praeterist interpretation as "the most certain or the best". This has the effect of blunting the impact of his argument before it is even begun: for if even the author of this commentary does not regard his interpretation as the best, why should anyone else be sufficiently impressed by it to modify his own views? It is scarcely surprising that this candour does not recur in Leibniz's later remarks on the Apocalypse. Elsewhere in the *Sonderbare Erklärung* and again in the first lines of the *Summaria Apocalypseos explicatio*, he refashions his political gambit into a confidently articulated hermeneutic principle: "While studying the Apocalypse recently, I judged that this rule of interpretation ought to be established: *It is probable that all things [treated in the text] ought as far as possible to be understood of events contemporaneous with John.*"[42] This is the positive tone which regularly recurs in his correspondence: while the precise degree of probability which he ascribes to the praeterist reading varies from one passage to another,[43] we encounter no further indications that Leibniz considers it to be untrue or less certain or satisfactory than some other interpretation.

More important still is the revelation that in 1677 Leibniz does not seem to regard praeterism as "the most certain or the best" interpretation of the Apocalypse. This raises an obvious question: which interpretation *does* Leibniz regard as best? An answer of a

---

[42] *Summaria Apocalypseos explicatio* (VE 2065): "Nuper in *Apocalypsin* meditatus, hoc interpretationis fundamentum ponendum putavi: V e r i s i m i l e   e s t   o m n i a   q u o a d   e j u s   f i e r i   p o t e s t   d e   r e b u s   J o h a n n i   c o n t e m p o r a n e i s   i n t e l l i g i   d e b e r e." Cf. *Sonderbare Erklärung der Offenbarung* (VE 2064): "Ich seze demnach zum fundament das was man füglich von denen zeiten so Johanni am nächsten verstehen kan auff die dinge nicht zu ziehen so sehr weit davon entfernet."

[43] Cf. for instance the passages listed in 36 above.

general kind is not difficult to deduce: if the view that all apocalyptic prophecies have been fulfilled in the past is not the best one, then the best interpretation would seem to be that at least some of these prophecies must be fulfilled either in the present era or in the future. Surprisingly enough, this deduction is supported by at least four short passages from Leibniz's correspondence between 1685 and 1693.[44] These passages, to be sure, no longer describe this alternative interpretation as 'better' or 'more certain' than the praeterist one. Rather, they posit a second, equally genuine, 'mystical' level of meaning coexisting within the sacred text which is evidently quite different from the 'literal' praeterist one which we have discussed thus far. On the significance of the literal sense Leibniz was consistently outspoken: it applied, as Grotius had argued and Leibniz's irenical strategy demanded, to the last centuries of pagan Rome. On the precise meaning of the mystical sense he was much more evasive, and with good grounds; for the more he revealed of it, the more it began once again to undermine his pragmatic, political agenda.

In one of these four passages, Leibniz simply pleads ignorance as to its meaning: "As for the mystical sense, since it is less certain, I can say nothing solid about it here.'[45] But why, one might ask, does he introduce this mystical sense if he knows nothing about it?

In a second passage, he reveals slightly more of his conception of this mystical meaning: it refers "to the last time and is therefore as yet unknown to us."[46] Even this tiny concession begins to reveal the perils of this mystical meaning for Leibniz's pragmatic praeterism: for a great number of Protestants and not a few Catholics believed that they were living in precisely that 'last time', and therefore that the prophecies of Daniel and the Apocalypse applied particularly to them.[47]

This objection applies still more forcefully to the final two descriptions of this mystical sense. In a third passage, Leibniz

---

[44] A I iv 358, 405-6; A I vii 203; A I ix 228. Occasional glimpses of this qualification of a consistently praeterist position can be found in a letter to Daniel Larroque of 21 (31) July 1691 (A I vi 588.20-23). Cf. also the *Essais de Theodicée,* § 274 (G VI 280).

[45] Leibniz to Landgraf Ernst von Hessen-Rheinfels, 7 Dec. 1691 (A I vii 203).

[46] Leibniz to Landgraf Ernst von Hessen-Rheinfels, 14 Mar. 1685 (A I iv 358).

[47] Cf. for instance the literature cited in notes 5, 7-15, 20 and 24 above.

suggests that it applies, not merely to the first three or four centuries of the Christian era, as the literal sense does, but to "a longer period of time".[48] This seems to imply that the mystical meaning of the Apocalypse pertains also to the post-Constantinian phase of church history, possibly extending from there through the present and into the future. In the last of these four passages to be written, this idea is made explicit in Leibniz's suggestion that in the Apocalypse "the entire future state of the church is prefigured."[49] This is the most puzzling variant of all, for what is the purpose of expending such effort to rule out the application of the 'literal' sense of the Apocalypse to the present, when one merely introduces another 'mystical' sense which *does* apply to the present?

Taken together, therefore, Leibniz's consistent qualification of his praeterist interpretation of the Apocalypse raises two difficult questions. Leibniz invested considerable energy in outlining, refining and advocating the praeterist interpretation of the Apocalypse. He also clearly articulated a strong and consistent practical necessity for doing so. Why then does he repeatedly and fatally undermine it? What advantages, in other words, does the mystical sense offer to counterbalance the threat which it poses to the irenical function of the praeterist 'literal' meaning? These questions are by no means easy to answer. But one thing is clear from the outset. Leibniz had compelling practical reasons for advocating the praeterist interpretation of the Apocalypse. It stands to reason that there must be equally compelling reasons of some kind to lead him to undermine it so fully in this way. The difficulty consists in determining what those reasons were.

4. 'Mystical' Theology and Poetic Language: Leibniz and J. W. Petersen's *Uranias*, 1706-1715

No absolutely straightforward answer to these questions is provided, so far as I can divine, in the works by Leibniz published to date; but hundreds of allusions to apocalypticism, millenarianism, and millenarians scattered throughout his writings shed a multitude of

---

[48] Leibniz to Landgraf Ernst von Hessen-Rheinfels, 12 Aug 1686 (A I iv 405-6).
[49] Leibniz to Gerhard Meier, 10 Jan. 1693 (A I ix 228).

individual points of light on it. Here we can consider only one cluster of such passages which perhaps shed more light than any other. It pertains, not to the young Leibniz, but to the old Leibniz in the final decade of his life. Its central protagonist is Johann Wilhelm Petersen – the leading Pietist advocate, not only of millenarianism, but also of the still more radical and unorthodox eschatological notion of the ¢pokat£stasij p£ntwn, the restitution of all things, the final absolute triumph of good and eradication of evil.[50] Specifically, it concerns Leibniz's encouragement of and collaboration in the composition of Petersen's grand poetic epic which culminates in an account of the millennium and the universal restitution.

Leibniz had been following Petersen's career with interest since 1691: discussing his ideas, attempting to shield him from persecution, reading, reviewing, praising, criticising and discussing his numerous works.[51] On 14 October 1706 he received from a mutual friend, Johannes Fabricius, a sample of Petersen's poetry, to which he responded with surprising warmth: "I have read Petersen's verses with great pleasure," he wrote; "I knew he was a learned man, but I had no

---

[50] For a brief overview, see Ernst A. Scherling, 'Johann Wilhelm and Johanna Eleonora Petersen', in Martin Greschat (ed.), *Gestalten der Kirchengeschichte*, vol. VII (Stuttgart: Kohlhammer, 1982), pp. 225-39. A definitive study of the early phase of their career is Markus Matthias, *Johann Wilhelm und Johanna Eleonora Petersen. Eine Biographie bis zum Amtsenthebung Petersens im Jahre 1692* (Göttingen: Vandenhoeck & Ruprecht, 1993). A fuller joint biography, but one based largely on the couple's autobiographical writings, is Stefan Luft, *Leben und Schreiben für den Pietismus. Der Kampf des pietistischen Ehepaares Johanna Eleonora und Johann Wilhelm Petersen gegen die lutherische Orthodoxie* (Herzberg: Traugott Bautz, 1994). On their eschatology, see Walter Nordmann, 'Die Eschatologie des Ehepaares Petersen, ihre Entwicklung und Auflösung', *Zeitschrift des Vereins für Kirchengeschichte der Provinz Sachsen* 26 (1930): 83-108; 27 (1931), 1-19; D.P. Walker, *The Decline of Hell* (London: Routledge & Kegan Paul, 1964), pp. 231-44; Friedhelm Groth, *Die 'Wiederbringung aller Dinge' im württembergischen Pietismus* (Göttingen: Vandenhoeck & Ruprecht, 1984), esp. pp. 38-51.

[51] Cf. esp. A I vii 29-52, 74-9, 100-108, 190-91; D V 278-9; G III 274-5, 283; Gu II, 342-7; *Essais de Theodicée*, § 17 (G VI 111-12, 202-3). See also Leibniz, *De l'Horizon de la Doctrine Humaine* – 'Apokat£stasij p£ntwn (*La Restitution Universelle*), ed. Michel Fichant (Paris: Vrin, 1991), pp. 16-28, 94-7, 119-24, 172-3; Coudert, *Leibniz and the Kabbalah*, pp. 111, 115-17, 120.

idea that he could accomplish so much in verse."[52] So delighted was he, in fact, that he immediately set about urging Petersen to undertake a monumental poetic project: on the back of a letter from Petersen dated the following day, Leibniz sketched the outline of a grand verse epic which he hoped Petersen would write, which is worth quoting at length:

> I, who am accustomed to thinking often about how the talents of great men might serve to advance the public good to the greatest degree, see that what I have often hoped for might come from you, namely a fit and comprehensive work about divine matters in the form of a heroic poem. For theology, which shines forth in prose, would be even more sublime if dressed in Virgilian majesty, which you of all people could do best. This would be the subject of such a great work: first, God, sufficient in his perpetual and secret eternity; then the creation of the cosmos; and finally the workings of providence in the governing of the world. But the second part should treat the future as it pertains to the body and the soul. Here the purification of souls and the restitution of all things, or rather their gradual improvement and elevation, could be discussed. I hope that the last, but not the least, part of the work will concern the grandeur of the celestial kingdom, or, as I call it, the divine court. There the astonishing virtues of the angels should be depicted in vivid colours and the happiness of blessed souls celebrated, blessed souls, who not only see the world under our feet but innumerable other worlds. From the different scenes of divine wisdom and goodness throughout the ages love and veneration for the supreme mind will burn ever more brightly. Here is the place for the most elegant fictions, although there is nothing that can be imagined by us, however beautiful, that is not surpassed by the truth. I do not know anyone from whom one could hope for such a work aside from

---

[52] Leibniz to Fabricius, 14 Oct. 1706 (D V 278-9).

you, you who have the gift of divine eloquence and to whom the hidden recesses of divine matters are visible.[53]

In 1711 Fabricius sent Leibniz another sample of Petersen's poetry; and this prompted Leibniz to urge him in even greater detail, via their mutual friend, to undertake a verse cosmogony which, Leibniz was convinced, would render him immortal:

> Thank you very kindly for the most beautiful poem by Petersen which you sent me; and thanks also through you to the truly quite outstanding author: at once a profound theologian and a marvellous poet. Although I might not agree [with them] everywhere, I never-the-less admire his meditations greatly.
>
> I have often thought to myself that no one would be more able than him to compose a poem called Uranias or rather entitled Uraniados, a work that is which would celebrate in Virgilian measure the city of God and the life eternal. It would have to begin with cosmogony and paradise, which would make up the first, or first and second books. The third, fourth and fifth, if this seemed right, would relate the fall of Adam and the redemption of mankind through Christ, and touch upon the history of the Church. Then I would certainly, for my part, permit in the sixth book a description of the millennial reign, and in the seventh the invasion of Antichrist with Gog and Magog and his destruction in the end by the breath of the divine mouth. Then in the eight book we would have the day of judgement and the punishment of the damned; in the ninth, tenth and eleventh the happiness of the blessed and the magnitude and beauty of the City of God and of the habitation of the Blessed, and excursions through the immense space of the universe for reviewing the marvellous work of God, and would add a description of the palace of heaven itself. The twelfth would conclude all with 'Apokat£stasij p£ntwn, the restitution of all things, with evil itself reformed and returned to happiness and to God – God now ordering

---

[53] Leibniz to Petersen, 15 Oct. 1706 (*De l'Horizon*, ed. Fichant, p. 25). Translation adapted from Coudert, *Leibniz and the Kabbalah*, pp. 115-16.

everything in all things without exception. Here a certain loftier philosophy mixed with mystical theology might suitably be introduced in appropriate places, where the origins of things are treated in the manner of Lucretius, Vida and Francastor. And things might be permitted to a poet which would be tolerated with more difficulty in a dogmatic theologian. Such a work would make its author immortal and could be of marvellous use in moving men's souls to hope for better things and in kindling the embers of a more genuine piety.[54]

This second suggestion was not without effect, for the entire work – in fifteen books averaging over one thousand verses each – was finished within four months![55] Leibniz asked to see the book before it was published, and upon receiving it he quickly discovered that the work composed in such a hurry did not fully live up to his expectations. He found, to be sure, innumerable things acutely, beautifully and worthily expressed; but not a few were imperfect, defying the laws of metre, poetry or even of grammar. As he read through the work, he immediately set about making improvements. "I have changed many things", he confessed to Fabricius on 28 January 1712, "and here and there entire verses ought to be altered."[56] Worse still, as he worked his way deeper into the work, he found that its later books were more seriously flawed than the early ones. "Between the two of us", he confided to Fabricius a month later,

> I am astonished in paging through the *Uraniados* at the negligence of our friend Petersen. There are many beautiful passages, but many are so languid, so irregular or careless that they can by no means be tolerated in so important a work. I often encounter whole pages which need to be improved, many verses which need to be deleted and substituted with others.[57]

---

[54] Leibniz to Johannes Fabricius, 3 Sept. 1711 (D V 293-4).
[55] Cf. Leibniz to Fabricius, 8 Dec. 1711 and 28 Jan. 1712 (D V 295, 296-7); and Leibniz to des Bosses, 6 January 1712 (G II 428).
[56] Leibniz to Fabricius, 28 Jan. 1712 (D V 296-7).
[57] Leibniz to Fabricius, 26 Feb. 1712 (D V 297).

As his awareness of the flaws in the later books grew, so also did the task of emending them. But although he could find time to devote to it only with difficulty, Leibniz clearly thought Petersen's work too important to publish in its imperfect state; and so he was gradually drawn into a full scale revision of the work himself. His labours are recorded in some detail in a series of further letters to Fabricius as well as fifteen leaves of draft emendations still to be found amongst Leibniz's papers.[58] As late as January 1715 he was still at work: "I have expended much effort upon it," he reported, "in order to polish and recall to order a thing far too quickly written. So I have changed numberless things and sometimes entire pages."[59] He finally returned the manuscript in July 1716, only four months before his death, still urging that it required more revision.[60] Six years later it was published under the title *Uranias*.[61]

This episode therefore presents a remarkable case of Leibniz conceiving a millenarian work, repeatedly urging its composition, and devoting considerable care over the last four years of his life to refining it. It thus provides an opportunity for seeking an answer to our two central questions: What is the nature of the mystical meaning retained by Leibniz? And why is he willing to jeopardise his irenical praeterism by preserving it?

The key to resolving both of these questions would seem to be the poetical nature of Petersen's work. Firstly, this helps to clarify the nature of the mystical meaning of the Apocalypse. In the second letter Leibniz states that "in appropriate places a certain loftier philosophy mixed with mystical theology might suitably be introduced,... And things might be permitted to a poet which would be tolerated with more difficulty in a dogmatic theologian." In the first letter he suggests that an epic treatment of the works of divine love and wisdom throughout the ages "is the place for the most elegant

---

[58] Leibniz to Fabricius, 10 Mar. and 17 Mar. 1712 (D V 297, 299); BH 366; Niedersachsische Landesbibliothek, Hanover: Leibniz-Handshriften XXXIX 18 Bl. 39-53: 'Leibn.'s Verbesserungen zu den Gedichte des J.W. Petersen: "Uranias, ...".'
[59] Leibniz to Fabricius, 22 Jan. 1715 (D V 301).
[60] Leibniz to Fabricius, 6 July 1716 (D V 301).
[61] *Petersen, Uranias qua opera Dei magna omnibus retro seculis et oeconomiis transactis usque ad apocatastasin seculorum omnium ... carmine heroico celebrantur* (Frankfurt and Leipzig, 1722).

fictions". His reference to Petersen's eschatological doctrine of the ¢pokat£stasij p£ntwn is especially revealing: 'Here', he writes, "might be discussed the restitution of all things, or rather their gradual improvement". In this general context, this clearly implies that the poetic description of the ¢pokat£stasij p£ntwn in Petersen's poetic masterpiece is not to be understood literally but is rather to be regarded as a metaphor for progress. Similar is the statement in the second letter regarding millenarianism: 'For my part, I would certainly permit to the poet a description of the millennial reign in the sixth book.' In short, millenarianism and universal salvation can be treated in a poetical work because it is in the very nature of poetry to employ tropes and figures which are not literally true. When in Petersen's great poem such matters are treated, they are not to be taken literally but understood as referring to the true manifestation of God's wisdom and goodness in history: unending progress.

Secondly, this project also helps to explain why Leibniz is willing to retain this mystical or allegorical level of meaning, even though it jeopardises the pragmatic function of the praeterist 'literal' level. "Theology", he remarks in the first letter, "which shines forth in prose, would be even more sublime if dressed in Virgilian majesty", that is, if presented in poetic form. He concludes the letter on a similar note: "From the different scenes of divine wisdom and goodness throughout the ages, love and veneration for the supreme mind will burn ever more brightly." Likewise, in the second letter, such an epic treatment "could be of marvellous use in moving men's souls to hope for better things and kindling the embers of a more genuine piety." It is another basic poetic and rhetorical principle that the concrete, vivid, imaginative, metaphorical language of poetry is far more effective in moving men to action than the objective, non-emotive, rational language of philosophy. In 1715, the last year in which he worked on the *Uranias*, Leibniz, acting partly on inspiration from Petersen and his old enemy, Adam Theobald Overbeck, worked out his own final combinatorial formulation of the doctrine of unending progress in a short work entitled *Apocatastasis*.[62] For all but the philosophical

---

[62] Leibniz, *De l'Horizon de la Doctrine Humaine*, ed. Fichant, pp. 66-77; cf. pp. 86-93, 111-119, 172-3. Cf. the first edition and German translation in Max Ettlinger, *Leibniz als Geschichtsphilosoph* (Munich: Josef Kösel and Friedrich Pustet, 1921);

minority, however, Petersen's sublime, poetic treatment of the millennium and *apocatastasis panton* would be far more effective in arousing love of God and hope for better things than the mathematical calculations and abstract reasonings of Leibniz's *Apocatastasis*. A poetic treatment of this material was not merely permissible but was positively desirable because it could advance Leibniz's ultimate goal – inspiring love of God, hope for the future, and zealous activity to promote the common good – more effectively in the great majority of human hearts than his own work of a purely philosophical nature could do.

Now if the characteristic of Petersen's greatest treatment of millenarianism and universal salvation which justifies its publication is its poetic language, this raises a possibility of crucial importance regarding Leibniz's conception of the Apocalypse itself. In a fragment published by Feller, Leibniz describes the Apocalypse itself as having been written in a 'poetic' style.[63] In the *Sonderbare Erklärung der Offenbarung*, he writes that it "is written in a magnificent and quite delightful manner".[64] In the *Summaria Apocalypseos explicatio*, he goes further to place the Apocalypse "amongst the most artful writings which have been passed down to us from antiquity." Plato's language in the famous passage on the immortality of the soul in the *Phaedo* is so powerful that upon reading it one almost yearns for death. Virgil's description of Livia's grief at the death of Marcellus in the *Aeneid* is so moving that one cannot read it without tears. Likewise, such is the simplicity of vocabulary, the propriety of diction, the majesty of its periods, and the luminous style of the Apocalypse that it is impossible to read it attentively without wonder and an intimate agitation of spirit.[65] It is this power which has produced many of the most

---

and Michel Fichant, 'Ewige Widerkehr oder unendlicher Fortschritt: Die Apokatastasisfrage bei Leibniz', *SL* 23/2 (1991): 133-50.

[63] Feller (ed., *Otium Hanoveranum*, p. 225: 'La traduction de l'Apocalypse par Martin Luther a des expressions fortes; Et le livre en luy même est ecrit d'un stile beau, fleuri, et poëtique.'

[64] Leibniz, *Sonderbare Erklärung der Offenbarung* (VE 2064): "Es sey aber dieses buch von wem es wolle, so ists auf eine herrliche und ganz entzückende weise geschrieben;...".

[65] *Summaria Apocalypseos explicatio* (VE 2065-6): "Alterum est quod noto *Apocalypsin* esse scriptum inter artificiosissima

dangerous enthusiasts, prophets and fanatics which Leibniz's praeterism is designed to discourage; but might it not also be turned to more beneficial purposes? If the Apocalypse is to be interpreted not primarily as a philosophical or theological treatise but as a work of 'poetry', might not the explanation which Leibniz applied to the publication of Petersen's *Uranias* apply also to the Apocalypse itself? Might not Scripture, in other words, like Petersen's poem, treat the theme of eternal progress and improvement in millenarian language precisely because the literal inaccuracies of such language are more than compensated for by its power to arouse hope for the future? Might therefore the mystical or analogical meaning of the Apocalypse which Leibniz wishes to retain despite its tendency to undermine his pragmatic praeterism be the vision of unending future progress during all the ages of church history contained not literally but poetically in the Apocalypse? Such would seem to be the most coherent explication of Leibniz's many scattered statements on the millennium – not only the few discussed here, but all the others located to date.

Does this interpretation make Leibniz a millenarian, although one of a extremely moderate variety? No, at least not the mature Leibniz. If the term 'millenarianism' is to retain a distinctive meaning, it must refer to those who believe that the twentieth chapter of the Apocalypse refers to a lengthy and distinct future period of greatly enhanced felicity, whether purely spiritual or also partly material, for the church on earth. Leibniz's mature position differs from this strict definition in one important respect: it refers the millennium not merely to the future but to the whole period extending into the future but beginning from the time at which the Apocalypse was written. The millennium for Leibniz is not simply to be awaited in the future but also experienced in the present and the past. In this chronological respect Leibniz's position is far closer to that of Augustine and mainstream Catholicism, which applied the prophecy of the millennium to the

---

censendum, quae nobis ex omni antiquitate reliqua sint. Ea in illo est simplicitas sermonis, et verborum proprietas, et sententiarum majestas, et lumina orationis, ut sine admiratione quadam atque intima animorum commotione legi attente non possit. Qualis dicendi ratio est Platonis cujus *Phaedo* de animae immortalitate, aliquibus mortem voluntariam persuasit; et Virgilii cujus de Marcelli morte versus Livia sine lacrymis legere non potuit."

entire period between the First and Second Advents.[66] But Augustine differs radically from Leibniz in allowing no room for fundamental improvement, whether spiritual or temporal, during this period. The essential spiritual improvement, he maintained, had already been performed by Christ's redemptive work; and even the preaching of the Gospel throughout the world would not create a new period of temporal or political felicity on earth, as the sack of Rome had demonstrated to his generation. Completely different from Leibniz's position was the mainstream Protestant interpretation of the Apocalypse in the Reformation era, which referred the millennium to a definite, thousand-year period in the past history of the church between the Apostles and the rise of the papal Antichrist. A fourth contemporary interpretation bears interesting similarities to Leibniz. A small minority of Protestants believed that the millennium had begun some time in the fairly recent past with the revival of evangelical preaching by Luther, Hus or Wycliff and would gradually issue in greater triumphs and joys for the church in the future.[67] The chief difference of this position from Leibniz's was that it excluded a lengthy period in the past history of the Christian church from the millennium.   This difference was crucial, for it maintained the dominant Protestant conviction that for many centuries the established church had been the kingdom not of Christ but of the Papal Antichrist, whose complete destruction was one of the most eagerly awaited causes of future happiness. In short, Leibniz's mature position seems typically to possess characteristics of all of these more or less standard alternatives, both Protestant and Catholic, and in doing so to elude the standard dichotomy between millenarian and amillenarian readings. What this interpretation of Leibniz's position does clearly imply is that it integrated the expectations of profound future progress stimulated

---

[66] In a variant formulation, it was applied to the period between the Resurrection of Christ and the rise of Antichrist, three and one-half years before the Second Coming. See Augustine, *De civitate Dei*, xx, 7-9, 11, 13.

[67] The best-known instance is Thomas Brightman, *Apocalypsis apocalypseos, id est, Apocalypsis D. Joannis analysis et scholiis illustrata* (Frankfurt, 1609); translated as *A Revelation of the Revelation* (Amsterdam, 1611, 1615), pp. 838-61, esp. 848-53. Others include Matthieu Cottière (*alias* Cotterius), *Apocalypseos Domini nostri Jesu Christi exposito* (Saumur, 1615); and James Durham, *A Commentarie upon the Book of Revelation*, ed. John Carstairs (London, 1658).

and sustained by millenarianism into a conception of the millennium closer in its chronology to the traditional Catholic one. It was, as such, a position admirably adapted to combining a quasi-millenarian optimism regarding future progress with a traditional, Catholic chronology in keeping with Leibniz's ecumenical and irenical purposes.

There is however one important exception to this conclusion, and it comes, significantly, from the pen of the young Leibniz. In the *Justa dissertatio* Leibniz places the beginning of this period of enhanced felicity, not in the past, but in the future: "verissimum inchoabimus ... chiliasmum". Unlike what we have described as Leibniz's mature position, this early vision is a fully (if moderate) millenarian one. The difficulty here resides rather in determining whether this text is to be taken at face value. Fortified by exposure to these later passages, let us now return to the final passage of the *Justa dissertatio* for a second look.

5. The *Justa dissertatio* Revisited

The issue at stake here is an important one and the questions raised by it, as usual with Leibniz, subtle and complex. We therefore take a cautious line of approach, asking first whether there is anything in this passage which contradicts what we know of Leibniz's views from elsewhere, and second whether there are any internal indications that this vision is genuinely Leibniz's own.

As a late seventeenth-century millenarian vision, the most remarkable aspect of this passage is its pronounced material, political and even military component. Its emphasis on mechanical inventions, medical discoveries, legal and political institutions and above all military victories places a striking emphasis on human agency as a cause of the millennium and on material prosperity as a characteristic of it. These external and material emphases place this passage not in the tradition of Pietist millenarianism but rather in the tradition of such Baconian universal reformers as Comenius, the Hartlib circle, and later British millenarians who associated the millennium with a reform of philosophy, science, education, agriculture, medicine, law and politics as well as religion.[68]

More difficult to reconcile with Leibniz is the role assigned to a military campaign in general and to Louis XIV's leadership of it in particular in inaugurating the millennium. Even this aspect of this vision, however, can be reconciled with Leibniz's later position more readily than it might seem. The mature Leibniz clearly believed that all the benefits outlined in this passage would be enjoyed in the future. The key discrepancy between this passage and his later views on progress is the supposed agency of crusade and king in bringing it about. One can therefore substantially reconcile this passage with Leibniz's later views by supposing that it represents a shift of emphasis from the ineluctable general course of progress and providence to the specific, contingent agencies which would bring that progress about. Leibniz may have believed, in other words, that all of the blessings described in this passage would come about in the future, whatever the Sun King chose to do, but that by turning his aggression on his European neighbours Louis XIV would delay the advent of these blessings while by leading a crusade to Egypt he might help to accelerate it.

If this passage can be at least partially reconciled with other aspects of Leibniz's thought, there can be no doubt that it directly contradicts his later irenical praeterism. In the *Summaria Apocalypseos explicatio* of 1677 and many later passages, Leibniz argues that all the prophecies in the Apocalypse ought to be applied to events of the distant past in order to avoid the turmoil and anguish caused by applying them to the present. In the conclusion of the *Justa dissertatio* of 1671-2, he explicitly applies the prophecy of the millennium to events of the near future precisely in order to inspire a grand religious and military crusade. The contradiction is inescapable; but it demonstrates not that the young Leibniz could not have been a millenarian but rather that he could not have been an irenical praeterist. In doing so, it confirms Leibniz's statement of in the

---

[68] In addition to the works cited above, notes 3-8, see especially Charles Webster, *The Great Instauration: Science, Medicine and Reform, 1626-1660* (London: Duckworth, 1975), esp. ch. 1; and *idem, From Paracelsus to Newton: Magic and the Making of Modern Science* (Cambridge: Cambridge University Press, 1982), ch. 2.

Summaria Apocalypseos explicatio that he reached his praeterist position "while studying the Apocalypse recently".[69] It is praeterism which is new upon Leibniz's disappointed return from France in 1677 and it is for pragmatic political grounds that it is introduced despite his lingering preference for another interpretation which he had held previously.

Although it has the hallmarks both of Leibniz's youth and of its diplomatic purpose, there is nothing in this vision which compels us to regard it as insincere. On the other hand, the presence of millenarianism in this scheme indicates Leibniz's sympathy for the doctrine in at least two important ways. Firstly and most importantly, there is the simple fact that the more general hopes and aspirations expressed in this passage are undeniably Leibniz's own. We would not need to look far for further expressions of Leibniz's conviction in the future intellectual, political and moral progress of mankind. It is therefore extremely significant that Leibniz chose in this early passage to characterise the realisations of his own hopes and aspirations as the beginning of the millennium. At the very least this shows that Leibniz recognised the striking similarity of his own aspirations with those of at least one school of millenarian predecessors and contemporaries.

But Leibniz not only recognised that his own vision and aspirations *could* be presented in millenarian terms; in the *Justa dissertatio* he *chose* to present them in this fashion. There was no need for him to do so. The logical coherence of Leibniz's plan in no way required him to depict the outcome of the Egyptian campaign as the inauguration of the millennium. He could have scored through the sentence which mentions the millennium, indeed he could have rubbed out the entire passage quoted above, without changing in the least the feasibility of the project in the eyes of a hard-headed military strategist. Leibniz would have chosen to add this concluding passage to the *dissertatio* only if he thought that this would strengthen its appeal to Louis XIV and his advisors. Even in the most sceptical reading of this text, the presence of millenarianism in it indicates that Leibniz thought of the idea as sufficiently attractive and respectable to lend weight to his

---

[69] Leibniz, *Summaria Apocaypseos explicatio* (VE 2065; quoted above, note 42).

argument.[70] Why then did Leibniz choose to conclude his treatise in this way? We seem to have here yet another example of his deep appreciation of the powerful language of the Apocalypse, of its capacity to arouse hope for better things in the future and to inspire the activity necessary to achieve them.

Even an appropriately cautious reading of the millenarian conclusion of the *Justa dissertatio* can therefore reach at least five firm conclusions. Firstly, there can be no doubt that the young Leibniz recognised the intimate resemblance between his own aspirations and those of a previous and indeed contemporary school of reformist millenarians. Secondly, it is equally certain that he had a high enough regard for the doctrine of millenarianism to suppose that his proposal to Louis XIV would be strengthened by portraying it as millenarian. Thirdly, there is nothing in this millenarian vision fundamentally irreconcilable with Leibniz's basic views as we know them from elsewhere, with the exception of his later, praeterist objection to the application of Biblical prophecy to contemporary events, and this one contradiction confirms, fourthly, that Leibniz's irenical praeterism was a later development, implying that Leibniz's views on the Apocalypse had evolved before the writing of the *Summaria Apocalypseos explicatio*. Finally, as in his inspiration and emendation of Petersen's *Uranias*, one can sustain the sincerity of the millenarian conclusion of the *Justa dissertatio* with the simple and relatively painless assumption that the young Leibniz, like the old, genuinely regarded the twentieth chapter of the Apocalypse as a prophecy of material, political, moral and intellectual progress. As for any residual embarrassment caused by this concession, this can perhaps be tempered by the recent discovery that the roster of seventeenth-century millenarians is far more distinguished and far less uniformly deranged than previous generations of scholars have generally supposed.

---

[70] This assumption on his part is in striking contrast to his position eleven years later, as manifested by his satirical broadside against Louis XIV, the *Mars Christianissimus* of 1683, where he portrayed the grandious pretensions and far-fetched biblical justifications of French policy as millenarian precisely in order to ridicule them (A IV ii 480; cf. 457; R 128).

G. H. R. PARKINSON

SUFFICIENT REASON AND HUMAN FREEDOM

IN THE *CONFESSIO PHILOSOPHI*

I

This paper is concerned with certain features of what is perhaps one of the most important and interesting works of the young Leibniz. The work in question is a dialogue which he wrote during the early months of his stay in Paris – probably between Autumn 1672 and the early months of 1673 – and which he entitled *Confessio Philosophi*. Its theme[1] is the justice of God, a topic which remained an abiding concern, culminating in the *Theodicy* of 1710. Here I shall be concerned with only a part of the dialogue, the part that concerns the question whether human beings can be called free.

The relevance of this question to the topic of the justice of God is easily seen. For Leibniz and for many others, God is not just a creator: he is also a judge, rewarding some with bliss and punishing others with the pains of Hell. What is more, God is not only a judge; he is a just judge. Now, if someone is to be justly rewarded or punished, that person must have free will. So it is essential for someone who argues for the justice of God to be able to establish that human beings do have free will.

There are several arguments which seem to threaten human freedom. One is an argument which is based on antecedent truth: another concerns God's foreknowledge. Yet another argument concerns God, not just as a being who has foreknowledge, but as a being who pre-ordains what is to happen. These arguments did not escape Leibniz's

---

[1] 116, 3. References, by page and line, are to the text of the *Confessio Philosophi* contained in A VI iii. Translations are my own.

S. Brown (ed.): The Young Leibniz and his Philosophy (1646-76). 199–222

attention:[2] they are not, however, discussed in detail in the *Confessio*. What Leibniz does discuss at length in this work is an argument which involves the principle of sufficient reason. One should say that Leibniz does not use the *term* 'principle of sufficient reason'[3] in the dialogue, but there is no doubt that he uses and discusses the principle itself, and that it constitutes one of the main topics of the work.

The principle enters quite early in the work. One of the speakers, the Theologian, asks the other, the Philosopher, whether he agrees that there is nothing without a reason[4]. He does not speak of a *sufficient* reason, but there is no doubt that this is in mind: when the Philosopher answers in the next sentence, he says that he does not merely grant this, but thinks that it can be *proved* "that there never exists anything such that it is not possible (at any rate for an omniscient being) to assign a sufficient reason why it should exist rather than not exist, and why it should exist in this way rather than in some other way"[5]. The same readiness to move from talking about a 'reason' to talking about a 'sufficient reason' is to be found in an interesting argument, to which I shall return shortly, contained in a paper entitled by the editors 'A demonstration of primary propositions', written between Autumn 1671 and early 1672.[6] Here, after setting out to prove that "There is nothing without a reason", Leibniz concludes that "Whatever exists, has a sufficient reason". There is no case, then, for distinguishing between a 'principle of reason' and a 'principle of sufficient reason'.[7]

---

[2] For Leibniz's approach to these problems, see G. H. R. Parkinson, *Leibniz on Human Freedom* (Wiesbaden: Franz Steiner, 1970), pp. 5-17.

[3] Two common formulations of this principle are that there must be a sufficient reason for everything that exists and happens (e.g. to Clarke, 5.125, G VII 419; cf. *Principles of Nature and of Grace*, section 7, G VI 602; *Monadology*, section 32, G VI 612) and that there is no true proposition whose reason could not be seen by anyone who had all the knowledge necessary to understand it properly (*Remarques sur le livre de l'origine du mal*, section 14, G VI 413; cf. to Clarke, 5.125; *Monadology*, section 32, G VI 612).

[4] *Confessio philosophi* 118, 2.

[5] *Confessio philosophi* 118, 3-5.

[6] A VI ii 483.

[7] Compare, for example, the remark that physics requires "the principle of the need for giving a reason" (*Specimen Inventorum*, G VII 309) with the assertion that it requires the "principle of the need for a sufficient reason" (to Clarke, 2.1, G VII 355).

As to the nature of the reasons of which the principle speaks, Leibniz makes clear in the *Confessio Philosophi*[8] that by a 'reason' he means an answer to the question 'Why?', and that a 'reason' may be either 'efficient', or, 'if the author is rational, an end' – a clear reference to the Aristotelian distinction between efficient and final causes.[9]

II

I have said that Leibniz, in the *Confessio Philosophi*, asserts that the principle of sufficient reason can be proved. In fact he offers two proofs, the first of which rests on the notion of a "requisite"[10]. Leibniz's argument is that anyone who denies the principle of sufficient reason

> destroys the very distinction between existence and non-existence. Whatever exists, will assuredly have all the requisites of existence; but all the requisites of existence taken together are the sufficient reason of existence, therefore whatever exists has a sufficient reason of existence.

This repeats, in an informal guise, the argument set out formally in the 'Demonstration of Primary Propositions' of 1671-2, to which I have just referred. The difference is that in the formal version, Leibniz defines both 'sufficient reason' and 'requisite'.[11] A sufficient reason is "that which, having been given, the thing exists", and a requisite is "that which, having not been given, the thing does not exist".[12] Leibniz is saying, in effect, that a requisite is a necessary, as opposed to a sufficient condition.

---

[8] *Confessio philosophi* 118, 9-10.

[9] In Leibniz's works, the principle of sufficient reason also takes the form of the assertion that there is nothing without a cause. It does not appear in this guise in the *Confessio Philosophi*; but see *Catena Mirabilium Demonstrationum*, 12 Dec. 1676, A VI iii 584, and a paper on existence, Dec.? 1676, A VI iii 587: PDSR 113.

[10] *Confessio philosophi* 118, 5-8.

[11] A VI ii 483, 12-13.

[12] See also *De Conatu et Motu, Sensu et Cogitatione* (1671), A VI ii 283: "A requisite is that which, if it is not thought, something cannot be thought".

In the *Confessio Philosophi*, Leibniz offers another proof of the principle of sufficient reason; this one appeals, not to definitions, but to human practice. Human beings, the Theologian says[13], always seek an answer to the question 'Why?', and having found one they then seek a reason for *that* reason, and so on. Philosophers will continue the process until they reach a being which is necessary, i.e. is its own explanation[14]; 'plain men' (the *vulgus*) will continue until they reach something that is common and familiar, and there they will stop. The Philosopher agrees, but adds that this is not just something that human beings *do*: it is something that they must do[15]. If one does not accept the principle of sufficient reason, he says, "the foundations of the sciences are destroyed". For

> Just as 'The whole is greater than the part' is the principle of arithmetic and geometry, which are the sciences of quantity, so the proposition that there is nothing without a reason is the foundation of physics and of morals. These are the sciences of quality[16] – or (since quality is nothing but the power of acting and being acted on) the sciences of action, namely thought and motion.[17]

The least and simplest theorem of physics or of morals, the Philosopher continues, cannot be proved unless it is assumed that the proposition that there is nothing without a reason can be demonstrated.[18]

One may note that, in claiming that the argument shows that the principle of sufficient reason can be demonstrated, the Philosopher is claiming more than he is entitled to. The argument shows only that we have to assume that the principle is *true*; but this truth might be a

---

[13] *Confessio philosophi* 118, 9ff.

[14] *Confessio philosophi* 118, 14.

[15] *Confessio philosophi* 118, 15.

[16] See also *Demonstratio Propositionum Primarum*, A VI ii 480: "I, as far as I know, was the first to demonstrate that the proposition that there is nothing without a reason is the foundation of the sciences of mind and motion".

[17] *Confessio philosophi* 118, 16-20.

[18] *Confessio philosophi* 118, 20-22.

primary truth, not capable of demonstration.   Still, the line of argument here is very interesting. Leibniz is not trying to prove the principle of sufficient reason by showing that it *follows from* certain primary truths by way of definitions: rather, he is arguing that it is the *presupposition* of some of the sciences.[19] Only *some* of the sciences, be it noted; we have here an early form of the thesis, perhaps best known from sections 31-2 of the *Monadology*, that our reasonings are based on "two great principles".[20] It is noteworthy, however, that the young Leibniz says that the sciences of arithmetic and geometry are based on the principle that the whole is greater than the part, and not (as he did later) on the principle of contradiction. This is the more surprising in that he had already claimed, in the 'Demonstration of Primary Propositions' of 1671-2[21] to offer a demonstration of the proposition that the whole is greater than the part.

This argument from presupposition seems to be absent from Leibniz's later writings. What of the argument from requisites? Certainly, the young Leibniz continued to use the argument; we find it in two papers written late in 1676[22]. It does not, however, seem to be present in the works of Leibniz's maturity. Leibniz continued to think that the principle of sufficient reason can be proved, but in his later years he put forward a different argument, based on his theory of truth and on the related theory of the complete concept of an individual substance. Such an argument is to be found as late as 1710[23], but it is most prominent in the *Discourse on Metaphysics* of 1686 and related works.[24]

III

---

[19] Elsewhere he argues for the principle of contradiction along similar lines. See PDSR xv-xvi, 48, 56; also to Foucher (1686), G I 382.

[20] Compare *Theodicy*, section 44, G VI 127 and *Remarques sur le livre de l'origine du mal*, section 14, G VI 413.

[21] A VI ii 482-3.

[22] *Catena Mirabilium Demonstrationum*, 12 Dec. 1676, A VI iii 584, PDSR 107; a paper on existence, Dec.? 1676, A VI iii 587, PDSR 111-3.

[23] *Remarques sur le livre de l'origine du mal*, section 14, G VI 414.

[24] *Discourse on Metaphysics*, section 13; to Arnauld, 14 July 1686, G II 56; *De Verum a Falso Dignoscendi Criteriis* (1685-7) G VII 301, VE 1174.

Now that the principle of sufficient reason has been accepted, the Theologian and the Philosopher explore its consequences.[25] One apparently damaging consequence appears to be that given this principle, the nature of God must be radically different from what theists believe it to be. The Theologian points out[26] that it has been conceded[27] that each thing which is not its own reason for existence must be analysed into its reason, and then into the reason for that reason, and so on until they are analysed into that which is its own reason, namely the Being in itself (*Ens a se*), i.e. God. But the things which require such analysis include sin and damnation[28], therefore God must be the ultimate cause of these. This unwelcome conclusion launches a long discussion, which turns on a distinction between God as cause and God as author. The Philosopher agrees that God, the ultimate reason of all things, is the cause of sin[29], but says that this is not theologically harmful. For God is not the *author* of sin[30]: that is[31], God does not *will* that there shall be sin.[32] God only *permits* sins.[33]

Most of this discussion does not concern human freedom, a topic which enters[34] only when Leibniz has completed his reply to the charge that the principle of sufficient reason implies that God wills that there shall be sin. However, in the course of his reply Leibniz makes a point that has an important bearing on the problem of human freedom, as he sees it. I am referring to what he says about our dependence on external things. The point is made when Leibniz is, in

---

[25] *Confessio philosophi* 118, 24ff.

[26] *Confessio philosophi* 120, 16-9.

[27] The Theologian says (120, 16), "You yourself have said". This seems to be a reference to a remark made earlier by the Philosopher (118, 15), in which he concedes that philosophers seek a series of reasons until they reach a being which is necessary, i.e. is its own reason.

[28] *Confessio philosophi* 120, 17.

[29] *Confessio philosophi* 121, 4.

[30] *Confessio philosophi* 129, 10.

[31] See the definition of "author", *Confessio philosophi* 127, 10.

[32] *Confessio philosophi* 130, 9ff.

[33] *Confessio philosophi* 131, 1; 131, 28-9.

[34] *Confessio philosophi* 132, 4.

effect, filling in some of the detail of what he has already said, in general terms, about God as the cause of sin. A starting point is provided by an account[35] of one particular sin, Judas' betrayal of his master; this has to be supplemented by a later passage[36] in which the Theologian sums up the argument by which the Philosopher has "absolved the will of God from sins".

Judas sinned, the Theologian says, because (a) he could do so and (b) he willed to do so[37]. Leibniz does not produce an express argument for this; he clearly regards it as evident that the sinner not only has the power to sin (the other disciples had the power to betray Jesus, but did not) but also wills to exercise that power. Now, both (a) and (b) – the power to sin, and the will to sin – have their reasons, and these come from external things. With regard to (a), when Leibniz discusses Judas' sin, he says curtly that Judas' being able to act as he did was given to him by God.[38] Later[39] he expands this, saying that the reason for our power to sin comes from what is born with us (*connatis*) and from what we receive – the former coming from our parents and the latter from food. Each of the two, then, comes from external things. As to (b) – the reason for an act of will – Judas willed as he did because he thought it good. In reply to the query why Judas thought it good[40] the Philosopher replies[41] that to think something good is to have a belief. Now, a belief has two causes – the temperament of the believer, and the disposition (*dispositio*) of the object; or in other words, the state (*status*) of the person and the circumstances of the thing.[42] Leibniz does not say expressly what such an 'object' or 'thing' is, but it is clear that (as a cause of belief) it *affects* the believer; Judas' state of mind, Leibniz says[43] is "altered by"

---

[35]   *Confessio philosophi* 120, 3ff.

[36]   *Confessio philosophi* 131, 17ff.

[37]   *Confessio philosophi* 120, 4: cf. 131, 18.

[38]   *Confessio philosophi* 120, 4.

[39]   *Confessio philosophi* 131, 19-20.

[40]   *Confessio philosophi* 120, 5.

[41]   *Confessio philosophi* 120, 7-9.

[42]   *Confessio philosophi* 120, 10.

[43]   *Confessio philosophi* 120, 11.

objects. When Leibniz reviews his argument later, it emerges[44] that objects affect us by way of sensation. "The cause of willing", he says, "is intellection" (he must, in this context, be thinking of belief). He then goes on to say, "The cause of intellection is sensation, the cause of sensing is the object, the state of the object comes from external things (*ab externis*): so the power and the will to sin come from external things".[45]

IV

It is these 'external things' that pose a problem for the defender of human freedom. The Theologian states the problem in the following way[46]. "What, I ask you, is human freedom if we depend on external things; if there are things which bring it about that we will (*quae nos efficiunt velle*); if a certain fatal connection governs our thoughts no less than it governs the swervings (*flexus*) and the collisions of atoms". Leibniz begins his reply by saying that there can be no question of abandoning the principle of sufficient reason. The Philosopher reminds the Theologian that they have agreed to accept this principle; there must, therefore, be a sufficient reason of the very act of willing.[47]

Leibniz's answer to the problem rests on a definition of free will[48], but before he offers this he says that it is necessary to define what it is to will.[49] This seems a logical procedure; it seems obvious that before we can say what *free* will is, we must say what *will* is. But in fact what Leibniz says about will in the passage which follows raises a number of problems. The definition of will is sought because Leibniz is looking for the sufficient reason of an act of will.[50] But Leibniz has

---

[44] *Confessio philosophi* 131, 20-22.

[45] Leibniz then elaborates on this, saying that the power and the will to sin come from the present state of things, and that in turn from the universal harmony and the immutable ideas contained in the divine intellect (131, 23-5). The point of this is to lead up to the assertion (131, 25) that there is no intervention of the divine will; God does not will sin, he only permits it.

[46] *Confessio philosophi* 132, 4 ff.

[47] *Confessio philosophi* 132, 8-9.

[48] *Confessio philosophi* 133, 4 ff.

[49] *Confessio philosophi* 132, 12.

[50] *Confessio philosophi* 132, 12.

already provided an answer: discussing Judas' sin earlier in the dialogue, he has said that Judas willed as he did because he thought it good, i.e. because he had a certain belief.[51] Perhaps what Leibniz is doing can be explained in terms of a distinction that he drew later in the *Meditationes de Cognitione, Veritate et Ideis* (1684). The account of Judas' act of will that has already been given is, he might say, an example of 'clear knowledge'[52], in that at this stage of the inquiry we can do no more than recognise *examples* of acts of will. What we need, however, is a *distinct* concept of will, which is provided by a satisfactory definition.[53]

However, the definition of will offered in this part of the *Confessio Philosophi* is far from satisfactory. Leibniz says that to will something is "to be pleased by its existence, whether we sense the thing as actually existing, or imagine the existence of something that does not actually exist".[54] But this is not to will something, in any standard sense of the term. At the most one could say that, if one is pleased by something that one senses, then what exists is *in accordance with* one's will; one cannot say that one *wills* that things shall be so. The same can be said of cases in which we are pleased when we imagine the existence of something that does not actually exist.[55] I might feel pleasure if I imagine the existence of some Utopia: but this is not the same as willing to bring about its existence. The Danish theologian and scientist Niels Stensen, who read the *Confessio Philosophi* in about December 1677, was surely right when he remarked of Leibniz's definition of will, "As if the act of will could not be distinguished from the perception of pleasure and pain".[56]

In the light of all this, one might suppose that what Leibniz has to say about free will can be of no value; but this need not be so. In fact, when Leibniz offers his definition of free will the topic of pleasure disappears, and the concept of will that is used is a different one, more

---

[51] *Confessio philosophi* 120, 4.

[52] G IV 422.

[53] G IV 423.

[54] As Leibniz notes (132, 13), this is a (slightly abridged) version of a definition given earlier in the dialogue (127, 8).

[55] *Confessio philosophi* 132, 14.

[56] *Confessio philosophi* 127, n.14.

in line with his later views. This later view of the will can roughly be explained as follows.[57] Suppose that I plan to do something: Leibniz regards planning as a purely contemplative activity, so that if my plan is to be translated into action, there must be some intermediate activity that comes between the planning and the action, and this is a volition or act of will. Such a three-part division is implied later in the *Confessio*, where it is stated to be between belief (namely, the belief that something is good), will and act.[58] A link between intellect, will and act is also present in another work of the young Leibniz, *Definitionum Juris Specimen* (Spring or Summer, 1676). Here, Leibniz says that "Will is the inclination of the agent to act because he understands"[59], and also that it is an "intellectual appetite" – a concept which comes from the Scholastics.[60]

Such a three-part theory of the will has been severely criticised by modern philosophers[61] , so one might think that Leibniz's theory of human freedom still rests on an insecure basis. I suggest, however, that such criticisms could be met by making a change which does not affect Leibniz's overall position too radically. One could take his theory of the will to be analogous to what philosophers of mind now call a 'black box' theory; that is, one could take him to mean that the will is that which, *whatever it may be*, comes between the act or planning or deliberating and the act. Let us, at any rate, now proceed to Leibniz's account of free will.

V

Concluding the discussion of the will as such, the Theologian says that the Philosopher has failed to answer his objection that our dependence

---

[57] Cf. Parkinson, *Leibniz on Human Freedom,* p. 18. For a fuller account of Leibniz's concept of the will, see *ibid.*, pp. 18-23.

[58] *Confessio philosophi* 133, 13-4; cf. the beginning of Section VI below.

[59] A VI iii 600, 6.

[60] See Anthony Kenny, *Aquinas on Mind* (London: Routledge, 1993), p. 60. Kenny cites Aquinas, *Summa Theologiae* I, Qu. 80, Art. 2.

[61] See Gilbert Ryle, *The Concept of Mind* (London: Hutchinson, 1949), p. 62.

on external things means that there can be no free will.[62]   The
Philosopher replies that the problem arises because of a faulty
definition of free will. Here, there is a change of focus. So far the talk
has been about the sufficient reason of an act of will; now, however,
Leibniz analyses the sufficient reason into the requisites – the
necessary conditions – that make it up. If, the Philosopher says[63], you
define free will as some do – namely, that it is "the power which is
able to act and not to act, given all the requisites of action, existing
outside and inside the agent alike" – then there is no free will. (The
reference to "some" people who define freedom in this way may be a
reference to Molina and his followers).[64] Leibniz establishes this as
follows.[65] Suppose that all the requisites of something (in this case, an
action) exist. Then if the action does not occur, one or other of the
requisites must be absent; but it has been assumed that *all* the
requisites exist. It seems, then, that the action must occur. To escape
this conclusion, and allow for free will, we have to define free will in
another way: we have to say that free will is the power of acting or not
acting, given all the *external* requisites of action.[66] This means that
"even if all the aids to action are at hand, I can still not perform the
action, if I am unwilling to act"[67].

What Leibniz is saying here can perhaps be made clearer by a
conjectural example. Let us suppose that I perceive that a glass of
beer is close at hand, that my muscles are not physically impeded (e.g.
I am not tied up) and that I am in good physical shape (e.g. I am not
paralysed). Let us, suppose, finally, that these are all the external

---

[62]   One could say, indeed, that the Philosopher's discussion of the will only
emphasises the difficulties that lie in the way of free will. He argues (132, 14) that
pleasure is a sensation of harmony, and that what is harmonious depends on the state
of the percipient, of the object and of the medium. His conclusion (132, 21-2) is that
we do not will to will – i.e. our acts of will are not in our power.

[63]   *Confessio philosophi* 132, 24-6.

[64]   Cf. Francesco Piro (ed.), *G. W. Leibniz: Confessio Philosophi e altri scritti*
(Naples: Cronopio, 1992), p. 114, n. 24. Leibniz says only that the definition was
stated by the "later Scholastics". (Conversation with Stensen, 7 Dec. 1677, VE 302:
C 25)

[65]   *Confessio philosophi* 132, 27–133, 4.

[66]   *Confessio philosophi* 133, 4-6. Cf. Leibniz's conversation with Stensen, *ibid.*

[67]   *Confessio philosophi* 133, 6-7.

requisites of my drinking the beer. Leibniz would say that I am free to drink or not to drink the beer in that, in these conditions, I have the power to drink or not to drink.

Leibniz does not claim originality for this definition of free will. On the contrary, he says[68] that his definition is in line with that of Aristotle, who defined 'free' as "spontaneous with choice" and 'spontaneous' as meaning "when the principle of action is in the agent". We need not ask here whether this is really Aristotle's definition of free will;[69] what matters is that Leibniz regarded it as stating his own views, and what matters still more is that he continued to use it right up to his last years.[70] It is clear why Leibniz should approve of calling a free act 'spontaneous' in the sense defined, but it is not clear from the *Confessio* why he should add "with choice". However, on the basis of later passages[71] we may take his point to be that the lower animals have spontaneity, i.e. the source of an animal's actions is in itself, but no such animal can be called free, in that it does not choose to act as it does. Or, as Leibniz also says,[72] the animals do not deliberate about their actions. In some passages, Leibniz also says that freedom involves spontaneity and intelligence,[73] the point being that to choose or deliberate is an intellectual activity.

What Leibniz has said about freedom in the *Confessio* so far suggests that any person can be called free who has and exercises that rational capacity which is called 'choice'. It is important to note that this does not entail that the choice is the *right* choice, or (to put the point in another way) that the good at which the agent aims is the *true* good. Judas, for example, was a free agent in the sense just explained,

---

[68] *Confessio philosophi* 133, 8.

[69] See Otto Saame (ed.), *G. W. Leibniz: Confessio Philosophi* (Frankfurt: Klostermann, 1967), pp. 173-4, notes 128-9.

[70] E.g. *Theodicy*, section 34, G VI 122; section 301-2, G VI 296. On 'spontaneity' and 'spontaneity with choice', see also Parkinson, *Leibniz on Human Freedom*, pp. 57-8.

[71] E.g. *Theodicy*, section 302, G VI 296; a paper on freedom (undated, but after 1676) G VII 108-9.

[72] *Theodicy*, section 302; *Causa Dei*, section 20, G VI 441; *Nouveaux Essais* 2.21.9.

[73] *Theodicy*, section 302; paper on freedom, G VII 108, 109; 'Remarks on Descartes' Principles', G IV 362.

even though what Judas thought to be good was not the true good.[74] But when Leibniz goes on in the *Confessio* to develop what he has said about freedom as spontaneity with choice, we get a very different concept of freedom. Leibniz writes:

> From which it follows that each thing is the more spontaneous, the more its acts follow from its own nature and the less they are changed by external things: and the more free, the more it is capable of choice, i.e. the more it understands with a pure and tranquil mind. Spontaneity, therefore, comes from power, and freedom comes from knowledge.[75]

The point is made again later in the dialogue. After saying that God is supremely free, even though he cannot err in the choice of the best, Leibniz continues "Freedom, then, arises out of the use of reason;[76] and according as this is pure or infected, we either advance along the royal road of duties, or we stumble through trackless regions."[77] It follows from this (though Leibniz does not say this explicitly) that in betraying his master, Judas did not act freely, for in so doing he did not use his reason properly.

This is clearly a different sense of freedom from that which Leibniz employed when he spoke of freedom as spontaneity with choice. In that sense, Judas was a free agent: in the sense just mentioned, he was not. Why, then, should Leibniz adopt this second sense? Why should he say that to be free is to use the reason, or more precisely is to use it in the most perfect way[78], or is to have a reason which is pure[79]? One answer (which is associated with the Stoics) involves a view about the nature of the passions. Briefly, the thesis is that to act in accordance with the passions is to be governed by something which is foreign or external to one's true nature, which is to act rationally. A person who is led by the passions is therefore not autonomous, and is therefore not

---

[74] *Confessio philosophi* 120, 4-12.

[75] *Confessio philosophi* 133, 9-12.

[76] Cf. 135, 5: "The true root of freedom is the use of reason".

[77] *Confessio philosophi* 135, 14-6.

[78] *Confessio philosophi* 135, 7.

[79] *Confessio philosophi* 135, 14.

free. There are indications of such a line of argument in Leibniz's later works,[80] but it is not certain that it is to be found in the *Confessio*. In that work, Leibniz does indeed speak of the passions[81] as clouding the way in which the intellect sees objects. But there is no hint, here or in the rest of the work, that the passions are external to our true selves. I suggest that we can make better sense of what Leibniz says about reason and freedom if we take him to be operating with a concept of freedom which is not associated with any particular philosopher or school, but is held by ordinary people. According to this way of thinking about freedom, to be free is to have the power to do what one wants to do.[82] The relation of reason to this sort of freedom can be put in the following way. In so far as the passions obstruct the reason, they impede something which enables us to achieve our ends. An intellect which is pure, therefore (i.e. not clouded by the passions) gives us the power to achieve our ends, i.e. to do what we want to do. That is, in so far as we follow the reason we are free.

VI

Leibniz insists that his defence of freedom does not imply a breach of the principle of sufficient reason. After saying that freedom comes from knowledge[83] he continues: "But given that there is within us a belief that something is good (*opinio bonitatis*) it is impossible not to will it, and given the will together with a knowledge of its supporting external aids it is impossible not to act"[84]. In other words, the connections between judgement and will, and between will and act, are *necessary* connections.

---

[80] See especially a paper on freedom, G VII 109-10: "The more we act from the passions, the more we are slaves to the power of external things". For other references, see Parkinson, *Leibniz on Human Freedom*, p. 63.

[81] *Affectus*, 135, 10.

[82] Much later, in the *Nouveaux Essais* (2.21.8), Leibniz was to recognise this as a kind of freedom, the 'freedom to do'.

[83] *Confessio philosophi* 133, 12.

[84] *Confessio philosophi* 133, 13-4.

Leibniz follows this by saying that nothing is more incongruous than to transform the concept of free will into some "unheard of and absurd power of acting and not acting without a reason" – which, he says, no sane person would want.[85] It is sufficient for a defence of free will that "We are so situated in life's cross-roads that we can strive to obtain (*indagare*) only what we will to do, and can will to do only what we believe to be good – meaning by the latter what are to be counted as good by the fullest permitted use of our reason".[86] The alleged power of acting without a reason is, he says, "a monstrous power of a sort of rational irrationality"[87]. To the objection[88] that there are people who say that they have this power, in that they can do or not do something out of sheer caprice, Leibniz replies that such people are either liars, or they deceive themselves. The pleasure that arises out of such an act is itself a reason;[89] and even if someone honestly says that he is unaware of a reason for his action, there *must be* a reason, though the reason is of an elusive kind[90]. Much later, Leibniz was to say that these "elusive reasons" are "little perceptions" or "imperceptible impressions"[91], but there is no hint of this idea in the *Confessio Philosophi*.

The argument now shifts to the prediction of human actions and the relation of freedom to such predictions. By 'prediction' here is not meant any forecast whatsoever, but predictions made by someone who *knows* the future, such as an omniscient God[92]. The connection of such predictions with what has gone before is not explained, but doubtless the point is that the principle of sufficient reason entails that every human action is in principle predictable. If it turns out that this

---

[85] *Confessio philosophi* 133, 14-7.

[86] *Confessio philosophi* 133, 17-9.

[87] *Confessio philosophi* 133, 20-1.

[88] *Confessio philosophi* 134, 1.

[89] *Confessio philosophi* 134, 3-4. In connection with what Leibniz has said earlier, about willing as a kind of pleasure (cf. Section IV above), one may note that in the present passage pleasure is treated as a *motive* for an act of will, not as will itself.

[90] *Subtilis*: 134, 7.

[91] *Nouveaux Essais*, 2.1.15; *Theodicy*, section 305, G VI 297.

[92] *Confessio philosophi* 134, 10.

is not the case, then the principle of sufficient reason is overthrown, as is any scepticism about human freedom that it seems to involve.

The argument is simple. Suppose that someone – whether a human being, an angel, or God himself – predicts what I will do. I can always do the opposite of what is predicted, and so "assert my freedom"[93]. Leibniz replies that this does not mean that the principle of sufficient reason is overthrown, for[94] the pleasure that I get from overturning the prophecy is itself a reason[95]. Further, an infallible prophet can still know what I will do. Suppose that he knows that, if he tells me what I will do, I will perform an act which is different from the one predicted. All that he has to do is to keep the prediction from me – either by foreseeing my act in silence, or by predicting it to some third person, without my knowledge.[96] Leibniz then faces an interesting objection to this reply. The objection is that, by supposing that the prophet can't communicate his knowledge to me, Leibniz is in effect contravening the logical grammar of the verb 'know'. For anyone can state what he knows, in the presence of any audience.[97] The prophet, then, does not have foreknowledge.

Leibniz's reply is less than satisfactory. In effect, he says[98] that what is at issue is what can be predicted by a being of whatever kind (*a quocunque*), and this must include the predictions made by an omniscient God. But there is such a God;[99] therefore to suppose a mind that can always do or will the contrary of what is predicted is incoherent. Clearly, this is at best an *argumentum ad hominem*: but even if one concedes the existence of an omniscient being, Leibniz's reply is not wholly satisfactory. All that Leibniz has said is that, because there is an omniscient God, there must be *some* way of reconciling foreknowledge with our capacity to act in a way that is

---

[93] *Confessio philosophi* 134, 10-11.

[94] As has been said before, 134, 3-4.

[95] *Confessio philosophi* 134, 12-13.

[96] *Confessio philosophi* 134, 14-5.

[97] *Confessio philosophi* 134, 15-6: *quivis ... quod scit dicere potest, audiente quovis.*

[98] *Confessio philosophi* 134, 19-22.

[99] The existence of such a being has in fact been conceded at the beginning of the dialogue (116, 2, 10-11).

contrary to the act predicted. But what this way might be, we are not told.

Leibniz continues with a sketchy account of a major problem of moral philosophy – the problem of *akrasia*, or weakness of will. He takes as the centre of discussion some well-known lines of Ovid, "I see and approve the better course; I follow the worse".[100] It is not made clear how this relates to the discussion that has preceded it, but perhaps the point is this. The person who acts in a way contrary to the way predicted, precisely because it *was* predicted, may find himself acting in a way which is not the best. From this, it is a short step to considering someone who *knows* that a certain course of action is the best, but actually follows a course of action which he knows to be inferior. The question is, how can this happen? Leibniz does not really answer this question. What he says[101] is that we always follow the line of action which we think to be the best overall; no one ever chooses what he believes to be worse *on the whole*. But this was not the question raised. This was, how can we not follow the line of action which we *know* ('see') to be the best?

VII

We come now to the last major topic related to free will that is considered in the *Confessio*. It was mentioned at the beginning of this paper that the discussion of free will is linked with the discussion of the presuppositions of praise and blame, reward and punishment. Only a free agent, it is argued, can properly be blamed or punished, praised or rewarded. Since Leibniz has already argued that the will is free, it might seem that no difficulty remains; however, he clearly thinks that this is not so. His discussion is in terms of theological concepts – sin and damnation – but it is not difficult to paraphrase it in secular terms.

---

[100] *Metamorphoses*, 7, 20-1, discussed in *Confessio philosophi* 134, 23. Cf. *Theodicy*, section 154, G VI 201 and section 297, G VI 292; also *Nouveaux Essais* 2.21.35.
[101] *Confessio philosophi* 135, 1-2.

He begins by repeating a point made earlier – namely, that freedom consists in understanding or knowledge.[102] The true root of freedom, the Philosopher says, is the use of the reason, or more exactly it is the *right* use of the reason.[103] The Theologian argues that it follows from this[104] that all sin arises from error, from which there follows the (unacceptable) consequence that all sin is to be excused. The Philosopher agrees that sin comes from error, but not that it is therefore to be excused.[105] We have in our power, he says, a method (*ratio*) of escape from our darkness (presumably he is referring to the right use of reason) provided that we are willing to use it.[106] The question now arises, why some people fail to use this method. Leibniz replies[107] that it has never occurred to such people that they can use this method fruitfully, or else it is present in their mind as if it were not there. That is, such people lack *reflection* or *attention*. Take, he says[108], such well-known precepts as 'Say why you are acting now', 'Consider the end', and 'Look at what you are doing'.[109] If people were to perceive even one of these properly, and if certain laws or penalties were attached to the precepts, then each person would at once become infallible, prudent and blessed. What, then, is Leibniz's answer to the objection that if one regards sin as coming from error, one therefore has to excuse it? He is in effect saying that sinners are to be blamed because of a sort of culpable negligence – negligence in respect of the sinner himself. Sinners fail to use, or even to note, certain principles which are in a way in their mind, and they can properly be blamed for this.

---

[102] *Confessio philosophi* 133, 9-12; cf. Section V above.

[103] *Confessio philosophi* 135, 5, 14-6.

[104] *Confessio philosophi* 135, 16.

[105] *Confessio philosophi* 135, 16-7.

[106] *Confessio philosophi* 135, 17-8.

[107] *Confessio philosophi* 135, 19-21.

[108] *Confessio philosophi* 135, 23-4.

[109] "Dic cur hic", "Respice finem" and "Vide quid agas". Such expressions are cited in works which are roughly contemporary with the *Confessio*: see *Demonstratio Propositionum Primarum* (1671-2), VI ii 482; *Wilhelmus Pacidius* (1671-2) A VI ii 511, G VII 362. Leibniz continued to cite them, e.g. 'Remarks on Descartes' *Principles*' (1692), G IV 362; *Nouveaux Essais*, 2.21.47.

Leibniz continues by pushing further his inquiry into the question, 'How do people come to neglect these principles?' Bad men, he says, are not to be compared to the insane.[110] The insane are incapable of reflection, and of thinking 'Say why you are acting now', in which respect they resemble people who are drunk or asleep.[111] But bad men (*malitiosi*), as well as fools and people who make mistakes, do use this precept. However, in using it they do not direct themselves to the supreme issue (*ad summam rerum*): they deliberate about anything rather than their happiness. Leibniz goes on to say that both fools and evil men have a kind of reason that perverts reason: a lesser reason that perverts the greater, a certain specific reason (*certa quaedam*) – instilled by temperament, education and habit – that perverts a universal reason.[112]

This idea of two reasons may seem strange; Leibniz has previously spoken as if there were just one reason, which can be pure or impure, used well or badly.[113] But the point that is being made seems clear enough. There are, Leibniz is saying, certain universal principles of action that are common to all human beings. We act wrongly in so far as we neglect these principles, and we neglect them because, when we reason, we use principles that are not common to all, but are to be explained by the particular circumstances of a person's temperament or upbringing. One is reminded of the *praejudicia*, the 'preconceived opinions' which Descartes regards as the causes of error.[114] But this leaves one vital question unanswered: namely, what is the difference between a fool and a rogue? Leibniz does not give a clear answer to this, but he does say that "There is no doubt that evil people appear as

---

[110] *Confessio philosophi* 136, 5.

[111] *Confessio philosophi* 136, 5-7.

[112] *Confessio philosophi* 136, 10-12.

[113] *Confessio philosophi* 135, 7, 14: cf. Section V.

[114] *Principles of Philosophy* I 71-2 (*The Philosophical Writings of Descartes*, trans. Cottingham, Stoothoff and Murdoch, Cambridge: Cambridge University Press, 1985, I 218-9); *Replies to Sixth Objections*, ibid. II 296-300. Leibniz could have added that, besides the circumstances of our temperament and upbringing, a cause of our use of principles which are not universal lies in the passions. These, it may be recalled, have previously been said (cf. Section V) to explain our failure to follow reason, and so be free. Leibniz could argue that the passions, which make us look to our own narrow interests, lead us to follow a perverted kind of reason.

foolish to the angels, as fools do to us".[115] Perhaps this means that the sinner is a fool of a special kind – someone whose folly can be discerned by superhuman intelligences, who can grasp the universal truths that escape the attention of sinners, bent as they are on their own narrow ends. One would expect Leibniz to say (though he does not) that there are some human beings who can approximate to such angelic knowledge.

The reference to temperament and upbringing leads Leibniz to consider a major difficulty. Bad men, the Theologian says, have something to complain about:[116] namely fortune, other human beings (presumably those who have influenced them badly) and the circumstances of their desperate life. The Philosopher agrees; in a passage which is underlined in the manuscript he says, "So it is; indeed it is necessary that it should be so. For no one has voluntarily made himself bad; otherwise he would be bad before he became bad".[117] Leibniz is asserting that this is a logically necessary truth,[118] following from the concept of a bad man. A man who is not bad cannot decide to make himself bad, since the decision to corrupt anyone – and 'anyone' includes the person who decides – is a mark of a bad man.

This brings us to what the Theologian rightly regards as the main difficulty.[119] The problem is stated in theological terms – namely, in terms of the justification of damnation – but the argument applies to anyone who is subject to punishment of any kind.[120] The damned, the Theologian says, will complain that "they were born, they were sent into the world, they fell in with times, people and occasions, in ways such that they could not fail to perish".[121] If any warnings were given to them, they lacked the attention or reflection necessary to profit from

---

[115] *Confessio philosophi* 136, 12.

[116] *Confessio philosophi* 136, 13-6.

[117] *Confessio philosophi* 136, 16-7. In his notes on his conversation with Stensen of 7 Dec. 1677, Leibniz quotes this nearly verbatim: Gr 272, VE 301.

[118] Compare the remark "The contrary implies a contradiction" (137, 26) which is made about the same thesis.

[119] *Confessio philosophi* 136, 18.

[120] *Confessio philosophi* 136, 21-9; 137, 1-8.

[121] *Confessio philosophi* 136, 21-22.

these.[122] It is therefore unjust that they should suffer punishment (*mactatio*) whilst others do not.[123]

This objection is of great interest in view of what contemporary philosophers – notably Thomas Nagel and Bernard Williams[124] – have said about "moral luck". The person who is damned may be called unlucky in two of the four ways recognised by Nagel; he lacks "constitutive luck", which relates to "the kind of person you are, where this is not just a question of what you deliberately do, but of your inclinations, capacities and temperament", and he is also unlucky in the way in which he is determined by antecedent circumstances, which make him the kind of person he is.[125] Leibniz's first answer to the problem is not satisfactory, and indeed he seems to recognise this. Consider, the Philosopher says[126], someone who is damnable but not yet damned, and suppose that he is shown the place in Hell that he will occupy if he sins. If he does sin, can he blame God? Surely not; he can blame only his own will. But, as the Theologian points out[127], this is not satisfactory. The sinner, whose will is held to blame, will blame his will on fortune, i.e. on God or at any rate on the nature of things.[128]

The Philosopher's reply is of great interest. He begins[129] by conceding that the Theologian's point is a powerful one; he himself has already pointed out[130] that no one voluntarily makes himself bad. But if the sinner is to be allowed to blame his will on fortune, then we must be prepared to grant that punishment has no objective basis

---

[122] *Confessio philosophi* 136, 26-7.

[123] *Confessio philosophi* 136, 28.

[124] Thomas Nagel, 'Moral Luck', in *Mortal Questions* (Cambridge: Cambridge University Press, 1979), pp. 24-38, and Bernard Williams, 'Moral Luck' in *Moral Luck* (Cambridge: Cambridge University Press, 1981), pp. 20-39.

[125] Nagel, *op. cit.*, pp. 28, 32-3, 35. The other two sorts of moral luck recognised by Nagel are (a) luck in one's circumstances, i.e. the kinds of problems and situations one faces (26, 33-4) and (b) luck in the way one's actions turn out (pp. 28-32). (E.g. a motorist might pass a red light, but by good luck there is no one on the crossing).

[126] *Confessio philosophi* 137, 11-23.

[127] *Confessio philosophi* 137, 23.

[128] *Confessio philosophi* 137, 25-6.

[129] *Confessio philosophi* 137, 26 - 138, 3.

[130] The reference is to *Confessio philosophi* 136, 16-7.

(*tollenda est poena de natura rerum*). "No one will be bad, no one will be punishable, no one will be without an excuse."[131] This, he implies, is clearly unacceptable, and his solution is this: "In all judgements made with a view to inflicting punishment, it is sufficient that it shall be thought (*censeri*) that there is a known, evil (*pessimam*) and deliberate will, wherever it has come from."[132] Critics of the divine justice (or, he could have added, of human justice as well) are therefore extremely foolish in trying to rebut punishment by going beyond the ascertained (*compertam*) will of the criminal, which would be an infinite process.[133]

This is a view which Leibniz had already put forward, and which he continued to hold until his last years. A passage from *Von der Allmacht und Allwissenheit Gottes*[134] is of particular interest.[135] Leibniz says here that punishment belongs to the evil will, wherever that will comes from; otherwise no misdeed would ever be punished. One can always find a cause of the will outside the person who wills; yet it is the will that makes of us human beings and persons, and either sinners, blessed or damned. It has to be said that Leibniz's argument, here and in the corresponding passage in the *Confessio*, is not absolutely clear. It is not clear whether he is laying stress on the infinity of the causes that determine the will; that is, whether the argument is that if we look for causes of the will we shall never stop, and therefore we should not even start to look for them. If so, one naturally asks, 'Why should we not look for causes of the will as far as we can?' If the answer is that only by not looking for such causes can the institution of punishment be preserved, then this begs the question: for the whole problem is whether it is justifiable to punish people. I would suggest that the line of argument is different, and that it is brought out most clearly in *Von der Allmacht und Allwissenheit Gottes*. Here, Leibniz says that we can always find a cause of the will

---

[131] *Confessio philosophi* 138, 1-3.

[132] *Confessio philosophi* 138, 3-5.

[133] *Confessio philosophi* 138, 5-6.

[134] About 1670-71 (section 13: A VI i 542).

[135] See also notes on three letters on Spinoza (October 1676?), A VI iii 368 n.16; conversation with Stensen, Gr 272, VE 301; *Discourse on Metaphysics*, section 30; *Theodicy*, section 264, G VI 274.

outside the person who wills. I take it that Leibniz is saying that in justifying punishment, one ought not to pay attention to what he has called "external requisites". In this way, his argument can be linked with his definition of freedom. It is agreed that someone who is punished for an act must be a free agent. But I am called free[136] in so far as I am able to act or not to act, given all the external requisites of the act. But the requisites to which the sinner appeals in trying to show that punishment is never justified are external requisites. One point must be emphasised here. Leibniz is not saying that an act which is punishable has no cause. This would contradict the principle of sufficient reason; and in any event we have already seen that, within the agent, belief determines will, and will together with knowledge determines the act.[137] The punishable act, then, is determined, but it is determined internally.

VIII

This account of the justification of punishment concludes Leibniz's discussion of free will in the *Confessio Philosophi*. It remains only to make a few remarks about the relation of this discussion to what Leibniz has to say about free will in his later philosophy. We have noted several important Leibnizian theses about human freedom that are defended in the *Confessio* and re-appear in his later thought: the idea of freedom as constituted by spontaneity with choice (Section V), the idea that to be free is in a way to be rational (Section V), the idea that there are no uncaused human actions (Section VI), and finally the thesis that when we punish someone, we look to the act and not to its external causes (Section VII). However, there are some noteworthy omissions. One of Leibniz's best-known phrases is that motives "incline, but do not necessitate"; this phrase, however, does not appear in the *Confessio*. Again, when the mature Leibniz discusses the way in which human actions can be caused and yet free, he uses the notion of hypothetical necessity, i.e. the notion of what is necessary given that such and such is the case. (Indeed, there is reason to think that this concept is closely related to the idea that motives incline but do

---

[136] *Confessio philosophi* 133, 4-6: Section V.
[137] *Confessio philosophi* 133, 13-4; Section VI.

not necessitate).[138] The concept of hypothetical necessity was known to the young Leibniz,[139] but he makes no significant use of it in the *Confessio.*[140]

One naturally asks why Leibniz, in his later discussions of the freedom of the will, should make use of the concept of hypothetical necessity. Perhaps he came to think that, in the *Confessio*, he had not succeeded in proving that when we choose to do something, we could always have chosen to do something else. Whether this can be established by means of the concept of hypothetical necessity, is something of which one may doubt;[141] but this is an issue which takes us beyond the philosophy of the young Leibniz.

---

[138] Cf. Parkinson, *Leibniz on Human Freedom*, pp. 50-53. When Leibniz says that motives incline without necessitating, he is thinking of the strongest among two or more motives. The connection with hypothetical necessity is this: Whenever I make a choice, I follow the strongest motive. If, in the present situation, X is my strongest motive, then I follow X. The conclusion is necessary, but only hypothetically necessary, for it remains logically possible that I should have chosen something else. Had there been no such logical possibility, the conclusion would have been what Leibniz calls "absolutely necessary".

[139] *Von der Allmacht und Allwissenheit Gottes*, section 11.

[140] There is a passing reference in 129, 24 and in a deleted passage, 127, note to 1. 16. Cf. 128, 8-9 and 129, 10 (*per accidens necessarium*).

[141] Consider an example given by Stuart Hampshire, *The Age of Reason* (New York: Mentor, 1956), p. 167. Suppose that a householder, Jones, has been bound and gagged by a robber. As such, Jones cannot prevent the robbery of his house, i.e. it is necessary that he does not prevent it. This proposition is hypothetically necessary, i.e. it is necessary *given that* Jones is bound and gagged. Hampshire points out that it *makes sense* to suppose that the man could have prevented the robbery (in Leibniz's terms, the proposition that he fails to do so is not absolutely necessary). But no one, says Hampshire, would suppose that such a man was *free* to prevent the robbery.

CATHERINE WILSON

ATOMS, MINDS AND VORTICES IN *DE SUMMA RERUM*:

LEIBNIZ *VIS-À-VIS* HOBBES AND SPINOZA

The recent translation of *De Summa Rerum* by G. H. R. Parkinson has
done much to revive speculation on the origins of Leibniz's later
metaphysics. Yet although *De Summa Rerum* is doubtless the most
coherent body of Leibniz's metaphysical writing between the
Confessio Philosophi of 1671 and the *Discourse* of 1686, the thoughts
expressed in it frequently seem to be related by dream logic rather than
logic – there is a swirl of statements relating to minds, particles, God,
and vortices which are highly resistant to systematic interpretation.[1]
Vortices, for example, are said to be associated with minds, with
worlds, and with solid bodies. They do not reappear in such a field of
associations, as far as I can determine, ever again: these vortices
(unlike the mathematically describable 'harmonic' vortices, Leibniz
preferred as a better fundamental explanation of planetary orbits than
Newtonian gravitation) are true singularities in Leibniz's theorising. In
this paper I shall suggest that they are intended to function as solutions
of what I will call the 'contouring problem', the problem of finding
stable individuals, substances – as opposed to substance – in the spare
ontology of the new philosophy. As Leibniz puts the question:

---

[1] For a previous approach to this problem, see G. H. R. Parkinson, 'Leibniz's *De
Summa Rerum*: A Systematic Approach', *SL* 18 (1986): 132-51.

S. Brown (ed.): The Young Leibniz and his Philosophy (1646-76). 223–43

> As the mind is something which has a certain relation to some portion of matter, then it must be stated why it extends itself to this portion and not to all adjacent portions; or, why it is that some body, and not every body, belongs to it in the same way.[2]

My argument will be that Leibniz had, for a period, a metaphysics without individual substances. It went something like this: the world is an aggregate of particles and fluids in which visible bodies are constantly changing, being generated and perishing, according to the rules of mechanics. Sensations, which are also generated and perish, depend on these motions and reactions, but there are also minds interspersed throughout the physical cosmos, and the enduring part of the mind − that which is not a temporary sensation − is a bit of the divine mind situated in matter. In other words, Leibniz married Hobbesian materialism to his version of pantheism.

In *De Summa Rerum,* a new scheme emerges in which each mind is associated with its own "vortex". Leibniz imagined that, as God was the soul of the great vortex of the world, so each mind was the soul of its own vortex, and each particle was a world (= vortex) animated by a mind. In a way, this scheme anticipated the theory of monads: when vortices drop out of the scheme what remains is the identification of each soul with its own world, and each particle of matter with its own soul. This, roughly is my account of how monads emerge from Leibniz's early encounters with mechanism and Spinozism. If this account in correct, it explains why Leibniz later confessed that he had been tempted by both atomism and Spinozism. It has not been easy to find atomistic and Spinozistic moments in Leibniz, but they are clearly in evidence in *De Summa Rerum.*[3]

---

[2] 'Notes on Science and Metaphysics', A VI iii 393: PDSR 45.

[3] Whether Leibniz can be seen as a 'Spinozist' is a matter of emphasis, attribution, and relevant comparisons. If Leibniz's focus on individuation is thought to be more important than his focus on perspectival harmony, he is not Spinozistic. If his references to creation by emanation are more properly described as Neo-platonic or as Scholastic, he is not Spinozistic. If the relevant contrast-class is given by Locke and Descartes, he is Spinozistic. Relevant discussions include Georges Friedmann, *Leibniz et Spinoza,* (2nd edition, Paris: Gallimard, 1962); Aaron Gurwitsch, *Leibniz und den Panlogismus* (Berlin: de Gruyter, 1974); Catherine Wilson, *Leibniz's Metaphysics* (Princeton: Princeton University Press, 1989), pp. 280-1, et *passim;* R.

The first question to be addressed is a simple one. Why is it wrong to think that Leibniz was always a substance-pluralist?

For a long time commentators thought it was fairly obvious that Leibniz was dissatisfied with Hobbes and Spinoza because they were not substance-pluralists and he always had been. According to Loemker, Leibniz's reading notes on Spinoza's *Ethics* of 1678 "show how his concern to establish a sound logical basis for his own pluralistic view of substance impelled him to search out and criticise the logical gaps and implicit assumptions in Spinoza's argument".[4] But recent research has forced a reassessment of this claim. As is well known, Leibniz became interested as a young student in the problem of individuation and its relation to matter, which he approached in his doctoral dissertation through the texts of the scholastics, and when he came to write the *Discourse* he thought of himself as breathing new life into the by then unfashionable theory of substantial forms. But the view that Leibniz had up to that date never wavered from his trademark substance pluralism is difficult to sustain. Rather, he seems to have been attracted within a short space of time both by a monistic emanation theory and by Cartesian mechanism. In the fragment 'On Transubstantiation' of 1668, he tries to explain how (in Aristotelian terms) bread can lose its nature as bread-substance and become the substance of the body of Christ when consecrated. Leibniz argues that the identity of a substance is given by its union with a particular or general "concurrent mind". Thus, different humans are different "substances" because they are united to different minds, and bodies which lack reason are the substances they are thanks to their union

---

M. Adams, *Leibniz: Determinist, Idealist, Theist* (New Haven: Yale University Press, 1993), pp. 126-30; pp. 157 ff.; G. H. R. Parkinson, 'Leibniz's Paris Writings in relation to Spinoza', *SL Supp.* 18 (1978): 73-91; Mark Kulstad, 'Did Leibniz incline towards Monistic Pantheism in 1676?', *Leibniz und Europa. Proceedings of the VIth International Leibniz-Kongress* (Hanover, 1994), pp. 424-8, and 'Leibniz's *De Summa Rerum;* the Origin of the Variety of Things, in Connection with the Spinoza-Tschirnhaus Correspondence', *SL Sond.* (1997).

[4] L 196.

with God.[5] When bread becomes the body of Christ, it is released from its union with God's mind, in virtue of which it is bread, and acquires a union with Christ's. A transmigration of souls, the 'appropriation' of a body by a particular mind, changes the substantiality of objects. But doesn't this imply that all of inanimate nature is one substance as it is informed by the same (divine) mind?[6] No! says Leibniz, the *concurrent* divine mind is different from the divine mind. "From this it is apparent that there is not one substantial form for all bodies but a different one for different bodies, for as the disposition of nature is varied, the form and idea are also varied."

Here, several years before Leibniz knew anything about Spinoza, there is a suggestion that inanimate nature is varied as the ideas of God are varied. And in the Supplement to the fragment, Leibniz says that the ideas of God and the substances of things (note that there is no restriction here to inanimate nature) are "the same in fact, different in relation; they are, moreover, as action and passion ... the substances of things are the act of God on species".[7] Evidently, Leibniz is here trying to effect a merger of Aristotelian and Platonic metaphysics. Before heaving a sigh of despair at the apparent futility of such an undertaking, it is well to recall that just such reconciliation was a prominent task of Renaissance philosophy. In the idea = form equation there are echoes of Plotinus' "seminal reasons" – the *logoi spermatikoi* – which mediate between material objects and immaterial ideas. Ficino says:

> The soul of the world possesses at least as many seminal reasons of things as there are ideas in the divine mind, and with these reasons [soul] makes the same number of species in matter. Thus each and every species corresponds through its own seminal reason to an idea, and through this reason, it can easily receive something of value from on high.[8]

---

[5] Leibniz, 'On Transubstantiation,' in A VI i 509: L 116.

[6] A VI i 511: L 118.

[7] A VI i 512: L 119.

[8] Marsilio Ficino, *Opera* I 531, quoted in Brian P. Copenhaver, 'Astrology and Magic', in *The Cambridge History of Renaissance Philosophy,* ed. Quentin Skinner,

And Leibniz never lets go of the idea that the substances of things are or are somehow equivalent to ideas in God's mind. Eight years later, in *De Summa Rerum,* he suggests that God and his creatures may be conceived as related as essence and properties or that things may originate from God as $1 + 1 + 1 + 1 + 1 + 1$ originate from 6.[9] Mark Kulstad has called attention to a frankly Spinozistic – but also Platonic in the sense indicated above – passage from April 1676. As Kulstad stresses, one of Leibniz's major preoccupations is the problem of explaining the differentiation of the world, how to explain the origins of mutability and multiplicity from the simplicity of God, and how to explain the variety of figures and motions of bodies from the attribute of extension.[10]

> That all things are distinguished not as substances but as modes, can easily be demonstrated, from the fact that if things are radically distinct, one of them can be perfectly understood without the other; that is, all the requirements of one can be understood without all the requirements of the other being understood. But it is not so in things; for since the Ultimate reason of things is unique ... it is manifest that the requirements of all things are the same. And thus the essence is too. If the only things that are really different are those that can be separated, or one of which can be perfectly understood without the other, it follows that nothing is really different from another thing, but all things are one, as Plato explains in the *Parmenides.*[11]

Eckhard Kessler and Jill Kraye (Cambridge: Cambridge University Press, 1988), pp. 264-301.

[9] 'On the Origin of Things from Forms', PDSR 77; A VI iii 518.

[10] Mark Kulstad, '*Leibniz's De Summa Rerum*: the Origin of the Variety of Things'.

[11] 'That a Perfect Being is Possible', in PDSR 93-5; A VI iii 573-4. Adams' subtle gloss on this passage confirms that Leibniz could not fully accept an ontological distinction between the creator and the created and creation of the latter in orthodox

Now, it can be argued that Leibniz is simply running through an argument on paper without the superposition of an attitude of belief, as Hume would put it. But the weight of the texts suggests that this is not the case, and that a relatively favourable early reception of Spinoza was facilitated by Leibniz's theological interpretation of Spinozism. Another passage, from 18 March 1676, appears to be a frank endorsement of the Aristotelian-Averroist doctrine of the universal intellect:

> It can easily be proved that matter itself is perpetually extinguished, or, becomes now this and now that. In the same way it can be shown that the mind also is continually changed, with the exception of that in us which is divine, or, comes from outside. In sum, just as there is something divine in space, namely the immeasurability of God, so there is something divine in the mind, which Aristotle used to call the active intellect, and this is the same as the omniscience of God ... .[12]

There is something, he goes on to say, something "eternal and indivisible" in matter "which seems to have been understood by those who said that God himself is the matter of things". But we should understand this as meaning that God is the principle of things, not that he is a part of them.

The remainder of this passage confirms that Leibniz grasped the possibility of giving a morally acceptable interpretation of Spinoza's doctrine that God and his modes are the totality of what is. For Spinoza this meant that nothing was actually good nor evil. Leibniz improves on Spinoza here by rendering God as the totality of "positive attributes", and so slips valuation into Spinoza's neutral universe. In the several papers written in November–December 1676, we can observe how, repeatedly, "absolute positive qualities" slide over into "perfections"[13], following the thought of 18 March that "Perfection is

---

fashion *ex nihilo*. Adams, *Leibniz*, p. 130-1. Cf. C. Wilson, *Leibniz's Metaphysics* pp. 275-81.

[12] 'Notes on Science and Metaphysics', A VI iii 391: PDSR 43.

[13] "I term a 'perfection' every simple quality which is positive and absolute, or, which expresses without any limits whatever it does express." (A VI iii 577: PDSR 99).

an affirmative, absolute attribute, and it always contains everything of its own genus, for there is nothing that limits it."[14] A being which has all "affirmative" properties is possible, he argues, – and necessary.[15]

The second reason for doubting that Leibniz was a continuous proponent of individual substances is that he was distinctly friendly to Gassendist-Cartesian-Hobbesian mechanism in 1670-71, when the *Hypothesis physica nova* was being written and presented.[16] Leibniz tried to get into friendly contact with Hobbes in 1670, and in the Nizolius Preface, written in the same year, he is categorical: "We may thus regard it as established that whatever cannot be explained in popular terms is nothing and should be exorcised from philosophy as if by an incantation unless it can be known by immediate experience (like many classes of colours, odours, and tastes)."[17] This position is amplified in the letter to Herman Conring, who had reproached Leibniz with going over to the moderns. Leibniz defended his position, while denying that he followed Descartes slavishly:

> I do not know why you should consider as most absurd the view that everything happens mechanically in nature, that is, according to certain mathematical laws prescribed by God. I recognise nothing in the world but bodies and minds, and nothing in minds but intellect and will, nor anything in bodies

---

[14] 'Notes on Science and Metaphysics', A VI iii 392: PDSR 45.

[15] 'A Most Perfect Being Exists', A VI iii 572-3: PDSR 91-3.

[16] On Leibniz and Hobbes, see Ferdinand Tönnies, 'Leibniz und Hobbes', in *Studien zur Philosophie und Gesellschaftslehre im 17. Jahrhundert*, ed. E. G. Jacoby (Stuttgart-Bad-Cannstatt: Frommann-Holzboog, 1975), 151-68; Konrad Moll, 'Die erste Monadenkonzeption von Leibniz und ihr Ausgangspunkt in Conatus-Begriff und Perzeptionstheorie von Thomas Hobbes', *Proceedings of the Vth International Leibniz-Kongress*, Hanover, 1988; H. M. Bernstein, 'Conatus, Hobbes and the Young Leibniz', *Studies in the History and Philosophy of Science* 11 (1980): 25-37; Jeffrey Barnouw, 'The Separation of Reason and Faith in Bacon and Hobbes and Leibniz's *Theodicy*', *Journal of the History of Ideas* 42 (1981): 607-28.

[17] 'Preface to an Edition of Nizolius', in L 124: G IV 143.

insofar as they are separated from mind but magnitude, figure, situation and changes in these, either partial or total. Everything else is merely said, not understood: it is sounds without meaning.[18]

Contrary to what Leibniz says, this is orthodox Cartesianism. Did Leibniz then really believe in *individual* substances in 1670-71 and thereafter? Or was he trying to carve out a notion of individuality within the framework of Cartesian dualism?

Leibniz's restricted ontology of 1670 is compatible, I would argue, with the doctrine of concurrent minds of 1668. But it is not compatible with either a) his later rejection of Cartesian dualism in favour of a conception of bodies as possessing both active and passive powers; or b) the importance he comes to attach to the *perceptive* and imagistic rather than purely intellective aspects of mentality. It is for this reason interesting to ask to what extent, in *De Summa Rerum,* Leibniz had moved away from the concurrent minds+matter ontology (fitted into a Neo-Platonic framework) towards what is old-fashionedly but quite correctly described as an ontology which makes the living animal the fundamental unit.

1. Excursus: 'Individuals' in a Mechanical World

It has always been somewhat puzzling how, out of their fundamental ontologies, Hobbes and Spinoza are able to generate a conception of the subject of action and experience. Contours are lacking. For Gassendi, Hobbes, Boyle, and Descartes, the physical world consists of subvisible particles in incessant motion which aggregate to form larger units and which move (Hobbes, Descartes) in a fluid ether. In the physical world of Hobbes, as Spragens puts it:

the Aristotelian configuration of purposeful finite movements had disappeared entirely. In their stead remained a homogeneous swarm of incoherent, aimless perpetuations of

---

[18] Letter to Herman Conring, L 189: G I 196-7.

momentum that had no capacity for growth, fulfilment or rest.[19]

But how then can there be *things* apart from corpuscles? How is macroscopic structural stability arrived at? Why does a grain of sand remain a grain of sand and not turn into powder? On the middle-sized object level, how does a human body remain an object capable of acting as a unit and not fragment into the individual parts composing it, as will happen after death? On the cosmological level, what keeps the system of planets moving smoothly in proper circles (or ellipses) around the sun and keeps the moving earth from being whirled to pieces? The old answer: 'form' was unavailable, as were appeals to natural place.

In Chapter XXVI of his *Elements of Philosophy*, 'Of the World and of the Stars', Hobbes enunciates a number of physical theses, the effect of which is to break down the ordinary conception of the world as an ensemble of middle-sized visible objects, most of them stationary, of relatively fixed appearance. All space is full of matter,[20] and its motion may be coeternal with it. Moveable bodies are "fluid", "inconsistent", that is to say "hard", and "mixed". Hardness and softness are degrees of consistency, but fluidity is primitive. "A fluid body is always divisible into bodies equally fluid and quantity into quantities and soft bodies of whatsoever degree of softness, into soft bodies of the same degree." Although the atomists say that a substance is fluid if it consists of small particles like grain, this is incorrect, according to Hobbes. Neither dust nor a house falling to pieces is fluid.[21] Air consists of small non-fluid bodies swimming through a fluid ether which fills the rest of space. Because of the physical interconnectedness of everything, "no motion can be so weak, but that it may be propagated infinitely through a space filled with

---

[19] Spragens, *The Politics of Motion* (Lexington, University Press of Kentucky, 1973), p. 73.

[20] Thomas Hobbes, *De Corpore* in *English Works* ed. W. Molesworth (London: Bohn, 1939), *De Corpore, Works,* I 414.

[21] *Ibid.*, 1 426.

body of any hardness whatsoever".[22] This we might call the 'principle of infinite effect'. Sensation implies a motion in the organ of sense which has been propagated through all media originating with the object; it begins with a pressing or touching of the organ of sense which yields to it and propagates further motion.[23] A body endeavours to resist the entry of another body attempting to enter it and this endeavour outward opposed to inward endeavour creates the phantasm.[24] The universe is full of percipient beings, as small as anyone likes.[25] All bodies which are moved and which take part in action and reaction have sense, but, lacking organs, some do not have the means to retain these motions. Lacking memory, they lack awareness.

Perception and mental imagery, according to Spinoza in turn, depend on relations of solidity and fluidity. "When external bodies determine the fluid parts of the human body, so that they often impinge on the softer parts, they change the surface of the last named, hence they are refracted there from in a different manner from that which they followed before such change." This refraction within the body endures, leading to later experiences of renewed presence in memory and imagination.[26] Any and every change in the action of liquids against solids in the body affects its ideation. "Whatever happens in the object of the idea [namely, as is shown later, the human body – C. W.] constituting the human Mind, must be perceived by the human Mind."[27] This claim is echoed later in Prop. XIV "The human mind must perceive all that takes place in the human body."

But what is it to be the same person? – a perceiving individual? "The being of substance", Spinoza declares, "does not pertain to the

---

[22] *Ibid.*, 1 530.

[23] *Ibid.*, I 399.

[24] *Ibid.*, I 391-2.

[25] There are living creatures so small we can scarcely see their whole bodies, "yet even these have their young ones; their little veins and other vessels, and their eyes so small as that no microscope can make them visible." We cannot imagine any magnitude so small but that our very supposition is exceeded by nature. *Ibid.*, I 446.

[26] *Ethics*, Pt. II, Prop. 17, *Collected Works of Spinoza* I 464.

[27] *Ethics*, Pt II, Prop. 12, *Collected Works of Spinoza* I 456.

essence of man, or substance does not constitute the form of man".[28]
This is said to follow from the truth of the claim that there cannot be
two substances of the same nature; if men were diversified by being
different substances, that claim would be false. The human mind is
"part of the infinite intellect of God". This leaves him with a serious
version of the contouring problem. Spinoza attempts to give a
relational definition of what it is to be 'the same' body, the
consequence of which is that everything in the world can be seen to be
part of one body: If the parts composing a body so move that "they
communicate their motion to each other in a certain fixed manner, we
shall say that these bodies are united with one another and that they all
compose one body or Individual, which is distinguished from others
by this union of bodies".[29] So long as mutual relations of motion and
rest remain the same, "the [body or the] Individual will retain its
nature...".[30] The human body or person thus remains 'the same one'
despite the continual coming and going and replacement of its parts.
But the human body itself is part of a larger whole in which parts
come and go, and: "if we proceed in this way to infinity, we shall
easily conceive that the whole of nature is one Individual, whose parts,
i.e. all bodies, vary in infinite ways, without any change of the whole
Individual."[31]

Propositions 11-13 contain a curious argument which attempts to
pull from the flux of parts and the unity of the whole a notion of
personal and psychological identity. The argument runs as follows:
(Notice how Platonic Ideas are employed in preference to Aristotelian
Forms!)

---

[28] *Ethics*, Pt. II, Prop. 10, *Collected Works of Spinoza* I 454.

[29] *Ethics*, Pt II, Prop. 13, Axiom 3, *Collected Works of Spinoza* I 460.

[30] *Ethics*, Pt II, Prop. 13, Lemma 4, Cf. Lemma 7, *Collected Works of Spinoza* I
461.

[31] *Ethics*, Pt II, Prop. 13, Lemma 7, *Collected Works of Spinoza* I 461-2.

1. The human mind is a part of the infinite intellect of God and is constituted by one of God's ideas.[32]

2. This idea has an object, which actually exists.[33]

3. This object is a (human) body. (Ibid.)

It seems that Spinoza has drawn a human individual out of the single divine substance, like a rabbit out of a hat. Even more amazingly, he goes on to find a basis for the hierarchical ordering of human individuals. This happens in Prop. XIII with the help of the proposition that:

4. Some ideas, like some objects, are more excellent than others and contain more reality.

> In proportion as a Body is more capable than others of doing many things at once, or being acted on in many ways at once, so its Mind is more capable than others of perceiving many things at once. And in proportion as the actions of a body depend more on itself alone, and as other bodies concur with it less in acting, so its mind is more capable of understanding distinctly. And from these [truths] we can know the excellence of one mind over the others, and also see the cause why we have only a confused knowledge of our Body...[34]

2. Leibniz and the Problem of Individuals

When we left him in 1670, Leibniz was still working with his basic ontology of concurrent minds and matter. There are several references in *De Summa Rerum* to the Hobbesian doctrine that "sensation is motion" and to Hobbes' doctrine of infinite effect. For example:

---

32 *Ethics*, Pt. II, Prop. 11, Corollary, *Collected Works of Spinoza* 1 456.

33 *Ethics*, Pt. II, Prop. 13, *Collected Works of Spinoza* I 457.

34 *Ethics*, Pt. II, Prop. 13, Scholium, *Collected Works of Spinoza* I 458.

> A body resists, and ... this resistance is sensation. That is to say, a thing resists that which endeavours to divide it. Sensation is a kind of reaction. A body is as incorruptible as a mind, ...[35]

and:

> Species themselves are merely undulations of a liquid that is subject to pressure. Every undulation is preserved for eternity even if, when put together with others, it becomes imperceptible.[36]

Substantial forms are not mentioned in *De Summa Rerum,* and Leibniz is clear, as indeed he was in 1670, that there are "minds" in addition to matter. Note however, the new emphasis on the *perceptual* capacity of mind-matter composites. "In fact the mind is added to matter, [though] without matter it would not perceive as it does."[37] The doctrine of 'confused omniscience' is not so much a theory of knowledge as a theory about what we sense:

> It seems to me that every mind is omniscient in a confused way; that any mind perceives simultaneously what happens in the entire world, and that these confused perceptions of infinite simultaneous varieties produce the sensations that we have of colors, tastes, and feels. For such perceptions consist, not in one act of the intellect, but in an aggregate of infinitely many acts.[38]

In *De Summa Rerum,* concurrent minds suddenly appear in a new context: as each associated with a "vortex" which it agitates:

---

[35] 'On Truths, the Mind, God and the Universe', A VI iii 510: PDSR 61.

[36] 'On the Union of Soul and Body', A VI iii 480-1: PDSR 35-6.

[37] 'On the Origin of Things from Forms', A VI iii 519: PDSR 77.

[38] 'On the Plenitude of the World', A VI iii 524: PDSR 85.

> In the liquid [in the brain] there is a kind of fountain of motion and dilation, as in a burning candle. Further, every sort of gyration seems to be performed in the cavities of the brain, as the soul observes its own vortex ... The soul itself agitates a vortex – that is wonderful.[39]

I think we can see these passages as articulating a temporary position midway between 'concurrent minds' and a later theory of individual substance. The vortex, as I shall try to argue, is the 'world' of an individual soul, just as God is the soul of the greater 'world.' Each particle of matter, as Leibniz had observed earlier, is a world.[40] Each world is a vortex animated by and perceived by a mind, hence each particle is a vortex animated and perceived by a mind. This is the series of equivalencies which I imagine Leibniz to be thinking through.

I give below the main statements, in Parkinson's translation, of the vortex theory.

(1) There are as many unsplittable bodies as there are vortices - that is, motions of surrounding sectors which are varied in relation to some one thing.[41]

(2) Every mind has a vortex around itself.[42]

(3) [T]he solidity or unity of ... body comes from ... mind ...; ... there are as many minds as there are vortices; ... there are as many vortices as solid bodies.[43]

(4) [T]he soul observes its own vortex.[44]

---

[39] 'On the Union of Soul and Body', A VI iii 480-1: PDSR 35-6.

[40] Leibniz, *Hypothesis physica nova*, A V ii 223.

[41] 'On the Plenitude of the World', A VI iii 525: PDSR 89.

[42] 'On the Secrets of the Sublime', A VI iii 476-7: PDSR 31.

[43] 'On Truths, the Mind, God, and the Universe', A VI iii 509-10: PDSR 61.

[44] 'On the Union of Soul and Body', A VI iii 480: PDSR 35.

(5) [T]here are as many minds, or little worlds, or perceptions, as there are vortices in the world.[45]

(6) It seems that there is some centre of the entire universe, and some general infinite vortex; also some most perfect mind, or God.[46]

(7) [T]he soul itself agitates a vortex – that is wonderful... [F]or we do not act as a simple machine, but out of reflection, i.e. of action on ourselves. Perhaps the whole vortex of the great globe is vivified by a soul of the same kind, which is the reason why the laws of the system are observed, and all things are compensated. The whole world is one vortex for God.[47]

But why exactly vortices?

We are accustomed to Leibniz's constantly repeated idea that mind somehow confers unity and permanence on things. Without it they would disperse into fragments. Leibniz's disparaging talk about "mere aggregates" – what Aristotle called "partial bodies" which are one only because of the proximity of their parts – is not just a kind of metaphysical snobbery. Behind it is the genuine fear that aggregates are temporary: mortalism. If anything is to be eternal, it must be an atom because all composites will be worn down by abrasion and dispersed by motion. "If there were no atoms, then, given a plenum, all things would be dissolved."[48] But the "atom" is indestructible only because of the presence of a mind. "Every body which is an aggregate can be destroyed. There seem to be elements, i.e. indestructible bodies because there is a mind in them... ".[49] But why does Leibniz take the additional step of associating atoms and minds with vortices?

A vortex is a moving aggregate of celestial bodies or particles which maintains its motion and, through motion, its contour eternally.

---

[45] 'Excerpts from Notes on Science and Metaphysics', A VI iii 393: PDSR 47.

[46] 'On the Secrets of the Sublime', A VI iii 474: PDSR 25.

[47] 'On the Union of Soul and Body', A VI iii 480: PDSR 37.

[48] 'On the Plenitude of the World', A VI iii 525: PDSR 87.

[49] 'On the Origin of Things from Forms', A VI iii 521: PDSR 81.

The entire history of 'vortex theory' from Empedocles onwards is based on this seemingly miraculous feature. And the mechanists – Hobbes, Descartes, Spinoza – all require vortices to explain what holds the universe together. At one point Hobbes avails himself indiscriminately of every ancient notion of cosmic unity, suggesting that the universe stays together (a) because it is like an animal, (b) through rotation; and (c) through a subtle spirit: "It is very probable that the parts of the earth, the outermost no less than the innermost are all rotated, at the same time, and in the same manner in which a living creature turns round, there being suffused through the whole earth a most subtle body, that is a spirit working within it."[50].

It is perhaps unclear whether we should read 'vortex' in Leibniz's texts in the technical sense, as a series of rings of rotating fluid or particulate matter. In light of the ideas we have encountered above in Hobbes and Spinoza about how coherence and consistency are given by conspiring motions, it is possible that Leibniz simply means that the presence of a body indicates the presence of a unity-preserving set of motions analogous to those of the typical 'whirlpool' shape. (Recall that Spinoza in Bk II Prop. 13 claims that the coherence of a body implies its relative immunity to the concurrent motions of other bodies.[51]) What vortices do, on my hypothesis, is keep the minds associated with them 'separate' and 'distinct'. They give contour.

This function is brought out in an argument in the paper of 18 March 1676. If two separate portions of matter, each animated by a mind, come into contact, Leibniz argues, one of three things can happen. First, it can happen that "it will follow from the contact alone that the minds will coalesce into one, since no vacuum is interposed, from which it will follow that the thoughts of each are mingled." This seems problematic, as the new mind would spontaneously remember two selves. Second, it can happen that the two original minds perish, and a new mind arises representing the new amalgamated body. This seems problematic because it amounts to the admission that minds can be destroyed. The only solution is to say that there are as many minds

---

[50] Thomas Hobbes, *Thomas White's* De Mundo *Examined,* trans. H. W. Jones (London: Bradford University Press, 1976), p. 254.

[51] *Ethics* Pt II, Prop. 13 Axiom 3, Lemma 4, *Collected Works of Spinoza* I 460-1.

as there are portions of matter which *cannot* be brought into contact. Now a solid atom, by its motion, generates a vortex in a fluid, and a vortex cannot be brought into contact with another vortex. So mind, vortices, and atoms coincide.

Leibniz avails himself of vortices for another reason. He is seeking a model for the way in which minds are implanted in matter and implanted in such a way that they are confusedly omniscient. The model is – God. And the God who animates or agitates the great vortex of the whole is not mere will and understanding or the power and the order of nature. His personhood consists in sensation and awareness. "It must be shown that God is a person, i.e., an intelligent substance. It must be demonstrated rigorously that he senses his own action on himself, for nothing is more admirable than for the same being to sense and to be affected by it."[52] Leibniz ascribes perceptual sensitivity and moral personality to God in order to borrow them back to support his comparison between God and our souls:

> God is not as some represent him – something metaphysical, imaginary, incapable of thought, will or action, so that it would be the same as if you were to say that God is nature, fate, fortune, necessity, the world. Rather God is a certain substance, a person, a mind.[53]

In making these statements, Leibniz is able to treat the universe – the great world – as a living animal without denying the personhood of God, or giving in to Spinoza's idea that the universe is just God in his physical manifestation: God's mind agitates the vortex, it is not identical with the vortex. The way is also open for him to treat each particle (= world = vortex) as a living animal. Moreover, Leibniz has now laid the basis for a genuine substance pluralism. Each mind is a separate world, and each world is eternal.

It remains to explain the puzzling refutation of Spinoza which occurs in the paper 'On the Origin of Things from Forms'. If the mind

---

[52] 'On the Secrets of the Sublime', A VI iii 474-5: PDSR 27.

[53] *Ibid.*

were the idea of the body, Leibniz argues, it would not remain the same when the body, as an aggregate of solids and fluids, is always changing. But if it were the idea of all that the body perceived, he goes on to argue, "any mind will [would] be the idea of a [the?] whole vortex, which is not the case".[54] Is the objection that our finite minds cannot each and every one be the idea of the whole (read: great) vortex? Or that an individual mind cannot be the idea of its own vortex because it does not distinctly perceive everything happening within its own vortex? The intention is obscure. Nevertheless, by 15 April 1676, Leibniz seems to have rejected once for all the idea, which he entertained earlier, that immortality is impersonal and pertains only to the divine element within us. After repeating Hobbes' view that "Sensation is a kind of reaction", Leibniz tells us that

> A body is as incorruptible as a mind, but various organs around it are changed in various ways... . It is credible that one persists in one's very last thoughts. So it is credible that the man who dies content, remains content. It is my view that all true entities or minds, which alone are one, always increase in perfection; that there is some effect of all the impressions occurring in a body, which proceeds to infinity. It is not credible that the effect of all perceptions should vanish in the future, even though the effect of all other actions endures forever; but this would happen if the mind were extinguished. So I do not accept the view of Spinoza, that the individual mind is extinguished with the body; that the mind in no way remembers what has gone before; that there remains only that which is eternal in the mind, ...[55]

Leibniz goes on to argue that if Spinoza were right and only the "idea or essence of the body" were to survive, this would

> in no way belong to us, for it will not be remembered, nor shall we have any sensation of it, and we labour in vain to perfect our mind on behalf of its state after death. For that ultimate

---

[54] 'On the Origin of Things from Forms', A VI iii 518: PDSR 75.

[55] 'On Truths, the Mind, God, and the Universe', PDSR 61: A VI iii 510.

perfect essence, which is all that will survive when we die, is nothing to us.[56]

The transcendental argument here is that 'it is rational that the perfection of the mind should not be sought in vain'. But I am more interested for the present in the argument that "it is not credible that the effect of all impressions should vanish in the future". A vanishing, Leibniz holds, is inconsistent with the claim that the effect of all other actions endures for ever. Here, a Hobbesian doctrine is converted into an argument for the inextinguishability of consciousness.

3. The 'Grounding of the Subject'

As I have shown above, even when a 'fundamental' ontology contains no human individuals, philosophers have their ways of pulling them out, leading us to wonder whether Hobbes and Spinoza are substance monists only in a parade sense, not for the purposes of ordinary working philosophy.

For the purposes of ordinary working philosophy, the psychological concept of the individual is of moral and practical importance to both Hobbes and Spinoza. The moral text of the *Ethics* tells how the individual can sustain himself (temporarily) against the abrasive wearing away which is caused by mere living, and the fragmenting effects of emotional upheaval. Hobbes' text, as Jeffrey Barnouw emphasises, reveals him as a purposive thinker who insists that men must not only strive to live "securely, happily and elegantly", but indulge their curiosity and drive for the acquisition of knowledge – "something independent of any animal concern with self-preservation".[57] Self-preservation is nevertheless a fundamental drive for both. Leibniz accepted their conception of striving, self-improving

[56] *Ibid.*, A VI iii 510: PDSR 63.

[57] J. T. Barnouw, 'Hobbes's Psychology of Thought', *History of European Ideas* 10 (1989): 519-45.

'active' subjects, but insisted on situating these subjects in a familiar context: the city of God, where their actions had not only moral but also theological meaning. He cuts a striking figure to us in his historical context because he seeks a metaphysical basis for workaday pluralism.

Let me explain this further. It is sometimes wondered in what way the cosmologies and physical theories of Hobbes and Spinoza might be said to 'ground' their political theory, and it is held up as a reproach to Spinoza, for example, that his determinism is inconsistent with his didacticism. Now a metaphysics may 'ground' a politics by the exploiting analogies: for example, Locke's corpuscularianism is thought by some to 'ground' his alleged liberalism and doctrines of tolerance: no one is special, everyone is an atom jostling against other atoms. In Hobbes and Spinoza, the notion of *conatus* grounds a conception of subjecthood. Here, a concept is displaced from the physical realm, in which it is conceived variously as inertia, or a tendency to restitution, or as active endeavour, to the psychological realm in which it is conceived variously as a struggle for self-presentation or self-advancement.[58] Leibniz provides this sort of 'grounding' when he draws analogies between the "primitive power of action" of substances, the *vis viva* of physical bodies, and the striving for perfection of souls. But there is another sort of grounding which involves clearing the ground, and this kind Hobbes and Spinoza engage in as well. *First,* they destroy the traditional moral-theological notion of the individual as a creature of God and King, reducing him to a chance congeries of fluids and solids, then they reconstitute this subject as a political or social one *ad libitum.*

This is why, in a sense, there is no contradiction in Spinoza's idea of an ethical subject who dissipates the causal nexus of emotion in which he is at the same time enmeshed and thereby frees himself from the temporal order. The causal nexus is described precisely by Spinoza to show that it contains no ethical subjects. You cannot find any there. Ethical subjects are radically self-made.

Leibniz felt an antipathy for these subjects, new men, who, he thought, were conceived in terms of power and will, not in ethical

---

[58] *Ethics,* Pt. IV, Props. XX-XXV: *Collected Works of Spinoza* I 557-9.

terms.   And he seems to have thought that, in the absence of a defensible metaphysical notion of personhood, individuality, and identity, morality itself was threatened.   If we were not persons, substances, rather than fragile and temporary constructions of particles, there would be no basis for saying that God was a substance or a person.   Our experiences would end at death.   The perfection of the mind would be sought in vain.

Cartesianism, as Leibniz had discovered by the mid 1670s, could not satisfy his needs.   For the idea of potentially disembodied minds was absurd: minds were implanted in matter, and perception, not just intellection, was an elementary function of such implanted minds.   But scholastic hylomorphism could not satisfy them either.   Conceived by pagans, hylomorphism naturally lent itself to an Aristotelian, hence mortalist, conception of generation and corruption.   When form loses control of matter, death and deterioration ensure.   Spinoza's Averroist impersonal immortality was not a good substitute.   Leibniz's invention in *De Summa Rerum* – and his solution to the contouring problem – was the theory that each person is as eternal as the whole cosmos; each person is a little God, with a distinct personality, acting, sensing, and living, united to a world.[59]

---

[59]   This image can properly be regarded both as a prefiguring of the doctrine of 'world-apart' monads and of the *Theodicy*'s influential theory of creative activity as the artist's imitation of divine creation.

MARK A. KULSTAD

LEIBNIZ, SPINOZA AND TSCHIRNHAUS:

MULTIPLE WORLDS, POSSIBLE WORLDS

The relationship of Leibniz and Spinoza has been much disputed, not least in connection with the young Leibniz, that is, Leibniz in the years before about 1685. A leading question is whether Ludwig Stein was right, more than a century ago, when he claimed that the young Leibniz entered into a 'Spinoza-friendly' period during and shortly after 1676.[1] Of course, some believe that Georges Friedmann, in his *Leibniz et Spinoza,* put to rest the persistent claim of a substantial connection between the two philosophers, not only for Leibniz's early years but also for the whole of Leibniz's life.[2] But the issue of Spinozistic strains in the young Leibniz has been raised again recently, by Robert Adams as well as myself, in connection with suggestions that Leibniz was a monist in 1676.[3] The complex and debated questions associated with this intriguing philosophical relationship obviously will not be put to rest in this paper. But perhaps new light may be brought to such questions from a familiar, but perhaps

---

[1] Ludwig Stein, *Leibniz und Spinoza* (Berlin: George Reimer, 1890); see especially chapter V, 'Die Spinoza freundliche Periode (1676-1679)', pp. 60-110.

[2] Third edition (Paris: Gallimard, 1975). See especially Appendix II, 'Note sur le livre de Ludwig Stein', and pp. 276-9.

[3] For Adams, see his *Leibniz. Determinist, Theist, Idealist* (New York & Oxford: Oxford University Press, 1994), pp. 123-34 (the section entitled, 'Is Leibniz's Conception of God Spinozistic?'). For my own perspective, see 'Did Leibniz Incline towards Monistic Pantheism in 1676?', International Leibniz-Congress, *Leibniz und Europa* 1 (1994): 424-28. It should be noted that Christia Mercer's much-awaited book on the young Leibniz – *Leibniz's Metaphysics: Its Origin and Development* (Cambridge: Cambridge University Press, forthcoming) – will take an opposing view.

S. Brown (ed.): The Young Leibniz and his Philosophy (1646-76) 245–62
© 1999 Kluwer Academic Publishers. Printed in the Netherlands.

To be sure, Tschirnhaus is well known as one of the contemporary critics, indeed, possibly the most penetrating contemporary critic, of Spinoza. He is also reasonably well known as the individual who, perhaps not altogether properly, initiated Leibniz into some of the secrets of the as yet unpublished *Ethics*. But the two roles have not typically been put together. It is a major point of this paper that they should be put together, that it is by focusing on the challenges that Tschirnhaus raised in his exchanges with Spinoza, including the interpretations of Spinoza implicit in these, that we can find major insights into some of the themes that may have engaged Leibniz most about Spinoza's philosophy in late 1675 and, especially, 1676 (basically, the time between Leibniz's establishing contact with Tschirnhaus and Leibniz's own face-to-face meeting with Spinoza in November of 1676). And what this means is that perhaps the best way to view the relationship between Leibniz and Spinoza in this period is not as a purely bipolar relationship – however much the image of the two philosophers finally conversing together alone in the Hague late in 1676 (not to mention the much greater fame of these two in comparison to Tschirnhaus) invites this reading – but rather as a three-cornered metaphysical dialectic, metaphysics à trois, if you will, beginning with Spinoza, continuing through Tschirnhaus' exchanges with Spinoza, and leading to the reflections by Leibniz on a Spinoza mediated by these exchanges.

The present paper will by no means try to address the whole of this three-cornered metaphysical dialectic. Rather, it sets itself the more modest goal of presenting a single important example of the sort of insight that this particular lens may make possible in considering the philosophical relationship of Leibniz and Spinoza. The example is, somewhat surprisingly, the critical Leibnizian topic of possible worlds. I say 'somewhat surprisingly' because Spinoza makes no mention of possible worlds. Indeed, according to the standard view that Spinoza is a necessitarian, his system does not even allow for merely possible worlds – that is, possible worlds that do not exist – without which Leibniz's doctrine of possible worlds loses its point. Yet on the view to be presented in this paper, it was in fact an aspect of Spinoza's metaphysics that – filtered through Tschirnhaus' critical interest in, and correspondence with Spinoza about this aspect of Spinoza's metaphysics – was crucial in Leibniz's unexpectedly radical ruminations[4] about multiple and then possible worlds during the last of Leibniz's Paris years, that is, during 1676.

Let us begin our explorations by setting out as a kind of benchmark a sample of Leibniz's early mature position on possible worlds. This will provide us with a standard of comparison for Leibniz's earlier work in the so-called *De Summa Rerum*,[5] the collection of short, unpublished papers from 1675-76 that will serve as the basic Leibnizian source for the present study. The paper from Leibniz's early maturity, 'On Freedom',[6] is a work well-known for its distinction between necessary and contingent truth, as well as its explanation of the latter via the theory of infinite analysis. It has the added advantage of indicating clearly that the development in Leibniz's thinking involving possible worlds played a key role also in his thinking about other important topics, most notably, necessity and contingency. Here is the quotation:

> When I considered that nothing occurs by chance or by accident unless we resort to certain particular substances . . ., and that nothing exists unless certain conditions are fulfilled from all of which together its existence at once follows, I found myself very close to the opinions of those who hold everything to be absolutely necessary. But I was pulled back from this precipice by considering those possible things which neither are nor will be nor have been. For if certain possible things never exist, existing things cannot always be necessary; otherwise it would be impossible for other things to exist in

---

[4] I argue more generally for the claim that the private papers in Leibniz's *De Summa Rerum* quite often took a more radical turn than we might be led to expect on the basis of his mature writings in 'Roads Not Taken: Radical Suggestions of Leibniz's *De Summa Rerum*'. A version of that paper was read at the Woburn conference that prompted the present anthology but it could not be included here because of a prior commitment.

[5] The name comes from the Academy editors, who grouped together most of the philosophical papers of this period under the label.

[6] The paper is undated. However, it has been tentatively assigned to 1689 by Gaston Grua, Gr 326.

their place, and whatever never exists would therefore be impossible.[7]

Here we have the unequivocal statement that there are possibles that "neither are nor will be nor have been", and the explicit connection of this to the rejection that everything is absolutely necessary. To be sure, there is no explicit mention of merely possible worlds, though the thought of these is close at hand.

It will be helpful to compare Leibniz's position with other related but distinct positions. There are two main contenders to consider, both present, or at least suggested, in the quotation above. One is what I shall call the 'multiple worlds' or 'many worlds' view, in which it is held that there is not just one world (very roughly, the one we know), but rather many worlds, all actually existing, but quite distinct from one another, for example, because of dramatic differences in space and/or time. A simple example of this type of view can be seen in the fact that, with the onset of Copernican theory and its development, it became possible to think of our solar system as a world of its own and to conceive that another star might have its own planetary system, which could then also count as a world of its own, and so on. Leibniz indicates his awareness of views like this in the continuation of the passage above from 'On Freedom' (note especially the second half of what follows):

> For it cannot be denied that many stories, especially those we call novels, may be regarded as possible, even if they do not actually take place in this particular sequence of the universe which God has chosen – unless someone imagines that there are certain poetic regions in the infinite extent of space and time where we might see wandering over the earth King Arthur of Great Britain, Amadis of Gaul, and the fabulous Dietrich von Bern invented by the Germans.[8]

A second contender to Leibniz's view of merely possible worlds is that, although not all possible things exist now, each possible thing

---

[7] FC 178-79: L 263.
[8] *Ibid.*

either has existed, is existing, or will exist at some point. This too is a position that Leibniz is aware of. In the continuation of the passage above, he sets out an example of it with a reference to Descartes, along with a clear statement of his rejection of it and his reasons for this rejection:

> A famous philosopher of our century does not seem to have been far from such an opinion [the one about many worlds], for he expressly affirms somewhere that matter successively receives all the forms of which it is capable *(Principles of Philosophy, Part 111, Art 47)*. This opinion cannot be defended, for it would obliterate all the beauty of the universe and any choice of matters, not to mention here other grounds on which the contrary can be shown.[9]

Insofar as the second view implies that there is no possible thing that never exists, it might be taken as having more obvious connections to Spinoza's necessitarian position than the 'many worlds' contender. But, as our examination of Tschirnhaus' questioning of Spinoza will reveal, there is a way of interpreting Spinoza's philosophy as a 'many worlds' position as well. To be sure, there is no logical incompatibility between the two positions. Spinoza could have held both views – and Leibniz seems indeed to see a link between the two positions. But reading Spinoza as a 'many worlds' theorist is perhaps a surprising approach. Because it may be crucial for Leibniz's developing views on 'worlds', let us consider the questions and challenges of Tschirnhaus that bring this reading to the fore.

The clearest exposition of the relevant position comes, not strictly from a letter by Tschirnhaus, but rather a letter by Schuller, who wrote to Spinoza on July 25, 1675 (letter 63), passing on to the latter some

---

[9] *Ibid.* The suggestion is that Leibniz takes the first view, the 'many worlds' view, to imply the second view, that all possibles will exist at some time in our universe, even if they do not all exist at any one time. We shall not take up this suggestion here, but it should at least be noted. The issue will come up again later in the paper.

questions Tschirnhaus had raised using Schuller as an intermediary. Here is what is said on the topic that concerns us:

> Would you be willing, Sir, to convince us by some direct demonstration, and not by a reduction to impossibility, that we cannot know more attributes of God than thought and extension? Moreover, does it follow from that that creatures which consist of other attributes cannot conceive extension, so that there would seem to be constituted as *many worlds* as there are attributes of God? For example, our world of extension, so to speak exists with a certain abundance. So also, with the same abundance, would there exist worlds which consist of other attributes. And as we perceive nothing besides extension except thought, so the creatures of those worlds would have to perceive nothing but the attribute of their own world and thought.[10]

Here Tschirnhaus clearly raises the possibility of reading Spinoza as presenting a 'many worlds' view. And, at least on one fairly obvious interpretation of this, each of these many worlds exists. Thus, this 'many worlds' view would be radically different from the theory of possible worlds on which at most one of the possible worlds exists. The distinctness of these worlds would turn on, not radical differences of space or time, as in Leibniz's example above about the "poetic regions", but on radical barriers of knowledge, perceivability or conceivability: "we [in our world] cannot know more attributes of God than thought and extension", and "as we perceive nothing besides extension except thought, so the creatures of those [other] worlds would have to perceive nothing but the attribute of their own world and thought".

Spinoza's answer to this is a bit unclear, and indeed, as the exchange continues through subsequent letters it becomes apparent that each of the two has some difficulty in comprehending the other's ideas. We will not follow out the later details of this exchange here, since it is not central to the impact on Leibniz. Rather, we turn

---

[10] C. Gebhardt, *Spinoza Opera* (Heidelberg: Carl Winter, 1925), v. 4, pp. 274-75, translation from E. M. Curley, A *Spinoza Reader* (Princeton: Princeton University Press, 1994), pp. 269-70, emphasis mine.

directly to the relations between Tschirnhaus and Leibniz, especially those having to do with the issue of 'worlds'.

In late September of 1675, after having received a letter from Henry Oldenburg, the Secretary of the Royal Society, recommending Tschirnhaus, Leibniz made the acquaintance of the young German in Paris. Soon the two were actively exchanging thoughts about metaphysics as well as mathematics, in the early stages of one of the clearly important intellectual relationships of Leibniz's life.[11] Although Tschirnhaus had received information about Spinoza's *Ethics* in confidence, it is perhaps not too surprising in this context that he shared some of the new philosophy with Leibniz. We have a record of this in a summary of key ideas from the *Ethics* written up by Leibniz apparently sometime in the period from October 1675 to February 1676,[12] beginning with words showing clearly Tschirnhaus' role in Leibniz's developing understanding of Spinoza: "Mons. Tschirnhaus m'a conté beaucoup de choses du livre Ms. de Spinosa."[13]

There has been some debate about the accuracy and fullness of the information Leibniz received,[14] but that need not concern us overly here, since our main focus is on Leibniz's reaction to what he understood to be Spinoza's view. For present purposes one long sentence from that paper is what most bears examination:

> He [Spinoza] thinks that there are infinite other affirmative attributes besides thought and extension, but that thought is in all of them as it is here in extension; but what these other

---

[11] See H. Breger, 'Leibniz und Tschirnhaus', in *Wissenschaft und Weltgestaltung* (Hildesheim: Olms, forthcoming), for more on the nature of this relationship, particularly as it has to do with mathematics.

[12] The Academy editors include it in a group of papers recording conversations, and they tentatively date the whole group to the months "October 1675 – Februar 1676 (?)". (A VI iii 380).

[13] A VI iii 384, 'Uber Spinozas Ethik': "Mr. Tschirnhaus has told me many things about the manuscript book of Spinoza."

[14] See G. H. R. Parkinson, 'Leibniz's Paris Writings in Relation to Spinoza', pp. 79-83, *SL Supp.* 18 (1978): 79-83 and Friedmann, *Leibniz et Spinoza* (1st ed., 1946; 2nd ed., Paris: Gallimard, 1962), pp. 100-05. I incline to Parkinson's side.

attributes are, cannot be conceived by us, [and] each attribute
is infinite in its own kind, as is space in our case.[15]

As might be expected, we do not find here the precise terminology of
Spinoza. But pretty clearly we find in this text both the view that there
are infinitely many attributes besides the attributes of thought and
extension, and the view that what these other attributes are cannot be
conceived by us. So far so good – for most, these views are clearly
Spinoza's.[16]

Tschirnhaus' unusual interpretation of Spinoza on these matters
seems to make its entrance next, in the statement that "thought is in all
of them as it is here in extension". Although the exact meaning of this
statement is not certain, the idea seems to be that in all attributes other
than thought and extension, the modes of each of these attributes are
linked with thought as modes of extension are here in the realm of
extended things. Thus, if attribute X is one of these attributes besides
thought and extension, then for each of the finite modes of attribute X,
there will be an idea of this mode, just as for each body, or each finite

---

[15] A VI iii 385. The original Latin sentence (Leibniz started the note in French, and
then quickly changed into the learned language he had known much longer) is as
follows: "Putat infinita alia esse attributa affirmativa praeter cogitationem et
extensionem, sed in omnibus esse cogitationem ut hic in extensione; qualia autem
sint illa a nobis concipi non posse, unumquodque in suo genere esse infinitum, ut hic
spatium." The translation is drawn from Parkinson, 'Leibniz's Paris Writings in
Relation to Spinoza', p. 82, where it is broken up into two pieces. The reference to
'space' at the end of the passage is a bit disconcerting, suggesting an identification of
space and the attribute of extension. As we shall see below, Leibniz's thought on
space was definitely in flux in this period, including among other things a
repudiation of the identification suggested here.

[16] Bennett raises questions about the standard view that the *Ethics* contains the thesis
that there are infinitely many attributes besides thought and extension, going so far as
to build a case "for interpreting the *Ethics* as not containing the doctrine that there
are more than two attributes". See Jonathan Bennett, *A Study of Spinoza's* Ethics
(Indianapolis: Hackett, 1984), p. 77. His position is a subtle one, however, and it
should not be overstated. For example, he also says, "I do not say that Spinoza
thought there were only two attributes." *(ibid.)* And he states his "central claim"
hypothetically, after having distinguished between what Spinoza had in mind and
what is in his text: "if he [Spinoza] took 'infinite attributes' to imply 'more than two
attributes', then that extra implication is negligible because in the *Ethics* it is idle."
(ibid., p. 79)

mode of extension, there is an idea of that mode.[17] As a final point of comparison, we find the statement that each attribute is infinite in its own kind, a clear reference to Spinoza's distinction between absolute infinity and infinity in its own kind, drawn in the 'Explication' to definition 6 of Part I of the *Ethics,* and perhaps also an echo of Tschirnhaus' thought that, "our world of extension, so to speak, exists with a certain abundance. So also, *with the same abundance,* would there exist worlds which consist of other attributes."[18]

Now Leibniz does not use the expression 'many worlds' in his notes on this part of Spinoza's philosophy, but he is arguably on the threshold of Tschirnhaus' position, as expressed in the statement of Schuller's letter, that

> there would seem to be constituted as many worlds as there are attributes of God ... [A]s we perceive nothing besides extension except thought, so the creatures of those worlds would have to perceive nothing but the attribute of their own world and thought.[19]

---

[17] Some might wonder if the idea of modes of attribute X are actually modes of an attribute of thought distinct from the one of our realm, that is, distinct from the attribute of thought that has as its modes ideas of extended things. If one rejects such multiplicity of attributes of thought, then one seems forced to the conclusion that for Spinoza the attribute of thought is more extensive than the other attributes, not only for the reason just given, involving both the attribute of extension and all those other attributes whose nature is unknown to us, but also for the reason that for each mode of a given attribute, say of extension, there is not just one associated mode of the attribute of thought, namely, the idea of this mode of extension, but rather an infinity of such ideas, since there is also an idea of this idea, and an idea of the idea of this idea, and so on to infinity, all constituting modes of this same attribute of thought.

[18] This is drawn from the fuller quotation above, Gebhardt, *Spinoza Opera, v.* 4, pp. 274-75; translation from E. M. Curley, *A Spinoza Reader,* pp. 269-70; emphasis added.

[19] Gebhardt, *Spinoza Opera*, vol. 4, pp. 274-75; translation from E. M. Curley, *A Spinoza Reader,* pp. 269-70. It is worth noting that Spinoza, in letter 66, seems to confirm at least part of what Tschirnhaus has in mind, for he says that, "although each thing is expressed in infinite modes in the infinite intellect of God, the infinite ideas in which it is expressed cannot constitute one and the same mind of a particular

The key, again, is Leibniz's statement that "thought is in all of them as it is here in extension".

In any case, we need not limit ourselves to Leibniz's words in the important note just quoted to get a sense of what he was thinking in this time frame. For in writings of the same period, ones taken from what the Academy editors have grouped together as 'De Summa Rerum', Leibniz takes up rather similar notions. A striking passage, central for present purposes, is the following long statement from the paper, 'De Formis Simplicibus' of April 1676:

> Perception and situation are simple forms. But change and matter, i.e., modifications, are what result from all other forms taken together. For there are infinitely various things in matter and in motion, and this infinite variety can result only from an infinite cause, that is, from various forms. From this it is easily understood that simple forms are infinitely many. But the modifications which result from them all, related to individual forms, constitute the variety in them. It seems that perception and situation are everywhere, but matter is different in various things, and so various laws arise. For example, if it is a law in our world that the same quantity of motion is always preserved, there can be another universe in which there are also other laws. But it is necessary that the latter space differs from the former; there will be position of some kind, and multitude, but it will not be necessary that there should be length, breadth, and depth. We see already that there are various kinds of quantities in time, in an angle, and in other things. It seems that perception, pleasure, and happiness are everywhere; for it is the wonderful nature of this that it duplicates – indeed, it

---

thing, but an infinity of minds. For each of these infinite ideas has no connection with the others". (18 August, 1675, Gebhardt, *Spinoza Opera*, p. 280; translation from A *Spinoza Reader*, p. 302). The idea seems to be that no single mind could have an idea of both a mode of the attribute of extension and a mode of one of the attributes other than thought and extension. But if one can conceive a certain attribute only if one can have an idea of a mode of that attribute, then this would block minds associated with an attribute other than thought or extension from being able to conceive the attribute of extension.

multiplies to infinity – the variety of things. But it seems that variety can come about in other ways, which do not come within the reach of our mind. There is the same variety in any kind of world.[20]

It would take us well beyond the central aims of this article to try to untangle all that is suggested here. What I shall offer is an hypothesis about some central points of the passage without giving the sort of argument – drawing on many of the other writings of the *De Summa Rerum* – that would be necessary in a fuller exposition.

I begin then by claiming that in talking about simple forms, Leibniz is talking about what he elsewhere calls attributes.[21] Further, I claim that Leibniz's perception is an attribute that is more or less equivalent to Spinoza's attribute of thought. Situation, on my interpretation, is more complex. It would be a mistake, I think, to call it more or less equivalent to Spinoza's attribute of extension. The key text is this:

> if it is a law in our world that the same quantity of motion is always preserved, there can be another universe in which there are also other laws. But it is necessary that the latter space differs from the former; there will be position of some kind, and multitude, but it will not be necessary that there should be length, breadth, and depth.[22]

Leibniz is here thinking quite abstractly. He conceives of a 'space' without 'length, breadth, and depth'. Let me call such a 'space' a 'non-standard space'. He also, of course, conceives of a space that does involve 'length, breadth, and depth' – a sort of space that I shall call a 'standard space'. On my reading of this passage, Leibniz's 'situation' and 'space' (in his wide sense of the latter term) are

---

[20] A VI iii 522-23, 'De Formis Simplicibus', April 1676, translation from Parkinson, PDSR 83, with a minor change (reading 'multiplies' instead of 'multiples' as the translation of '*multiplicet*').

[21] A VI iii 513-14: PDSR 69.

[22] *Ibid.*

equivalent, and each includes both 'standard space' and 'non-standard space'. What Leibniz gives as the essential characteristics of such situation or space are 'position of some kind' and 'multitude'.

I see Leibniz here as thinking through ideas quite close to Spinoza's, but adding more detail on some points than Spinoza offered. For instance, Leibniz, probably following Tschirnhaus, seems inclined to draw a fundamental distinction between the attribute (or attributes[23]) of thought and all the other attributes. These latter attributes, the non-thought attributes, I shall sometimes call 'basic attributes' to give a convenient form of reference.[24] Even though in some sense basic attributes other than extension are, on Leibniz's view, "not within the reach of our mind", he thinks that in another sense we can know things about them, at least in very general terms – and this is where he goes beyond Spinoza. Specifically, we can know that the basic attributes besides extension are attributes that have something in common with extension, namely, what Leibniz calls situation, involving, as we have seen, multiplicity and a 'position' of some kind. But of course these other basic attributes are different from extension also: again as we have seen, "it will not be necessary that there should be length, breadth, and depth" as in extension there obviously is. And the laws of the modes of these other basic attributes can be different as well: "various laws arise", or at least can arise, in connection with different basic attributes.

At this point an objection based on the mature Leibniz might be raised. The point about "various laws", it may be objected, is not one about the modes of different attributes of the actual world, but a point about different laws in different possible worlds, only one of which is actual. Leibniz is here presenting, the objection might continue, an early version of his distinctive mature view that laws of nature are not

---

[23] See the note above on the interpretative possibilities that (a) there might be just one attribute of thought, but more extensive than any other attribute, or (b) there might be multiple attributes of thought.

[24] The idea behind the term 'basic attribute' is that the modes of thought always involve ideas of the modes of some other attribute, e.g., the idea of a body involves a mode of the attribute of extension. (There are, of course, ideas of ideas in Spinoza's system, but these can always be traced down to an idea that is not of an idea, but rather of a mode of some attribute other than thought.) Thus, in a sense, ideas as modes of thought are 'based on' other attributes; hence, the term 'basic attributes' to refer to attributes other than thought.

necessary, that the laws of nature of different possible worlds can differ, and that some worlds which are possible but do not exist have laws of nature that differ from those of this world, which does exist.

Although I will not attempt here to demonstrate that Leibniz does not have this interpretation in mind in the present text, I can at least make clear that I am well aware of this rival interpretation, based on the familiar position of Leibniz's maturity, and that my own interpretation of this passage differs sharply from this. I contend that Leibniz is here saying that laws may differ in two worlds, both of which actually exist. To be sure, Leibniz uses a confusing terminology in this passage: he talks of "our world", "any kind of world", "another universe", a "former" and a "latter space", and items which are "everywhere". But on my interpretation, this is all talk about actually existing things. 'Our world' is the world of standard space and the perception of items in standard space. (Or to put it in other, more Spinozistic terms, 'our world' is a world of thought and extension.) 'Another universe', or another world is one that has a 'non-standard space', but which also has 'perception' or thought, for "It seems that perception ... is] everywhere", that is, thought or perception exist in every (actual) world with each world defined in terms of a different situation, that is, a different basic attribute. Thus, each world has an extension-like attribute of situation, and also perception or thought. Also, as Leibniz says, "simple forms [or attributes] are infinitely many", so it seems that there are infinitely many such actually existing worlds. Leibniz's own words would seem to confirm this, for he says that his conception is such that it "multiplies to infinity ... the variety of things". Additionally, according to Leibniz, "there is the same variety in any kind of world", by which he may conceivably refer, via Tschirnhaus, to an extension of Spinoza's assertion of *Ethics* II Prop. 7 – to which Spinoza firmly directed Tschirnhaus' attention in their exchange, and which Tschirnhaus explicitly discussed later in the correspondence (letter 65) – namely, that "The order and connection of ideas is the same as the order and connection of things".

Two more points are important in the examination of this passage. First, although Leibniz seems less pessimistic than Spinoza about knowing the general structure of basic attributes other than extension, he still states that "it seems that variety can come about in other ways [than it does in our world of extension and thought], which [ways] do not come within the reach of our mind". That is, much as Tschirnhaus conceived of things, there would be 'many worlds', each with an extension-like attribute and also perception or thought, with the minds of each world unable to conceive of the extension-like attributes of the other worlds, so that there would be, as it were, an epistemological barrier establishing a clear separation among these many worlds.

Secondly, although it would not appear absolutely necessary that a 'many worlds' view would be linked to one in which all possible things exist, the suggestion is that Leibniz experimented with such a link, indeed, in the very paper we are examining. The key passage here involves its own complexities, but is worth including in our examination. It deals with the productions of things in the universe:

> Things are not produced by the mere combination of forms in God, but along with a subject also. The subject itself, or God, together with his ubiquity, gives the immeasurable, and this immeasurable combined with other subjects brings it about that *all possible modes, or things,* follow in it.[25]

If the present interpretation is on the right track, then in April of 1676 Leibniz had a theory of multiple worlds that was very different from his mature theory of 'possible worlds'. It was a 'many worlds' theory, a theory of multiple actual worlds, rather than the familiar theory of possible worlds, with at most one world being actual. It was a theory, moreover – and this is the point of the passage just quoted – in which all possible things are actualised. And it was a theory in which we, in our world of perception and extension – or space *with* length, breadth, and width –, could not adequately conceive of the other worlds of different basic attributes or simple forms. Thus, it was a theory with intriguing connections to the metaphysics of Spinoza – or at least to the metaphysics of Spinoza as understood by Tschirnhaus.

---

[25] A VI iii 523: PDSR 85. Emphasis mine.

But this, after all, is not the metaphysics that we find in the mature Leibniz. So it is reasonable to ask what happened to this system. Interestingly enough, I think the answer can also be found in the same period we have been discussing, the period of the *De Summa Rerum.* The key writings come from December 12, 1676, eight months after the one we have just examined, but less than a month after Leibniz's conversations with Spinoza in the Hague. As in most of the writings of the *De Summa Rerum,* there are many unclarities. But here as before we can at least present the relevant texts and offer our basic interpretation of them within the confines of the present brief investigation.

The first text is *Catena Mirabilium Demonstrationum De Summa Rerum.* It speaks directly against a 'many worlds' view, and ties this opposition to a rejection of the notion of the existence of all possibles. Leibniz says,

> *There is only one kind of world,* or, there are no entities besides bodies and minds, i.e., what we sense, nor are there any bodies except those which are at a certain distance from us. For if there were any, it could not be said whether they exist or do not exist now, which is contrary to the first principle. *So it follows that not all possibles exist.*[26]

---

[26] 'Catena Mirabilium Demonstrationum De Summa Rerum', A VI iii 584: PDSR 107, emphasis mine. As Parkinson tells us in his notes on this paper, the "first principle" referred to here is probably the one with which Leibniz begins the paper. "Nothing is and is not at the same time, or anything either is or is not." (PDSR 139, n. 5 to the paper in question.) At the Woburn conference, 'The Young Leibniz and his Philosophy (1646-76)', October 18-20, 1996, Francesco Piro raised points in discussion indicating that he had already independently come to the view of an important shift in Leibniz's thinking about worlds at this period and that he had views about the theory or theories of space and time that underlay that shift. As far as I know, it is not part of his view that Tschirnhaus and Spinoza may have played a role in the fact of, or the natuure of, some of the views involved in such a shift. Here and for many questions about the young Leibniz, Piro's work *Varietas Identitate Compensata. Studio sulla formazione della metafisica di Leibniz,* Napoli: Bibliopolis, 1990, should be consulted. My emphasis in this paper is not on the

The "bodies" of the only "kind of world' that there is are of course entities having length, breadth, and depth.[27] They are entities of 'standard space', and, since entities of a 'non-standard space' would not have length, breadth, and depth, neither they nor any non-standard space can exist in the universe that Leibniz now conceives: "There is only one kind of world", the world of bodies and the minds perceiving them. Moreover – and here Leibniz is typically subtle – there are no bodies that are not "at a certain distance from us", which I take to mean that there cannot be two or more worlds of this one kind. That is, it is not just that there is "only one *kind* of world" (my emphasis), a kind of world having bodies and standard space. It is also the case that there is only *one* world, only one standard space, and the test of this seems to be that if there were two standard spaces, then entities in one world would not be "at a certain distance" from entities in the other world. But as Leibniz tells us, there are no bodies but those which are at a certain distance from us (that is, one assumes, from our bodies).

The second text is 'Principium Meum Est, Quicquid Existere Potest, Et Aliis Compatible Est, Id Existere'. In some ways it is less direct in its opposition, but in others it provides a clearer comparison to the position of eight months before. For instance, as we have seen, Leibniz held in the central earlier writing, 'De Formis Simplicibus', that "it is the wonderful nature of this [the 'many worlds' theory] that it duplicates – indeed, it multiplies to infinity – the variety of things".[28] In 'Principium Meum', Leibniz appears to put this idea to rest once and for all: "*There is no need for the multitude of things to be increased by a plurality of worlds;* for there is no number of things which is not in this one world, and indeed in any part of it."[29]

---

argument by which Leibniz rejected the 'many worlds' view, although that is surely important. It is rather on the fact of the shift and the context in which it took place, a context which, on my interpretation at least, fundamentally involved Spinoza and Tschirnhaus.

[27] But not just these three qualities. Leibniz at one point in the *De Summa Rerum* says that these three would not be sufficient for impenetrability, which he seems also to take as essential for bodies: "The best proof that body differs from space or extension is derived from this: that one cannot, from extension alone, or, from the notion of length, breadth, and depth, demonstrate impenetrability." ('De Existentia', A VI iii 587: PDSR 111)

[28] A VI iii 523: PDSR 83.

[29] A VI iii 581: PDSR 103.

Returning to the Latin term, *'genus'*, which had played a role in his description of the 'many worlds' theory in his earlier work, a theory constructed in terms of simple forms, attributes, or kinds, he proceeds to give an additional argument against a multitude of worlds:

> To introduce another genus of existing things, and as it were another world which is also infinite, is to abuse the name of existence; for it cannot be said whether those things exist now or not. But existence, as it is conceived by us, involves a certain determinate time; or, we say that that thing exists of which it can be said at some certain moment of time, 'That thing now exists'.[30]

In 'Principium Meum' there is also a connection of this rejection of the 'many worlds' view with the rejection of the idea that all possibles exist, although the connection is not as direct as in *Catena Mirabilium Demonstrationum*. In the paragraph following the quotation just given, we find Leibniz saying:

> It can be shown that not all things which are possible *per se*[31] can exist together with other things. For otherwise there will

---

[30] A VI iii 581: PDSR 103, 105. I should note that, despite some ambiguity in Leibniz's actual language, I do not think that he is here objecting to "another world *which is also infinite*", (emphasis mine) while allowing for 'another world', so long as it is finite. Rather, I think he is speaking against a 'many worlds' view quite generally.

[31] This term, *'possibilia per se'*, is more technical than what we have seen in the other writings. It is followed, in the next paragraph, by the phrase, *'possibilis in se'*. Both suggest Robert Adams' notion of things possible in their own nature, that is, things whose essences do not imply a contradiction in themselves, considered apart from the essence of any other substance. (See Adams' *Leibniz. Determinist, Theist, Idealist*, pp. 12-15.) If this is the sense that Leibniz had in mind in 'De Formis Simplicibus' when he said that "all possible modes, or things, follow", and if he meant to refer to actual existence in this passage in talking about things following, then this would be a strong statement indeed – and would perhaps count as one of those moments when, as he recounts in 'On Freedom', he found himself "very close to the opinions of those who hold everything to be absolutely necessary". (FC 178: L 263)

be many absurdities; nothing can be conceived which is so absurd that it does not exist in the world – not only monsters, but also evil and miserable minds, and also injustices, and there would be no reason why God should be called good rather than evil, and just rather than unjust.[32]

In both these texts, the statements about possibles come close to the statement with which we began, the quotation from 'On Freedom' that we set out as a kind of benchmark for comparison with earlier views. Not all possibles exist, and this is important in connection with the goodness and justice of God.[33]

In sum, the interpretation presented in this paper – albeit without all details filled in and without all arguments made – is that Leibniz at least experimented with some widely divergent views in connection with God, world(s), and possibility in 1676, in part in response to information about Spinoza, as filtered through Tschirnhaus, and that the position that ultimately emerged was close, in essentials, to what we might call the 'mature position' as it is presented, for example, in 'On Freedom'. Speaking more generally, but without major pronouncements on the question whether Leibniz was a Spinozist, we can say that there is evidence that in 1676 Leibniz engaged in rather wide-ranging reflections on ideas deriving ultimately from Spinoza, with special emphasis on ideas that had played a key role in the latter's exchanges with Tschirnhaus. In this paper I have tried to provide some evidence of this in connection with the question of Leibniz's changing views on 'worlds'. Elsewhere, I have tried to provide[34] and hope to provide in the future – additional evidence of such a potentially illuminating three-cornered metaphysical dialectic among Spinoza, Leibniz, and Tschirnhaus.

---

[32] A VI iii 581: PDSR 105.

[33] The very first paragraph of 'On Freedom', right before the section we quoted at the outset of this paper, highlights the question of, and the challenges to, divine justice. (FC 178: L 263)

[34] See my 'Leibniz's *De Summa Rerum* in relation to the correspondence of Tschirnhaus and Spinoza', forthcoming in a *Studia Leibnitiana Sonderheft* edited by Dominique Berlioz and Frédérick Nef providing the proceedings of the conference, 'Actualise de Leibniz: Les deux labyrinthes', held at the chateau, Cerisy-la-Salle, France, June 15-22, 1995.

STUART BROWN

THE PROTO-MONADOLOGY OF THE *DE SUMMA RERUM*

In his instructive encyclopaedia article on 'Monad and Monadology', Leroy Loemker[1] characterised a 'monad' as "a simple, irreducible, self-determining entity whose activity is the source of all composite beings". "A monadology [he goes on] is a metaphysical system that interprets the world as a harmonious unity encompassing a plurality of such self-determining simple entities." Loemker, of course, allows Leibniz a special place in the history of monadology. But part of the interest of his entry is the way in which he sketches its earlier history. He suggests, for instance, that three conceptions have been particularly operative: the Christian Platonist tradition of the soul as a simple substance possessing self-certainty in immediate unity, especially mediated by Augustine; the Neo-Platonic-Stoic conception of the one that is essentially represented in each of its parts; and a spiritualised atomism ultimately derived from this Neo-Platonic-Stoic conception.

A fuller account of the tradition up to Leibniz would, I believe, bring out how widely diffused it had become in Germany and the extent to which monadological ideas were resources available to the young Leibniz and his contemporaries. The young Leibniz did study some of the classical sources of this tradition, such as Plotinus and Augustine.[2] But some of the influences on him, for instance by his

---

[1] See his entry on 'Monad and Monadology' in *The Encyclopedia of Philosophy*, ed. Paul Edwards (New York: Macmillan Publishing Co., 1967), vol. V, p. 361f.

[2] In a letter to Nicolas Remond of 1714 he mentions that he "discovered Aristotle as a lad" but then "Plato too, and Plotinus, gave me satisfaction". (L 655: G III 607) Catherine Wilson has suggested that "Plotinus is perhaps his [Leibniz's] closest

S. Brown (ed.), The Young Leibniz and his Philosophy (1646-76), 263-87.

teacher Erhard Weigel[3] and by the Herborn school[4], are also in a monadological direction.   More broadly he was influenced by a pervasive European tradition of Neo-Platonism which included such diverse representatives as Ficino, Nicholas of Cusa and Giordano Bruno. Mention should also be make of the related occult tradition of Jakob Böhme[5] and others, including, it has been claimed, J. B. van Helmont.[6]   Leibniz's acquaintances in the early 1670s already included some of the leading Christian Cabbalists, such as Knorr von Rosenruth and the younger van Helmont.[7] These are among the ways monadological ideas may have been absorbed by Leibniz as if they were obvious or at any rate possessed a high degree of intellectual authority and credibility.

A fuller account of the monadological tradition is beyond the scope of this paper, which is concerned with how far the young Leibniz can be said to have had a monadology.   I will only be concerned

---

relative". (*Leibniz's Metaphysics*, Princeton: Princeton University Press, 1989, p. 4) Augustine was one of the authors Leibniz first encountered when he gained access as a child to his father's library.

[3] For a fuller account of of Weigel, see Christia Mercer's chapter in this volume.

[4]   See L. E. Loemker, 'Leibniz and the Herborn Encyclopedists', *Journal of the History of Ideas* 22 (1961): 323-38. On the influence of Alsted and Bisterfeld, see respectively the contributions of Howard Hotson and Maria Rosa Antognazza to this volume.

[5] See, for a full account, S. Edel, *Die Individuele Substanz bei Böhme und Leibniz*, *SL Sond*. 23 (1995).

[6] Particularly by W. Pagel in his *Religious and Philosophical Aspects of Helmont's Science and Medicine*, Baltimore, 1940.

[7] Leibniz met F. M. van Helmont in 1671 and, probably through him, came to know Knorr von Rosenruth. See S. Brown, 'Leibniz and More's Cabbalistic Circle', in *Henry More (1614-1687): Tercentenary Studies*, ed. Sarah Hutton (Dordrecht: Kluwer, 1990), pp. 77-95. See also Allison P. Coudert, *Leibniz and the Kabbalah* (Dordrecht: Kluwer, 1995). No details survive of the early contacts between Leibniz, van Helmont and von Rosenruth, except that Leibniz seems to have had extensive conversations with van Helmont (A I iii 260) and von Rosenruth thought it appropriate to send him a copy of Boyle's paper on the possibility of the resurrection: a topic which, it seems, was seminal for the formation of Leibniz's early monadology.   See S. Brown, 'Some Occult Influences on Leibniz's Monadology', in *Leibniz, Mysticism and Religion*, ed. A. Coudert, R. H. Popkin and G. Weiner (Dordrecht: Kluwer, 1998).

incidentally and to a limited extent[8] with how far his later monadology is anticipated in the *De Summa Rerum*. Hence I do not want to define a monadology by reference to the later Leibniz alone. I begin by noting some of the features that are characteristic of the monadological tradition. In particular I focus on certain principles, on how they connect with one another and how they connect with other monadological doctrines.

Largely following Loemker,[9] I count as a 'monad', at least in the full sense, whatever meets the following conditions, which I am taking as separately necessary and jointly sufficient:

(a) is simple and irreducible:

(b) is eternal or at least not naturally destructible:

(c) is spontaneous /self-determining:

(d) is the source of other (composite) beings.

A monadology is a system which exhibits these entities as the fundamental entities of the universe and shows how they came into existence, how they are related to one another and how other entities depend on them. In a Neo-Platonic scheme of things the monads are characteristically those entities that God produces from within himself by some process of emanation, which entities will bear (perhaps in varying degree) the marks of divinity, including unity, durability and

---

[8] I am not here concerned, for instance, with the requirement of the later Leibniz that his monads should be individual substances. Many traditional monadologies are monistic in direction. I agree with Catherine Wilson's claim in the previous chapter that the metaphysics of the *De Summa Rerum* is also. She, however, reserves the word 'monad' for the entities of the later metaphysics. While I agree with her that there is a significant development in the direction she notes, I think it is illuminating to consider the earlier system as at least a proto-monadology.

[9] I do in fact add a further criterion, namely that a monad is eternal or not naturally indestructible. This may be implicit in Loemker's account and be an aspect of the spiritual atomism he identified as one of the most operative conceptions in the tradition of monadology. Nonetheless it is worth identifying explicitly. Leibniz for his part constantly argued that being indestructible was a consequence of being simple and indivisible, at least from his *Catholic Demonstrations* of the late 1660s to the *Monadology* (see sect. 4).

activity.   A central monadological principle is that the universe, expressing as it does the divine nature, must be the most perfect possible universe.   A number of principles follow, including *the principle of harmonious unity* which Loemker included in his characterisation of a monadology.[10]   This principle in turn has consequences for the nature of monads, for instance that they are all fundamentally alike.   Characteristically each monad not only bears traces of the divinity but is also in some sense a *microcosm* of the universe as a whole (macrocosm).   This doctrine is the usual Neo-Platonic[11] way of meeting the requirement that a universe expressive of the divine nature – a perfect universe – must be an harmonious unity.

The   principle   of   perfection   also   gives   rise   to   another characteristically Neo-Platonic principle, the principle of plenitude. According to Plotinus[12], all beings "send forth as much of themselves as they can".   Since God is a perfect and unlimited being, it follows that the world is as full as it can be: as Plotinus put it, "the whole earth is full of a diversity of living things, mortal and immortal, and replete with them up to the very heavens".[13]   These principles are characteristic of a monadology.   Their employment indicates that an author is writing within the same Neo-Platonic tradition.

In choosing to focus on the *De Summa Rerum* I have been particularly influenced by the publication of the Yale edition which encouraged me, as it no doubt has many others, to attempt a closer study of these difficult early writings.   The usual view is that Leibniz did not adopt a monadology until late in life and indeed many commentators assume that it evolved with his use of the term 'monad' in the 1690s. I myself used to think[14] that, while the monadology pre-dated Leibniz's adoption of the word to refer to his fundamental

---

[10]   Maria Rosa Antognazza, in her contribution to this volume, argues for the direct influence of Bisterfeld on Leibniz's conception of harmony.

[11]   See, for instance, G. P. Conger's *Theories of Macrocosms and Microcosms in the History of Philosophy* (New York: Columbia University Press, 1922).

[12]   *Enneads* V 4, 1.   Quoted from A. O. Lovejoy's *The Great Chain of Being* (Cambridge, Mass.: Harvard University Press, 1936 & 1964), p. 62.

[13]   Quoted from Lovejoy, *The Great Chain of Being*, p. 64.

[14]   In my *Leibniz* (Brighton: Harvester Press, 1984), for instance on pp. 137 ff.

entities, it evolved in 1686 sometime after he wrote his *Discourse on Metaphysics*. It seemed to me then to be a development to which Leibniz was driven by Arnauld, one reflected in doctrines that are not present in the *Discourse*. I had been inclined to date this development to late 1686–early 1687, when Leibniz begins to make much of the doctrine that in every particle of matter there is contained a world of infinitely many creatures.[15] Finding that this apparently[16] monadological doctrine was clearly affirmed in the *De Summa Rerum* and in other works of the Paris period[17] made me realise that I was wrong in taking it for a new development in the post-*Discourse* period. On the contrary, Leibniz seems to have been turning back at this stage to views he had expressed previously, which were later to feature in standard presentations of his system but which were missing from the *Discourse* itself.[18]

In the introduction to his admirable Latin-English *en face* edition of the *De Summa Rerum* for the Yale Leibniz series, G. H. R. Parkinson notes that Leibniz was already sketching a metaphysical system – "a system, far from immature, which contains many of the doctrines for which Leibniz is best known".[19] It is, he goes on, "Leibniz's first major attempt at presenting his philosophy in a systematic form".

---

[15] See PW 82: C 315; PW 91: C 17. This doctrine is affirmed a number of times in the period 1687-90 and it is included in the shorter summary of Leibniz's views sent to Arnauld in 1690.

[16] It is presented in that period as a consequence of the doctrine that there are no material things that are indivisible, which – following Leibniz's account in the *New System*, I then took to be the crucial point at which he passed from belief in corporeal substances to a belief in entities which have the chief characteristics of monads.

[17] See PDSR 2: A VI iii 474 and also, for instance, A VI iii 501 and 565.

[18] In *Discourse*, Sect. 9, Leibniz announces several of his most characteristically monadological doctrines as "notable paradoxes", which he claimed followed from what he had already established. In view of the ecumenical uses he seems to have envisaged for the work, it is likely that he left out some of the other paradoxical opinions which he was later willing to acknowledge. Another such opinion is that animals are not strictly born, nor strictly do they die, which is missing in the *Discourse*, emerges in the Arnauld correspondence but was already more or less explicit in the writings of the early 1670s.

[19] *De Summa Rerum: Metaphysical Papers, 1675-1676*, trans. G.H.R. Parkinson (New Haven & London: Yale University Press, 1992), p. xii.

Parkinson made good these claims by identifying a number of important elements of the later philosophy which are already established in this early work. His concern in an editorial introduction was, however, a broad one. He did not consider the narrower question which is the concern of this paper, namely, how far it already contains a monadology.

I here approach this question by considering some of the principles I have already mentioned, particularly the principle of plenitude and the principle of harmonious unity. In part II, I go on to consider each of the four conditions I listed earlier in greater detail and consider, in relation to the *De Summa Rerum*, what entities are candidates for being monads so far as each condition is concerned. I then consider whether there are any entities, according to this work, which meet all the conditions. Though I note that one condition is not fully met and that therefore the early monadology is not fully developed, it is nonetheless concluded that there is at least a proto-monadology already to be found in the *De Summa Rerum*.

I

The principle that the universe reflects the divine perfection is one that yields three further principles: the principle of plenitude, the principle that created things strive to imitate their creator, and the principle of microcosm and macrocosm, which I will consider shortly in relation to the *De Summa Rerum*. Leibniz had already adopted some of his most characteristic principles by this stage and both the principle of the best and the principle of sufficient reason are more or less explicit in these writings.[20] A related principle of what is called "the harmony of things" is, however, more characteristic of the *De Summa Rerum* and is invoked on several occasions.[21] What is most harmonious, he writes

---

[20] For instance, respectively: "For things to exist is the same as for them to be understood by God to be the best" (PDSR 113: A VI iii 587) and "There is nothing without a reason..." (PDSR 113: A VI iii 587).

[21] This topic is discussed more fully by Fabrizio Mondadori in his 'A Harmony of One's Own and Universal Harmony in Leibniz's Paris Writings', *SL Supp.* 18 (1978): 151-68.

at one point, is what "is most pleasing to the most perfect mind".[22] It will contain, as he puts it, "a certain simplicity in multiplicity"[23]. For instance it is in accordance with "the harmony of things" that "...the wisest being chooses the simplest means to achieve the greatest ends"[24]. Particular minds like ourselves exist because God judges it to be harmonious that they should.[25] Again it seemed to Leibniz that eternal damnation was consistent with "the harmony of things"[26].

This principle of "the harmony of things" is one from which the other three principles can all be derived. In the case of the principle of plenitude, indeed, it appears in one place as virtually equivalent. Leibniz began his paper 'On the Secrets of the Sublime': "After due consideration I accept the principle of the harmony of things: that is, that the greatest amount of essence that can exist, does exist..."[27]. This involves a particular gloss on plenitude. Harmony requires the maximisation of simplicity and order, so far as Leibniz is concerned, as well as plenitude. The principle of simplicity gives Leibnizian harmony a particularly Modern flavour, since it explains God's preference for a Copernican universe. Thus the principle of harmony presupposes two separable principles and is, strictly speaking, not equivalent to the principle of plenitude taken by itself but rather to the conjunction of both principles. Plenitude was, however, particularly in Leibniz's mind when he produced these notes and is one of the leading principles of his monadology. Indeed, at least according to Leibniz's later memory, this principle was crucial in leading him away from the naive atomism of his youth to a belief in monads. For this reason it merits particular attention.

---

[22] PDSR 29: A VI iii 476.

[23] PDSR 113: A VI iii 588.

[24] PDSR 13: A VI iii 466.

[25] PDSR 25: A VI iii 474.

[26] PDSR 29: A VI iii 476.

[27] A VI iii 472.

The Principle of Plenitude

In a postscript to his fourth paper in the controversy with Samuel Clarke, written in the last year of his life, Leibniz offered the following reflection on his youthful philosophy:

> When I was a young man, I also fell into the snare of the void and of atoms; but reason brought me back. The imagination was a pleasing one. On this theory a limit is set to our researches; reflection is fixed and as it were pinned down; we suppose ourselves to have found the first elements – a *non plus ultra*. We should like nature to go no further; we should like it to be finite, like our mind; but this is to ignore the greatness and majesty of the Author of things. The least corpuscle is actually subdivided *ad infinitum* and contains a world of new created things, which the universe would lack if that corpuscle were an atom, that is a body all of a piece and not subdivided.[28]

This remark encourages the speculation that Leibniz may have been led to reject atoms because he embraced the view that every particle of matter contained an infinite number of creatures and that he accepted this view because of his principles of perfection and plenitude. In 1704 he argued in a similar way in response to Damaris Cudworth's criticism that it was not clear why the organisational complexity of bodies was necessary in his system:

> Our body is a kind of world full of an infinity of creatures that also deserve to exist, and if our body were not organised, our Microcosme or little world would not have all the perfection it ought to have, and the Great World also would be less rich than it is.[29]

The principle of plenitude applies not only to the Macrocosm but also to our body and even to any particle of matter – each is a Microcosm

---

[28] PW 220: G VII 377f.
[29] G III 356.

containing an infinity of creatures, as many as there can be. This doctrine, though not always linked to Neo-Platonic views about plenitude or microcosms, is an integral part of Leibniz's mature monadological theory.

Though it is not in that context linked to the rejection of atomism, Leibniz commonly identified his monads as "atoms of substance" in contrast with material atoms, which he rejects on the ground that the smallest particle of matter can still be divided to infinity. Thus, for instance, when Bayle compared the Leibnizian soul or monad to an Epicurean atom, surrounded by a void, Leibniz replied:

> I do in fact regard souls, or rather monads, as atoms of substance, since there are no material atoms in nature, according to my view, and the smallest particle of matter still has parts.[30]

The doctrine that in every particle of matter there is an infinite number of creatures provides a bridge in Leibniz's later philosophy between earlier views he came to reject and his acceptance of a monadology. It is linked with his rejection of both atomism and of the view that there are, strictly speaking, corporeal substances. This suggests that, if he did give up atomism for the reason he gave to Clarke, namely, that acceptance of plenitude led him to believe that every material thing was subdivisible *in infinitum*, then his move away from atomism was in the direction of a monadology. As it happens there is some direct evidence in the *De Summa Rerum* that he was making this move away from atomism in 1676. In his paper 'On the Secrets of the Sublime...' dated 11 February, he remarks:

> If it is true that any part of matter, however small, contains an infinity of creatures, i.e. is a world, it follows also that matter is actually divided into an infinity of points. But this is true, provided it is possible, for it increases the multitude of existents and the harmony of things.[31]

---

[30] L 579: G III 561.
[31] PDSR 25: A VI iii 474.

In the same paper he notes that it follows from the principle of plenitude not only that there is no vacuum among forms but that "there is no vacuum in place and time".[32]   He had probably given up belief in bare physical atoms and possibly for the same reason, as his remarks in the paper for Clarke implies. But in the *De Summa Rerum* his position about atoms is shifting and is difficult to pin down. He seems to have wanted to retain atoms in some sense even after he had ceased to believe in them in the way he had as a youthful follower of Democritus or Gassendi.[33] Atoms in the new sense were consistent with a plenum and inconsistent with materialism. In the undated 'De plenitudine mundi' he argues both for a plenum in nature and an infinite number of spherical atoms.[34] The context makes it clear that each of these atoms or "unsplittable bodies" is united to a mind. For he is concerned from the beginning to explain how it could be that "every mind is omniscient". He argues that it follows from the plenitude of the world that "there is no body that is too small to sense all other things". And so, he says, "it is not surprising that any mind should perceive what is done in the entire world".[35]

He invokes the analogy of the town seen from different places that becomes familiar in his later writings, with at least some of the implications. He seems here to think that each atom, because it is in a slightly different space from any other, enables its mind to have a unique perspective on the universe. He does not go so far as to assert in this context that the universe is represented from every possible point of view but that is clearly what plenitude would call for. And, as I will now argue, this view is already implicit in the *De Summa Rerum*.

---

[32] PDSR 23: A VI iii 473.

[33] In the *New System* account of his early development, he accepted "the void and atoms" after a rebellion against "the yoke of Aristotle". (PW 116: G IV 478). In a letter of 1714 he gave his correspondent to believe that he had taken up "the void of Democritus or Epicurus, together with their incorruptible atoms" when still a schoolboy, when he was satisfied with the views of Gassendi. (L 657: G III 620)

[34] PDSR 91: A VI iii 525.

[35] PDSR 85: A VI iii 524.

The Harmonious Unity of the Universe

Leibniz attached himself himself to a philosophical tradition which stressed the underlying similarities between the universe and its Creator. All the marks of perfection are, from the standpoint of this tradition, to be found both in God and, despite necessary qualifications, in the universe. A perfect being will maximize unity and variety. For this reason, Leibniz argues, God must be a mind:

> A most perfect being is that which contains the most. Such a being is capable of ideas and thoughts, for this multiplies the varieties of things, like a mirror.[36]

One reason why God should create minds will have to do with his desire to create things in his likeness or, what comes to the same thing, to create a universe that is is as perfect as possible. This seems to have been what Leibniz had in mind in saying "Particular minds exist...simply because the supreme being judges it harmonious that there should exist somewhere that which understands, or, is a kind of intellectual mirror or replica of the world."[37] If I am right, however, this understates what the supreme being's sense of the harmonious requires, on Leibniz's account. There should, rather, be as many minds as possible, in what turns out to be a strangely extended sense of the word 'mind'. Leibniz does not say this in so many words in the *De Summa Rerum*. But he does imply that it would increase the perfection of a world to increase "the multitude of existents"[38]. And he also makes it clear that, in his view, minds are the only "true entities".[39] It may be claimed as an implication of the *De Summa Rerum*, therefore, that a perfect world, which reflects the perfection of its Creator, will contain as many minds as possible, each of which is a mirror of the universe from its point of view. This indeed appears, for Leibniz, to be their *raison d'être*.[40]

---

[36] PDSR 29: A VI iii 475.

[37] PDSR 25: A VI iii 474.

[38] *Ibid.*

[39] PDSR 61: A VI iii 510.

[40] I infer this from Leibniz's claim that God created so many minds in order to produce the wonderful variety of so many different perspectives on the same world.

The doctrine that each substance expresses the entire universe from a particular point of view is a cardinal one in Leibniz's later monadology. A version of the doctrine may be detected in the *De Summa Rerum*. It would be wrong, however, to read the later doctrine into the earlier writings. The view of the young Leibniz that "any mind perceives *simultaneously* whatever happens in the entire world" obviously falls short of his mature view that "every substance ... expresses, although confusedly, everything that happens in the universe, *past present and future*"[41] More importantly, perhaps, the earlier doctrine of universal expression fixes upon the passive, representative, role of the mind. Missing in these papers is the later thought that "it is the nature of every substance to express the whole universe *by its power of acting and being acted upon*"[42] That thought is concluded from two doctrines: (1) that it is in the nature of any substance to have a complete notion which contains all its predicates; and (2) that everything is connected with everything else. Only the second of these doctrines is evident in the *De Summa Rerum*.[43] Even in the *Discourse on Metaphysics*, where the doctrine of expression is prominent, it is still a passive one and the conclusion that each substance "extends its power over all the others" depends upon the additional premise that all substances "agree" with one another. The extension of the doctrine of expression to include the active aspects of created substances was not done in a clear or consistent manner. It sometimes involved a recognition that substances are expressions of God as well as of the universe and therefore strive to imitate Him but Leibniz vacillated between saying this was true of all substances and saying it was true only of rational minds, who were made in the image of God.[44] The 'mirror' analogy frequently used in connection with the

---

(PDSR 85, A VI iii 524) This compares with the later remark that "the whole nature, end, virtue and function of substance is merely to express God and the universe" (*Discourse on Metaphysics*, § 35)

[41] *Discourse on Metaphysics*, § 9, italics mine.

[42] G vii 317: PW 84, italics mine.

[43] Parkinson suggests that the absence of the doctrine that a substance has a complete concept is perhaps 'the most striking gap in the *De Summa Rerum*' (PDSR li) compared with his 1686 writings.

[44] The vacillation is between the Neoplatonic doctrine and the more limited Christian doctrine that man is made in the image of God. The *Discourse* view is that

doctrine is an essentially passive one, as Leibniz himself seems to have recognized by adopting, in his later writings, the curious phrase "living mirrors" to describe his monads.[45] This difference between the earlier and the later work is, I believe, the most important difference between the earlier and the later monadology.[46]

The principle of the harmonious unity of the universe is connected with Leibniz's thought that created things are, because of their capacity to represent the whole universe, microcosms. Minds are everywhere, according to the *De Summa Rerum*, and always implanted in bodies. As we have already seen, every part of matter contains an infinity of creatures. Leibniz added that it is a world.[47] Each little world, moreover, has a mind in which the macrocosm is represented. Each mind is also said to be a little world.[48] Elsewhere he writes that every change in the world I perceive brings about a change in me. In this way "all things are in a way contained in all things".[49] Leibniz was evidently familiar with the dictum that "all things are contained in all things"[50] which was one of the cornerstones of Neo-Platonism. His agreement with the received doctrine, however, is not unqualified. For he goes on to say that all things are contained in things in a quite different way from the way in which they are contained in God. God is the creator and sustainer of all things. Each created thing, however, only contains every other thing as a representation.[51] Thus Leibniz distinguished his version of this doctrine from those, like that of

---

all substances express God and that those capable of knowledge do it much better than others. (§ 35) Elsewhere, however, he says that only rational minds express God. See, for instance, PW 85: G vii 316.

[45] For instance, in *Principles of Nature and Grace*, he wrote that "each monad is a living mirror, or a mirror endowed with inner activity".

[46] This difference is one I return to at the end of this paper.

[47] PDSR 25: A VI iii 474..

[48] PDSR 47: A VI iii 393.

[49] PDSR 85: A VI iii 523.

[50] The dictum appears to derive from Anaxagoras but became a fundamental doctrine of Neo-Platonism. See R. T. Wallis, *Neoplatonism* (London: Duckworth), p. 33. The Cusanus source is *De docta ignorantia* II 5.

[51] Here Leibniz already anticipates his later denial of extrinsic denominations, though he has apparently not yet worked out its connections with other doctrines.

Bruno[52], which entailed pantheism.   At this point he clearly thought that there was clear water between his position and that of a monist even though, by his later standards[53], there was not enough clear water.   He later claimed that his system provided a rational underpinning for "the one and the whole of Parmenides and Plotinus, yet without any Spinozism" as well as "the Stoic connectedness, which is yet compatible with the spontaneity held to by others"[54]   It would have been more difficult to support such a claim for his earlier system.   For, though it gives a full place to the unity and connectedness of the universe, it is not enough to distinguish true individuals that they have a unique representational perspective. They need somehow to have creativity or 'spontaneity' for created substances which the later, but not the earlier, philosophy sought particularly to accommodate.

II

I turn now to the four conditions I listed at the beginning as necessary to an entity being a monad in the full sense:

(a) Simplicity and irreducibility

I have already suggested, on the basis of Leibniz's later account in the Clarke correspondence, that he was earlier led away from a crude physical atomism early on by considerations to do with plenitude. This suggestion is, as we have seen, supported by certain passages in the *De Summa Rerum*.   There is, however, another text which invites us to believe that Leibniz's change of direction was motivated by other

---

[52] Bruno's pantheism is clearly expressed in his version of the dictum: "Substance is in all things and all things are in substance" (*Opera Latina Conscripta*, ed. F. Fiorentino and others, Naples & Florence, 1879-91, I iv 73).

[53] In order entirely to avoid monism (Leibniz later used the word 'Spinozism'), as the occasionalists, Cabbalists and others failed to do, it was necessary to distinguish adequately between the actions of God and those of creatures. Leibniz was not keenly aware of the problem until later, when it appears to drive much of the argument of the *Discourse on Metaphysics*. (See especially § 8) The later stress on the active nature of substances is missing in these early papers.

[54] PPL 496, G iv 523.

considerations, to do with simplicity or "true unity". This is the *New System* of 1695, which is largely presented in the form of an intellectual autobiography. Leibniz's account of his rejection of atomism runs as follows:

> At first, when I had freed myself from the yoke of Aristotle, I had believed in the void and atoms, for it is this which best satisfies the imagination. But returning to this view after much meditation, I perceived that it is impossible to find *the principles of a true unity* in matter alone, or in what is merely passive, since everything in it is but a collection or accumulation of parts *ad infinitum.* Now a multiplicity can be real only if it is made up of *true unities*...to find these *real unities*, I was constrained to have recourse to what might be called a *real and animated point* or to an atom of substance...[55]

This passage suggests a rather different reason for rejecting atomism from the one I discussed earlier. Leibniz, however, did not claim that this was one of his original reasons and indeed the phrase "after much meditation" is consistent with it belonging to a much later period. So far as I can make out, this objection first makes an appearance in the Arnauld correspondence. Arnauld, in his letter of September 1686, alluded to the fact that some of the Cartesians, in order to find unity in bodies, were led to deny that matter was divisible to infinity and to accept indivisible atoms. In his reply, Leibniz recalled that Cordemoy, in his *Treatise on the Distinction between Body and Soul*, "to save substantial unity in bodies, felt himself obliged to admit atoms or extended indivisible bodies so as to find something fixed to constitute a simple being".[56] Cordemoy's book had been published in 1666 and it is not known when it first came to Leibniz's attention. The objection, however, seems to be one which was brought home to him by Arnauld's arguments against the view of corporeal substance he himself had been defending. In 1690 he offered Arnauld an abstract of views he had been discussing in Italy, which more closely resembles a

---

[55] PW 116: G IV 478.
[56] G II 78.

full-blown monadology in its contention that "in all bodies there must be found indivisible substances which cannot be generated and are not corruptible, having something analogous to souls".[57] The critique of atomism provided a direct route from atoms of matter to what Leibniz called "atoms of substance" and in the *New System* he came back to it again. Cordemoy rightly saw, according to Leibniz, that if there were no substantial unities there would be nothing real or substantial in the material world. And it was this consideration that compelled him to abandon Descartes and adopt Democritus' theory of atoms.[58] But Cordemoy was mistaken in believing that material atoms were substantial unities. According to the author of the *New System*, only atoms of substance "can be the sources of actions, and the absolute first principles of the composition of things".

But, even if the thought that there is no reality unless there are true unities only comes into prominence at a later stage, it is possible to find suggestions of it in the *De Summa Rerum*. In this work minds play the pivotal role later assigned to substances and monads. Minds alone are *vera entia*, they are *sola una*.[59] "Every body which is an aggregate can be destroyed. There seem to be elements or indestructible bodies because there is a mind in them."[60] The mind as a unity can confer unity on a parcel of matter: "... thought enters into the formation of matter, and there comes into the body which is one and unsplittable, i.e. an atom, of whatever size it may be, whenever it has a single mind."[61] By minds in this sense Leibniz does not mean only rational minds. In the curious sense of the *De Summa Rerum*:

> There are innumerable minds everywhere; there are minds in the ovum even before conception, nor do they perish, even if conception never follows...[62]

---

[57] G II 135.

[58] PW 116: G IV 478.

[59] 'On Truths, the Mind, God, and the Universe', PDSR 61: A VI iii 510.

[60] 'On the Origin of Things from Forms', PDSR 81: A VI iii 521. Elsewhere he writes that "the solidity and unity of the body comes from the mind" (PDSR 61: A VI iii 509).

[61] 'Notes on Science and Metaphysics', PDSR 47: A VI iii 393.

[62] 'On the Secrets of the Sublime', PDSR 31: A VI iii 476f.

Strictly, perhaps, Leibniz meant to say that the unity or substantiality of matter has to be conferred on it by something analogous to a mind. There is more than a hint of monads in this conception of a mind as what can create an atom or unsplittable body by sharing its unity and irreducibility with it. At this time, however, he was willing to use the word 'atom' in ways he would not have done later without qualification and as he would not later have used the word 'mind' at all. [63]

(b) Eternity or indestructibility

God is the only mind who, for Leibniz, is truly eternal. Nonetheless, in the *De Summa Rerum*, he was willing to say, even of finite minds, "Every mind is of endless duration."[64] Minds, moreover, do not float free of the material world but are, on the contrary, "indissolubly implanted in matter"[65] This suggests that atoms not only derive their unsplittability from an associated mind but also derive indestructibility in the same way.[66] Though he does not put it in this way, the relationship seems to have been similar to that he later conceived between substances and substantial forms.

This seems to be confirmed by the accounts given in the papers on 'The Seat of the Soul' and 'On the Union of Soul and Body'. They suggest that there is something – called in the one a *flower of substance* and in the other an *ethereal substance* – which is diffused throughout the whole body. According to the first, the soul is firmly implanted in this flower of substance.[67] In the second, Leibniz is disagreeing with the view that the soul is in the whole body equally.[68] If the soul were in the whole body equally, then it would itself be lost

---

[63] In the *New System*, for instance, he accepts "atoms of substance" in contrast with "atoms of matter" (G IV 482), whereas he wants to distinguish sharply between minds and brute souls (G IV 479f.).

[64] 'On the Secrets of the Sublime', PDSR 31: A VI iii 476.

[65] *Ibid.*, PDSR 31: A VI iii 477.

[66] 'Notes on Science and Metaphysics', PDSR 47: A VI iii 393.

[67] 'On the Seat of the Soul', PDSR 33: A VI iii 478.

[68] 'On the Union of Soul and Body', PDSR 35: A VI iii 480.

or alternatively multiplied when the body itself lost all or some of its matter – for instance, when someone is eaten by cannibals.[69] In either case such a view of the soul seemed to pose a serious problem for the orthodox doctrine of the resurrection of the same body, a topic to which Leibniz gave his attention both in the *De Summa Rerum* and at greater length in some writings[70] of 1671. It is in this connection that he invokes the *flos substantiae,* which "persists perpetually in all changes" and indeed which remains even when the body is to all appearances destroyed. "Hence", he claims, "it is easy to see how cannibals, in eating a man, have no power at all over the *flos substantiae.* It is diffused through the whole body; somehow comprises the whole form."[71] The meaning of this last sentence is not entirely clear and the best translation uncertain. But the substantial form is also something indivisible which is nonetheless present in all parts of a substance. So it is possible that Leibniz was already attempting to give a good sense to the embattled notion of substantial form by linking it with what he may then have regarded as the more promising notion of a *flos substantiae.*

Leibniz's curious remark that "the flower of substance is our body"[72] suggests, however, that it is not merely to be equated with substantial form. It suggests, on the contrary, that the *flos substantiae* is something material. This is implied by his acknowledgement that the idea was foreshadowed by the Rabbinical doctrine of the '*Luz*' ,

---

[69] The cannibals problem arises acutely for the view that the soul is in the whole body equally. For, on that account, a cannibal who consumed part of a man's body would thereby be consuming part of his soul and a group of cannibals might thus between them have consumed his entire soul, amalgamating it and his body with themselves and their own. The resurrection of the dead is far from straightforward on these suppositions. Leibniz, unlike Boyle, thought this was no problem if one had the right view of the union of the soul and the body. His account seems to have remained the same, though the clearest statement is in a work of the mid-1680s commonly know as the *System of Theology* (Ru 164), a critical edition of which is in draft form in VE 2411-99 and will be published in A VI iv.

[70] A letter to Duke Johann Friedrich (A II i 105-110) and an appendix on the resurrection of the body (A II i 5-7).

[71] A VI iii 478. This is the translation given by L. E. Loemker in the Appendix to his 'Boyle and Leibniz', *Journal of the History of Ideas* 16 (1955): 43.

[72] 'On the Seat of the Soul', PDSR 33: A VI iii 478.

which explained the possibility of the resurrection by postulating an irrefragible bone in the spine which natural processes could not destroy.[73]   It is also implied by a remark made later in the same passage, "that the soul seems to be firmly implanted in this flower of substance". The *flos substantiae* is thus the seat of the soul. Leibniz's point is not only that the soul cannot be destroyed (on which he has other arguments) but that neither can the seat of the soul in the body be destroyed.   The resurrection of the same body is not, he wanted to conclude, contrary to the nature of things.   Writing to Duke Johann Friedrich on the same topic in 1671, he had expressed himself to the same purpose though in rather different language:

> I am almost of the opinion that all bodies, as well those of men as those of beasts, vegetables and minerals, have a seminal principle (*Kern*) of substance....This seminal principle is so subtle, that it remains even in the ashes of the substance when consumed by fire, and has the power, as it were, of collecting itself in an invisible centre...[74]

The *Kern* seems to play a similar role to the flower of substance, underwriting continuity of the same bodily being throughout the most destructive of natural calamities. Its ability to do this is based on its capacity both to contract to "an invisible centre" and to provide the basis for subsequent regrowth.

Leibniz's use of the term 'Kern' in the writings on the resurrection of the body of 1671 has been linked with the monadological doctrine of J. B. van Helmont and indirectly with that of Augustine[75] according to which God in the beginning scattered the invisible seeds of all things. Leibniz was content, much later, to claim that his reasoning about all brute souls being created at one time "agrees well with the

---

[73]   I have discussed this doctrine and the references to it in Leibniz's writings in 'Some Occult Influences on Leibniz's Monadology'.

[74]   A II i 108.

[75]   See *On the Trinity* III 8.13, *Literal Commentary on Genesis* IX, 17.32. Cf. *The Essential Augustine*, ed. V. J. Bourke, 2nd edition (Indiapolis: Hackett, 1974), p. 102-3.

Holy Scriptures, which suggest that there were seeds (*semences*) in the beginning".[76]

One must exercise great caution in using later texts to illuminate earlier ones. But if, as is possible, Leibniz's earlier view of the *Kern* derives from Augustine's interpretation of Genesis, perhaps mediated by J. B. van Helmont[77], it may be that he was already disposed to hold that the "hidden seeds of all things that are born corporeally and visibly are concealed in the corporeal elements of this world", the hidden seeds being created at the beginning by God himself.[78] At any rate there appear to be significant points of continuity here between the earlier and later doctrines of indestructibility.

Leibniz's early theories of how the resurrection is possible are linked with his constantly repeated, though curiously neglected, doctrine that there is something indestructible about all living things and that, strictly speaking, there is no such thing as death – nor, for that matter, is there such a thing, strictly speaking, as birth. Though animals and, for that matter, humans, are complex substances, their indestructibility is derived from their special monadic character, from the way in which souls are implanted in them. In the later writings, as in the earlier, Leibniz wished to confer monadic benefits on complexes. Among these benefits is indestructibility.

(c) Active/self-determining

There is plenty of evidence in Leibniz's early writings of the [Neoplatonic] doctrine that the mind is active and that matter as such is passive. Only God is pure activity and God is the *ens realissimum*. A substance, as Leibniz understood the term, was something that "has a principle of action within itself"[79]. No body has a principle of action within itself without a concurrent mind.[80] The *De Summa Rerum* has

---

[76] L 557: G VI 534. In a letter to Arnauld he alludes, in a similar context, to "the fertility of seeds mentioned in Genesis". (G II 75)

[77] See Pagel, Walter, *Religious and Philosophical Aspects of Helmont's Science and Medicine* (Baltimore, 1944).

[78] *De trinitate* III viii 13, quoted from *The Essential Augustine*, ed. Bourke, p. 102.

[79] L 115: A VI i 508.

[80] L 116: A VI i 509.

less to say about the activity of mind than some of the earlier writings. Leibniz's remark that "whatever acts cannot be destroyed"[81] is connected with his remark elsewhere that minds alone are *vera entia*, as is confirmed by his comment that there can only be elements or indestructible bodies because there is a mind in them. But, while a number of the doctrines about substance are in position by this stage, it seems that Leibniz has not yet arrived at the view that everything that happens to an individual arises spontaneously from its nature.[82]

In addition to the absence of firm evidence that Leibniz's principle of spontaneity dates from the early period, there is some evidence that points positively to his having first articulated it much later. In the first place, the principle is the cardinal point at which Leibniz's theory of pre-established harmony puts him at variance with Malebranche's occasionalism. In 1686 he communicated to Foucher his hypothesis of concomitance or agreement that "God created the soul in the first place so that everything that happens to it arises out of itself without its having to accommodate itself to the body". He stressed that his view was "very different from [that of] the author of the *Recherche*", going on immediately to explain: "I believe that every individual substance expresses the universe in its manner and that its next state is a consequence (though often free) of its previous state, as if there were only God and it in the world."[83] Though the first of these doctrines is present in the *De Summa Rerum*, the second (which is the point of incompatibility with occasionalism) is not.

Though Leibniz may never have been an unqualified occasionalist,[84] he did not succeed until well into the 1680s in

---

[81] 'On Truths, the Mind, God, and the Universe', PDSR 81: A VI iii 521.

[82] The only passage I have found that suggests to the contrary is in some notes on Foucher's reply to the critique of his *Critique de la Recherche de la Vérité*, where Leibniz writes: "The essence of substances consists in the primitive force of action, or in the law of the sequence of changes, as the nature of the series consists in the numbers." (L 155: A VI iii 326) However not all of these notes were written in 1676 and it is possible, as Loemker himself suggests, that this is a revision note of a much later date. (The Akademie editors place it around 1690.) It cannot therefore be taken as a firm basis for identifying Leibniz's first articulation of this idea.

[83] MB 131: G I 382.

[84] He seems to have rejected body-body and body-mind causality. But there is no evidence that he ever seriously doubted that minds could act on bodies.

establishing a position for himself that was properly disengaged from occasionalism. In 1679 he could still write to Malebranche that he "heartily" agreed with him that bodies cannot act on us[85] and, though he insisted he had come to such doctrines independently, he made no mention of what he was later to highlight as a major point of difference between his system and that of the occasionalists. Although Leibniz had arrived at his view that it was in the nature of a substance to have a complete concept in 1679, it seems as if he only gradually came to formulate this key element of his system of pre-established harmony – perhaps as late as 1686, when it first makes a strangely late appearance in his *Discourse on Metaphysics*. This suggests that he had become dissatisfied with the tendency of occasionalism to say that God does everything and to deny the actions of creatures,[86] a position he came to represent as sailing too close for comfort to Spinozism. It seems indeed that he himself had held, in his *Systema Theologicum*, that "it is only through the medium of God that our ideas represent to us what passes in the world" and claims in defence of this that "on no other supposition can it be conceived how the body acts on the soul, or how different created substances can communicate with one another".[87] As I construe this passage, Leibniz is crediting God in occasionalist manner, with being directly[88] responsible for all causality or at least body-mind causality (as in veridical perception) and body-body causality.[89] The account introduced in Sections 14 and 15 of the *Discourse* bears all the marks

---

[85] L 210: G I 330. Leibniz also endorsed the vision in God.

[86] A central part of the philosophical project of the *Discourse* is to distinguish the actions of God from those of creatures, which Leibniz does first by propounding his doctrine of the complete notion of an individual substance (Section 8), from which the spontaneity doctrine is ultimately derived (Section 33).

[87] *System of Theology*, Ru 73.

[88] Leibniz continued to hold that God is necessary since without Him there would be no pre-established harmony. But, if Leibniz had already arrived at his important point of departure from occasionalism at this stage, it is surprising that he should have glossed over the differences as he appears to be doing in this passage.

[89] It is not clear in what way the supposition that God is a kind of mirror of the world helps to explain how created substances can communicate with one another except insofar as perception of the external world involves body-body causality as well as body-mind causality.

of a theory being worked out which is new and quite different, offering an account of what is happening when one substance is said to act on another which is based on differences between the substances.

This interpretation fits with Leibniz's own account in the *New System*, where he gives his reader to believe that he had already arrived at his view of the nature of substance before being cast out to sea by the difficulty about explaining how substances could communicate with one another. He suggests that he came to it both unexpectedly and insensibly while reflecting on what is wrong with the occasionalist account of the union of the soul and the body.[90] The idea he had was that "God first created the soul, and every other real unity, in such a way that everything in it must spring from within itself, by a perfect spontaneity with regard to itself, and yet in a perfect conformity with things outside"[91]. It seems to have made its first appearance late on in the *Discourse on Metaphysics*. At all events it seems to be a significant development in the period after the *De Summa Rerum*.

From this perspective, even if we agree that much of the framework for Leibniz's later theory of substance is already established by the *De Summa Rerum*, we should be struck by what is *not* there as well as what is. Most of the "paradoxes" which Leibniz derives as conclusions in Section 9 of the *Discourse* already feature as doctrines of the earlier work – the identity of indiscernibles[92], the doctrine of natural indestructibility, substances as microcosms and as bearing the marks of the divinity. But whereas the *Discourse* has substances imitating, in their way, the divine omnipotence as well as the divine omniscience, the *De Summa Rerum* only includes the imitation of God's knowledge. Leibniz was not worried in the mid-1670s by the problem that came to pre-occupy him and make him reject any form of occasionalism, namely, how to distinguish adequately between the actions of God and those of creatures. That was to be an important

---

[90] G II 484.

[91] PW 122: G IV 458.

[92] That "it is impossible that there should be two things which are perfectly similar" is put forward in PDSR 51: A VI iii 491.

item on the agenda[93] of the *Discourse*. His earlier work certainly provides for substances to be active. But it stops short of proposing that they are 'spontaneous' or self-determining in the way in which they are claimed to be in the later system.

(d) Basis of all other things

The *De Summa Rerum* does not have the fully developed distinction between simple substances and complex ones. The two strands of the later monadology – that leading to the "atoms of substance" and that leading to the doctrine of the dominant monad – are present, though there is no attempt at bringing them together in a single theory. In both strands, minds are the basis of the solidity, irrefragibility and unity and, in short, the substantiality of all other things. This is quite explicit in the 'atomistic' writings. When acknowledging that matter can be solid and unbreakable, Leibniz nonetheless insists that thought enters into its formation and it is only where there is a single mind that unsplittable bodies come into existence.[94] Again, he remarks: "Every body which is an aggregate can be destroyed. There seem to be elements, i.e. indestructible bodies, because there is a mind in them."[95] Likewise, it is because the soul is firmly implanted in the body, that there is something material – the *flos substantiae* perhaps – which is indestructible. The resurrection of the same body is possible not because all the matter is retained or restored. It is rather because a body cannot be destroyed and is only reduced when it appears to be destroyed to an essence which is no longer visible but from which it can regrow at another time. The single mind corresponds to the simple monad of the later philosophy and the essence (etc.) corresponds to the central or dominant monad.

To note such correspondences is not to deny that there are doctrinal differences between Leibniz's earlier and his later views. He moved away from the residual atomism of the *De Summa Rerum*. He also

---

[93] The summary of section 8 makes this clear: "In order to distinguish the actions of God from those of creatures, an explanation is given of the notion of an individual substance".

[94] 'Notes of Science and Metaphysics', PDSR 47: A VI iii 393.

[95] 'On the Origin of Things from Forms', PDSR 81: A VI iii 521.

dropped the alchemical basis of the earlier doctrine of essences, relying even more on the microscopists in support of his doctrine that, strictly speaking, living things do not die but are merely transformed. Nonetheless the young Leibniz had already arrived at many of the characteristic doctrines of his later monadology by 1676. The *De Summa Rerum* contains a proto-monadology which shows both continuity with the later work as well as relative discontinuity with some of the writings in Leibniz's middle period, including the *Discourse of Metaphysics*. It also shows, to a degree that has not yet been fully recognized, a continuity with a tradition of monadological writing.

STUART BROWN

SELECT BIBLIOGRAPHY OF THE YOUNG LEIBNIZ AND HIS
BACKGROUND

1. Select List of Leibniz's Early Writings (up to 1676)

Disputatio metaphysica de Principio Individui... . Leipzig, 1663. A
VI i 11-19 (Title-page A VI i 9) [Abbreviated to '*De Principio
Individui*'].

Specimen Questionum Philosophicarum ex Jure collectarum... .
Leipzig: Wittigau, 1664. A VI i 73-95. (Title-page A VI i 69)
[Abbreviated to '*Specimen Questionum*'].

Disputatio juridica de Conditionibus ... . Leipzig, 1665. A VI i 101-
124. (Title-page A VI i 99).

Disputatio juridica posterior de Conditionibus ... . Leipzig, 1665. A
VI i 129-150. (Title-page A VI i 127).

Notae ad Joh. Henricum Bisterfeldium. Unpublished, 1663-66. A VI
i 151-61.

Dissertatio de Arte Combinatoria ... . Leipzig, 1666. A VI i 168-
230: selections in L 73-82. (Title-page A VI i 165) [Abbreviated to
'*De Arte Combinatoria*'].

Disputatio de Casibus perplexis in Jure ... . Nuremberg, 1666. A VI i
235-256. (Title-page A VI i 233) [Abbreviated to '*De Casibus
perplexis*'].

Nova Methodus discendae docendaeque Jurisprudentiae ... .
Frankfurt, 1667. A VI i 263-364: selections from Part I in L 85-90.
(Title-page A VI i 261) [Abbreviated to '*Nova Methodus*']

*Specimen Demonstrationum politicarum pro Rege Polonorum
eligendo ... .* Vilna, Lithuania (pseud.), 1668. A IV i 3-98.
[Abbreviated to '*Specimen Demonstrationum Politicarum*']

S. Brown (ed.), The Young Leibniz and his Philosophy (1646-76). 289-307

Confessio Naturae contra Atheistas. In Theophilus Spizelius, *De Atheismo Eradicando* .... Augsburg, 1669. A VI i 489-493: L 109-113. [Abbreviated to '*Confessio Naturae*']

Demonstrationum Catholicarum Conspectus. Unpublished, 1668-9. A VI i 494-500.

De transsubstantiatione. Unpublished, c. 1668 ?. A VI i 508-513: L 115-119.

Defensio Trinitatis contra Wissowatium. Unpublished, 1669 ?. A VI i 518-30. [Abbreviated to '*Defensio Trinitatis*']

Specimina Juris ... . 1669. A VI i 369-430. (Title-page A VI i 369-430).

Elementa juris naturalis. Unpublished, c. 1669-71. A VI i 431-85. [There are three pieces entitled 'Elementa juris naturalis' (A VI i 459-85: extract in L 131-37) which are here referred to as the '*Elements of Natural Law*'. The previous studies are referred to as 'preparatory works to the *Elements of Natural Law*'].

Commentatiuncula de judice controversiarum. Unpublished, 1669-71. A VI i 548-59. [Abbreviated to '*Commentatiuncula*']

Elementa Juris civilis. Unpublished, 1670-72. A VI ii 49-93.

Dissertatio praeliminaris for a new edition of Nizolius' *Anti-Barbarus seu de veris principiis et vera ratione philosophandi contra Pseudophilosophos.* 1670. A VI ii 401-76: selections in L 121-130. [Abbreviated to '*Dissertatio praeliminaris*']

Hypothesis physica nova ... . Mainz, 1671. A VI ii 222-57. [Title-page A VI ii 222]

Theoria Motus abstracti ... . 1671. A VI ii 261-76. [Title-page A VI ii 259).

Justa dissertatio. 1671-2. A VI i 347-82.

Grundriss eines Bedenkens von Aufrichtung einer Societät in Deutschland. 1671. A IV. i. 530ff. [Abbreviated to '*Grundriss*']

Confessio philosophi. Unpublished, 1672-3. A VI iii 115-49.

'De vera Methodo Philosophiae et Theologiae ac de Natura Corporis.' Unpublished, 1673-75. A VI ii 154-159: W 58-65. [Abbreviated to 'De vera Methodo']

'Extrait d'une Lettre de M. Leibniz à l'Auteur du Journal touchant le principe de justesse des Horloges portatives de son Invention (avec une planche)'. *Journal des Sçavans*, 25 March, 1675, pp. 94-99. D III 135.

2. Editions of Leibniz's Writings

Works cited in the Abbreviations list (pp. xi-xii) are excluded.

Barone, F. (ed.). *G. W. Leibniz: Scritti di logica*. Bologna: Zanichelli, 1969.

Belaval, Y. (ed.). *G. W. Leibniz: Confessio Philosophi*. Paris: Vrin, 1961.

Bodéüs, R. (ed. & French trans.). *Leibniz-Thomasius: Correspondance (1663-72)*. Paris: Vrin, 1993.

Cook, D. J. & Rosemont, H. Jr. (ed. & trans.). *Leibniz: Writings on China*. Chicago: Open Court, 1994.

Dosch, H. G. and others (ed. & German trans.). *Leibniz Specimen Dynamicum*. Hamburg: Meiner, 1982.

Erdmann, J. E. (ed.). *Leibnitii Opera philosophica quae existant Latina, Gallica, Germanica omnia*. Berlin: Eichler, 1840; repr. Aalen: Scientia Verlag, 1974.

Fichant, M. (ed.). *Leibniz, G. W.: La réforme de la dynamique*. De corporum concursu (1678) *et autres textes inédits*. Paris: Vrin, 1994.

Gerland, E. (ed.). *Gottfried Wilhelm Leibniz, Nachgelassene Schriften, mechanischen und technischen Inhalts*. Leipzig: Teubner 1906; repr. Hildesheim: Olms, 1995.

Gruber, D. (ed.). *Commercii epistolici Leibnitiani ... recensuit Io. Daniel Gruber Tomi prodromi pars altera*. Hanover and Göttingen 1745.

Huggard, E. M. (trans.). *G. W. Leibniz: Theodicy: Essays on the Goodness of God, the Freedom of Man, and the Origin of Evil*. London: Routledge & Kegan Paul, 1951.

Jolley, N. 'An Unpublished Leibniz MS on Metaphysics.' *SL* 7 (1975): 161-189.

Knobloch, E. (ed.). *Gottfried Wilhelm Leibniz, De quadratura arithmetica circuli ellipseos et hyperbolae cujus corollarium est trigonometria sine tabulis.* Göttingen: Vandenhoeck and Ruprecht, 1993; *Abhandlungen der Akademie der Wissenschaften in Göttingen, Mathematisch-Physikalische Klasse,* Series 3, No. 43.

Piro, F. (ed.). *G. W. Leibniz: Confessio Philosophi e altri scritti.* Naples: Cronopio, 1992.

Saame, O. (ed.). *G. W. Leibniz: Confessio Philosophi.* Frankfurt: Klostermann, 1967.

Wiater, W. (ed.). *G. W. Leibniz. Philosophische Schriften,* vol. 5: *Briefe von besonderem philosophischen Interesse.* (Latin/German) Darmstadt: Wissenschaftliche Buchgesellschaft, 1989.

3. Leibniz Reference Works

Bodemann, E. (ed.). *Der Briefwechsel des Gottfried Wilhelm Leibniz in der Königlichen Öffentlichen Bibliothek zu Hannover.* Hanover: Hahn, 1895; repr. Hildesheim: Olms, 1966.

Finister, R. and others. *Leibniz-Lexicon. A Dual Concordance to Leibniz's Philosophische Schriften.* Hildesheim: Olms, 1988.

Müller, K. and Krönert, G. *Leben und Werk von Gottfried Wilhelm Leibniz. Eine Chronik.* Frankfurt: Klostermann, 1969.

Ravier, É. *Bibliographie des oevres de Leibniz.* Paris, 1937; repr. Hildesheim: Olms, 1966.

4. Other Relevant Primary Literature

Alsted, J. H. *Diatribe de mille annis apocalypticis.* Herborn: Christoph Corvinus, 1627.

------ *Encyclopaedia.* Septem tomis distincta. Herborn: Christoph Corvinus, 1630.

------ *Prodromus religionis triumphantis. In qvo methodicè repetuntur et breviter examinantur libri sex de vera religione; qvorum primus à Johanne Crellio, quinque reliqui a Johanne Volkelio sunt conscripti.* Alba Julia: Typii Celsissimi Principis Transylvaniae, 1635.

Arnauld, A. *La perpétuité de la foy de l'Eglise Catholique touchant l'Eucharistie...* 3 vols. Paris: Savroux, 1669-74.

Bisterfeld, J. H. *De uno Deo Patre, Filio, ac Spiritu Sancto, Mysterium Pietatis, contra Johannis Crellii, Franci, De uno Deo Patre, libros duos, breviter defensum.* Lugduni Batavorum: ex Officina Elzeveriana, 1639.

------- *Philosophiae Primae Seminarium ita traditum, ut omnium disciplinarum fontes aperiat, earumque clavem porrigat.* Lugduni Batavorum: Apud Danielem et Abrahamum Gaasbeeck, 1657.

------ *Elementorum Logicorum Libri tres: ad praxin exercendam apprimè utiles. Atque ita instituti, ut Tyro, trimestri spatio, fundamenta Logices, cum fructu jacere possit. Accedit, Ejusdem Authoris, Phosphorus Catholicus, Seu Artis meditandi Epitome. Cui subjunctum est, Consilium de Studiis feliciter instituendis.* Lugduni Batavorum: Ex Officina Henrici Verbiest., 1657.

Claude, J. *Réponse au livre de Mr. Arnauld intitulé La Perpétuité de la Foy de l'Eglise Catholique touchant l'Eucharistie défenduë.* Rouen: J. Lucas, 1670.

Comenius, J. A. *De rerum humanarum emendatione consultatio catholica.* (Posthumous 1st edition.) Prague: Academia, 1966.

------ *Sapientiae primae usus triertium catholicum appellandus hoc est humanarum cogitationum, sermonum, operum, scientiam, artem, usum aperius clavis triuna* (1681); repr. in *Dílo Jana Amose Komenského* 18, Prague: Academia, 1974, 239-366.

Ficino, M. *Opera.* Basle, 1576; repr. Torino: Bottega di Erasmo, 1963.

Gassendi, P. *Opera Omnia.* Paris 1658; repr. Stuttgart-Bad Cannstatt: Frommann-Holzboog, 1964.

Grotius, H. *De Iure Belli ac Pacis libri tres.* Paris: Buon, 1625.

Hobbes, T. *Elementa Philosophiae de Corpore.* London: Crook, 1655.

------ Collected by W. Molesworth. *Opera philosophica.* 5 vols. London: Bohn, 1845.

------ Collected by W. Molesworth. *The English Works.* 11 vols. London: Bohn, 1845; repr. Aalen: Scientia Verlag, 1966.

Huygens, C. 'A Summary Account of the Laws of Motion.' *Philosophical Transactions* 46 (1669): 925-928.

Huygens, C. in: *Journal des Sçavans* 3 (1672), Amsterdam 1678, p. 112f. (C. Huygens, *Oeuvres complètes*, Den Haag: Nijhoff, 22 vols., 1888-1950, vol. 7, pp. 201-206).

Leo Hebraeus (Abarbanel Juda Ben Isaac). *De Amore Dialogi tres, a Ioanne Carolo Saraceno purissima latinitate donati.* Basle, 1587. (Latin edition included in *Ars Cabalistica, hoc est recondita theologia et philosophia.*)

Pallavicino, S. *Del bene libri quattro.* Roma: Corbelletti, 1644.

Pico della Mirandola, G., Garin, E. (ed.). *De hominis Dignitate, Heptaplus, De Ente et Uno, e scritti Vari.* Florence: Vallechi, 1942.

---- trans. Wallis, C. G. and others. *On the Dignity of Man, On Being and One, Heptaplus.* Indianapolis: Bobbs-Merrill, 1965.

Scherzer, J. A. *Vade mecum sive manuale philosophicum quadripartitum.* Leipzig: Kirchner, 1658.

------ *Trifolium orientale, continens commentarios R Abarbenelis in Haggaeum, R Sal. Jarchi in Parsch I. Geneseos & R Mos. Maiemonidae Theologiam, cum versione, notis philologico-philosophiciis & Appendice Specimenis Theologiae Mythicae Hebraeorum, junctis Autoritatum SS Scripturae....* Leipzig: Bauer, 1663.

---- *Collegii Anti-Sociniani.* 3rd ed., Leipzig & Frankfurt: Scipio, 1702.

Spinoza, B., ed. C. Gebhardt. *Spinoza Opera.* Heidelberg: Winter, 1925.

------- trans. E. M. Curley. *The Collected Works of Spinoza.* Princeton: Princeton University Press, 1985.

------- ed. E. M. Curley. *A Spinoza Reader.* Princeton: Princeton University Press, 1994.

Stahl, D. *Compendium Metaphysicae in XXIV. Tabellas redactum.* Jenae: Typis et Sumtibus Georgii Sengenwaldi, 1655.

Sturm, J. C. *Philosophia eclectica.* Altdorf, 1686.

Thomasius, C. *Paulo plenior historia juris naturalis.* Halle, 1719; repr. Stuttgard-Bad Cannstatt: frommann-holzboog, 1972.

Thomasius, J. *Origines historicae philosophiae & ecclesiasticae.* 3rd ed., 1699.

---- *Physica* (1670), *Logica* (1670), *Metaphysica,* and *Rhetorica,* published together. Leipzig, 1692.

---- *Origens philosophiae gentiles & 4 in ea sectarum apud Graecos praecipuarum; haereseos item Simonis Magis, Gnosticorum ...; denique Theologiae Mysticae pariter ac Scholasticae* [check with author]

---- *Dissertationes LXIII. Varii argumenti magnam partem ad historiam philosophicam & ecclesiasticam pertinentes.* Leipzig: Zeitler, 1693.

---- *Exercitatio de Stoica mundi exustione: cui accesserunt argumenti varii, sed inprimis ad historiam Stoicae philosophiae facientes, dissertationes XXI.* Leipzig, 1676.

---- *Praefationes sub auspicia Disputationum suarum in Academia.* Leipzig, 1681.

---- *Schediasma historicum ... ad historiam tum philosophicum, tum Ecclesiasticam pertinentia: imprimis autem inquiritur in ultimas Origens philosophiae gentiles & 4 in ea sectarum apud Graecos praecipuarum; haereseos item Simon is Magis, Gnosticorum ...; denique Theologiae Mysticae pariter ac Scholasticae.* Leipzig, 1665.

---- *Breviarium Ethicorum Aristoteles ad Nicomachum.* Leipzig, 1674.

---- ed. Marcus Antonius Muretus. *Orationes, epistolae, poemata.* Leipzig, 1672.

---- ed. Paulus Manutius. *Epistolarum.* (Libri XI) Leipzig, 1681.

---- ed. Johann von Wower. *De polymathia tractatio.* Leipzig, 1665.

Valla, L. *Opera.* Basle, 1540; repr. Torino: Bottega di Erasmo, 1962.

Weigel, E. *Analysis Aristotelica ex Euclide restituta.* Jena: Grosius, 1658.

------ *Idea Matheseos universae cum speciminibus Inventionum Mathematicarum.* Jena, 1687.

----- *Philosophia Mathematica. Theologia Naturalis Solida, per singulas Scientias continuata.* Jena: Sirckner, 1693.

5: Secondary Literature

Aarsleff, H. 'Bisterfeld.' *Dictionary of Scientific Biography*. New York: Charles Scribner's Sons, 1970.

Aceti, G. 'Indagini sulla concezione leibniziana della felicità.' *Rivista di Filosofia neo-scolastica* 49 (1957): 99-145.

Adams, R. M. *Leibniz: Determinist, Idealist, Theist*. New York & Oxford: Oxford University Press, 1994.

Aiton, E. J. *Leibniz: A Biography*. Bristol & Boston: Hilger, 1985.

Allen, D. 'Mechanical Explanation and the ultimate Origin of the Universe according to Leibniz.' *SL Sond.* 11 (1983).

Antognazza, M. R. 'Inediti leibniziani sulle polemiche trinitarie.' *Rivista di Filosofia neo-scolastica* 83 (1991): 525-550.

------ 'Die Rolle der Trinitäts- und Menschwerdungsdiskussionen für die Entstehung von Leibniz' Denken.' *SL* 26 (1994): 56-75.

------ 'Die Polemik des jungen Leibniz gegen die Sozinianer.' In *Leibniz und Europa: VI Internationaler Leibniz-Kongress*. Hanover: G. W. Leibniz-Gesellschaft, Vol. 1 (1994): 17-24.

------ 'Leibniz e il concetto di persona nelle polemiche trinitarie inglesi.' In V. Melchiorre (ed.), *L'idea di persona*. Milano: Vita e Pensiero, 1996, 207-237.

------ 'The Defence of the Mysteries of the Trinity and the Incarnation: an Example of Leibniz's "Other" Reason.' In M. Dascal and Q. Racionero (eds.), *Leibniz the Polemicist*. Dordrecht: Kluwer (Boston Studies in the Philosophy of Science), forthcoming.

Armogathe, J. R. *Theologia cartesiana: l'explication physique de l'Euchariste chez Descartes et Dom Desgabets*. The Hague: Nijhoff, 1965.

Barnouw, J. 'The Separation of Reason and Faith in Bacon and Hobbes and Leibniz's Theodicy.' *Journal of the History of Ideas* 42 (1981): 607-28.

Baruzi, J. *Leibniz et l'organisation religieuse de la terre d'après des documents inédits*. Paris: Alcan, 1907.

Beck, L. W. *Early German Philosophy: Kant and his Predecessors*. Cambridge, MA: Harvard University Press, 1969.

Beeley, P. 'Leibniz und die vorsokratische Tradition. Zur Bedeutung der Materietheorie von Anaxagoras für die Philosophie des jungen Leibniz.' In I. Marchlewitz and A. Heinekamp (eds.), *Leibniz' Auseinandersetzung mit Vorgängern und Zeitgenossen.* Stuttgart: Steiner 1990 (*SL Supp.* 27: 30-41).

------ 'Les sens dissimulants. Phénomènes et réalité dans *l'Hypothesis physica nova.*' In M. de Gaudemar (ed.), *La notion de nature chez Leibniz.* Stuttgart: Steiner 1995 (*SL Sond.* 24: 17-30).

------ *Kontinuität und Mechanismus. Zur Philosophie des jungen Leibniz in ihrem ideengeschichtlichen Kontext.* Stuttgart: Steiner, 1996 (*SL Supp.* 30).

Belaval, Y. *Leibniz: Critique de Descartes.* Paris: Gallimard, 1960.

------ *Leibniz: Initiation à sa Philosophie.* Paris: Vrin, 1962.

Bernstein, H. M. 'Conatus, Hobbes and the Young Leibniz.' *Studies in the History and Philosophy of Science* 11 (1980): 25- 37.

Breger, H. 'Elastizität als Strukturprinzip der Materie bei Leibniz.' In A. Heinekamp (ed.), *Leibniz' Dynamica,* (*SL Sond.* 13): 1984, 112-121.

------ 'Leibniz und Tschirnhaus.' In *Wissenschaft und Weltgestaltung.* Hildesheim: Olms, 1997.

Brown, S. 'Leibniz and More's Cabbalistic Circle.' In S. Hutton (ed.), *Henry More (1614-1687): Tercentenary Studies.* Dordrecht: Kluwer, 1990, pp. 77-95.

---- 'Some Occult Influences on Leibniz's Monadology.' In A. Coudert, R. H. Popkin and R. Weiner (eds.), *Leibniz, Mysticism, and Religion.* Dordrecht: Kluwer, 1988.

Buntz, H. 'Das "Buch der heiligen Dreifaltigkeit". Sein Autor und seine Überlieferung.' *Zeitschrift für deutsches Altertum und für deutsche Literatur* 101 (1972): 150-160.

Cassirer, E. *Leibniz' System in seinen wissenschaftlichen Grundlagen.* Marburg: Elwert, 1902.

------ and others (eds.). *Three Renaissance Philosophies of Man.* Chicago: University of Chicago Press. 1956.

Conze, W. 'Leibniz als Historiker.' In *Leibniz zu seinem 300 Gebürstag.* Berlin: De Gruyter, 1951, Fascicle 6.

Cook, D. 'Leibniz: Biblical Historian and Exegete.' In I. Marchlewitz and A. Heinekamp (eds.), *Leibniz' Auseinandersetzung mit Vorgängern und Zeitgenossen.* Stuttgart: Steiner 1990 (*SL Supp.* 27: 267-76).

------ 'Leibniz and Millenarianism.' In *Leibniz und Europa.* Hanover: G.W. Leibniz Gesellschaft, 1994, vol. I, pp. 135-142.

------- 'Den "Anderen" Leibniz zu verstehen.' *SL* 24 (1992): 59-72.

Copenhaver, B. P. and Schmitt, C.B. *Renaissance Philosophy.* Oxford: Oxford University Press, 1992.

Coudert, A. P. *Leibniz and the Kabbalah.* Dordrecht: Kluwer, 1995.

Couturat, L. *La logique de Leibniz d'après des documents inédits.* Paris: Alcan, 1901; repr. Hildesheim, Olms, 1961.

Dascal, M. 'Reason and the Mysteries of Faith: Leibniz on the Meaning of Religious Discourse.' In *Leibniz. Language, Signs and Thought: a collection of essays.* Amsterdam: Benjamins, 1987, 93-124.

------ and Yakira, E. (eds.) *Leibniz and Adam.* Tel Aviv: University Publishing Projects, 1993.

Davillé, L. *Leibniz Historien.* Paris, 1909; repr. Aalen: Scientia Verlag, 1986.

----- 'Le Séjour de Leibniz à Paris 1672-1676.' *Revue des études historique* 78 (1912): 5-57.

de Olaso, E. 'Leibniz and Scepticism.' In R. H. Popkin C. B. Schmitt (eds.), *Scepticism from the Renaissance to the Enlightenment.* Wiesbaden: Harrassowitz, 1987 (Wolfenbütteler Studien vol. 35), pp. 133-167.

Döring, D. *Der junge Leibniz und Leipzig. Ausstellung zum 350. Geburtstag von Gottfried Wilhelm Leibniz im Leipziger Alten Rathaus.* Berlin: Akademie Verlag, 1985.

Duchesneau, F. Review of *Leibniz-Thomasius Correspondance, Dialogue* 33 (1994): 457-72.

Edel, S. *Die Individuele Substanz bei Böhme und Leibniz, SL Sond.* 23 (1995).

Fichant, M. 'Neue Einblicke in Leibniz' Reform seiner Dynamik (1678).' *SL* 22 (1990): 48-68.

------ 'La notion de système dans la physique de Leibniz.' In M. de Gaudemar (ed.), *La notion de nature chez Leibniz*. Stuttgart: Steiner 1995 (*SL Sond.* 24): 43-57.

Fischer, K. *Gottfried Wilhelm Leibniz: Leben, Werke, und Lehre*. Heidelberg: Winter, 1920.

Fouke, D. C. 'Leibniz's Opposition to Cartesian Bodies during the Paris Period (1672-76).' *SL* 23 (1991): 195-206.

------ 'Metaphysics and the Eucharist in the Early Leibniz.' *SL* 24 (1992): 145-159.

Friedmann, G. *Leibniz et Spinoza*. 1st ed., 1946; 2nd ed., Paris: Gallimard, 1962.

Ganzenmüller, W. 'Das Buch der heiligen Dreifaltigkeit. Eine deutsche Alchemie aus dem Anfang des 15. Jahrhunderts.' *Archiv für Kulturgeschichte* 29 (1939): 93-146.

Garber, D. 'Physics and Philosophy.' In N. Jolley (ed.), *The Cambridge Companion to Leibniz*, pp. 270-352.

Gensini, G. 'Leibniz: Linguist and Philosopher of Language: Between "Primitive" and "Natural".' In M. Dascal and E. Yakira (eds.), *Leibniz and Adam*, pp. 111-136.

Gerhardt, C. I. 'Leibniz und Spinoza.' *Sitzungsberichte der Berliner Akademie der Wissenschaften zu Berlin* 49 (1889): 1075-1080.

Goldenbaum, U. 'From Adam to Alexander and Caesar: Leibniz's Shift from Logic and Metaphysics to a Theory of History.' In M. Dascal and E. Yakira (eds.), *Leibniz and Adam*, pp. 365-76.

Guéroult, M. *Dynamique et Physiques Leibniziennes*. Paris: Les Belles Lettres, 1934.

Guhrauer, G. E. *Quaestiones criticae ad Leibnitii opera philosophica pertinentes*. Bratislava, 1842.

------ *Gottfried Wilhelm Freiherr von Leibniz. Eine Biographie*. 2 vols., Breslau: Hirt, 1846; repr. Hildesheim: Olms, 1966.

Gurwitsch, A. *Leibniz: Philosophie der Panlogismus*. Berlin: de Gruyter, 1974.

Hannéquin, A. *Études d'histoire des sciences et d'histoire de la philosophie*. (2 vols.) Paris: Alcan, 1908.

------ 'La Première Philosophie de Leibnitz.' In *Études d'Histoire des Sciences*, vol. 2. Paris: Alcan, 1908.

Hecht, H. *G.W. Leibniz: Mathematik und Naturwissenschaften im Paradigma der Metaphysik.* Leipzig: Teutner, 1992.

Hein, I. 'Ein neu gefundener Brief von Leibniz an Lambert van Velthuysen.' *SL* 22 (1990).

Heinekamp, A. and others (eds.). *Leibniz à Paris. SL Supp.* 18 (1978).

Hirsch, E. *Geschichte der neueren evangelischen Theologie im Zusammenhang mit den allgemeinen Bewegungen des europäischen Denkens.* 2. vols. Gütersloh: Bertelsmann, 1951.

Hostler, J. *Leibniz's moral philosophy.* New York: Harper & Row, 1975.

Hotson, H. 'Johann Heinrich Alsted: Encyclopaedism, Millenarianism and the Second Reformation in Germany.' Oxford DPhil dissertation (unpublished), 1991.

------ 'Alsted and Leibniz: A Preliminary Survey of a Neglected Relationship.' In International Leibniz-Congress, *Leibniz und Europa* 1 (1994): 356-363.

International Leibniz-Congress (1994), *Leibniz und Europa*, Hanover: G. W. Leibniz Gesellschaft, Vol. 1 (1994), Vol. 2 (1995).

Kabitz, W. *Die Philosophie des jungen Leibniz. Untersuchungen zur Entwicklungsgeschichte seines Systems.* Heidelberg: Carl Winter's Universitätsbuchhandlung, 1909. Repr. Hildesheim: Olms, 1974.

Kalinowski G. and Gardiés J. L. 'Un logicien déontique avant la lettre: G. W. Leibniz.' *Archives für Rechts- und Sozialphilosophie* 60 (1974): 79-112.

Kristeller Paul O. 'Humanism and Scholasticism in the Italian Renaissance.' *Byzantion* 17 (1944-45): 346-74.

------ *The Classics and Renaissance Thought.* Cambridge, MA: Harvard University Press, 1955.

------ *Studies in Renaissance Thought and Letters.* Oram: Storia Letteratura, 1956.

Kulstad, M. 'Did Leibniz incline towards Monistic Pantheism in 1676?' In International Leibniz-Congress, *Leibniz und Europa* 1 (1994): 424-28.

------ 'Leibniz's *De Summa Rerum*; the Origin of the Variety of Things, in connection with the Spinoza-Tschirnhaus Correspondence.' *SL Sond.* (1997)

------ 'Roads Not Taken: Radical Suggestions of Leibniz's *De Summa Rerum.*' *Synthesis Philosophica* 12 (1997): 403-13.

Kvacsala, J. 'Johann Heinrich Bisterfeld.' *Ungarische Revue* 13 (1893): 40-59 and 171-197.

Jolley, N. (ed.) *The Cambridge Companion to Leibniz.* Cambridge: Cambridge University Press, 1995.

Lamarra, A. 'Leibniz e la περιχώρησις.' *Lexicon philosophicum. Quaderni di terminologia filosofica e storia delle idee,* 1 (1985): 67-94.

Leinsle, U. G. *Reformversuche protestantischer Metaphysik im Zeitalter des Rationalismus.* Augsburg: Maro Verl., 1988.

Lewalter, Ernst. *Spanisch-Jesuitische und Deutsch-Lutherische Metaphysiker 17. Jahrhunderts.* Darmstadt: Wissenschaftliche Buchgesellschaft, 1967.

Loemker, L. E. 'Boyle and Leibniz.' *Journal of the History of Ideas* 16 (1955): 22-42.

------ 'Leibniz and the Herborn Encyclopedists.' *Journal of the History of Ideas* 22 (1961): 323-338.

------ *Struggle for Synthesis. The Seventeenth Century Background of Leibniz's Synthesis of Order and Freedom.* Cambridge, MA: Harvard University Press, 1972.

------ 'Leibniz and Our Time.' In I. Leclerc (ed.), *The Philosophy of Leibniz and the Modern World.* Nashville: Vanderbilt University Press, 1973, pp. 3-10.

------ 'Leibniz's Conception of Philosophical Method.' In I. Leclerc (ed.), *The Philosophy of Leibniz and the Modern World.* Nashville: Vanderbilt University Press, 1973, 135-57.

Look, B. Review of M. Dascal and E. Yakira, eds., *Leibniz and Adam. Leibniz Society Review* 5 (1995): 29-32.

Lorenz, St. 'Leibniz und Gottlieb Johann Hansch. Zur Frühgeschichte der Wirkung der Essais de Théodicée in Deutschland.' In *Leibniz und Europa. Vorträge zum VI. Internationalen Leibnizkongreß,* part 2. Hanover, 1995, 206-211.

Lovejoy, A. O. *The Great Chain of Being,* Cambridge, MA.: Harvard University Press, 1936 & 1964.

MacDonald Ross, G.   'Leibniz and the Nuremberg Alchemical Society.' *SL* 6 (1974): 222-48.

------ 'Leibniz and Alchemy.' *SL Sond.* 7 (1978): 166-80.

------   'Alchemy and the Development of Leibniz's Metaphysics.' *SL Supp.* 22 (1982): 40-45.

Mahnke, D.   *Leibnizens Synthese von Universalmathematik und Individualmetaphysik.* Halle: Max Niemeyer, 1925.

Mancosu, P.   'Aristotelian Logic and Euclidean Mathematics: Seventeenth-Century Developments of the *Quaestio de certitudine mathematicarum.*'   *Studies in History and Philosophy of Science* 23 (1992): 241-65.

------   *Philosophy of Mathematics and Mathematical Practice in the Seventeenth Century.*   New York and Oxford: Oxford University Press, 1996.

McCullough, L. B.   *Leibniz on Individuals and Individuation.* Dordrecht: Kluwer, 1996.

Menk, G.   'Die Restitutionsedikt und die kalvinistische Wissenschaft. Die Berufung Johann Heinrich Alsteds, Philipp Ludwig Piscators und Johann Heinrich Bisterfelds nach Siebenbürgen.' *Jahrbuch der Hessischen Kirchengeschichtlichen Vereinigung* 31 (1980): 29-63.

------   *Die Hohe Schule Herborn in ihrer Frühzeit (1584-1660). Ein Beitrag zum Hochschulwesen des deutschen Kalvinismus im Zeitalter der Gegenreformation.*   Wiesbaden: Selbstverlag der Historischen Kommission für Nassau, 1981.

------   'Johann Amos Comenius und die Hohe Schule Herborn.' *Acta Comeniana* 8 (1989): 41-59.

Mercer, C.   'The Vitality and Importance of Early Modern Aristotelianism.' In Sorell, T. (ed.), *The Rise of Modern Philosophy.* Oxford: Clarendon Press, 1993, pp. 33-67.

------ and Sleigh, R. C., Jr. 'Metaphysics: The early period to the *Discourse on Metaphysics.*' In Jolley, N. (ed.), *The Cambridge Companion to Leibniz,* pp. 67-123.

------   'Mechanizing Aristotle: Leibniz and Reformed Philosophy.' In M. A. Stewart (ed.), *Studies in Seventeenth Century European Philosophy, Oxford Studies in the History of Philosophy* 2 (1997): 117-52.

------ 'Humanist Platonism in Seventeenth-Century Germany.' In J. Kraye and M. Stone (eds.), *Humanism and Early Modern Europe. London Studies in the History of Philosophy*, vol. I. London: Routledge, forthcoming.

------ 'Clauberg, Corporeal Substance, and the German Response.' In T. Verbeek (ed.), *The Philosophy of Johann Clauberg*. Dordrecht: Kluwer, 1998.

----- *Leibniz's Metaphysics: Its Origins and Development.* Cambridge: Cambridge University Press, forthcoming.

Meyer, R. W., trans. J. P. Stern. *Leibniz and the Seventeenth-Century Revolution.* Cambridge: Bowes & Bowes, 1952.

Moll, K. 'Von Erhard Weigel zu Christiaan Huygens, Feststellungen au Leibnizens Bildungsweg zwischen Nürnberg, Mainz und Paris.' *SL* 14 (1982): 56-72.

------ 'Die erste Monadenkonzeption von Leibniz und ihr Ausgangspunkt in Conatus-Begriff und Perzeptionstheorie von Thomas Hobbes.' *Proceedings of the Vth International Leibniz-Kongress.* Hanover: Leibniz-Gesellschaft, 1988.

------ 'Überlegungen zur Aktualität von Leibniz angesichts der Krise der europäischen Wissenschaften.' In International Leibniz-Congress, *Leibniz und Europa* 1 (1994) 487-94.

------ *Der junge Leibniz*, 3 vols., Stuttgart-Bad Cannstatt: Frommann-Holzboog, 1978, 1982 & 1996.

Mondadori, F. 'A Harmony of One's Own and Universal Harmony in Leibniz's Paris Writings.' *SL Supp.* 18 (1978): 151-68.

Mugnai, M. 'Der Begriff der Harmonie als metaphysische Grundlage der Logik und Kombinatorik bei Johann Heinrich Bisterfeld und Leibniz.' *SL* 5 (1973): 43-73.

------ *Leibniz' Theory of Relations. SL Supp.* 28 (1992).

Mulvaney, R. 'The early development of Leibniz's concept of justice.' *Journal of History of Ideas* 29 (1968): 54-71.

Parkinson, G.H.R. *Leibniz on Human Freedom. SL Sond.* 2 (1970).

------ 'Leibniz's Paris Writings in relation to Spinoza.' *SL Supp.* 18 (1978): 73-91.

------ 'Leibniz's *De Summa Rerum*: A Systematic Approach.' *SL* 18 (1986): 132-51.

Parmentier, M. 'Conceptes juridiques et probabilistes chez Leibniz.' *Revue d'histoire des Sciences* 46 (1993): 439-85.

Piro, F. 'Leibniz e il progetto degli *Elementa de mente et corpore*.' *Il Centauro* 11-12 (1984): 106-16.

------ *Varietas Identitate Compensata. Studio sulla formazione della metafisica di Leibniz.* Napoli: Bibliopolis, 1990.

------ 'Leibniz et l'Ethique à Nicomaque.' In R. Cristin (ed.), *Leibniz und die Frage nach der Subjektivität.* Stuttgart: Steiner, 1994, 179-96.

Pichler, A. *Die Theologie des Leibniz*, 2 vols. München, 1869/70; repr. Hildesheim: Olms, 1965.

Popkin, R. H. 'Leibniz and the French Sceptics.' *Revue Internationale de Philosophie* 20 (1966): 228-48.

------ & Schmidt, C. (eds.) *Scepticism from the Renaissance to the Enlightenment.* Wiesbaden: O. Harrassowitz, 1987.

Poser, H. 'Apriorismus der Prinzipien und Kontingenz der Naturgesetze. Das Leibniz-Paradigma der Naturwissenschaft.' In A. Heinekamp (ed.), *Leibniz' Dynamica. SL Sond.* 13 (1984): 164-79.

Pring-Mill, R. 'The Trinitarian World Picture of Ramon Lull.' *Romantisches Jahrbuch* 7 (1955-6): 229-56.

Rescher, N. 'The Contributions of the Paris Period (1672-76) to Leibniz's Metaphysics'. *SL Supp.* 18 (1978): 43-54.

Riley, P. *Leibniz's Universal Jurisprudence: justice as the charity of the wise.* Cambridge, Mass.: Harvard University Press, 1996.

Robinet, A. *G. W. Leibniz. Le meilleur des mondes par la balance de l'Europe.* Paris: P. U. F., 1994.

Rossi, P. *Clavis Universalis. Arti mnemoniche e logica combinatoria da Lullo a Leibniz.* Milano-Napoli: Riccardo Ricciardi, 1960.

Rudolph, H. 'Kosmosspekulation und Trinitätslehre. Ein Beitrag zur Beziehung zwischen Weltbild und Theologie bei Paracelsus.' *Beiträge zur Paracelsusforschung* 21 (1980): 32-47.

Russell, B. *A Critical Exposition of the Philosophy of Leibniz.* Cambridge: Cambridge University Press, 1900.

Schepers, H. 'Leibniz' *Disputationes de conditionibus*. Ansätze zu einer juristischen Aussagenlogik.' *SL Supp.* 15 (1975): 1-17.

------ Art. 'Leibniz.' In *Neue Deutsche Biographie*, vol. 14, pp. 121-31. Ed. Historical Commission of the Bayern Academy of Sciences. Berlin: Durcher & Humblot, 1985.

Schmitt, C. B. 'Perennial Philosophy: From Agostino Steuco to Leibniz.' *Journal of the History of Philosophy* 27 (1966): 505-32.

------ *Aristotle and the Renaissance*. Cambridge, MA: Harvard University Press, 1983.

------ and Q. Skinner (eds.). *The Cambridge History of Renaissance Philosophy*. Cambridge: Cambridge University Press, 1988.

Schneider, H.-P. *Justitia Universalis. Quellenstudien zur Geschichte des "christlichen Naturrechts" bei G. W. Leibniz*. Frankfurt on Maine: Klostermann, 1967.

Schneiders, W. 'Naturrecht und Gerechtigkeit bei Leibniz.' *Zeitschrift für philosophische Forschung* 20 (1967): 607-50.

----- *Naturrecht und Liebesethik. Zur Geschichte der praktischen Philosophie im Himblick auf Christian Thomasius*. Hildesheim & New York: Olms, 1971.

------ 'Sozietätpläne und Sozialutopie bei Leibniz.' *SL* 7 (1975): 58-80.

------ 'Aufklärung durch Geschichte. Zwischen Geschichtstheologie und Geschichtsphilosophie: Leibniz, Thomasius, Wolff.' In A. Heinekamp (ed.), *Leibniz als Geschichtsforscher. SL Sond.* 10 (1982): 79-99.

Seivert, J. *Nachrichten von Siebenbürgurgischen Gelehrten und ihren Schriften*. Pressburg: im Weber und Korabinstischen Verlage, 1785.

Sleigh, R.C., Jr. 'Notes on Harmony.' In *Leibniz – Werk und Wirkung*. Hanover, 1983, 716-23.

Sparn, W. 'Das Bekenntnis des Philosophen. Gottfried Wilhelm Leibniz als Philosoph und Theologe.' *Neue Ztschr. f. Systemat. Philosophie u. Religionsphilosophie* 28 (1986): 139-78.

Specht, R. *Innovation und Folgelast, Beispiele aus der neueren Philosophie- und Wissenschaftsgeschichte*. Stuttgart-Bad Cannstatt: Fromann Holzboog, 1972.

Stammel, H. *Der Kraftbegriff in Leibniz' Physik.* Mannheim, 1982.

------ 'Der Status der Bewegungsgesetze in Leibniz' Philosophie und die apriorische Methode der Kraftmessung.' In *Leibniz' Dynamica, SL Sond.* 13 (1984): 180-88.

Stein, L. 'Neue Aufschlüsse über den litterarischen Nachlass und die Herausgabe der Opera posthuma Spinoza's.' *Archiv f. Gesch. d. Philos.* 1 (1888): 553-65.

------ 'Leibniz in seinem Verhältnis zu Spinoza auf Grundlage unedirten Materials entwickelungsgeschichtlich dargestellt.' *Sitzungsberichte der Kgl.-Preuss. Ak. d. Wiss. zu Berlin* 25 (1888): 615-27.

------ *Leibniz und Spinoza.* Berlin: Reimer, 1890.

Tönnies, F. 'Leibniz und Hobbes.' In E. G. Jacoby (ed.), *Studien zur Philosophie und Gesellschaftslehre im 17. Jahrhundert.* Stuttgart-Bad-Cannstatt: Frommann-Holzboog, 1975, 151-68.

Tognon, G. 'G. W. Leibniz: Dinamica e Teologia. Il carteggio inedito con Jacques Lenfant [1693].' *Giornale Critico della Filosofia Italiana* 61 (1982): 278-329.

Trausch, J. F. *Schriftsteller-Lexikon, oder biographisch-literärische Denk-Blätter der Siebenbürger Deutschen.* Kronstadt: J. Gött und Sohn, 1868-1870.

Trendelenburg, A. 'Ist Leibniz in seiner Entwicklung einmal Spinozist oder Cartesianer gewesen und was bedeutet dafür die Schrift *de vita beata?*' *Monatsberichte der Berliner Akademie der Wissenschaften* (1847): 372-86.

Troeltsch, E. 'Protestantisches Christentum und Kirche in der Neuzeit.' In P. Hinneberg (ed.), *Die Kultur der Gegenwart, ihre Entwicklung und ihre Ziele,* Berlin & Leipzig: Teubner, 1909, pp. 431-755.

Tuck, R. 'The "modern" theory of natural law.' In H. Pagden (ed.), *The Languages of Political Theory in Early-Modern Europe.* Cambridge: Cambridge University Press, 1987.

Utermöhlen, G. 'Die Literatur der Renaissance und des Humanismus in Leibniz' privater Buchersammlung.' *SL* 23 (1983): 221-38.

Walker, D. P. *The Decline of Hell. Seventeenth-Century Discussions of Eternal Torment.* London: Routledge & Kegan Paul, 1964.

------ *The Ancient Theology: Studies in Christian Platonism from the Fifteenth to the Eighteenth Century.* New York: Cornell University Press. 1972.

Watkins, J. W. N. *Hobbes' System of Ideas. A Study in the Political Significance of Philosophical Theories.* London: Hutchinson, 1975.

Watson, R. 'Transubstantiation among the Cartesians.' In T. Lennon and others (eds.), *Problems of Cartesianism.* Montreal: McGill/Queen's University Press, 1982, pp. 127-48.

Wiedeburg, P. *Der junge Leibniz. Das Reich und Europa. Part 1. Mainz.* Wiesbaden: Steiner, 1962. *Part 2. Paris.* Wiesbaden, Steiner, 1970.

Williams, G. H. *The Radical Reformation.* 3rd. rev. ed., Kirsville, MO: Sixteenth Century Journal Publishers, 1992.

Wilson, C. 'De Ipsa Natura. Sources of Leibniz's Doctrines of Force, Activity and Natural Law.' *SL* 19 (1987): 148-72.

------ *Leibniz's Metaphysics.* Princeton: Princeton University Press & Manchester: Manchester University Press, 1989.

------ 'The Combinatorial Universe: Scientific Language and Metaphysics in Leibniz.' In N. Rescher (ed.), *Leibnizian Inquiries: A Group of Essays.* Lanham, MD: University Press of America, 1989, pp. 159-69.

------ *The Invisible World. Early Modern Philosophy and the Invention of the Microscope.* Princeton: Princeton University Press, 1995.

Wilson, M. 'Leibniz: Self-Consciousness and Immortality in the Paris Notes and After'. *Archiv für Geschichte der Philosophie* 58 (1976): 335-52.

Wundt, Max. *Die Philosophie an der Universität Jena.* Jena: Fischer, 1932.

----- *Die deutsche Schulmetaphysik des 17. Jahrhunderts.* Tübingen: Mohn, 1939. Reprinted Hildesheim: Olms, 1964.

INDEX